Advance Praise for M

"Jim Simpson recognized the Red/Green Axis—a revolutionary, anti-American alliance between the radical Left and the Sharia-supremacists—long before it was 'a thing.' Now, in this important book, he exposes the strategies those domestic enemies are pursuing to destroy our beloved America—and what we must do to defeat them. Please read it and heed it!"

—**Frank Gaffney**, Executive
Chairman, Center for Security Policy

"With care and precision, Jim Simpson takes a whole-of-country approach to exposing the decades of systematic attacks on American society, economy, law, culture, and constitutional governance. He ties everything together to prove the scope and duration of the strategic attack. Most importantly, he shows what Americans can do to confront and reverse some of the damage."

—**J. Michael Waller, PhD**, Senior Analyst
for Strategy, Center for Security Policy; Author,
*Big Intel: How the CIA and FBI Went from Cold
War Heroes to Deep State Villains* (2024)

"Jim Simpson has written a fascinating and necessary book that describes in-depth the massive challenges that America is facing, and what we must do to respond. An important read."

—**Peter Schweizer**, *New York Times*
Bestselling Author of *Red-Handed: How
American Elites Get Rich Helping China Win*;
Investigative Journalist; Cofounder and President,
the Government Accountability Institute

"Jim Simpson has compiled an enormous amount of information that is truly an indictment of the American Left, and their now wholly owned subsidiary, the Democratic Party. He shows how it is all connected for the overarching goal of stealing our nation from under our feet, just as surely as they stole the 2020 election and intend to do the same in 2024. This should be required reading for every American."

—**Catherine Engelbrecht**, Founder and Director, True the Vote

"Democratic Party leader Rahm Emanuel once said, 'Never let a good crisis go to waste.' Jim Simpson's new book *Manufactured Crisis* demonstrates that when the Left doesn't have a crisis to manipulate to their political advantage, they manufacture one. *Manufactured Crisis* is essential reading for everyone seeking to understand what's going on in the world today and how the Left has manufactured a decades-long series of crises to undermine Western civilization and American constitutional liberty to establish a new Marxist world order."

— **Richard A. Viguerie**, Conservative Fundraising Pioneer and Chairman, ConservativeHQ.com

MANUFACTURED CRISIS

THE WAR TO END AMERICA

JAMES SIMPSON

Post Hill
PRESS

A POST HILL PRESS BOOK
ISBN: 979-8-88845-674-3
ISBN (eBook): 979-8-88845-675-0

Manufactured Crisis:
The War to End America
© 2024 by James Simpson
All Rights Reserved

Cover design by Maureen Mead

This is a work of nonfiction. All people, locations, events, and situations are portrayed to the best of the author's memory.

Post Hill Press
New York • Nashville
posthillpress.com

Published in the United States of America
1 2 3 4 5 6 7 8 9 10

To My Children

CONTENTS

FOREWORD

The United States today faces multiple seemingly insurmountable problems. The country is beset by skyrocketing debt, social breakdown is evident on almost every front, global war could break out any day, and we can't trust our leaders to prevent it, or even to try to win it. Unease is the order of the day.

The country is in crisis, and nobody seems to know what to do. The main reason there seems to be no clear path forward is that very few people seem to understand the root cause of our problems. How can we fix America, if we don't know what's ailing her?

The key question is this. Is the decline of the United States of America simply an inevitable historical process that we must make peace with, or is it primarily the result of a methodical program implemented over decades by our enemies?

If the answer is the former, we'd best all give up now. If it is the latter, we'd better quickly identify those enemies, and implement counter-strategies immediately. If a mega-wealthy octogenarian starts to rapidly physically deteriorate, it could be the natural aging process. Or it could be that a greedy relative has been quietly slipping cyanide into the coffee pot?

The title of James Simpson's latest book *Manufactured Crisis: The War to End America* makes it clear that he believes America is being economically, politically, culturally, and spiritually poisoned.

As a professional economist, James Simpson is well-placed to expose the economic sabotage that this great nation has been enduring for more than a century. However, Mr. Simpson goes way further. In a very straightforward way, he ties it all together. He analyzes all the major problems we face and looks for the common thread.

He looks beyond the economic factors, he examines the roots of our massive vote fraud programs, and he gets to the root of the "climate change" scam. He digs into weaponization of our culture and the indoctrination of our children.

Simpson also exposes the deliberate impoverishment of the middle class and the equally intentional fostering of racial division, the destruction of our borders, and the systematic corruption of our government.

And this is what I love most about this book—James Simpson talks about evil. Few commentators do this, but is evil not at the root of all our problems? If the deliberate indoctrination and perverted sexualization of our children is not pure evil, then what is? If the destruction of our borders and the cruelty of the human traffickers, drug dealers, and revolutionaries who exploit the situation is not evil, then what is? If the deliberate impoverishment, division, and catastrophic weakening of the greatest nation that has ever existed on the face of the Earth is not evil, then does the word have any meaning left at all?

James Simpson names and confronts the evil forces behind our threatened destruction head-on. He doesn't mince words. He writes clearly and unflinchingly. I like that, and I think you will too. Mr. Simpson names the forces, identifies their programs and plans. He brings clarity to the confusion that is overwhelming even the brightest and the bravest among us. Even better—once identifying the programs, the problems, and the perpetrators, Simpson lays out solutions.

To win any war, we must first understand that we are in a war—we're not just suffering an inevitable decline. Secondly, we must identify our enemies and their strengths and weaknesses. Thirdly, we must devise plans and strategies to counter these enemy forces. Fourthly, we must rally our allies around those strategies. Fifthly, we must decisively defeat our enemies, destroy their infrastructure, drive them from our institutions, and hold them legally accountable wherever possible. Lastly, we must strengthen our institutions, our schools, our churches, our judicial system, and our military, so that what little remains of the enemy is not able or willing to attack us again for centuries.

I am reminded of my favorite passage from the Bible, James 4:17 (KJV):

> *Therefore, to him that knoweth to do good, and doeth it not, to him it is sin.*

We are not in our present predicament because the Marxists and globalists deliberately wrecking our country are so clever. We are here because our leaders, religious, political, and cultural, have been too damned weak and too damned cowardly for too damned long. And so, frankly speaking, have been most of us.

To counter that weakness, to avoid the wages we are all owed for knowing the right thing to do but seldom doing it, and to ensure that our children and grandchildren live free, we must all act now.

James Simpson's great book clearly exposes our enemies. It points the way out of this mess, towards a much better future for us, our families, and our country.

James Simpson does us all a great service with this work.

Trevor Loudon
Free Florida
July 4, 2024

PREFACE

This book represents the culmination of almost forty years of research, study, writing, speaking, and in other ways opposing the radical Left, part of the international Communist movement. That is the greatest threat our nation has ever faced. And it has been with us for much longer than those forty years. As this book will describe, it was kicked off by Communism's best salesman, Karl Marx, followed by individuals and movements that developed and honed strategies and tactics to impose Communism throughout the world.

In 1985, as a newly minted economist fresh out of grad school, I became fascinated with Communism. Why, I wondered, would so many people in so many nations be so totally entranced with the Communist idea, when a first-year economics student could easily recognize the absurdity of Marxist economic theories? Economics is essentially the science of survival, so why would so many people go to the mats to destroy the Western free market idea—which has made survival more secure and delivered more prosperity to more people throughout the world than any other system ever created—to advocate a system of repeatedly proven failure, which invariably leads to mass murder?

It launched me on a personal quest to answer these questions. The answers, I discovered, were hard to find. Even then, and well before, the effort to silence or suppress criticism of the radical Left had long been active. For example, the book *Toward Soviet America*, written in 1932 by American Communist Party leader William Z. Foster, had been stripped from virtually every library in the US and denounced by Foster himself, because it was a little too forthright about Communist goals. You can find it available online now, but for a long time, most of the copies in circulation were from reprints ordered by the Un-American Activities Committee of the US House of Representatives in 1961. (This committee was put out of business in 1975—another Communist victory).

The vilification of Senator Joseph McCarthy was probably the best example of cancel culture in action during the 1950s, though certainly not the only one. "McCarthyism" is a slur that intimidates people to this day, yet McCarthy was right about Communist infiltration of the federal government. But as a researcher, I tend to be relentless. The answer, I found, is as old as the hills: money and power. As an economic system, Marxism is an absolute failure, but as a methodology for seizing power and obtaining virtually unlimited wealth, it is unmatched, as long as its practitioners abandon any and all morality, and are willing to engage in lies, deception, threats, grizzly torture, and mass murder to gain and keep that power.

I found more and more evidence that the entire Communist movement was a Trojan horse, designed to trick us into ceding ever more power to people with very evil intent, despite the fact that many Communist true believers were ardent in thinking it was the answer to all the world's ills. But they were perhaps the most deluded. One of the influential books I found was *The Great Terror* by Robert Conquest. It described in detail the horror faced by the Russian people during Soviet leader Joseph Stalin's reign of terror.

Another book, which should be considered a national treasure, was *New Lies for Old: An Ex-KGB Officer Warns How Communist Deception Threatens Survival of the West*, published in 1984 by Soviet defector Anatoliy Golitsyn. In that book, Golitsyn predicted the coming "fall" of the Soviet Union, years before it actually happened. He described it as a deliberate fake, in the planning stages for decades, and designed to make us lower our guard against the Communists.

It worked out even better than the Soviets planned. Following the so-called "fall" of Soviet Communism in 1991, Democrats said, "See, they were never *really* a threat!" Republicans cheered over Reagan's victory gained by outspending the Soviets on defense. (It didn't happen.) Both parties declared themselves the victor and went home. Then both presidents H. W. Bush and Bill Clinton cut defense spending successively to hollow force levels, and abandoned anti-Communist guerrillas in the field, where they were rapidly defeated. Never one to pass up a ripe opportunity to squander taxpayer dollars, Democratic senator Teddy Kennedy jumped in to propose domestic spending on the "peace dividend" before any defense spending cuts were even made.

When in 1987 I fully realized what the Communist plan was for America, I didn't sleep for three days. Over the following years I kept up my research but was too busy earning a living, paying back student loans, running a business, and raising a family to make it a full-time effort. Following 9/11, however, I was motivated to write about all I had learned, both through research and through years spent working in the White House budget office, where I saw the deception Golitsyn predicted being played out in real time.

Looking over the years, it is so sad to reflect on what our collective delusion has cost us and our allies. Do you ever wonder, for example, why we have not won a single major war since WWII? In Korea we were forced to accept a stalemate. In Vietnam, a war that could have been easily won in six months or less with very few casualties was instead a humiliating loss after a ten-year effort, 58,220 deaths, and thousands of remaining MIAs. It also enabled the complete takeover of Laos and Cambodia, dominoes that fell with enormous human cost. We did not really even win the first Gulf War. We only succeeded in rolling back Saddam's army to the Iraqi border. During the second Iraq war, President Obama essentially ceded Iraq to the Iranians. I don't need to tell you what happened in Afghanistan.

In virtually every case, our own leaders betrayed us. And in these and many other cases, those same leaders betrayed our allies and friends across the globe. The so-called "peace" movement, which built momentum for our exit from Vietnam, was led by Communists. Many of these, like Weather Underground terrorist Bill Ayers, were receiving guidance from Cuban intelligence and other hostile actors. They were not "anti-war" at all. They were anti–US victory against the Communists. We supposedly didn't know this at the time. Why not?

We have repeatedly been outmaneuvered by our Communist enemies abroad, and tricked, misled, and subverted by the many Communists and their useful idiots in the BLM/Antifa movements active in the US. These people and their stooges saturate our institutions today and pretty much own the entire Democrat Party apparatus. These people should be facing trials for treason. Instead, they are calling the shots.

This does not bode well for us. Our nation is at the tipping point, staring into the abyss. If you are not yet fully primed to the dangers we face, my hope is that this book will help elucidate them. It is further my hope that it will help you see where our priorities must lie for the immediate future and beyond, and what we must do for our nation to survive. Yes, literally survive.

I will leave you with the last words ever written by the wonderful entertainer and polemicist Lloyd Marcus, the "Unhyphenated American," shortly before he died in June 2020—a great sorrow and loss for us all.

"We must do everything in our power to reelect our remarkable president. This election is our last stand to save America as founded. America is counting on you."

Amen.

James Simpson
Baltimore
August 19, 2024

INTRODUCTION

I dunno man, I dunno. Seems the last few years, life's gotten cheap. The monsters ain't just in the shadows; they're in broad damn daylight. Country's got the devil in it Joe, and no one is calling him to account....
—Sheriff Sena, *Dark Winds*, Season 2, Episode 3

I n an unfortunate turn of events, on July 13 of 2024, as I was editing this book for final review, twenty-year-old Thomas Matthew Crooks attempted to assassinate President Donald Trump at a rally in Butler, Pennsylvania. He killed another man and wounded two others. He was quickly shot dead before he could do any more damage. But more than anything else, this one event defines where we are today.

I was discouraged but not surprised. The Democrats and their media allies have been demonizing, attacking, and lying about Trump since he descended the golden escalator at Trump Towers in 2015 to announce his first run for the presidency.

His treatment can only be described as barbaric. It is unprecedented in America politics, from Hillary Clinton's never-ending campaign to discredit Trump through the Democrats' contrived Russian collusion hoax and subsequent nonstop FBI investigations, to the two unprecedented impeachment trials based on wholly fabricated pretexts, the endless contrived Justice Department and New York district attorney investigations, multiple lawsuits, and on and on.

Or how about the repulsive beheaded Trump effigy photo shot by Kathy Griffin, an actress and comedian who needed to up her flagging career? Or what about statements by numerous prominent Democrats saying they would like to kill Trump, with California Rep. Maxine Waters exclaiming to a crowd, "I will go and take him out tonight!" or actor Johnny Depp asking, "When was the last time an actor assassinated a president?"[1] Ironically it was Republican President Lincoln shot by a Democrat, John Wilkes Booth, although Depp is probably too ignorant to know that. Or perhaps most memorably when Joe Biden said five days before the shooting, "It's time to put Trump in the bullseye." In any case, it has been a virtually nonstop effort to deliberately vilify, marginalize, and destroy Trump, and his supporters as well.

All this nonstop vitriol, hyped and repeated by the media, has raised division and hatred in this country to a fever pitch. It was therefore not surprising at all that this kid, supposedly a bullied loner, who, among other things, was rejected by his high school shooting team and asked not to return, would try to make a name for himself by shooting Trump. In fact, given all of the obscene hate rhetoric spewed by many high-profile individuals, like the "don't miss Trump next time" statement by a Jack Black band mate, it is more likely than not that someone will try again. One prominent Democrat even had the gall to suggest that the assassination attempt was "encouraged and maybe even staged" by candidate Trump.[2] You simply cannot make this stuff up.

Did Crooks work alone? He was found to have bomb-making materials in both his car and home, including an IED.[3] How did he get hold of those materials? He also had two cell phones and three encrypted overseas apps on one of his phones.[4] As of this writing, little more is known, but I have long believed that many of these so-called "lone wolf" shooters are in fact not alone. They are recruited online by enemy actors sophisticated enough to do so. Many online predators successfully target young girls and boys for victimization. Why would malevolent state actors not do the same thing? Reportedly, the Secret Service received intelligence that Iran was plotting to assassinate Mr.

Trump *before* the July 13 event and *increased security.*[5] While there is as yet no known Iranian connection to Crooks, if that represents increased security it's hard to imagine what security would have looked like otherwise.

As for the security situation, back in the early 1990s, I wrote budgets for the US Secret Service. At that time, you would never have seen such rank incompetence among the Service as witnessed on July 13. While they rapidly took steps to protect Trump and dispatched the shooter, Crooks was in a location easily visible from the venue and at a distance that would not be a difficult shot for anyone with any experience. That building should have been secured well before the event started. It is inexplicable that it wasn't. Furthermore, people were shouting warnings about the man on the roof well before he began to shoot, and law enforcement was aware of his presence for at least an hour beforehand. It must be asked, was this really incompetence? Had the speaker been Joe Biden, I guarantee you this shooting would not have happened.

Most readers of this book are well aware that we are in dangerous, uncharted waters today. The nation is at a tipping point, and the Left is agitating for full-on revolution. Candidate Trump was very lucky, and must be protected. The Service has denied more up until now, with the laughable excuse that they couldn't afford it.

I did not intend to make this introduction, or even the book, strictly partisan, but I will say now that if Mr. Trump loses this election, those who have brought us to this point will have won the day. And that will prove cataclysmic. However, if he wins, the Left will likely make the 2020 George Floyd riots look like a picnic. Hopefully President Trump won't hesitate to call out the National Guard if that happens.

Now that Biden has dropped out, we have Kamala Harris to deal with. If she defeats Donald Trump, what do we have to look forward to? Well, if you thought another four years of Biden would be bad, get ready. It will be magnitudes worse. My colleague, Trevor Loudon, who wrote the preface to this book, did a Counterpunch video for the *Epoch Times* prior to the 2020 election, where he described Harris's extreme left connections. The people she has surrounded herself with are Marxists, Communists, Socialists, "progressives," and Maoists with myriad ties to the Chinese Communist government. He predicted that she will be "China's best friend in the White House if, God forbid, she gets into that position."[6]

Well, she did, and while Joe Biden was the best friend China could ask for, Kamala was and is just as bad if not worse, because unlike Biden, she still has most of her faculties, and her list of Communist co-conspirators is truly frightening. Behind that flaky, seemingly mindless personality, Harris is an avowed Marxist. We need to state it plainly. Her list of Communist and especially pro-Chinese Communist connections spans most if not all of her life.

As described by Loudon:[7]

Harris's father was a Marxist professor at Stanford University. Both parents were active in a pro-Castro Marxist group called the Afro-American Association, headed by radical black activist Don Warden. Warden helped birth the Black Panthers and later changed his name to Khalid al-Mansour. Under that name he helped Barack Obama get into Harvard.

Harris's husband, Doug Emhoff, has a law firm that does business with Communist China, and some of their staff are actual Chinese Communist Party members.

Harris is good friends with Alicia Garza. Garza co-founded Black Lives Matter with help from the Freedom Road Socialist Organization, a Maoist group, and the Chinese Progressive Association—a San Francisco Bay area Communist Chinese front. Harris is an enthusiastic supporter of BLM, and cheered them on while they burnt down cities.

Harris parlayed her sexual affair with the sixty-year-old former California assembly speaker and San Francisco mayor, Willie Brown, into a series of increasingly high-level political jobs. First San Francisco district attorney, then California attorney general, US senator, and finally vice president. Brown himself owed his political career to numerous prominent California Communists, one of whom even won the Order of Lenin from the Soviet Union.

But Harris had help from others, particularly Stephen Phillips, a Marxist-Leninist member of the League of Revolutionary Struggle, a pro-Chinese Communist group. Phillips married Susan Sandler, daughter to Herb and Marion Sandler, former owners of Golden West Financial, the second largest savings and loan bank in the US. The Sandlers sold Golden West to Wachovia Bank just before the subprime mortgage collapse. It sent Wachovia into bankruptcy but the Sandlers walked off with billions.

Hardcore leftists themselves, the Sandlers showered money on numerous radical causes and eventually partnered with George Soros and other radical billionaires.[8] Radical son-in-law Phillips made good use of his wife's share by starting PowerPAC, a political action committee that, according to Loudon, helped elect Barack Obama in 2008 and has been a driving force behind the massive advances the radical Left have made in turning red states blue.

So, it is Phillips and people of his pedigree financing the political fortunes of Kamala Harris. And a Harris victory would invite many of these people into the White House. Many are already there. The Biden administration went a long way to disassemble our nation. A Harris administration would finish the job. Finally, her newly chosen vice presidential candidate, Tim Walz, has been partnering with the Communist Chinese in various roles both as a private citizen and elected leader since the 1980s. So in a Harris administration, we would essentially be turning our nation over to a pair of Communist Chinese agents of influence.

All you need to do is look around and see where we are today. Where does one begin? Crises are everywhere. Some are very real: borders flooded with illegal aliens, child and drug trafficking, inflation, massive and growing government debt, supply chain disruptions, the war in Ukraine, growing threats from China, Iran, and Russia, continued fallout from COVID, unprecedented division, vote fraud so enormous many people don't believe it could be real, and other threats. Some are entirely contrived, like the so-called global warming "crisis," a fraud imposed as an excuse to banish fossil fuels and increase our dependency on the government while making all the wrong people filthy rich.

As our cities are overwhelmed with crime waves that malevolent prosecutors refuse to prosecute, even allowing killers to go free without bail;[9] as record numbers of people, especially the young, die from overdoses enabled by the flood of drugs through open borders; as suicides, especially among the young and military, reach unprecedented levels; as educators seek to indoctrinate and mutilate our children with horrific transgender and hateful CRT propaganda; as rampant spending and unchecked inflation threaten to destroy our economy, we see our beloved nation circling the drain.

But in every case, the source of these crises can be traced directly to leftist policies, agendas, and lies. None are necessary or without simple solutions.

Simple—but not easy.

Columnist Victor Davis Hanson observed, "Things are becoming so strange, so surreal, so nihilistic in contemporary America that the chaos can only be deliberate. Chance, incompetence, and accident could not alone explain the series of disasters we now daily witness that are nearly destroying the country."[10]

He's right. Our government is literally at war with us. But this is true for most, if not all, Western governments. Just look at Canada. With the 2022 trucker protest against the COVID mandates, Canadian prime minister Justin Trudeau declared war on those protesters, jailing many, cutting their access to credit and savings, and assuring many lost their jobs. Thirty-nine trucking companies were shut down.[11] Where in Canadian law is such despotic rule given to the Canadian leader? The Parliament is even considering a law to impose life sentences for certain speech.[12]

At the start of the 2015 refugee invasion into Europe from Africa and the Middle East, German chancellor Angela Merkel threw open the doors to these refugees, virtually guaranteeing the unprecedented terrorism that occurred throughout Western Europe. Today, Germany, France, England, the Netherlands, Denmark, and Sweden are experiencing growing "no go" zones, rapes, violence, and terrorism from these same "refugees." And you can be arrested for just complaining about it. Italy is finally saying, "Enough!" But we don't hear a peep from most leaders of those other countries. Politicians brave enough to speak up are smeared as bigots and "Islamophobes" and must hire teams of security professionals just to stay alive.

The migrant invasion of Europe was a precursor of what was planned for us, as predicted in my books, *The Red-Green Axis* and *The Red-Green Axis 2.0*. The response by European governments stripped the façade of "democracy" and showed the world that Europe's "deep state" hated their people as much as today's American government appears to hate us. We dodged a bullet in 2016 with election of President Donald Trump, but Democrats redoubled their efforts to win, no matter what it would take, in 2020. And here we are. They will steal 2024 also if we let them.

To most people, these many-faceted crises are considered individually and simply reflect policy differences. The migrant crisis is sold as a humanitarian response to needy people. If you oppose open borders, you are heartless. You must be "compassionate." The Biden administration's efforts at ending fossil fuel are billed as "essential" to countering the threat of "cataclysmic" global warming.

Rampant government spending on credit exploded our national debt to over $30 trillion in 2022, which along with skyrocketing energy costs, has fueled unprecedented inflation. The Biden administration's answer was to propose the hilariously misnamed "Inflation Reduction Act," which pumped $1 trillion more printed dollars into the economy. National debt now stands at $34 trillion, and $1 trillion more is being added every one hundred days.[13] Any rational economist will tell you such policies will increase, not decrease, inflation. In fact, such debt spending is unsustainable without triggering hyperinflation.

But rarely are all these different agendas viewed as part of a larger whole, and their true purpose is either not understood or carefully overlooked. News analysts love to debate policy because it keeps them in business. They can call Joe Biden and the Democrats "stupid," "wrongheaded," or simply "ignorant." Political pundits do this all the time. But it is a cop-out. It generously credits people who advance these agendas with good motives, even if their ideas are crazy.

However, you don't spend a lifetime surviving in Washington, DC, being an idiot. These people know exactly what they are doing. And while Joe Biden may be suffering dementia, he cheerfully goes along with those pulling the strings—*he always has*—and is aware of the damage they cause. He takes pleasure in watching it. He is the person-ification of evil.

Consider Richard Levine, the man they appointed assistant secre-tary for Health and Human Services, and recently, admiral in the Public Health Service. We know him as Dr. Rachel Levine. He is not female. Today he is referred to as "transgender," but he is just a transvestite, i.e., a cross-dresser. He is a really ugly fat guy who likes to dress up as a woman. Is he what you would call a picture of health? He's the polar opposite. Why on earth would they appoint a blatantly obese cross-dresser to a leadership position in the Health Department? Because they want to make a mockery of public health. Everything being inflicted on us today is specifically designed to shock, demoralize, confuse, enrage, and ridicule us. It is also a great way to smoke out political enemies, something the Left is always trying to do.

The people who dreamed up this entire agenda are literally evil. They rejoice in our misery. They want to convince us that *we* are evil, that *we* are the problem, that *we* are standing in the way of "progress." And they have convinced and intimidated lesser individuals to believe they are right. The Left does not need a reason. They only need a pre-text, and the cultural narrative has given them that. So they call us hat-ers, Nazis, bigots, fill-in-the-blank-phobes, with impunity, when really, they are projecting characteristics of *their* behavior. And the intimidated public goes along with it.

America faces an existential threat. The threat is apparent today to those of us whose heads are not completely buried in the sand. But it is really the accumulation of a death by a thousand cuts administered by the anti-American Left for decades. At first it was subtle, underhanded, and dismissed as unimportant by those who saw it happening, while the rest of us shrugged or ignored it. "There go those crazy liberals again," we would say, shaking our heads. The few who spoke out were ignored, attacked, or censored—much as they are today. ·

For almost a century, the agitators, propagandists, and rioters of the radical Left (the true insurrectionists)—today represented primar-ily by the Democratic Party and its "progressive" allies—have been on a relentless crusade to achieve the "fundamental transformation" of

America into the Socialist paradise of their fantasies. Along the way, they have caused countless crises that tear at the fabric of our society from all directions.

At the same time, they have sought to undermine and sabotage our foreign policy at every turn, making us vulnerable to enemies both within and without, and have *often colluded directly with those enemies*. Although it is difficult to believe, they are aware of the misery and chaos they create. Generating chaos, pain, and strife is actually *a critical component of their game plan*.

People unfamiliar with the Left's fundamental depravity reject this proposition as the product of a conspiracy theorist's fevered imagination. But they are simply ignorant of the facts. The Left utilizes proven strategies with firmly established and easily traceable pedigrees. The increasingly aggressive implementation of these strategies defines the Left today—enthusiastically personified during the administration of President Barack Hussein Obama and now on steroids under the deranged but even more destructive Joe Biden. Even the Clinton administration, mistakenly considered "moderate" by Democrat standards, got the ball rolling with the *premeditated* subprime mortgage crisis, Bill Clinton's degenerate predilections, and his *outright treason*.[14]

The Left operates under one guiding principle. Former radical David Horowitz described it: "The issue is never the issue. The issue is always the revolution."[15] In other words, for all the agendas they promote—whether it's climate change, transgender rights, illegal immigration, unrestricted abortion, or free housing—they only care about that issue so much as it serves the purpose of advancing their revolution. As described below:

> No matter what issue they were fighting about…it was a mere pretext to hide their radical goal: a communist revolution in America. While most Americans were debating the merits of the issue itself, SDS and other radical leftists were framing the debate, inflaming emotions, neutralizing opponents, and weaponizing

it in order to overthrow American institutions and destroy society.[16]

The widespread chaos we see everywhere across America is all part of a comprehensive plan by our nation's enemies—both within and without—to destroy America once and for all. Every aspect is a *Manufactured Crisis*, conceived, planned, and advanced by an international movement that correctly identifies America as the last impediment to its worldwide domination. That movement has a name. You can call it the "Deep State," the "Swamp," the "Establishment," the "Elite," the "Globalists," "Wokeism," "Progressivism," or whatever name you choose. Its true name is *Communism*. And while many in the "Establishment" or the "Swamp" may not even realize this, it is the strategies employed by the worldwide Communist movement that they are advancing. And if America falls, the world will fall with it.

Tucker Carlson recently interviewed Xi Van Fleet, a woman who survived the horrific Cultural Revolution in Communist China. It was very similar to what is happening in America today—and that is not coincidental, as this book will prove. This short snippet at the end of the interview says it all:[17]

> Tucker: You survived all of this, this first [Chinese cultural] revolution. What advice would you give to Americans for how to respond to our revolution right now happening in our country?
>
> Xi: I would say, you understand what's going on. Only when you understand what's going you can fight back. Otherwise, you can't fight something you don't understand. And it's not some kind of crazy, kind of Democrats, they just do some crazy things. No. This is absolutely a full-blown Communist revolution. And the goal is very simple, it's just one: destroy this country so some people can have total control of power.

Tucker: So it has nothing to do with improving any-body's life?

Xi: No.

We are experiencing the end stages of a Communist revolution that has been conducted against America for over one hundred years but has only recently come fully out of the shadows. What happens in the next few years will determine whether the great American Experiment surges back to life or dies an ignoble death. This book will explain to you the who, what, where, when, and how of their diabolical plans—and what has to happen to stop them.

THE SEEDS OF CRISIS

*We must organize the intellectuals and use
them to make Western civilization stink.*

—Willi Münzenberg

n 1869, a twenty-two-year-old Russian anarchist named Sergey
Nechayev penned a short pamphlet titled *The Revolutionary Catechism*.[18] While notorious in his day, few of today's historians speak
about him or apparently even know of him. I call him the most
important radical no one's ever heard of, and in my book *Who Was Karl
Marx?*, I devote an entire chapter to him.[19] This is because in *Catechism*
he laid out a strategy that became the blueprint for Communist revolu-
tions worldwide, first implemented by the Russian Bolshevik[1] Vladimir
Ilyich Lenin, who took power in Russia with the birth of the Soviet
Union in 1917.

Nechayev's *Catechism* states, "Our task is terrible, total, universal,
and merciless destruction." Karl Marx and all the revolutionaries of his
day agreed. In one of his writings, Marx proclaimed, "There is only one

---

[1]   Literally meaning "Majority," Lenin's Bolsheviks were a small, extreme-left minority
within the Russian Social-Democratic Workers' Party. In 1903 at the party's second
congress, Lenin's group gained temporary control of the party leadership and declared
themselves the "Majority." They named the much larger group within the party the
"Mensheviks" or "Minority." See: https://www.britannica.com/topic/Bolshevik.

way in which the murderous death agonies of the old society and the bloody birth throes of the new society can be shortened, simplified and concentrated, and that way is revolutionary terror."[20]

Pol Pot move over.

In his 1848 *Communist Manifesto* co-authored with fellow Communist Friedrich Engels, Marx wrote, "The Communists disdain to conceal their views and aims. They openly declare that their ends can be attained only by the forcible overthrow of all existing social conditions."[21]

The anarchist Mikhail Bakunin, one of Nechayev's colleagues who is sometimes cited as co-author of the *Catechism*, stated, "In this revolution we will have to awaken the Devil in the people, to stir up the basest passions. Our mission is to destroy, not to edify. The passion of destruction is a creative passion."[22]

Keep that last quote in mind. From these short statements and many other similar ones, we can see that the seeds were planted very early on in the Communist movement to foment crises manufactured by the Communists themselves. The *Catechism* states it concisely in the following passage:

> The Society [of revolutionary conspirators] has no aim other than the complete liberation and happiness of the masses—i.e., of the people who live by manual labor. Convinced that their emancipation and the achievement of this happiness can only come about as a result of an all-destroying popular revolt, *the Society will use all its resources and energy toward increasing and intensifying the evils and miseries of the people until at last their patience is exhausted and they are driven to a general uprising.* (Emphasis added.)

Reflect on that. Nechayev advocated actions that would literally drive people mad. Today's Left has taken this idea to heart. Nechayev laid out the entire plan, summarized below:

1. Penetrate all segments of society, pretending to fit in, while plotting destruction.

2. Attack property rights, traditional society, and morality.
3. Create so much chaos and division that the society declares war on itself.
4. Create an order of execution to exterminate all people not useful to the Left.

Somehow he never got around to saying how this would make us all happy. And this is the case for all the Marxist revolutionaries. They seek to destroy rather than build, and that fact is made clear by their repeated statements and actions. Marx was vague on how his brave new world would actually function. Communist ideology only provided a pretext for the destruction they planned.

Lenin was obsessed with Nechayev and reprinted and widely distributed Nechayev's writings. Nechayev's strategy for destroying the West became known as "catastrophism." And while Lenin did not refer to the term specifically, he is alleged to have described it as follows:

> Deepen the contradictions [i.e., exaggerate, exacerbate existing crises, problems, social and ethnic differences and disparities, opinion discrepancies, rifts, etc.], and if they don't exist, create them or, if you can't create them, convincingly claim that they exist, and then deepen them, and in the process, profit the most from them in any way you can—politically, ideologically [and financially, to bankroll the Left] and, in the resulting chaos, blame our enemies for the whole mayhem, and finally, come up with 'solutions' that will favor us, and that will be the root of new future crises to be exploited in the future, and so on, until the targeted capitalist society is destroyed completely, to then build—under Bolshevik supervision and control—a socialist society enroute to communism.[23]

This statement sounds eerily familiar to what we are seeing from the Left almost every day now, doesn't it? But as we shall see in later chapters, many of the "solutions" brought to us by the Left have already made matters much worse, and true to form, the Left is there with the answer: more of the same.

Lenin's strategies were further developed by the German Communist, Willi Münzenberg. Münzenberg was a Bolshevik in Lenin's inner circle and consummate true believer. He became known as the Red Millionaire.[24] Using funds provided through the Communist International (Comintern)[2] and money he could sponge from his wealthy contacts, he spent lavishly to develop a network of newspapers, magazines, theaters, and film outlets with which he could promote Communist propaganda throughout Europe and America.

He is credited with creating popular fronts—organizations like the Hollywood Anti-Nazi League—where the ostensible purpose (fighting fascism) hides the true purpose (promoting Communism). Many prominent writers and actors came under his spell, including Upton Sinclair, Sinclair Lewis, Ernest Hemingway, Lillian Hellman, Dashiell Hammet, Bertolt Brecht, and others. His work inspired the British "Cambridge Five" spy ring, led by Kim Philby, the notorious MI-6 official who spied for the Soviets from 1933 to 1963 until finally exposed, whereupon he fled to the Soviet Union and died there in 1988.[25]

Both Lenin and Münzenberg realized after World War I that the working class would not carry out the revolution they sought. Instead, it would come, as one brilliant French polemicist put it, through "the treason of the intellectuals."[26] Why the "intellectuals"? Because, as Ruth Fischer, friend of Münzenberg and prominent German Communist, observed, "Willi knew that you don't have to buy the intellectuals—you just have to flatter them."[27]

This statement rings so true. Liberal elitists, including college professors, news pundits, Hollywood actors, and for that matter, most outspoken liberals, are some of the most conceited people you will ever meet. It is not simply that they think they know better (they usually

---

[2] The Third International, or Communist International (Comintern), was created by Lenin and his Bolsheviks in 1919 to cement the most radical goals within the international Socialist movement. Moderates were to be expelled, and only those parties agreeing to align with the Soviet Union could join. See: https://www.britannica.com/topic/Third-International.

don't) but that they are fueled by pride and ego—enthralled by their imagined intelligence. Thus when a leading Communist flatters them, they are only too eager to help out. They thrill at the idea of contributing to "the revolution," while safely ensconced in comfortable positions that risk little as long as they have "right think."

But Münzenberg was primarily targeting academia. With this in mind, he articulated a strategy that would use the intelligentsia to corrupt Western culture. He said:

> We must organize the intellectuals and use them to make Western civilization stink. Only then, after they have corrupted all its values and made life base, can we impose the Dictatorship of the Proletariat.[28]

Münzenberg was a leader and regular speaker at Comintern meetings, and his extensive influence may well have shaped the future of Europe.[29] His ideas, and those of another Bolshevik, the Hungarian Communist Georg Lukacs, launched a school to accomplish just that. In 1923, with Lenin's approval, and Comintern money and funds from the Marxist son of a wealthy German industrialist, they helped found the Institute for Social Research, a school housed at the University of Frankfurt in Germany.

Given this bland name to hide their radical agenda, the professors were prominent and doctrinaire Marxists, like Max Horkheimer and Friedrich Pollock, and Communist espionage agents, such as Hede Massing and Richard Sorge.[30] Over time, it became known as simply "the Frankfurt School." The goal was to churn out Communist-indoctrinated students and teachers while providing a cover for secret agents to do their spy work. With the rise of the Nazis in the 1930s, the school relocated to Geneva, Switzerland, and in 1934, to Columbia University's Teachers College.

But while in Frankfurt, the school's leading scholars, primarily Horkheimer and Lukacs, began development of a new "philosophy" they called "Critical Theory." This idea came directly from Karl Marx. In 1843, well before *The Communist Manifesto* was published, Marx had exhorted his comrades, saying:

The proclamation of ready-made solutions for all time is not our affair, when we realize all the more clearly what we have to accomplish in the present—I am speaking of a *ruthless criticism of everything existing*, ruthless in two senses. The criticism must not be afraid of its own conclusions, nor of the conflict with the powers that be. (Emphasis in the original.)[31]

Later on that year, he expanded on the idea:

The immediate task of philosophy, which is in the service of history, is to unmask human self-alienation in its *secular* form now that it has been unmasked in its *sacred form*. Thus, the *criticism of heaven* is transformed into a *criticism of earth*, the *criticism of religion* into the *criticism of law*, and the *criticism of theology* into the *criticism of politics*. (Emphases his.)[32]

The goal of Critical Theory was aptly described by William Lind of the Free Congress Foundation in 2004:

Critical Theory was essentially destructive criticism of the main elements of Western culture, including Christianity, capitalism, authority, the family, patriarchy, hierarchy, morality, tradition, sexual restraint, loyalty, patriotism, nationalism, heredity, ethnocentrism, convention and conservatism.[33]

Clearly, this was what Münzenberg referred to when he outlined the goal to corrupt Western values to the point where Western civilization would "stink."

The move to Columbia's Teachers College really magnified the Frankfurt School's influence on culture. Ralph de Toledano writes: "The influence of Teacher's College, in fact, reached out across the country, as its graduates filled more than 60 percent of all teaching and educational administrative posts in the country."[34]

In 1937, Max Horkheimer formalized Critical Theory in an essay titled "Traditional and Critical Theory." It aimed at "critiquing and changing society as a whole."[35] From the beginning, Frankfurt School's Critical Theory relentlessly accused Western societies of being "the world's greatest repositories of racism, sexism, xenophobia, homophobia, anti-Semitism, fascism, and Nazism."[36]

Critical Theory, today often identified as "political correctness" or "Cultural Marxism," has been further refined into smaller subsets as thinking has evolved. For example, "criticism of law" has become Critical Legal Theory, which sees our Constitutional Republic as a system of oppression that favors the privileged over the oppressed.[37] Therefore, the US Constitution is not merely a "living document" to be altered at will but rather the foundation of our "oppressive," "racist," "imperialist," nation that supports "white privilege." Therefore, it is justifiable to completely ignore the US Constitution as a basis for law and work and to replace it with a system that promotes diversity, equity, and inclusion in pursuit of "social justice." Once again, the Left does not need a valid reason to do what they do, just the pretext.

Further subclassifications include Critical Race Theory (CRT), Feminist Legal Criticism, Latino Critical Legal Theory, Critical Race Feminism, Critical White Studies, and Critical Pedagogy (criticism of education as a construct of white privilege).[38]

The list goes on forever. But everywhere, the goal is to deconstruct our society through relentless criticism and usually flawed reasoning or blatant lies, giving leftists the pretext to rewrite, enforce, or ignore the law to their liking. The *New York Times'* "1619 Project," which rewrites American history to reinforce leftist narratives on race, is a case in point.

And as those ideas spread like metastasizing cancer, action followed thought, delivering us to the state we're in today where all aspects of American society are under attack, fomenting crisis after crisis and creating ever more divisions, breaking our nation into warring fragments. It has brought America to the point where the literal survival of our society is threatened. One can hear echoes of Nechayev: "increasing and intensifying the evils and miseries of the people until at last their patience is exhausted and they are driven to a general uprising."

Critical Legal Theory and many of its offshoots continue to be taught in law schools across the US, putting Constitutional law in the back seat and producing a vanguard of attorneys who not only believe the Constitution to be irrelevant but a source of oppression that needs to be abolished. In a 2023 *California Law Review* article titled "The Purpose of Legal Education," the author states:

> This Article argues that the anti-racist, democratic, and movement lawyering principles advocated by progressive legal scholars should not be viewed merely as aspirational ideals for social justice law courses. Rather, querying whether legal systems and political institutions further racism, economic oppression, or social injustice must be viewed as endemic to the fundamental purpose of legal education…it demonstrates the urgency of moving beyond liberal legalism in legal education by *integrating critical legal theories and movement law principles throughout the entire law school curriculum.* (Emphasis added.)[39]

The many district attorneys who today flout the law, letting criminals run free while going after police officers, are a good example of Critical Legal Theory's end product—creating manufactured crises across the nation, essentially penalizing those dedicated police officers who attempt to uphold the law, while allowing crime to escalate the chaos. It punishes Americans, well, simply because we are Americans.

Herbert Marcuse was perhaps the best-known and definitely the most influential Frankfurt School Communist. Younger than most of the others when the school was started, he became notorious throughout American higher education in the 1950s and '60s, first at Columbia University, then Harvard; Brandeis, where he first mentored Black Communist Angela Davis, and later the University of California at San Diego.

He was admired by the so-called "red diaper babies" of the 1960s, most prominently represented by Students for a Democratic Society (SDS). Primarily offspring of American Communists, SDS members abandoned party membership but retained its ideology. They were called the New Left, a term coined by Columbia University Socialist professor C. Wright Mills,[40] and Marcuse—who credits Mills's work—was referred to as the "Father of the New Left."[41] The New Left students later took up careers in academia, law, and media, and we are seeing the long-term results today.

Marcuse was also considered the father of the sexual revolution. In his 1955 book *Eros and Civilization*, he attempted to combine Marxist theory with that of Sigmund Freud, founder of psychoanalysis. Whereas Freud thought that sexual urges should be controlled, Marcuse argued that moral standards were "repressive" and that human sexual instincts should be given free rein. He supposedly coined the phrase, "Make love, not war."

There were, of course, many other factors that drove the sexual revolution: invention of the pill, growing drug use, and an increasingly permissive atmosphere driven by post-war affluence and the nation's gradual slide away from Christianity and God. But most of these other influences were in turn encouraged by the Left. And the inspiration goes way back. Recall the anarchist Bakunin's quote: "We will have to awaken the Devil in the people, to stir up the basest passions."

Marcuse was also influenced in this regard by Georg Lukacs, the Hungarian Communist who helped inspire the Frankfurt School. As the minister of culture in the very short-lived Hungarian Soviet Republic, Lukacs advocated using sex to corrupt culture. Specifically, he imposed explicit sex education to children in public schools and launched a nationwide campaign urging women to leave their husbands and be promiscuous. His intention was to attack Christian morality, stand traditional culture on its head, and create a new generation that would reject the mores of the old. He called his program "Cultural Terrorism."[42]

During its formative years from 1923 to 1933, Lukacs and Münzenberg saw Berlin as a test bed for Critical Theory and the Frankfurt School's planned corruption of society. Ralph de Toledano described it in his seminal book, *Cry Havoc*:

> Berlin was the Frankfurt School's dream and plan
> in microcosm, for Germany as it would be for the
> United States. It was the testing ground for the Lukacs-
> Horkheimer Critical Theory, and the elimination of
> family, morality and religion...there was the *cabaret*
> Berlin: nightclubs in which nude waitresses not only
> served drinks but themselves to the customers, and
> prostitutes on the street snapping whips to entice
> masochists.[43]

Berlin became the most decadent city in Europe. Novelist Christopher Isherwood wrote, "In the vilest perversions of the oriental mind, you couldn't find anything more nauseating than what goes on there quite openly, every day. That city is doomed more surely than Sodom ever was...."[44]

Screenwriter Anita Loos wrote, "The night life was pretty decadent. Any Berlin lady of the evening might turn out to be a man; the prettiest girl on the street was [prominent male actor] Konrad Veidt."[45]

There was another facility called the Institute for Sexual Research, which, according to de Toledano, "plumped for nudism, homosexuality, sadomasochism, voluntary sterilization to eliminate the family, the sexual encouragement of children and free psychoanalytic clinics to spread...Critical Theory."[46]

Marcuse turbocharged Lukacs's ideas with his 1955 book *Eros and Civilization*, which harmonized with the "free love" attitudes of the 1960s, and has been credited with inspiring the gay rights movement. As aptly described here:

> Marcuse believed that sexual liberation was achieved
> by exploring new permutations of sexual desires,
> sexual activities, and gender roles—what Freud called
> "perverse" sexual desires, that is, all nonreproductive
> forms of sexual behavior, of which kissing, oral sex, and
> anal sex are familiar examples. Marcuse was himself
> heterosexual, but he identified the homosexual as the
> radical standard bearer of sex for the sake of pleasure,

a form of radical hedonism that repudiates those forms of repressive sexuality organized around genital heterosexuality and biological reproduction. "Against a society which employs sexuality as a means for a useful end," Marcuse argued, "the perversions uphold sexuality as an end itself…and challenge its very foundations.[47]

So like Lukacs, Marcuse sought to subvert traditional morality by advocating sex as an end in and of itself, totally detached from procreation, and a direct attack on Christian morality. Marcuse described sex and sexual liberation as the ultimate form of satisfaction in an atheistic world where no God exists and no morality restrains this impulse. Marcuse called it "libidinal rationality."

But in reality, instead of freeing us, it has virtually destroyed our society. In *The Center That Holds*, Anthony Costello writes:

> Should it strike us as odd that two generations after the "Sexual Revolution" our nation has had to grapple with the devastating aftermath of that revolution? This aftermath has been most poignantly revealed in justice movements like *#MeToo* and devastating, social endemics like fatherless homes… Moreover, as we begin to see what is likely just the tip of the iceberg of the sexual damage that has been wrought since the Sexual Revolution, is it any wonder that we also see the number of suicides in our homeland at record highs? Is it not entirely evident that sexual brokenness and depression are inextricably linked? Do we not sense that we are all, in some way, damaged goods and that this is mostly on account of our vain, Marcusean attempts at the phantom of sexual liberation? Is it not obvious that "libidinal rationality" is not only a myth, but that even if it were not, it would always be subservient to our more innate sense of right and wrong?[48]

Now step back from this dense discussion and ask yourself: Did Marcuse really believe that the world's problems could be solved by a society unleashed to engage in unrestrained sexual activity? Or, given what we have already identified as the Left's universal desire to see our society destroyed, wasn't that the result intended all along?

Communists study history. They know that Rome fell as its citizens were given over to debauchery. They saw firsthand how the pre-war German Weimar Republic had become the most depraved society in the West. You might recall the movie *Cabaret*, starring Liza Minnelli, which depicted the decadence of Berlin before World War II.

Why is moral corruption important to the Communists? It is because a morally corrupt society becomes so preoccupied with its debauchery, it becomes weak, cowardly, and blind to dangers at its doorstep. Toward the end of *Cabaret*, the camera pans to the people in the front row of the theater, all wearing Nazi uniforms. The performers were blissfully unaware of the implication, but they'd learn soon enough.

So wasn't Marcuse simply following Willi Münzenberg's instructions to "make Western civilization so corrupt it stinks?" Of course he was.

But Marcuse wasn't finished. He was probably the most influential critical theorist of all the Frankfurt School professors but was also one of the most effective advocates for what we today call "cancel culture." In a 1965 essay titled "Repressive Tolerance," Marcuse argued that an oppressive imbalance exists in Western societies, which he said "favors and fortifies the conservation of the status quo of inequality and discrimination." [49]

Marcuse argued that it was therefore justifiable to impose repressive tolerance in the opposite direction, silencing all thought and speech that the Left disapproved of:

> Not "equal" but more representation of the Left would
> be equalization of the prevailing inequality.... Given
> this situation, I suggested in "Repressive Tolerance"
> the practice of discriminating tolerance in an inverse
> direction, as a means of shifting the balance between
> Right and Left by restraining the liberty of the

Right, thus counteracting the pervasive inequality of freedom (unequal opportunity of access to the means of democratic persuasion) and strengthening the oppressed against the oppressors....[50]

Despite the First Amendment allowing alternative ideas and philosophies to be discussed, promoted, and even supported by political parties, it wasn't enough, because the Left wasn't getting the traction it wanted with its propaganda. Did it never occur to them that maybe *their message* was the problem? But never mind. This effort to silence their enemies came to be called "partisan tolerance," i.e., tolerance of the Left and complete intolerance, even down to the level of thought, of the Right.

Thus, we all have to shut up! And don't you dare say anything that disagrees with the Left, especially when whatever you are saying reveals the truth. And the truth is what they are trying to suppress with cancel culture, because if the American people were apprised of what they are really up to, people would be calling for their heads.

One more historical figure deserves mention here. Antonio Gramsci, a prominent Italian Communist in the 1920s, spent the bulk of 1922 and 1923 in the Soviet Union and attended the 4th Comintern Congress, where he was exposed to Münzenberg. In 1924, he became the leader of Italy's Communist Party. Jailed by Mussolini in 1926, he further developed Nechayev's and Münzenberg's ideas in what came to be known as the *Prison Notebooks*. Gramsci never left prison and died there in 1937. But his *Notebooks* survived him and were picked up with enthusiasm by American Marxists, most notably '60s radicals.

In his *Revolutionary Catechism*, Nechayev said:

> Aiming at implacable revolution, the revolutionary may and frequently must live within society while pretending to be completely different from what he really is, for he must penetrate everywhere, into all the higher and middle-classes, into the houses of commerce, the churches, and the palaces of the aristocracy, and

into the worlds of the bureaucracy and literature and
the military....

According to Gramsci, capitalism's power or "hegemony" rested in
its institutions, that is, churches, schools, the media, Hollywood, the
military, government, and political parties. The answer of course was
to infiltrate, subvert, dominate, and control these institutions to serve
Communist ends, as Nechayev had specified. It became known as the
"long march through the institutions."

Because he died in prison, and his notebooks were written in Italian,
they didn't receive as much attention as the Frankfurt School, which
had essentially been carrying out the infiltration plan since its relocation
to Columbia. Joseph Buttigieg, father to failed presidential candidate
and now secretary of transportation, Pete Buttigieg, was a prominent
Marxist and Notre Dame professor who was well known in leftist circles
as a leading scholar of Gramsci.[51] He co-founded and presided over the
International Gramsci Society and translated all of Gramsci's work in a
project that took him three decades before its initial 1992 publication.[52]
Joseph's son is following Gramsci's infiltration plan as a prominent
player in the Biden administration, doing his part to "make Western
civilization so corrupt it stinks."

In 1971, Marcuse found the perfect vehicle for his "partisan tolerance," the Southern Poverty Law Center. The SPLC is an extreme
Left, Communist-inspired, if not Communist-led, influence operation
designed to demonize and silence critics of the Far Left's agenda for
America. With the SPLC's "Hate Watch," "Hate List," and "Hate Map,"
you can find practically every conservative organization in America.

We are relentlessly vilified. SPLC's "Teaching Tolerance" program
has been adopted by many public schools, and of course, the tolerance
only goes in one direction. It teaches hateful *intolerance* of America,
the Constitution, and our Judeo-Christian values. SPLC's vilification
inspired Floyd Corkins, a homosexual activist, to attack the Family
Research Council in Washington, DC, in 2012. He said he "wanted to
kill as many people as possible."[53] It also inspired James Hodgkinson,

who in 2017 attempted to murder GOP congressmen playing baseball at a field in Alexandria, Virginia.[54]

The SPLC is one of the major epicenters of cancel culture. It is referenced by media, employers, and governmental organizations, *including the FBI*, that use it as a source to justify targeting individuals who need silencing.[55] Not surprisingly, the SPLC was behind the effort to call parents and organizations that oppose radical sex education and CRT "anti-government extremists."[56] The Biden administration took the cue, labeling them "domestic terrorists," and requested the FBI investigate.[57] You simply cannot make this stuff up.

The SPLC was co-founded in 1971 by promoter Morris Dees and radical leftist Julian Bond. Bond presided over the SPLC until 1979 and remained on the board of directors until his death in 2015. Bond spent his life allied with Communist Party organizations, agendas, and activities and was a founding member of Democratic Socialists of America (DSA), the US arm of the Socialist International and the largest Communist organization in America.[58] (Note: DSA is not Democratic and only includes "Socialist" because it doesn't sound as scary as what the organization truly stands for.)

Marcuse and Bond knew each other since at least 1967, when they were both organizers for the National Conference for New Politics (NCNP), an event that attempted to unify all the forces of the radical Left under one banner. Marcuse and Bond also connected through Angela Davis. Marcuse had mentored Davis at Brandeis and later at UCLA San Diego, where Davis went for postgraduate studies specifically to continue to receive his tutelage.[59]

Both Marcuse and Bond supported Davis during her 1972 trial for participation in the murder of a California judge. Later on, Marcuse and Bond would together help co-found *In These Times*, a Communist newspaper that is still published today. Interestingly, you have to look to the internet archive to find Marcuse's name among the paper's founders.[60] With all we know about Marcuse today, it is not surprising that the paper would want to suppress his name. Canceling one of their own... Ironic, no?

But all the leftists were on board with the agenda to vilify their opponents, going all the way back to Lenin, who said, "We can and must write in a language which sows among the masses hate, revulsion, and scorn towards those who disagree with us."[61]

So today, when you watch media personalities lie into the TV, smearing and misrepresenting conservatives, and in fact, anyone who challenges the narrative with facts, know that you are witnessing partisan tolerance in action. And partisan tolerance, as well as Critical Theory, libidinal rationality, and every other Communist machination targeted at the West, comes directly from the sick mind of Karl Marx and those who followed him.

THE CRISIS STRATEGY

*Create crisis, because crisis is that
edge where change is possible.*
—Anarchist Lisa Fithian

Never let a good crisis go to waste.
—Rahm Emanuel

*In my view, this crisis is a genuine opportunity.
An opportunity to do things we wanted to do.
And only now it becomes so apparent.*[62]
—Joe Biden

Yuri Bezmenov was a Soviet propagandist who defected to the West in 1970. In a series of explosive interviews, he described the Soviet strategy for destroying the West—and America, particularly. It would come in four stages, summarized below from the description in *Big Intel*, a book by J. Michael Waller that should be required reading for every American:[63]

Stage 1. Demoralization. Students are the target. They will be taught to hate America, its constitution, its values and its position in the world. Without aggressive challenge, these beliefs will become engrained in our youth over one to three or more generations. As they build careers in academia, media and corporate America, they will carry this poisonous ideology with them.

With the Frankfurt School's Critical Theory and its downstream offshoots, this stage has been pretty well accomplished.

> Stage 2. Destabilization. Takes two to five years. Any and all reasoned debate is thrown out the window. The powers that be don't care in the least for your beliefs or your circumstances. They use the levers of media, economy, foreign and policy defense policy to destabilize everything.

Our economy is teetering on collapse, Joe Biden has become the laughing stock of the world, and our defense complex is more preoccupied with transgender "rights" than defending our nation. Stage two looks pretty much in the bag. It will only get worse if Kamala Harris wins, now that Biden has bowed out of the race. She will be totally controlled by the Obama crowd, and probably Red China too.

> Stage 3. Crisis. This stage seeks permanent crisis. It will take advantage of both natural and manufactured crises. All will be used to cripple our country and bring anxiety and uncertainty to a fever pitch. Trust in institutions will be lost (*a la* the FBI). Some people will lose the ability to reason, as lies replace truth and reason itself is turned upside down.

Manufactured crises have been instigated by the Left at an exponentially increasing rate since the 1960s, and if you read the news, it looks like quite a few people are going crazy.

> Stage 4. Normalization. This occurs after the Left has taken absolute power, and with it, permanent changes in the economy and all aspects of life. Bezmenov says it is a cynical term. This new normal is not a time of

peace. "You are in a state of war and have precious little time to save yourself."[64]

Stage three reiterates Lenin's idea to "deepen the contradictions… and if they don't exist, create them or, if you can't create them, convincingly claim that they exist, and then deepen them, and in the process, profit the most from them in any way you can…."

Both Lenin and Bezmenov described the general idea, and the Frankfurt School effectively targeted culture to compromise our societal immune system, but two Socialist college professors devised and implemented a complimentary plan that would bring about the kind of sustained, overwhelming crises Lenin referred to "that will be the root of new future crises to be exploited in the future, and so on, until the targeted capitalist society is destroyed completely…."

Richard Cloward and Frances Fox Piven were a married pair of sociology professors who taught at Columbia University during the heyday of the 1960s. While their names remain unknown to most Americans, they were very prominent in left-wing circles. From the 1960s to today, they have had a profound impact on American society. Cloward died in 2001, but Piven lives on, continuing to spout revolutionary drivel into her nineties.

Cloward and Piven were instrumental in developing crisis strategies that today literally threaten to destroy America as we know it. The best summary can be found, surprisingly, on Wikipedia:

> It is the strategy of forcing political change leading to societal collapse through orchestrated crises. The "Cloward–Piven Strategy" seeks to hasten the fall of capitalism by overloading the government bureaucracy with a flood of impossible demands, amassing massive unpayable national debt, and other methods such as unfettered immigration thus pushing society into crisis and economic collapse.[65]

The Cloward–Piven Strategy of Manufactured Crisis, also called "break the bank" or simply the "crisis strategy," was outlined in a May

1966 *Nation* magazine article titled "The Weight of the Poor: A Strategy to End Poverty."[66] Cloward and Piven believed that when organized as a unified force, the poor's "weight" could be "used as a battering ram against the welfare system, and by extension, against the American system itself."[67]

There were thirty thousand reprints of the article, and Cloward and Piven's ideas helped to popularize modes of operation that have since been adopted by radicals and subversives everywhere, including Presidents Clinton, Obama, and Biden. No matter where the strategy is implemented, it shares the following features:

- The offensive organizes previously unorganized groups eligible for government benefits but not currently receiving all they can.
- The offensive seeks to identify new beneficiaries and/or create new benefits.
- Government funding purchases permanent new voting blocs wholesale and further solidifies current beneficiaries' support for politicians who back these policies.
- The overarching aim is always to impose new stresses on target systems, with the ultimate goal of forcing their collapse.
- The strategy accomplishes a number of complimentary goals:
- Chaos makes the system difficult if not impossible to control.
- Demands for services provide both actual and psychic benefits to the Left's voting demographic. To the extent that actual benefits are supplied, the Left's supporters are materially better off than they were before.
- If all benefits cannot be supplied, the simple fact that an identifiable political party is calling for them endears that party to potential beneficiaries (who vote), offers a defensible—if duplicitous—justification for demanding such benefits, and helps build public pressure to provide them.

In 1966, many people had not taken full advantage of all the benefits now available to them under President Johnson's new Great Society program, whether out of ignorance or because of the stigma traditionally attached to accepting government handouts. Cloward and Piven believed that if Americans signed up for every benefit the law entitled them to, it would overwhelm state and local government budgets, creating a "profound financial and political crisis" that would generate demands for "major economic reform at the national level." The "reform" they envisioned was income redistribution through a new guaranteed annual income program—Socialism, in other words.[68]

Yet if their goal was a guaranteed income, would that not further increase the burden on government? Of course it would. While they offered it as a replacement to the current system, *it would not replace other benefits currently available*; it would be added on. Remember, government programs are rarely abolished, and the Left certainly wouldn't want that. Their *real* goal, as stated by virtually *all* prominent radicals including Cloward and Piven, is the collapse of capitalism. To facilitate their planned crisis, Cloward and Piven proposed "a massive drive to recruit the poor *onto* the welfare rolls." They were very specific about the kind of crisis they hoped to create:

> By crisis, we mean a *publicly visible* disruption in some institutional sphere. Crisis can occur spontaneously (e.g., riots) or as the intended result of tactics of demonstration and protest which either generate institutional disruption or bring unrecognized disruption to public attention. (Emphasis theirs.)[69]

And:

> Advocacy must be supplemented by organized demonstrations to create a climate of militancy that will overcome the invidious and immobilizing attitudes which many potential recipients hold toward being "on welfare." In such a climate, many more poor people are likely to become their own advocates and will not need to rely on aid from organizers.[70]

Cloward said the only way the poor could gain power was "when the rest of society is afraid of them."[71] And when will that be? When they are rioting, damaging property and people—much like what we saw with the George Floyd and other riots. But what would create that atmosphere of rage? The societal collapse Cloward and Piven were trying to engineer with their strategy.

Cloward and Piven openly acknowledged it. In creating the crisis strategy, they asserted that welfare was not actually helping the poor but driving them into lethargy. With the safety net, they argued, the rich were "dousing the fires of rebellion."[72] By overwhelming and bankrupting the system, Cloward and Piven hoped to drive angry welfare beneficiaries into the streets, violently demanding their benefits.

In other words, as Nechayev preached, Cloward and Piven deliberately sought to orchestrate a crisis that would *intensify "the evils and miseries of the people"* until they were provoked to violent rebellion.

Cloward and Piven were founders of many extreme Left organizations including the National Welfare Rights Organization (NWRO), the Association of Community Organizations for Reform Now (ACORN), Human Service Employees Registration and Voter Education Fund (Human SERVE), and the Democratic Socialists of America (DSA).

The NWRO was organized by Cloward and led by black activist George Wiley to implement their strategy. According to author Richard Poe, "By 1969, NWRO claimed a dues-paying membership of 22,500 families, with 523 chapters across the nation."[73] A 1970 *New York Times* article reported on the NWRO's disruptive activities in carrying out the crisis strategy:

> There have been sit-ins in legislative chambers, including a United States Senate committee hearing, mass demonstrations of several thousand welfare recipients, school boycotts, picket lines, mounted police, tear gas, arrests—and, on occasion, rock-throwing, smashed glass doors, overturned desks, scattered papers and ripped-out phones.[74]

Poe described the phenomenon:

> The flood of demands was calculated to break the budget, jam the bureaucratic gears into gridlock, and bring the system crashing down. Fear, turmoil, violence and economic collapse would accompany such a breakdown—providing perfect conditions for fostering radical change.[75]

The guaranteed annual income "solution" the NWRO demanded was a minimum of $5,500 per year for a family of four, with assistance provided until income reached $10,000.[76] It doesn't sound like much today, but median family income in 1970 was $9,870.[77] In today's dollars, $5,500 would be equivalent to about $44,000, while $10,000 equals approximately $80,000.[78] Median household income in 2022 was $74,580.[79] So they were really talking about a wholesale redistribution of income. Wiley's NWRO said it out loud.[80]

Cloward and Piven were pivotal in creating the welfare state they were working so hard to destroy. In 1961, Richard Cloward co-founded an organization in New York City called Mobilization for Youth. A sympathetic description reads:

> In 1962, the pioneering social work agency Mobilization for Youth (MFY) began its anti-juvenile delinquency program in New York's Lower East Side. Within two years, energized by the civil rights movement, residents and staffers together transformed MFY from a social service program into a hotbed of direct action organizing. Low-income African American and Puerto Rican mothers, together with MFY organizers, generated social movements that forever changed New York City and shaped the national War on Poverty.[81]

The organization worked with gang members, and Cloward argued that their delinquency resulted from lack of opportunity rather than any individual behavioral problems. In Cloward's Marxist mind, capitalism was at fault for creating poverty, thus criminals were just pursuing their rational self-interest in a corrupt system not of their making.[82]

Not surprisingly, according to the FBI, Cloward's organization was "a hot bed of communist activity."[83] In any event, Cloward argued the problem could be solved with massive welfare spending. Mobilization for Youth became *the model* for President Johnson's "Great Society."[84]

Now just reflect on that for a moment. Did Johnson know he was enabling the crisis strategy, or did he simply see this as a way to win votes? It's also interesting to note that Johnson borrowed the name for his program, "Great Society," from the title of a 1914 work by British Socialist Graham Wallas.[85]

Johnson's program birthed the Office of Economic Opportunity. Conservative activist Howard Phillips ran the OEO in 1973 and identified Cloward and Piven as the OEO's "ideological architects." He said the OEO financed "10,000 organizations employing several hundred thousand people" to radically transform US policy outside the political process.[86] There are many more than that today.

Liberal black commentator Juan Williams offered a humorous reflection on Cloward and Piven in a 1982 column for the Cleveland *Plain Dealer*. With the election of Ronald Reagan in 1980, the Left came unglued. Cloward, Piven, and other leftists exhorted inner city blacks to launch violent street riots as they had in the 1960s. Williams responded:[87]

> I had planned on going to the beach this summer, but the liberals seem to want me on the city streets. The tom toms of progressive thinking are beating out the message that blacks should riot....
>
> In the Nation magazine, social scientists Frances Fox Piven and Richard A. Cloward write "Large scale protest in the United States now seems certain...."
>
> "Riots or Marauding Gangs—Will They Strike Our Cities?" was the headline on a late April column by

Neal Pearce that began, "The voices are so responsible, so widespread that they have to be taken seriously...."

Therefore "burn baby burn" so we can all point at those Republican idiots and say "I told you so." Well, as a young black, I'd prefer the beach.

Williams pointed out that while it might be enjoyable for white liberals to sit around a coffee table fomenting revolution, for the inner-city blacks they want to use as cannon fodder for their class war, it's not so much fun:

> For the people who are the poor, another round of riots would mean living through days and nights of fear and watching neighborhoods just now on the mend from the '60s devastated again.

During the race riots of the 1960s, most of the damage fell on inner-city neighborhoods and the businesses that served them. Today, some sixty years later, many of those neighborhoods have still not recovered, and have suffered even more destruction thanks to the Freddie Gray, Michael Brown, George Floyd, and other riots.

But the white liberals might finally be getting those race wars they seem to want. Stanford University economist and commentator Thomas Sowell, who is black, believes we have been witnessing the opening salvos of a race war. Writing in 2015, even before the latest rounds of race-stoked violence, Sowell stated:

> For American society, a dangerous polarization has set in. Signs of this polarization over the years include opposite reactions between blacks and whites to the verdict in the O. J. Simpson murder case, the "rape" charges against Duke University students, and the trials resulting from the beating of Rodney King and the death of Trayvon Martin.

More dangerous than these highly publicized episodes over the years are innumerable organized and unprovoked physical attacks on whites by young black gangs in shopping malls, on beaches, and in other public places all across the country today.[88]

While Cloward and Piven did not get their guaranteed income directly, the crisis strategy managed to explode the welfare rolls. Between 1965 and 1974, single-parent households on welfare grew 151 percent, from 4.3 million to 10.8 million, during a period of relative economic prosperity. In New York City, where the crisis strategy had its greatest "success," there was one person on welfare for every two people working in the private sector.[89] This precipitated New York City's near bankruptcy in 1975. Speaking of that crisis in 1998, then New York mayor Rudolph Giuliani accused the pair of economic sabotage.[90]

ACORN

ACORN was the largest radical leftist community organization ever created. In its heyday, it boasted four hundred thousand members and 1,200 field offices in 120 cities nationwide.[91] In addition, *Subversion, Inc.* author Matthew Vadum uncovered a total of 370 "affiliates, subsidiaries, political action committees, branch offices and shell corporations" controlled by ACORN.[92] He did not rule out the possibility that there could be more.

In 2009, undercover reporters James O'Keefe and Hannah Giles posed as pimp and prostitute to record a series of videos of ACORN officials showing them how to circumvent the law in order to set up prostitution rings using underage illegal aliens.[93] They successfully replicated this sting in several cities around the country. Though one of the filmed ACORN workers in California subsequently sued the pair because surreptitious videos are against California law, ACORN closed its doors in 2010 citing declining revenues.[94]

This was just a tactical retreat. ACORN resurfaced under a variety of new names employing many of the same people, often at ACORN's old addresses. Former ACORN chief organizer Bertha Lewis bragged that they created "18 bulletproof community-organizing Frankensteins" to replace the old structure.[95] In fact, there are probably many more. Vadum identified twenty-seven in nineteen states plus the District of Columbia.[96] Some of these groups are still up to no good. But in its heyday, ACORN did its best to implement the Cloward–Piven Strategy, agitating for welfare, engaging in massive vote fraud, and pumping sub-prime mortgages that caused the 2008 recession. More about that later.

Richard Cloward mentored ACORN founder and chief organizer Wade Rathke and helped get the organization off the ground in 1970.[97] ACORN persisted in following the crisis strategy after the NWRO folded in 1975, but Rathke renamed it "maximum eligible participation." He admits this slyly in a backhanded effort to refute Cloward and Piven's critics:

> The irony of all of this is that we are dealing with the power of an article that Fran wrote with her partner Dick Cloward in *The Nation* in the 1960's which argued famously for a so-called "break the bank" strategy to achieve what I now call "maximum eligible participation…."[98]

He called the "break the bank" strategy nothing more than a "rhetorical flourish" designed to frighten bureaucrats into increasing the "grossly inadequate [welfare] benefits to something more humane."[99] In light of NWRO's decade-long, violent nationwide campaign, his statement is pure sophistry. But this is what leftists do: lie, dissemble, ridicule, obfuscate, mislead.

Cloward and Piven, however, were forthright. They wanted systemic failure and created the organizations to make it happen. Wade Rathke's ACORN continued the NWRO tradition by relentlessly promoting "maximum eligible participation" in welfare programs.

Minimum Wage Eugenics

Consider the $15 minimum wage. ACORN was promoting that idea, as well as the guaranteed annual income, for decades. Starting about ten years ago, states and municipalities caught on and began targeting a $15 minimum. The current federal minimum wage remains at $7.25 per hour, but most states have increased it substantially, some to $15 or more.[100] Washington State, for example, has set its minimum wage at $15.74. Massachusetts provides $20 per hour.[101] As of this writing, eight states have adopted a minimum wage that meets or exceeds $15 per hour. Another ten are $12 or above, fifteen states maintain the current federal rate or less, and five have no minimum wage law at all.[102]

Raising the minimum wage to such an extent has devastating consequences for both businesses and employees. Businesses must increase prices to pay higher employee costs, fire some employees, or both, and higher wages also put upward pressure on inflation. More of the same results from the guaranteed income—pushing more and more people onto the dole and away from gainful employment. The net result is fewer businesses, more unemployment, and higher inflation that cancels out the benefit of the increased income. So we lose everywhere.

While it is promoted as a way to help the poor obtain a "living wage," as usual, the leftists are wrong. Because it forces companies to squeeze their budgets, the minimum wage automatically makes it more difficult for people with handicaps or less experience—often minorities—to find work. Of course that contributes to the perception of the market as being biased. California raised its minimum wage for fast food restaurants to $20 in April 2024. The reaction among the business community was immediate and entirely predictable:

> There have already been repercussions. Ahead of the wage hike, some pizza chains began laying off delivery drivers and farming out deliveries to third-party apps, according to the *Wall Street Journal*. Other companies are considering raising prices, slowing hiring, cutting back on employee hours, closing their doors during slower periods, installing more ordering kiosks, and pausing expansion plans or expanding in other states instead.[103]

Originally, the minimum wage was openly advocated as a form of eugenics. And note that, just like the World Economic Forum and other "woke" organizations of today, it is always the "progressive" elitists who come up with these sick ideas. In the *Princeton Review*, Thomas C. Leonard writes of the minimum wage's early (1890–1930) proponents:[104]

> Progressive economists, like their neoclassical critics, believed that binding minimum wages would cause job losses. However, the progressive economists also believed that the job loss induced by minimum wages was a social benefit, as it performed the eugenic service ridding the labor force of the "unemployable."
>
> Sidney and Beatrice Webb (1897 [1920], p. 785) put it plainly: "With regard to certain sections of the population [the "unemployable"], this unemployment is not a mark of social disease, but actually of social health." "[O]f all ways of dealing with these unfortunate parasites," Sidney Webb opined in the *Journal of Political Economy*, "the most ruinous to the community is to allow them to unrestrainedly compete as wage earners."
>
> A minimum wage was seen to operate eugenically through two channels: by deterring prospective immigrants (Henderson, 1900) and also by removing from employment the "unemployable," who, thus identified, could be, for example, segregated in rural communities or sterilized.

This was similar to the original ideas behind abortion and birth control. The eugenicist founder of Planned Parenthood, Margaret Sanger, described her work in black communities as an effort to exterminate "human beings who never should have been born."[105] In this category, she also included anyone considered "the unfit." In a letter, she wrote, "We do not want word to get out that we are trying to exterminate the

Negro population."[106] It still has the same discriminatory effect on the labor force.

How about the guaranteed annual income? The idea was considered in Biden's Build Back Better monstrosity, and a pilot program was proposed in Congress in September 2023.[107] Other pilot programs have been launched in some fifteen large US counties already.[108] Participating in the pilot would not affect recipients' ability to receive other welfare assistance, like food stamps or Medicaid. So, as described earlier, this would not replace welfare but simply add more to it, straining government budgets further and forcing up taxes and debt while increasing dependency and unemployment. It is now called universal basic income (UBI). Because it dictates income redistribution, it is Socialism by another name.[109] Over 140 mayors in cities throughout the US have joined the Mayors for a Guaranteed Income, a group that advocates for it.

But even that isn't enough. Socialist senator Bernie Sanders recently proposed a new thirty-two-hour work week, while employees would still get paid for forty hours. That would actually increase pay by about 25 percent. How can you make a bad situation worse? In describing the bill, Charles Lipson of the *American Spectator* called Bernie, "the bottomless cup of bad ideas."[110]

The Cloward–Piven Strategy has had a major impact both in growing government spending and shifting its priorities. In 1960, healthcare and welfare—both components of Johnson's Great Society—took up a mere 4.6 percent of federal government spending. Today it consumes 36 percent, almost twice the amount spent on national defense (19.6 percent). If you add in Social Security, it rises to 59 percent.[111]

Democratic politicians justify the burgeoning welfare state—now including millions of illegal aliens—as reflecting compassion for the "poor and oppressed." Cloward and Piven were much more honest: "If organizers can deliver millions of dollars in cash benefits to the ghetto masses," they wrote, "it seems reasonable to expect that the masses will deliver their loyalties to their benefactors."[112]

Democrats had the same thing in mind during the Great Depression, as Cloward and Piven reveal:

> During the realignments of 1932, a new Democratic coalition was formed, based heavily on urban working-class groups. Once in power, the national Democratic leadership proposed and implemented the economic reforms of the New Deal. Although these measures were a response to the imperative of economic crisis, *the types of measures enacted were designed to secure a new Democratic coalition.* (Emphasis added.)[113]

This plan enabled Democrats to control both houses of Congress for most of the twentieth century, and it is largely responsible for their vice-grip control over our nation. So, while they planned for the collapse of capitalism, which they hoped would drive armies of the "oppressed" poor onto the streets, they were spending our money to garner the votes from those same people to bring it about.

It is difficult to swallow the notion that this was actually a deliberate strategy conceived by Americans, but this is what happened, and Cloward and Piven share the blame for the ballooning deficits at all levels of government and for the fractured families, drugs, poverty, and misery associated with the burgeoning welfare state. Cloward and Piven, like Marx, Nechayev, Lenin, and others, were fine with this. *And they say so!* Cloward and Piven observed the result of their strategy with enthusiasm:

> Mass influence...stems from the consumption of benefits and does not require that large groups of people be involved in regular organizational roles. Moreover this kind of mass influence is cumulative because benefits are continuous. *Once eligibility for basic food and rent grants has been established, the drain on local resources persists indefinitely.* (Emphasis added.)[114]

If you ever find occasion to drive through a typical inner-city neighborhood, where every other building is boarded up and abandoned, think of the overburdened police and fire departments, the pitted streets, failing schools, runaway crime, prostitution, drugs, and feral lifestyles, and recall Cloward and Piven's thrill that "the drain on local resources persists indefinitely…."

Today, the strategy has been turbocharged by application to all left-wing agendas, from open borders to massive government spending, from defunding the police to letting criminals go free to wreak havoc in inner cites. Wash, rinse, repeat—creating, as Lenin said, "new future crises to be exploited in the future, and so on, until the targeted capitalist society is destroyed completely."[115]

Key Role of Media

The Left must establish the moral high ground to get the credibility necessary to push their outrageous demands. Convincing the public that government intervention is essential to "solving" any "problem" is a necessary prerequisite to making the Left's demands sound worthy and admirable. A successful PR campaign to convince the public that the need is genuine automatically makes opponents out to be the bad guys and puts them on the defensive. After all, how could you *not* want to help the poor!

This narrative can then be resurrected again and again to pummel opponents into submission. Thus "racist," "sexist," "homophobe," "xenophobe," (for opponents of illegal alien amnesty), and now "transphobe" are really all the same negative term, "bigot," applied to any and all opponents of the Left's destruction strategies. It is unethical, it is brutal and mean-spirited, it is dishonest (and they know it), but it is also effective, which is all they really care about.

The media bears much of the responsibility for the bad things happening in the US today. This is because, as one of the most essential components of the Left, the media constantly assaults us with attacks, lies, and misinformation. They deliberately mislead us into seeing a world of their construct, which is the polar opposite of the truth.

This of course has become much more blatant over the past few years, with COVID misinformation flying everywhere, the many attacks on President Trump and his supporters, and social media colluding with the government to silence critics. Even the value of the First Amendment is now regularly questioned—even mocked—by left-wing Democrat politicians. It is part and parcel of the totalitarian mindset embedded in "woke" ideology.

We think of media bias as a new phenomenon. But even in the 1960s, Cloward and Piven knew they could rely on the heavily left-biased mass media to carry their water, writing, "As the crisis develops, it will be important to use the mass media to inform the broader liberal community about the inefficiencies and injustices of welfare…. And throughout the crisis, the mass media should be used to advance arguments for a new federal income distribution program."[116]

In a footnote, they even went so far as to explain just how the media should present the argument, in case there was any question: "In public statements, it would be important to distinguish between the income distributing function of public welfare, which should be replaced by new federal measures, and many other welfare functions, such as foster care and adoption services for children, which are not at issue in this strategy."[117] (In other words, it bears repeating, those other programs wouldn't be touched).

THAT ALL CHEATERS MIGHT VOTE

*We have put together I think the most extensive
and inclusive voter fraud organization in
the history of American politics.*[118]

—Joe Biden

This chapter delves deeply into the history of Left's long-term strategy for stealing our elections to obtain permanent, irrevocable political power. It is another dimension to the crisis strategy. But if you read nothing else, read and take action on the following. In a May 7, 2024 episode of *Tucker Carlson*, Tucker interviewed Catherine Engelbrecht, President of True the Vote, one of the most effective voter integrity organizations in America.[119] Catherine discovered a little-known provision in federal law that allows non-citizens to vote in federal elections. You heard that right. The criminal code, 18 U.S.C. Section 611 (c)3, states explicitly that, while it is illegal for non-citizens to vote in federal elections, penalties do not apply if "the alien reasonably believed at the time of voting in violation of such subsection that he or she was a citizen of the United States."[120]

How is one supposed to adjudicate that person's state of mind when he/she voted illegally? It can't be done. Furthermore, as Ms. Engelbrecht points out, once the vote is counted, it is too late to figure out who it was that voted. This, then, is a major component of the Democrat plan to once again steal the election. And in case you had any doubts, Joe Biden has called illegal aliens "model citizens."[121] Of course, for the Democrats, illegals are "model" citizens, because they will give the Democrats what they want if something isn't done. Of course nothing will change under a Harris administration either.

The Biden administration is currently flying in hundreds of thousands of illegal aliens by abusing immigration parole, a system designed to provide legal pathways to certain individuals on an emergency, case-by-case basis in particularly trying circumstances. President Trump authorized an average of 5,623 per year. Biden had authorized 1,598,325 as of January 2024.[122] He is flying in migrants from over fifty different countries, according to the House Homeland Security Committee, "to help process into the country more than 400,000 inadmissible aliens through the administration's unlawful Cuban, Haitian, Nicaraguan, and Venezuelan (CHNV) mass-parole program."[123]

And that's only part of the open-borders agenda. The plan should be clear. Biden, Harris, and Co. know they will not win an honest election, so they are importing massive numbers of illegal aliens to do the job for them. If this agenda is not stopped *right now, before the 2024 election*, we will never have a free election again. Our nation will die in the voting booth on November 5, 2024. This cannot be emphasized enough. *The Democrats fully intend to steal this election*, and this is how they plan to do it. Only massive public pressure will stop them.

Vote Fraud Crisis Strategy

The Cloward–Piven Strategy is the intellectual foundation for mass vote fraud. The ever-expanding welfare state is also a great recruitment tool for more Democratic votes. So, next on Cloward and Piven's menu was nationalizing the voter apparatus. Once again, just as with welfare, using the "compassion" argument, they claimed the poor need government help getting registered to vote, thus shifting responsibility from the individual to the state. It is a ridiculous argument, just as the claim that voter ID is voter "suppression." The Left encourages helplessness because, using the government, it directs all processes to their advantage, legally or otherwise.

In 1982, Cloward and Piven founded the Human Service Employees Registration and Voter Education Fund (Human SERVE) to build political momentum for laws that would use government agencies (and taxpayer dollars) to facilitate low-income voter registration. This was articulated in their 1988 book, *Why Americans Don't Vote*:

> In 1982, we developed an analysis of the way we thought registration reform might be accomplished in the United States, and formed an organization to try to enlist public and nonprofit agencies to register their clients to vote. The potential reach of this approach is enormous. People would be able to register at unemployment and welfare offices, motor vehicle bureaus and departments of taxation, hospitals and public health centers…. Everyone has some dealings with public and nonprofit agencies…and poorer and minority people…are more likely to have contact with health, housing, welfare and unemployment agencies. If citizens could register in the course of using these services, *access* to voter registration would become nearly universal.[124]

Note the last line in that passage. Their ultimate goal was universal voter registration, or UVR. Throughout the 1980s, Human SERVE field-tested legal and political strategies and developed legislative language to promote this plan. The final fruits of its labor were realized with passage of the 1993 National Voter Registration Act, signed into law by Bill Clinton with Cloward and Piven standing directly behind him at the signing ceremony.

Also called "Motor Voter," the National Voter Registration Act (NVRA) was designed primarily to facilitate easy voter registration for the poor, elderly, and disabled. Never mentioned of course, but hiding in the background, was the plan to use Motor Voter to register illegal aliens to vote. It applies to all but six states. Idaho, Minnesota, New Hampshire, North Dakota, Wisconsin, and Wyoming are exempted because they have no voter registration requirements, or offer same-day registration at polling places.

Key provisions:

Section 5 specifies that all new motor vehicle driver's license applications, renewals, and change of address forms double as voter registration applications, including mail, telephone, or internet applications, and that information must be forwarded to state election officials. This is where the law got its nickname "Motor Voter."

Section 7 requires that all public assistance, military recruiting, and state-funded disability offices offer voter registration services. The state must identify other offices as well, such as public libraries, public schools, state colleges, universities, and community colleges, city and county clerk offices, marriage license offices, fishing and hunting license offices, government revenue offices, and unemployment compensation offices. They must provide the same level of service as they would for any other type of application and forward applications to election officials. This applies to all application, renewal, recertification, and change of address transactions. Rigorously meeting all these requirements poses significant challenges for these agencies, and execution has been inconsistent.

Section 8 spells out requirements for state maintenance of voter registration lists for federal elections. The state must follow a multi-step, multi-year procedure to remove voters from the rolls. It is an arduous, lengthy, and confusing process. According to a study by the American Constitution Society, Section 8 "may be the least understood and most contravened subsection of the NVRA as a whole. Several provisions have proven especially problematic for local election officials."[125] For example, if someone moves, their name cannot be removed from the voter list for two federal election cycles after the voter does not respond to a forwardable mail notification.

While the NVRA Section 8 nominally provides procedures for cleaning up voter rolls, the process is extremely slow and difficult. Unsurprisingly, relatively few lawsuits have been joined for Section 8 violations. There is no incentive for left-wing groups to improve the integrity of voter rolls. All the momentum goes in the other direction. Even when there are lawsuits to force compliance, the Left goes out of the way to fight them. Under the Obama DOJ, Attorney General Eric Holder announced he would not even make any effort to enforce Section 8 and instead would focus on Section 7, requiring states to implement voter registration aggressively.

The Left's election stealing operation began in earnest with Cloward and Piven but has grown substantially since. They have constructed an entire industry devoted to this task and pursue a multifaceted strategy to accomplish it:

1. Swamp election officials with overwhelming numbers of registrations and/or absentee mail-in ballots at the last possible minute, a huge proportion of which are fraudulent, in order to create *systemic chaos*. This accomplishes numerous goals:
    a. Makes verification of registrations and absentee mail-in ballots difficult, if not impossible, given the small size and limited budgets of state and local election offices.
    b. Provides multiple opportunities for vote fraud, especially in states where ID requirements are minimal or through absentee ballots.
    c. Throws the entire voting process into question, improving prospects for settling close results in court, where the Left has an advantage.

    d. Goads some election officials to challenge registrations, whereupon the Left's legal arm sues for "voter suppression." This in turn serves complementary goals:

        1) Charge of "voter suppression" reinforces the Left's narrative about America as an oppressive, "racist" country.

        2) Publicity and lawsuits intimidate election officials, making them hesitant to identify vote fraud.

    e. People instinctively doubt claims of such a massive effort. The large numbers involved raise suspicion in the minds of everyday people that the numbers are exaggerated, reinforcing the "voter suppression" narrative.

    f. Provides a pretext for enacting the biggest systematic change the Left wants: universal or automatic voter registration, which would guarantee effortless, 100 percent registration of low-income groups and institutionalize system-wide vulnerability to fraud.[126]

2. Activist groups like the ACLU sue state authorities for "voter suppression," creating further chaos, hamstringing agencies, setting agencies up for future suits, and pressuring them to become de facto taxpayer-funded, low-income voter registration drives.

3. The Justice Department tacitly supports voter intimidation tactics, sues states, and backs private lawsuits, selectively enforcing voting laws while actively resisting reform, challenging all efforts to ensure vote integrity as "voter suppression."

4. Leftist institutions, think tanks, and media discredit allegations of vote fraud, supporting the "suppression" theme, while pursuing public policy changes like universal voter registration, illegal alien amnesty, and the National Popular Vote.

The Vote Fraud Swamping Method

ACORN got in the voter registration business almost from its founding in 1970. Ironically, it was a liberal Republican governor who got them started. Arkansas governor Winthrop Rockefeller gave ACORN $3,000 in cash in the hopes they would induce Arkansas blacks to vote for him. *Subversion, Inc.* author Vadum writes:

> ACORN kept the money and registered Democrats. "[T]hey thought we were going to register Republicans" [ACORN organizer Gary] Delgado snickers, but "[w]e did not register a single Republican. However we did use those resources early on to build the organization...." After it became clear that Democratic challenger Dale Bumpers had ousted Rockefeller, Rathke took his leaders to the winner's victory party.... Because Rockefeller's payment had been in cash, he couldn't very well demand an accounting. Metaphorically, Rockefeller's was the first head ACORN placed over its mantle.[127]

After the Motor Voter law was passed, ACORN implemented the Cloward–Piven Strategy with voting by using the NVRA's loose registration requirements to garner as many registrations as possible and then swamp registrar offices with them. The intent, as with welfare, was to overwhelm the process. In this case, it would make policing the election more difficult and thus make vote fraud easier.

ACORN hired marginal workers at very low rates and used incentive bonuses or quotas to encourage them to collect as many voter registrations as possible. The resulting flood of registrations was fraught with duplicates, errors, omissions, and many overtly fraudulent ones, including made-up names like "Donald Duck," "Mickey Mouse," "Dallas Cowboys," and the like.[128]

Numerous ACORN employees were implicated in registration fraud schemes in dozens of states over a number of election cycles. This was extensively documented by the Employment Policies Institute's 2006 report, *Rotten ACORN*,[129] and in Vadum's book, *Subversion, Inc.*[130]

In one notorious case, an Ohio man was bribed by ACORN workers to register seventy-two times.[131] Citing individual examples from only eight states, Discover the Networks identified 187,000 fraudulent registrations submitted by ACORN during the 2008 elections alone.

According to Vadum, a total of four hundred thousand bogus registrations were thrown out in 2008.[132]

ACORN was permanently banished from Ohio in 2010 when it settled a state racketeering case there.[133] The organization and two of its top leaders were convicted of vote fraud charges in Nevada stemming from the 2008 election. As quoted in the *Wall Street Journal*, then Las Vegas registrar Larry Lomax said that almost half of ACORN's registrations "were clearly fraudulent," a statement confirmed in a phone interview with the author.[134] Of ninety thousand registrations submitted, only twenty-five thousand became voters who actually voted. Nevada Democratic attorney general Catherine Cortez Masto added that ACORN's training manuals "clearly detail, condone and…require illegal acts."[135]

While capitalizing on the vote fraud swamping strategy enabled by the NVRA, ACORN, Project Vote (an ACORN offshoot, where Frances Fox Piven still serves on the board), and others picked up the torch for SERVE, which closed its doors in 2000. Using tactics developed by SERVE, they sued states that didn't aggressively execute the voter registration activities required by Section 7.

The narrative has always been "voter suppression," and settlements have forced state agencies to become de facto low-income voter registration drives. Not only must states develop, maintain, and execute plans for assuring comprehensive registration, they are forced to report regularly to radical Left lawyers. A 2009 settlement between ACORN and Missouri's Department of Social Services (DSS) is illustrative:[136]

- DSS must create a NVRA state coordinator position for the Family Support Division's (FSD) Income Maintenance branch.
- Each FSD office must designate an NVRA site coordinator.
- Each office must keep detailed records of client visits and registration activities.
- The county must immediately send a letter offering registration to any individual who "may not have been given the opportunity to register…."

- The NVRA coordinator must collect and report detailed monthly data to ACORN lawyers regarding:
  - numbers of persons visiting DSS offices,
  - responses to voter registration inquiries,
  - numbers of voter registrations completed and submitted to election authorities,
  - number of letters sent, and
  - additional information.
- State coordinator's performance review will be judged by NVRA compliance.
- ACORN received $450,000 in settlement.

Under this settlement, ACORN, a private, radical Left entity, effectively assumed an executive function over state agencies. State employees implicitly had to answer to ACORN for their job performance, and some requirements were vague and open-ended. There was no guidance, for example, regarding how the coordinators are to determine whether clients "may not have been given the opportunity to register…." Notably, there is no corollary requirement for them to ascertain the legality of registrations or to clean up the rolls. This agreement was signed by ACORN, Lawyers' Committee for Civil Rights Under Law, Project Vote, and others. Similar settlements were obtained from New Mexico, Indiana, and Ohio, to name a few, and Colorado was forced to improve NRVA compliance following a published report by Project Vote.[137]

The administrative burdens, the noncompliance lawsuits, and consent decrees are designed, in part, to build pressure for universal voter registration. "Wouldn't it be easier?" they all argue.[138] It is critical to understand that the NVRA was an *intermediate goal*. As Cloward and Piven clearly elucidated in their book, the ultimate goal is universal voter registration.[139] Chaos and unreliability were created deliberately to propose UVR as the solution, just as the welfare system was overwhelmed to create a pretext for their solution, the guaranteed annual income. And both of those goals had the further objectives of creating chaos, collapsing the country, and delivering it into the Left's hands permanently.

It is difficult to overestimate Cloward and Piven's impact. The NVRA has become a beacon for vote fraud. Its complicated procedures and minimal verification requirements invite fraudulent registrations. The fraud danger was recognized early on, and one of former president Obama's only trial cases involved a lawsuit he joined with ACORN and others against then Illinois governor Jim Edgar, when Edgar refused to execute the law for fear of vote fraud.[140]

Illegal Alien Voting

A 2024 poll conducted by I&I/TIPP asked the question, "How concerned are you about letting those who are in the U.S. illegally to participate in local and federal elections?" An overwhelming 71 percent said they were very concerned (50 percent) or somewhat concerned (21 percent). This included 60 percent of Democrats, very concerned (36 percent) or somewhat concerned (24 percent); 89 percent of Republicans, very concerned (73 percent) or somewhat concerned (16 percent), and 66 percent of Independents very or somewhat concerned. Sixty percent of all parties agreed that we must "rigorously vet voter records to ensure non-citizens don't vote."[141] Americans are genuinely concerned that illegal aliens are voting and with good reason.

Consider, for example, that federal registration forms do not require a voter to prove US citizenship. Therefore, immigrants, both legal and illegal, can easily be registered to vote. This was *a deliberate oversight*. Proof can be seen in their response when someone tries to correct this "oversight." They face leftist wrath.

The former Kansas secretary of state, Attorney General Kris Kobach, attempted to require proof of citizenship for voter registrations. The state was successfully sued by the League of Women Voters and other groups.[142] Requiring proof of citizenship to register to vote is not difficult, nor is voter ID, but the Left always objects, because those changes would make it harder to cheat.

But the Left has gone further. Eighteen jurisdictions in California, Maryland, Vermont, and Washington, DC, have enacted laws that allow illegal aliens to vote in local elections.[143] It's been proposed in

Connecticut and other states as well.[144] But if local elections are held on the same day as state and national elections, what is to prevent illegals from also voting on those races?

There are other states that, while not directly condoning illegal alien voting, weasel out of responsibility for policing the vote and allow it by default. For example, from the Arizona secretary of state, the regulation reads:

> A person who submits valid proof of citizenship with his or her voter registration form (regardless of the type of form submitted) is entitled to vote in all federal, state, county and local elections in which he or she is eligible. The voter registration form otherwise must be sufficiently complete.
>
> *A person is not required to submit proof of citizenship with the voter registration form, but failure to do so means the person will only be eligible to vote in federal elections (known as being a "federal only" voter)....* (Emphasis added.)[145]

This regulation indicates no provision for identifying the legal status of the person in question. So Arizona has essentially told illegal aliens they can vote in federal elections, which of course is where it matters most.

Even more radical is the idea that some votes should count more than others, a form of electoral reparations. Some Democrats have said that because minorities and the poor have little influence, "extraordinary measures (for example, stretching the absentee ballot or registration rules) are required to compensate."[146] Democrat election officials do this all the time, and a form of it became official Justice Department policy under Barack Obama in its effort to boost Hispanic representation.[147]

In 2021, the Biden administration issued Executive Order 14019 on "Promoting Access to Voting."[148] This executive order showed just how far the Democrats have come in enlisting the government to recruit new Democratic voters and enable vote fraud. It directs hundreds of federal agencies and those state agencies under its control to enable mail-in ballots and automatic voter registration, which opens the door to illegal alien voting, duplicate registrations, and other forms of errors that can enable vote fraud.

The order explicitly facilitates voting for those incarcerated in federal prisons—illegal in most states. It essentially turns the government into a get-out-the-vote operation for Democrats. It has also opened the door to illegal alien voter registration and likely voting. And now, with the revelation you read at the start of this chapter, we know that the Democrats will use that little-known provision in law to encourage illegals to vote. To recap, Title 18 U.S.C. Section 611 (c)3, states specifically that penalties do not apply to non-citizens if they "reasonably believed at the time of voting in violation of such subsection that he or she was a citizen of the United States."[149]

The executive order furthermore tells those agencies to work with "'nonpartisan third-party organizations' that have been 'approved' by the administration to supply 'voter registration services on agency premises.'"[150]

Let that sink in. The Biden administration, the most corrupt administration in US history, gets to determine which "nonpartisan third-party organizations" are allowed to work with federal agencies in registering voters. The Biden administration went to great lengths to suppress the names of these organizations, but to no one's surprise, they turned out to be radical Left groups like the ACLU and the voter activist organization, Demos.[151]

In March 2024, Mississippi secretary of state Michael Watson wrote to Attorney General Garland expressing his concern that "agencies under [Garland's] charge [are] attempting to register people to vote, including potentially ineligible felons and to coopt state and local officials into accomplishing this goal."[152]

"It is quite shocking," Watson wrote, "in the midst of a crisis at our southern border and an unprecedented crime wave, that the Biden administration has chosen to expend tax dollars and vital law enforcement resources on a program that risks bloating state voter rolls with ineligible and non-citizen voters."[153]

This new initiative has already paid off for Democrats in Michigan, who were able to flip control of the state House to Democrats in 2022 with the help of an illegal alien group that bragged of its efforts:

> Through sustained, long-term organizing in rural communities, undocumented folks in Michigan are demonstrating that we ultimately wield the power to effect change and can use elections as a powerful tool in winning campaigns for our rights.[154]

Key operators in this campaign were the tax-exempt groups We the People Michigan and We the People Action. Though they were only formed in 2020, between the two of them, they had over $9 million of income in 2021 and retained $6.6 million in net assets.[155] The executive director of both organizations is Arturo Reyes, who received compensation of $95,699 from each for a total of $191,398. Not bad for a thirty-hour work week.[156] Most of the money these groups received was from dark money organizations,[157] and leaders were veteran Michigan left-wing organizers.[158]

The payoff for illegals was to get a Michigan law allowing them to obtain driver's licenses. And of course, with a driver's license, you can easily register to vote under the NVRA. The predictable propaganda goes along the lines, "If you live in Michigan and have proven you can be a responsible driver, you should be able to obtain a license, regardless of your immigration status. The safety of our residents should not depend on whether the federal government has figured out our broken immigration system."[159]

There goes that "compassion" argument again. As long as you are a "responsible driver," we care about your "safety." And "broken immigration system" is code for amnesty. The system is not broken. The system is ignored today by the Left, because they aren't getting the amnesty they want by legal means. Repeating "broken immigration system" over and over builds momentum for "doing something." And of course that something is always what the Left wants; in this case, amnesty. By flinging the borders open, Democrats hope the massive numbers entering will be able to stay and at some point be amnestied. That will spell doom for our Republic.

Congress has already passed successive legislation deliberately intended to increase *legal* immigration from everywhere in the world on the slightest pretext. Today, we allow about one million legal immigrants per year, many from Communist nations like China and Russia. And in the past ten years, only 16 percent of that million immigrated for employment purposes. About 65 percent have taken advantage of chain migration, which allows relatives of naturalized citizens to immigrate.[160]

Furthermore, there is an entire industry devoted to anchor babies. Women come to the US from all over the world, especially Russia and China, to have their babies here.[161] Pew Research estimated about 340,000 in 2010—doubtless a low-ball even then.[162] Those babies are granted birthright citizenship. Of course, that will mean amnesty and eventual citizenship for their mothers and other relatives sooner or later. President Trump vows to end this kind of birthright citizenship through executive order on his first day in office.[163]

Democrats know that most of those immigrants will become Democrat voters. In the cases of China and Russia, they are also potential spies and saboteurs. In 2017, before the latest migrant caravans, renowned national defense writer Bill Gertz estimated there were at least twenty-five thousand, and maybe as many as forty thousand, Chinese Communist spies already in the US.[164] Who knows how many there are now? If there is anything broken about our legal immigration system, it is that it has become too liberal. But even that isn't enough for the Democrats. So now they've flung open US borders to the world, and it has literally turned into an invasion.

In the meantime, the Department of Justice has become the new ACORN. DOJ attorney general Merrick Garland claims to have doubled the size of the voting section of the civil rights division and is going after states that implement voter ID, restrict mail-in voting, drop boxes, and other methods that prevent Democrats from stealing elections.[165] He calls this voter "suppression."

Jocelyn Benson, current Michigan secretary of state and former SPLC staffer, described "coordinating" with other secretaries of state in the battleground states of Arizona, Wisconsin, Pennsylvania, Georgia, and Nevada to be prepared for 2024. She called it the "battle for the future of our democracy."[166] They have so far refused to name who or what they are battling, but referring to 2020, Benson said, "We were all battling a common adversary: a really nationally coordinated effort to undermine the will of the people both before, during, and after Election day."[167]

So to "save democracy," they will coordinate to defeat President Trump. You can bet they will not be targeting any Democrat. Is that a legitimate role for secretaries of state? They are supposed to administer elections, not attempt to influence them. But these overtly partisan Democrat secretaries of state have become a fixture in modern elections with the help of George Soros money and other left-wing funders.

Benson was an early beneficiary of George Soros's now-defunct Secretary of State Project, an organization replaced by iVote. iVote also lobbies for UVR. Benson received support from iVote as well.[168] Benson is a poster child for corruption. Ruth Johnson, chair of the State Senate Election Committee, said that during the 2020 election, Benson's office mailed out 7.7 million absentee ballots, eight hundred thousand of which were to non-qualified voters. All were filled out. How did they vote? We'll never know. Benson took over the whole voting apparatus to do this. Formerly, absentee ballots were handled by local registrars.[169] Biden won Michigan by 154,000 votes. How many were among those eight hundred thousand non-qualified voters? We'll never know. Does that sound like a "secure" election to you?

We do know, however, what happened in Muskegon, Michigan. Secretary of State Benson, Attorney General Dana Nessel, the FBI, and other officials have remained silent in the face of a vote fraud operation there in 2020 that was investigated by the Michigan State Police.[170] A Muskegon elections clerk noticed multiple fraudulent voter registrations with fake or nonexistent addresses, erroneous phone numbers, many forms completed by the same person, and signatures that didn't match records.

The ACORN registration fraud operation continues, this time with a shady Democrat operation named GBI Strategies. GBI has no website and scant online presence, but it did receive $4.7 million from the DNC, the Biden and Senate Democrat campaign operations, the League of Conservation Voters, and other leftist groups in 2020 according to OpenSecrets.[171]

The Michigan State Police investigated and found the evidence. Additionally, when they searched GBI premises, they found semiautomatic pistols with silencers.[172] Unless those silencers are registered with the feds, possessing them is a serious felony. State GOP chairwoman Kristina Karamo asked, "Who were they about to shoot? Who were they prepared to shoot?"[173] Despite all this, Attorney General Dana Nessel refused to prosecute GBI. Instead, she went after sixteen "fake GOP electors," in what GOP legislators called "malicious prosecution."[174]

Shortly after, Michigan legislators introduced articles of impeachment against Nessel for corruption.[175] Specifically included in the articles of impeachment was the charge that she refused to prosecute the clear case of vote fraud that occurred in Muskegon. It reads, "Despite the fact that an October 2020 investigation found evidence that an organization submitted clearly 29 fraudulent voter registration applications to the Muskegon City Clerk, Attorney General Nessel has failed to charge those responsible for forging and filing these documents."[176]

Unfortunately, this impeachment will go nowhere because of the illegal alien vote fraud noted earlier in this chapter that allowed Democrats to obtain a slight majority in the state House in 2022. This is the kind of endemic corruption we are dealing with.

And Michigan has more troubles. A Michigan sheriff is investigating Dominion software and its apparent willingness during the 2020 election to grant access to its voting machines by Serbian nationals living overseas. In a March 2024 letter to US Rep. Jim Jordan, he wrote:

> I have evidence in my file of Serbian foreign nationals entering our election system while the votes were being counted, and prior to certification.... I am investigating the role that some individuals inside the United States have played in conspiring with these foreign nationals, and who have even directed and instructed

them to access and interfere with electronic voting machines and electronic voting systems during past elections, including the November 2020 election.... Moreover, I have evidence that U.S. Dominion and its affiliates (Dominion) instructed its employees to alter or otherwise falsify the integrity of the software and hardware in its voting machines and systems to attain certification by the Election Assistance Commission (EAC), even when they knew that the systems could not be properly verified and certified.[177]

Much of this information came from Stefanie Lambert, an attorney working for former Overstock.com CEO Patrick Byrne, who has been battling a defamation lawsuit filed by Dominion over allegations of vote fraud it allegedly enabled during the 2020 election. Lambert and Byrne leaked emails and other confidential information they believe supports their case. Dominion protested this latest release to a judge, and Lambert was arrested for it.[178] It will be interesting to see what the sheriff turns up. Perhaps this law enforcement officer will be able to get to the truth.

A mayoral election in Bridgeport, Connecticut, was thrown out after surveillance video leaked of Democratic Town Committee vice chairwoman Wanda Geter-Pataky repeatedly stuffing ballot drop boxes with multiple ballots in different locations.[179] The challenger, another Democrat, ultimately lost, but not before presenting irrefutable evidence of the crime.

Practically everything Democrats are doing is in service to their ultimate goal of securing permanent majorities. This could be said of any political movement; however, the Left doesn't limit that effort to *legal* voters. Vote fraud is an integral part of the strategy. Some years ago, when New York actually enforced the law, two NY Democrats caught in a vote fraud scandal told police, "Voter fraud is an accepted way of winning elections...."[180]

Traditional politicians of both parties are not above engaging in vote fraud. The left-liberal political/media establishment makes sure these cases receive maximum publicity when they involve conservatives or Republicans. But this kind of corruption is relegated to individual campaigns or areas where corrupt political establishments have been able to develop unchallenged for many years, for example, in Alaska, with the serially corrupt GOP senator, Lisa Murkowski.[181] With Republicans, it is not a systematic component of an overall national strategy as it is with the Democrats.

The Left seeks fundamental structural change to our entire form of government. They are playing for keeps. They will register any voters, dead or alive, legal or illegal, who will then vote as many times as possible. The ultimate aim is to systematize a taxpayer-funded voting machinery that will guarantee maximum participation from low-income groups while undermining our ability to manage elections and prevent fraud. The NVRA was designed to accomplish this.

Mail-in ballots are limited or banned completely in most other countries because of concerns with vote fraud.[182] In 2005, former president Jimmy Carter co-chaired the Commission on Federal Election Reform, which found that "absentee ballots remain the largest source of potential voter fraud."[183] Even the *New York Times* expressed concern about it back in 2012.[184]

But Democrats had an election to win in 2020. Nancy Pelosi used the COVID pandemic as the pretext for widespread use of mail-in ballots in the 2020 election—the updated, and as it turned out, much more effective way to swamp and steal elections.[185] But it is not a new idea. Democrat-sponsored bills pushing mail-in ballots had been around since at least 2009, and Pelosi proposed congressional legislation mandating mail-in ballots well before the pandemic hit.[186]

Many of these proposals also included provisions for automatic voter registration (AVR) at motor vehicle departments—a double whammy. AVR is the latest innovation on the road to UVR. There would be numerous duplications, and with mail-in ballots, cheaters could have a heyday. In 2021, the US House passed HR 1, the "For the People" Act. It essentially nationalized all aspects of elections and included automatic voter registration as well as nationwide mail-in voting, with no ID verification requirements. Election expert Hans von Spakovsky called it a "threat to American democracy," saying, "HR 1 would usurp the role of the states, wipe out basic safety protocols, and mandate a set of rules that would severely damage the integrity of elections."[187]

As of March 2023, it is now on the table again with HR 1439 and the Senate companion S 700, the "Vote at Home Act." The identical bills mandate automatic voter registration through state motor vehicle departments and widely expanded mail-in voting.[188] Since 2016, automatic voter registration through motor vehicle and other state agencies has already been passed in the District of Columbia and twenty-four states, including the swing states of Georgia, Michigan, Pennsylvania, Nevada, and Virginia.[189] This is how the voter rolls get swamped. And the Democrats can find ways of utilizing those registrations whether they are legitimate or not. So Cloward and Piven show their faces again.

Meanwhile, Biden's Executive Order 14019 appears to have a function similar to Facebook founder Mark Zuckerberg's "Zuckerbucks" that illegally interfered in the 2020 election on Biden's behalf. Two organizations, the Center for Tech and Civic Life (CTCL) and the Center for Election Innovation and Research (CEIR), together received over $400 million from Zuckerberg's own Chan Zuckerberg Foundation prior to the 2020 election.[190] There is little doubt that this skewed the election in Biden's favor.

A report by the Amistad Project of the Thomas More Society, a national constitutional litigation group, described in a report how Zuckerberg's money corrupted the election and may have changed the outcome:[191]

> Zuckerberg's $500 million intervention included a $350 million donation to the Center for Technology and Civic Life (CTCL), which used the money to illegally inflate turnout in key Democratic swing states as part of this effort. This network injected hundreds of millions of dollars into the election, violating state and federal election laws in the process and ensuring an unequal distribution of funding that favored

Democratic precincts, depriving voters of both due process and equal protection.

Amistad Project Director Phill Kline said:

> This network pumped hundreds of millions of dollars into local election systems using the COVID crisis as a pretense. Our report proves that in reality it was nothing more than a naked attempt to purchase an election. "Zuckerbucks" and local election officials invited a billionaire into the consolidated ballot counting centers while kicking out the American people.

These two foundations were tiny and obscure. Perhaps that is why they were chosen. CTCL's contributions increased from $2.8 million in 2019 to $354.6 million in 2020, a 12,564 percent increase.[192] CTCL also received an additional $24.8 million from the left-wing New Venture Fund.[193] CEIR received two donations from Zuckerberg, totaling $69.5 million, increasing CEIR's donation receipts by 7,500 percent from 2019.[194] CTCL sent funds to beef up local election offices with left-wing staff and equipment to handle a vast increase in mail-in ballots, while CEIR sent money for the same purposes to secretaries of state under the guise of COVID-19 "relief grants."[195]

Both organizations are run by veteran members of the radical Left. CTCL was founded by Tiana Epps-Johnson, Donny Bridges, and Whitney May, all veterans of the radical Left's New Organizing Institute.[196] They each earn six-figure salaries.[197]

CEIR is run by David Becker, a hardcore leftist former member of the radical People for the American Way—an ironic title if there ever was one. PFAW is another anti-American smear merchant like the SPLC. CEIR pays Becker about $242,000.[198] CEIR grants totaling $64.3 million went to twenty-three states. The four swing states of Arizona, Georgia, Michigan, and Pennsylvania received $35.6 million or 55 percent of the total.[199]

Becker was also a founding member of the Electronic Registration Information Center (ERIC), a left-wing operation with about thirty member states. It claims ability to cross-check with member states to find and remove dead or duplicate voters. In fact, during the 2020 election, it partnered with CEIR by sharing voter roll data in an effort to turn out Democrats for the election.[200] In 2020, it identified about three million invalid voters on the rolls but identified seventeen million new voters. A report by Judicial Watch found that 353 counties in twenty-nine states had voter rolls that exceeded 100 percent of eligible voters.[201] ERIC has not been doing its supposed job.

Michelle Obama has created a new website, WhenWeAllVote.org. She tweeted:

> Together, we can stand up for what we believe in, and we must do that at the ballot box this year. The issues that impact us most are on the ballot across the country—from equal pay and racial justice to reproductive healthcare and climate change. And as Queen Bey says at the end of Ya Ya, we need to "keep the faith" and "VOTE!"
>
> You can register to vote with @WhenWeAllVote in the time it takes you to listen to your favorite song on the album. Visit WhenWeAllVote.org to register now.[202]

The site brags: "The voter registration hub is your one stop shop to get registered to vote and cast your ballot. Check your voter registration status, find your polling place, and know your voting rights in your state."[203]

The registration page asks you to fill out all of your personal information. It acknowledges that you cannot register to vote by doing this but promises to direct you to your secretary of state where you can.

It says, "We have you fill out this form so that we can contact you if your registration gets rejected."[204] If it's legitimate, your registration will not be rejected. And this is one of the ways they nudge us all toward automatic voter registration. The next step will be to automate the connection to the secretary of state's website so that this one step can be avoided, and bingo, AVR. But they also will have your personal information. They will now have ways to contact you from a database that very likely goes into ERIC.

They will make sure you vote, even if you didn't.

Michigan passed automatic voter registration in 2019. Through the efforts of ERIC and CEIR, thousands of unregistered voters were identified and mailed. Because Michigan has automatic registration, 114,000 new voters were registered in one day, even though they never responded to the mailing.[205] Michigan also received $11.9 million from CEIR, an amount only exceeded by Pennsylvania. Over 90 percent of it went to Democrat political consulting firms, supposedly for "non-partisan" voter education.[206]

These kinds of activities between CEIR, ERIC, and CTCL were happening all over the nation in 2020. Many states are fighting to stop a similar abuse of the system in 2024. Ten GOP states have dropped their memberships in ERIC, and some twenty-seven states have either restricted or outright banned private funding of elections offices a la "Zuckerbucks." The Biden administration's EO 14019 looks to be replacing what Zuckerbucks did, only financed by we the taxpayers.

CTCL battled relentlessly against disclosure of where and how its funds were spent, but ultimately some of that information was disclosed. CTCL sent $327 million to forty-seven states and Washington, DC.[207] Of the total, 31 percent went to the five swing states shown in the table below. And consider Georgia, which received almost half of that. The rest focused on specific districts where more Democratic votes were needed or where they thought they could more easily boost the numbers with fraudulent counts.

State	CTCL	Electors
Arizona	$5,169,724	11
Georgia	$45,013,990	16
Michigan	$16,862,654	15
Pennsylvania	$25,011,085	19
Wisconsin	$10,108,644	10
Total	$102,166,097	71

Green Bay, Wisconsin, is a good case in point. William Doyle of the *Federalist* reported:[208]

> Of the 26 grants CTCL provided to cities and counties in Arizona, Georgia, Michigan, North Carolina, Pennsylvania, Texas, and Virginia that were $1 million or larger, 25 went to areas Biden won in 2020. The only county on this list won by Donald Trump (Brown County, Wisconsin) received about $1.1 million—less than 1.3 percent of the $85.5 million that CTCL provided to these top 26 recipients.
>
> But even in Brown County, Wisconsin, where heavily Democrat Green Bay is located, the funding disparities are glaring. The Wisconsin legislature provided roughly $7 per voter to the city of Green Bay to manage its 2020 elections. Rural counties in Wisconsin received approximately $4 per voter.
>
> The CTCL funds boosted Democratic-voting Green Bay resources to $47 per voter, while most rural areas still had the same $4 per voter. Similar funding disparities occurred near Detroit, Atlanta, Philadelphia, Pittsburgh, Flint, Dallas, Houston, and other cities that received tens of millions of dollars of CTCL money.
>
> Preliminary analysis shows this partisan targeting of CTCL funding was repeated in battleground states across the country.

Eric Genrich, the mayor of Green Bay, allowed Michael Spitzer-Rubenstein, a partisan Democrat who worked for a CTCL partner organization, to essentially run the election, according to GOP state senator Eric Wimberger. Wimberger called for an investigation, saying in a press release:

The City Clerk was pressured by a partisan actor, the National Vote at Home Institute, who the Mayor's Chief of Staff actively assisted. A private citizen, not affiliated with the City of Green Bay, and not a Wisconsin resident, effectively became the chief elections officer for Green Bay during a presidential election. They were allowed direct access to absentee ballots, and directed how, where, and when ballots should be collected.[209]

Wisconsin bills aimed at stopping CTCL and groups like it from influencing elections this way were vetoed twice by Democratic governor Tony Evers. So Wisconsin passed a referendum for a constitutional amendment that bans private donations to election officials for running elections and allows only lawful elections officials to manage elections. So no more Zuckerbucks in Wisconsin.

CTCL and CEIR have not given up, however. CTCL is now using a different strategy, conducting online seminars for election officials, urging them to partner with left-wing groups to counter "misinformation." CEIR has a new electronic messaging tool called REVERE. Its supposed purpose is the same. Using data mined from ERIC, it can access voter records to send texts, emails, and voicemails to prospective voters to "assist state election officials in combating foreign and domestic disinformation on social media and email."[210]

One of CTCL's senior project managers, Kurt Sampsel, is quoted as saying, "Trump's statements on voting by mail, voter fraud, and whether or not he'll accept the results of the election have had the effect of undermining confidence in our democratic processes on just a bigger scale than we've ever seen before."[211]

And why has it undermined confidence in our "democratic processes"? It is not Trump's statements that have undermined confidence in elections; it is the relentless Democrat campaign of lies, misinformation, suppression of facts, and outright fraud that has undermined faith in *all* our institutions.

Do they need listing? How about the four-year effort by the Democrats to convince people President Trump was working with the

Russians, when it was the Democrats, with help from the FBI, who used Russian disinformation in a shameless, transparent effort to mislead voters about candidate and then president Trump—all at the behest of Hillary Clinton? How about repeated "impeachments" on wholly invented charges? Or the phony "trials" they've cooked up in an attempt to bankrupt and sideline Trump?

How about the massive examples of unprecedented vote fraud conducted by groups like ACORN? How about the blatantly partisan and illegal activities of CTCL itself? Democrats use this inversion of the truth as a *strategy*. We've seen it over and over again. They accuse others of doing what they, themselves, are doing.

And CTCL's latest campaign is merely a repeat of the kind of censorship campaign carried out by Facebook, Twitter, other social media platforms, mass media, and countless Democrat operatives during the 2020 election. It calls for countering misinformation (incorrect information), disinformation (deliberately misleading or false information), and even *malinformation*.

Now what is "malinformation"? According to CTCL, it is truthful information that is harmful. Kurt Sampsel says an example "would be to highlight cases of voter fraud or election irregularities with the implication that this is a really common, widespread problem."[212]

Unfortunately, because of actions by people like Sampsel, Mark Zuckerberg, Hillary Clinton, and too many others to count, *it really is a common, widespread problem*. President Trump told the truth, and it is the kind of truth we all need to hear in order to be properly warned and take action. But the Democrats don't want that. So when we reveal an inconvenient truth, we'll be accused of *malinformation*. Once again, we hear Lenin's words echoing down the centuries: "We can and must write in a language which sows among the masses hate, revulsion, and scorn towards those who disagree with us."

CTCL advocates the use of "fact checkers." Where did that come from? If you spend any time on Facebook, you already know. If the truth can be ridiculed or labeled as "malinformation," it simply provides them with another excuse to censor online speech. Following are two examples of malinformation that could be censored by "fact" checkers. These are direct quotes of CTCL leaders:[213]

- "[I]f a voter discourages participation on Election Day by simply tweeting a photo of a really long line at a polling place." [Are we going to guess the voter's motives, or was he/she just tweeting out helpful information? How do we find out if that tweet discouraged participation?]
- "It could also be a social media campaign that uses accurate information about an example of voter fraud or election fraud to intensify support for a candidate whom the target audience may already support." [Again, how could they deduce motive? And would the Left not use such information, or even invent lies, to bolster favored candidates? They do it all the time.]

CTCL wants election administrators to get directly involved in "educating" legislators so they don't erroneously propose legislation based on "misinformation." CTCL senior project manager Josh Simon Goldman said, "You can think of persuading as motivating public officials to support your stance, or move them towards even a neutral standpoint, limiting their opposition. Sometimes the facts aren't enough.... The bottom line, you are an expert. You are an election official, community leader, source of truth, steward of democracy, a public official in your own right."[214]

Another CTCL leader encouraged administrators to provide this information in multiple languages to "build inclusive, empowering connections" with "communities of foreign language…that also allows you to reflect on where your organization is in regards to diversity and inclusivity."[215]

And that would encourage illegal alien voting as well. Citizens, i.e., those who can legally vote, are supposed to understand English.

Consider what all this means. Unelected election administrators are being encouraged, possibly with money, to become censors. As of January 2023, CTCL had $79.5 million in net assets.[216] Not quite as much as the $350 million they had for 2020, but still a lot. CEIR had net assets of $11.7 million as of May 2023, the latest data available.[217]

If this program takes off, we will likely see more Zuckerbucks coming in. And don't expect any leftist individual or outlet to be censored, no matter what they post. They lie with impunity daily, with Joe Biden and Kamala Harris as the standard-bearers.

The Democrat Party also received huge, very questionable contributions from another source: foreign nationals. Tax-exempt 501(c)(3) and (c)(4) organizations are not required to disclose foreign donors on their tax filings. This is an enormous loophole through which foreign money has poured into Democrat coffers. The US House of Representatives Ways and Means Committee held a hearing about this in December 2023.

In a press release, the committee reported: "One Swiss billionaire alone donated over $200 million to political groups that the *New York Times* found 'helped Democrats in their efforts to win the White House and control of Congress.'"[218] One Democrat political action committee even called these foreign donations "the single most effective tactic for ensuring Democratic victories."[219]

The obvious concern is that foreign nationals could and are using this vehicle to influence the outcome of US elections. But don't look to Democrats to turn down a gift horse. Many Democrat organizations have taken advantage of this loophole, including Arabella Advisors, a huge Democrat "dark money" consulting firm that directs donors to Democrat causes and candidates without having to disclose who the donors are. It spent $1.2 billion on the 2020 election.[220] And this short description illustrates the importance of having Congress in GOP control. If Democrats controlled the House, this would never be a subject of public hearings. And that brings up another question.

Communist Chinese Election Interference?

True the Vote (TTV) is an election integrity organization founded by Catherine Engelbrecht in 2009 that reviews voter registrations. Engelbrecht gained notoriety in 2008 when she and a small group discovered some twenty-five thousand bogus registrations submitted by Houston Votes, a left-wing voter registration organization that used tactics very similar to ACORN.[221] The local registrar publicly characterized it as "an organized and systematic attack" on the voter rolls in Harris County, Texas.[222]

Engelbrecht is one of the most underappreciated patriotic heroes in the US today. The story is too long to recount here, but suffice it to say that since that fateful day in 2008, Engelbrecht has faced the full wrath of the Democrat Party and the federal government. She and her businesses have been sued multiple times by the Democrats, and her businesses faced twenty-three audits, investigations, and inquiries by the IRS, DOJ, FBI, ATF, and OSHA during the Obama administration. She won a multi-year battle with the IRS in 2019, in a case that cost millions, over securing tax-exempt status for TTV and has yet to receive the promised $1.9 million settlement.[223] Her fight publicized the effort by the IRS to deny conservative groups tax-exempt status, when liberal groups got easy access.

In January 2021, Engelbrecht's business partner, Gregg Phillips, honed in on an election software company called Konnech with direct ties to Communist China. He and his staff found that Konnech files containing detailed records of 1.8 million US election workers, including names, addresses, phone numbers, social security numbers, bank accounts, routing numbers, and even information about their children, were being stored on servers in Communist China.[224]

Konnech is based in Michigan, and CEO Eugene Yu is a naturalized citizen from Communist China who lives in Lansing, Michigan. During the 2020 election, Michigan and many other states and districts used Konnech vote scanning software. In a 2024 interview with Steve Bannon of *War Room*, Engelbrecht said, "By all appearances, Konnech software, which is being used in some of the largest counties and states in our country, is developed in, and run by, and monitored from China."[225]

TTV turned their information over to the FBI and worked with the FBI over the next sixteen months. Their suspicions were further confirmed when company whistleblowers came forward. However, in April 2022, the FBI turned its investigation over to the head office in Washington, DC, whereupon FBI cooperation immediately stopped. A sympathetic FBI agent warned Engelbrecht that she should be prepared to "go nuclear," meaning go public, because the Bureau was going to come after TTV. Shortly thereafter, the FBI accused TTV of illegally accessing this information.

Los Angeles County, which was using Konnech to manage its election workers, arrested Yu in October 2022 for possible theft of their election workers' data.[226] It was confirmed that not only was election information stored in China, but Konnech was using China-based contractors to do its work. However, one month later, charges were dropped by District Attorney George Gascon, one of the anti-police DAs responsible for letting murderers go bail-free. Gascon cited "potential bias" as a reason for dropping the case—a clear reference to TTV as the source of these revelations.[227]

About the same time, Yu sued Engelbrecht and Phillips for defamation and unlawful access to its database. Engelbrecht and Phillips were arrested and placed in jail, without bond, in solitary confinement, because they refused to disclose to the court the name of their informant. They were able to appeal to the Fifth Circuit and nine days later were freed. This all happened in late October through early November 2022.[228] Engelbrecht stated, "Konnech's aggressive litigation to shut down all conversation about their activities resulted in the wrongful imprisonment of Gregg Phillips and me. It required the intervention of a higher court to release us. We are more dedicated than ever to our mission of fostering a public conversation about voting integrity."[229]

In April 2023, Konnech dropped its lawsuit without explanation. TTV responded, "Konnech's litigation was meritless and intended to harass this organization. They have failed.... We believe Konnech dismissed its lawsuit because it saw that it would lose."[230]

According to Engelbrecht, Konnech shared data with CTCL and may have accessed ERIC voter information.[231] It was also learned that Konnech may have gained access to Department of Defense databases through the DoD's Uniformed and Overseas Citizens Absentee Voting Act (UOCAVA) program, which registers US military and civilian overseas voters. Prominent writer, commentator, and former CIA operations officer Sam Faddis asks, "Is it possible the Chinese really did hack our elections?"[232] He's not sure they didn't. Faddis writes, "In the four years leading up to the 2020 election roughly 350,000 'people' registered to vote using the UOCAVA system. That system may well have been compromised. All indicators point to mainland China."[233]

In testimony before the Arizona Senate regarding recounts of the 2020 election, Paul Harris, a Maricopa County manager auditing the election, described the difference between Maricopa County UOCAVA ballots received in 2016 and 2020. According to official figures, in 2016, there were 6,180 UOCAVA ballots returned. In 2020, 10,396 were returned, a 68 percent increase.[234]

There was no increase in Maricopa County overseas military members during that period. Overall, the population of US citizens overseas increased by 11–12 percent. But most stunning, Mr. Harris testified, was that approximately 95 percent of those UOCAVA ballots were for Joe Biden.[235] It is inconceivable that 95 percent voted against Trump in 2020. Furthermore, that only counted Maricopa County. What were the results for the entire state? Biden won that state by 10,457 votes. Then GOP attorney general Mark Brnovich had no interest in exploring the issue further.

Similar concerns were raised in other states over the UOCAVA vote. In a more recent development, in March 2024, Kimberly Zapata, deputy director of the Milwaukee, Wisconsin, Election Commission, was convicted for obtaining three military ballots using fake names and social security numbers.[236] Zapata said she did this to demonstrate how easy it is to commit fraud. She sent the ballots to GOP state representative Janel Brandtjen, who has been active in trying to identify the various forms of vote fraud she believes occurred in 2020.

The 2020 Election Was Stolen

Many credible reporters and voting experts, even conservative ones, say that Joe Biden legitimately won the election. Was there cheating? Almost certainly, but after many recounts, with a few adjustments, the numbers come up with Joe the winner. That is the claim. But it does not tell the full story. Far from it.

You have to begin with the recognition that the Left has no ethics of any kind. They believe "the ends justify the means." Notably, it was our friend Sergey Nechayev who adopted that slogan as his creed, and the Left has followed suit ever since.[237] The Left's greed for absolute power is unquenchable. If they can get away with it, they will do it. It may even be true that the vote count legitimately went to Biden. But the election was stolen all the same. Here is a partial list of the tactics used:

- $450 million to enlist partisan election workers in key districts
- Creating election chaos with mass mail-in ballots
- Implied and explicit threats
- Lawfare
- Smear campaigns
- Rampant disinformation
- Censorship of negative Biden news and positive Trump news
- Dispensing with longstanding rules:
  - Inadequate identity validation on absentee ballots
  - Banning GOP poll watchers from poll locations
- Partisan judges dismissing vote fraud allegations without examining evidence
- Partisan judges consistently deciding cases in support of Democrats
- Widespread use of remote drop boxes
- Massive ballot harvesting
- Automatic voter registration
- Illegal alien and felon voting
- Denying left-wing minority party listing on general election ballots
- Possible interference from Communist China

Some of these activities may not technically have been illegal, but they are all an unethical way to assure victory that undermines the entire electoral process. For example, there was no precedent with Zuckerbucks. Republicans had no idea how to handle it—if they even knew it was going on. Democrats, however, knew exactly what they were doing. Even in the very unlikely event that the vote count was largely legitimate, the 2020 election was essentially purchased by Mark Zuckerberg with help from partisan election workers, partisan judges, secretaries of state, big tech censorship, and news manipulation.

And with all those factors in play, there were many opportunities for vote fraud. It would be more surprising if there weren't any. John R. Lott directs the Crime Prevention Research Center and is known for his many studies on firearms use. He did an analysis of swing state voting patterns and found as many as 255,000 "excess" votes in swing states.[238] He found that while most heavily Democratic counties had slightly lower turnout in 2020, in counties where vote fraud was alleged, Democrat turnout was extremely high.

Lott evaluated the heavily Democratic Fulton County, Georgia, and four surrounding counties that were majority Republican. In all the GOP counties, President Trump's proportion of mail-in ballots was similar, but in Fulton County, there was a huge drop in the percentage of mail-in ballots for Trump. Lott estimated that drop to be as high as 11,350 votes, a number almost equal to Biden's 11,779 vote margin of victory.[239]

And that raises another question. How did vote counts in Georgia's Fulton County supposedly stop at 10:30 because of some questionable "plumbing" problem but then continue after poll watchers and other election observers were told to go home? Counting didn't stop until 3 a.m. No one has been able or willing to explain why that happened. In fact, similar things happened in many states. When the polls closed, Trump was ahead by large numbers, but magically, by the next morning, his advantage had vanished. What happened in the dead of night in some of those polling locations remains unanswered.

President Trump won eighteen of nineteen "bellwether counties." Since 1980, no presidential candidate who won those counties lost the election.[240] This was less important than previous elections because Biden got votes in the big cities. But that is where the vote fraud is alleged to have occurred, as described by John Lott. Trump is the first candidate since 1888 to have lost the election despite having more votes—eleven million more votes—than his first election.

In September 2023, Pennsylvania became the twenty-fourth state to allow automatic voter registration. Democratic governor Josh Shapiro imposed that by executive order. That is a major change and will make PA elections even more suspect than they are now. Republican state legislators objected. Election law is a legislative responsibility. GOP Caucus chairman George Dunbar said, "Gov. Shapiro knows this is a complete bypass of the General Assembly's authority."[241]

That is a major problem, as it was in 2020. GOP legislators could have done more to stop the shenanigans then, but they didn't. Commonwealth secretary Al Schmidt, a Republican, even celebrated Shapiro's announcement.[242] And as secretary of state, Schmidt is in charge of overseeing elections. He was appointed by Shapiro, likely for just such a time as this, giving Shapiro the appearance of bipartisanship, and got a Republican to endorse his action, when it was a wholesale usurpation of legislative authority.

Anyone who obtains a driver's license will now be automatically registered to vote in PA. Since many states provide driver's licenses to illegal aliens, this will likely spike votes for Democrats in 2024. Governor Shapiro is now calling for the legislature to pass a bill proposed in 2021 that would give illegals driver's licenses.[243] That will not bode well for the GOP in 2024 if it passes, but given the difference in overall registrations, PA is still an uphill battle.

Pennsylvania pulled another fast one thanks to the majority Democratic state Supreme Court. In 2016, the Green Party took fifty thousand votes that would have otherwise gone for Hillary Clinton. Trump won PA in 2016 by forty-four thousand votes. Democrats were not going to make that mistake again, so in 2020, the Supreme Court's five-seat Democrat majority ruled that the Greens' candidate, Howie Hawkins, had not used proper procedures in filing the paperwork needed. CNN reported, "Hawkins' campaign manager, Andrea Mérida Cuéllar, said the Democrats are playing 'legal shenanigans just to knock legitimate competition off of the ballot. I think that they should be afraid of having Greens on the ballot....'"[244]

Democrats pulled the same thing in Wisconsin, where, in 2016, the Green Party took thirty thousand votes. In 2016, Trump won in Wisconsin by twenty-three thousand votes. In 2020, the three Democrats on the Wisconsin Election Commission voted to reject about half of the signatures collected to put Hawkins on the presidential ballot, because his running mate's address was different on those petitions. That left him 211 short of the two thousand needed.[245] The three Republicans on the WEC objected, putting the issue in deadlock. A lawsuit went to the Wisconsin Supreme Court, which predictably ruled for the Democrats.[246]

And what about maintaining the voter rolls? This is not a difficult thing to do, except that the Democrats pull out all the stops to prevent it. Why would they do that if not to enable vote fraud? You can have dozens of recounts, but if those recounts include votes by ineligible voters, how can you determine the legitimate winner? Or, if they destroy the records before they can be properly evaluated, how do you know the votes were legal? Catherine Engelbrecht's True the Vote found that in Georgia:[247]

- 67,284 ineligible votes were cast in 2020
- 48,207 of those were made by people who no longer lived in the county
- 19,077 votes were cast by people no longer living in Georgia
- 16,986 of the out-of-state votes were mail-in ballots
- 8,984 of the mail-in ballots were from inactive voters

How many of those should have been tossed out? Probably well more than enough to swing the state for Trump, given Biden's slim margin of victory. Engelbrecht met with Georgia secretary of state Brad Raffensperger after the 2020 election. She told him they were preparing 364,000 voter record challenges based on ineligible residency. He was not surprised. He knew that the voter rolls had not been maintained. Democratic gubernatorial candidate Stacey Abrams and her "Fair Fight" group had sued in 2019 to prevent the state from cleaning the rolls of ineligible voters, e.g., those who had moved or died.[248]

While the state won that suit in 2021, Raffensperger didn't take any action beforehand. So the rolls remained cluttered with invalid registrations during 2020. True to form, the Democrats used them. In the post-election January 2021 runoff for the open US Senate seat, True the Vote worked with citizens across the state in an effort to file voter record challenges. Abrams's Fair Vote and Marc Elias (the sleazy Democrat operative who helped peddle the phony Trump/Russia hoax) threatened to sue every county that tried to use TTV's challenges. This is the kind of epic corruption that we face in elections. Engelbrecht asks:

> Mail ballots, drop boxes, no ID requirements, no monitoring, all catalyzed by inaccurate voter records. What actions were taken in 2020 to prevent illegal votes from being cast? Were any eligibility checks done before Georgia's vote count was certified?

She concluded:

> Georgia's lack of voter roll maintenance, together with rules that lowered identification standards for mail-in and inactive records, created an expressway for fraud. Make no mistake, this is not the only problem with our elections, but inaccurate voter rolls are where election fraud begins.

> True the Vote is now preparing for an October trial in the Fair Fight lawsuit over our work in supporting elector challenges. Where is the state? Clearly, they could intervene in our defense. After all, they pre-cleared our plan. But curiously, they too have sued True the Vote in another matter involving our findings related to dropboxes, arguing for data they already have in their possession but choose to keep covered up.[249]

In January 2024, TTV won the above-referenced October trial, based on a lawsuit by Stacey Abrams's Fair Fight group, which had accused TTV of "voter intimidation," a ridiculous charge. Abrams and the Left are the ones who use intimidation, and as usual, they've simply inverted the truth. To no one's surprise, they are appealing— another example of the lawfare leftists use to financially cripple effective opponents.[250]

The Trump candidacy came under full-scale, sustained attack from many directions starting well before President Trump took office in 2016 and lasting four years. There were the endless FBI investigations started in summer 2016, Congressional hearings, a phony impeachment, and nonstop vilification in media. Did this have an effect on the 2020 outcome? How could it not? Meanwhile, facts were suppressed or discredited by the media that would have sunk Joe Biden's prospects, such as the story of Hunter Biden's laptop or the many findings of Biden's criminal pay-for-play with some of our nation's biggest enemies. These were known facts, but the mass media suppressed them.

Then we had the COVID-19 pandemic and the George Floyd riots. Confusion and chaos reigned, much of it engineered by the Left, and they exploited the pandemic to stack the deck in their favor, especially with the use of extensive mail-in balloting, and loosened voting regulations.

Mollie Hemingway, best-selling author and editor-in-chief of the *Federalist*, has written a new book, *RIGGED: How the Media, Big Tech, and the Democrats Seized Our Elections.*[251] Hemingway's book points to many of the questionable events and actions taken during the 2020 election. In Pennsylvania, for example, in some jurisdictions, different procedures were used for counting GOP and Democrat mail-in ballots that gave Democrats a winning advantage. Mail-in ballots are required by Pennsylvania law to have a declaration on the outside envelope that is signed and dated.[252] If the voter does not fully complete that declaration, that vote is supposed to be rejected. In Republican districts, GOP election workers rejected those ballots, because they were following the law. In Democrat-controlled districts, they were counted.

For example, Nicole Ziccarelli, a GOP state senate candidate, was winning in her district by ten thousand votes until mail-in ballots were counted. She lost by less than one hundred votes, because while incomplete ballots in the majority GOP area of Westmoreland County were rejected, in the heavily Democratic Alleghany County, they were counted. Ziccarelli challenged the election outcome and won a court case where 2,349 improperly marked votes were rejected.[253]

The Democrats appealed, and the majority Democrat state Supreme Court allowed those votes to be counted.[254] That same decision allowed the counting of 8,329 incomplete ballots from Philadelphia County.[255] Thus, those two counties alone allowed 10,678 Democrat votes to count that should have been rejected. How many incomplete ballots from other jurisdictions were counted? We don't know.

In PA, there were 2.6 million votes cast by mail in 2020, 77 percent of which went to Biden.[256] The 8,329 incomplete ballots from Philadelphia represented 2.3 percent of mail-in ballots cast in Philadelphia. If we apply that percentage to the total mail-in vote throughout the state, then about sixty thousand votes should have been rejected, and 77 percent of those, about forty-six thousand, would come out of the Biden vote. This still leaves a thirty-four-thousand-vote margin for Biden.

In Ziccarelli's race, 4.4 percent of the ballots were incomplete. If we applied that rate to the same exercise as above, Biden loses PA by ten thousand votes. It depends on the number of incomplete ballots statewide that would have been rejected if the corrupt Supreme Court had not stepped in and decided for the Democrats. We will never know. And that assumes the Philadelphia County vote counts were accurate. Since GOP poll watchers were prevented from watching the count, we will never know. And why were they prevented?

The issue is still under litigation. Most recently, in November 2023, an Obama-appointed US district judge declared that incomplete ballots must be counted.[257] (Note: the media calls her a "Trump-appointed" judge to make her decision sound reasonable. Trump simply endorsed her to remain on the bench as part of a deal he made with Senate Democrats in 2017.) In any event, her decision was appealed, and the Third District Court of Appeals will hear the case.

There was a similar situation for "naked" ballots—that is, mail-in ballots that had not been sealed inside the signed and dated external envelope. No one has estimated how many of those there were, but it would have been treated by Democrats as the incomplete ballot envelopes were.[258]

Maricopa County, Arizona, had serious problems in both the 2020 and 2022 elections that could have thrown the elections for Trump, gubernatorial candidate Kari Lake, and others. America First Legal, headed by Stephen Miller, a former top advisor to President Trump, filed suit in February 2024 against Maricopa County, Arizona, election officials, alleging:

- Maricopa County refuses to maintain the mandatory chain of custody for ballots. In 2022, these failures resulted in a discrepancy of over 25,000 votes—larger than the margin of victory in the state governor's race.
- Maricopa County ignores mandatory reconciliation procedures to track each ballot printed or issued to a voter. The law requires tracking and reconciling ballots cast and voters checked in to stop fraud, but the Defendants do not perform any reconciliation procedures *at all*.
- Maricopa County's election day "voting centers"…are situated in a racially discriminatory way, having a disparate impact on the County's White and Native American citizens who are more likely to vote in person. Furthermore, these centers are poorly run; during the 2022 general election, a majority had issues with their ballot-on-demand printers. Malfunctions included printing 19-inch ballot images on 20-inch paper and/or using an ink-saving "eco" function that rendered ballots unreadable, disenfranchising lawful voters.
- Starting in 2020, the Defendants have been wrongly canceling the voter registrations of hundreds, and possibly thousands, of Maricopa County residents. This has been happening without voters' knowledge, thus making it impossible for canceled voters to protest…. These voters were forced to cast provisional ballots, which the Defendants never counted. The number of voters disenfranchised during the 2022 general election by the Defendants' unlawful cancellations was larger than the margin of victory in some races.
- Maricopa County violates state laws mandating ballot curing procedures that require that a voter actually see a suspect signature and confirm its authenticity *in person*.

- Arizona law requires ballot drop boxes to be staffed by at least two election officials positioned close enough to view each person who deposits ballots into it. Maintaining an unstaffed drop box is a felony. However, Maricopa County maintains unstaffed, unsupervised ballot drop boxes, facilitating illegal ballot harvesting.[259]

These are only some of the details that have raised serious questions about the electoral processes in many states and not only for 2020. So what actually happened in 2020? A mere ten days after the election, CBS News quoted alleged "experts" claiming 2020 was "the most secure election in history."[260] And of course, the story cited here discredited President Trump's allegations that the election was stolen, saying, "President Trump continued to spread *baseless claims* of widespread voter fraud in key battleground states." (Emphasis added.)[261]

How do so-called experts know ten days after the election that Trump's claims were "baseless"? Nine days after the elections, all fifty states and the District of Columbia were still counting.[262] But the media-Democrat complex started early in the effort to discredit any allegations of vote fraud, because the massive allegations of vote fraud came from every direction in *all* the swing states.

Consider, too, that Joe Biden, who barely campaigned, whose rallies didn't attract enough people to fill a Starbucks, supposedly received eighty-one million votes, the largest amount of any presidential candidate in US history. Meanwhile, Trump, who held huge rallies with overflow crowds almost daily for months, received seventy-four million, more votes than any other candidate in history...except Biden? It does not pass the smell test.

If you questioned the election outcome, you were immediately labeled an "election denier." This is the height of hypocrisy. Hillary Clinton claimed the election was rigged against her in 2016 and went after Trump for four years with the Russia collusion hoax. She's still at it. And Democrats still mentally litigate the outcome of the 2000 election between George W. Bush and Al Gore. So apparently all elections are free, fair, and secure unless a Republican wins. Then they are immediately suspect?

But the opposite is true. As is apparent from everything presented here, Democrats use every device possible to win elections, legal or not. The Biden campaign was further helped by partisan judges and a sympathetic media. Since Biden took office, he's opened the borders for the specific purpose of importing millions of people Democrats are confident will vote for them at some point.

Finally, the hand of Barack Obama can be seen in much of what happened and continues to happen with our electoral system. When Obama ran for office in 2009, he created an organization called Organizing for America. For his second run, he changed the name to Obama for America. Finally, in 2013, it changed again to Organizing for Action. It has now morphed into All on the Line (AOTL) after merging with former Justice Department attorney general Eric Holder's group, National Democratic Redistricting Committee, and the National Redistricting Action Fund, also directed by Holder.[263] It seeks to redraw electoral maps in a manner more favorable to Democrats, especially targeting Arizona, Colorado, Florida, Georgia, Michigan, North Carolina, Ohio, Pennsylvania, Texas, and Wisconsin.[264] According to GOP Wisconsin Assembly Speaker Robin Vos, Democrats have already been successful in redrawing the legislative districts that will remove most of the advantages Republicans have now, which have given them substantial majorities in the state legislature for a long time.[265]

Actually, in one sense, 2020 may have been the most secure election. The Democrats made absolutely sure they secured the election for Joe Biden. But calling an election "secure" is not the same as calling it clean. And it most certainly was not that. We have reviewed the activities of CTCL and CEIR, which alone illegally skewed the election in Biden's favor, whether all the votes he received were legitimate or not. We have cited all the other unethical and borderline criminal activity that enabled Biden's win. Would you call that a secure, free, and fair election? The election was stolen, as surely as if the Democrats had bought every vote in America.

STRATEGIC CORRUPTION

The rich get richer and the poor get poorer.
—Percy Bysshe Shelley

The Left's constant refrain is that the rich get richer while the poor get poorer in capitalist countries. The trouble is, like most of what the Left says, it simply isn't true. Now, it may be true that in good economic times, the rich get richer *faster* than the poor, but everyone benefits. In fact, America's "poor" are materially better off than most people in the world.[266]

The whole argument that the rich get richer while the poor get poorer implicitly assumes that wealth creation is a zero-sum game. If someone becomes better off, it is always at someone else's expense—robbing Peter to pay Paul. This is the rationale used to justify Socialism. It is an utterly fallacious argument.

When Steve Jobs created the iPhone, did he steal from someone else to do it? Did anyone else lose? Of course not. He brought an entirely new product to the market and in doing so, created vast wealth *that did not exist before*. It provided tens of thousands of new jobs and many more downstream. If you had purchased seven thousand shares of Apple stock on September 1, 1985, it would have cost you $480.00. As of this writing, those shares would be worth over $1.2 million. Nobody lost anything; many people gained a great deal.

Like most of the Left's arguments, it is idiotic on its face. But it appeals to people's *emotions*. They feel cheated. "Why didn't I make that money?!" they squeal. Well, because you didn't work for it. The leftists appeal to people's baser emotions to ply their trade, and one of the basest human emotions is envy.

The Left has been stumped at every turn in their effort to destroy our market economy. The economy simply adjusts and moves on. So while they continue to try to wreck the economy with endless crisis strategies, they have worked on the inside to make their erroneous assumptions about markets a self-fulfilling prophesy.

It is less than a conspiracy perhaps, but more than a coincidence, that starting in the 1990s, leftist ideologues began infiltrating the financial markets. They did indeed rob Peter to pay Paul at first with the subprime mortgage debacle and subsequently with economy, social, and governance (ESG) concepts in investing. Today, the investment firm BlackRock is the best example of this. With $10 trillion in assets under management, it can literally move markets. And it is one of the most prominent advocates for ESG, forcing corporations to focus investments on money-losing projects like climate change and diversity, equity, and inclusion (DEI).

The World Economic Forum dubbed it "stakeholder capitalism," which advocates focusing investments not on what provides a monetary return but rather what the latest leftist political fad is. The biggest example of this is "climate change." So while, for example, it might be more lucrative to invest in oil and gas exploration, ESG concepts would demand institutional investors steer toward money-losing "green" solar and wind energy projects. And that is where the "G" for government comes in, because wind and solar *require* government subsidies and mandates to be even remotely competitive with oil and gas. And even then, they are unreliable, expensive, and produce very little energy. So most of these companies become involved in "public/private partnerships."

We had our first big taste of that with President Barack Obama's "green energy" program, where the only "green" from that list of multibillion-dollar failures went to Obama's political allies and supporters.[267] Ironically, given the endless left-wing name-calling against "fascist"

America, public-private "partnerships," in which private companies are recruited to serve government interests, are the essence of fascism.[3]

The World Economic Forum and others have a partner in this effort that has gone virtually unnoticed, proxy advisory services; Institutional Shareholder Services (ISS) and Glass Lewis are two of the most prominent ones. Because institutional investors hold so many proxy votes at one time, they seek the advice of such services. This has enabled ISS and Glass Lewis to literally dictate to corporate boards where they must place their investments. They can see to the turnover of entire boards if board members don't endorse their "advice."[268]

The Sidley law firm, famous for its former associates, Barack and Michelle Obama, pointed its clients to the latest "advice" from ISS and Glass Lewis, which very explicitly warned board members that they'd better toe the line on "climate change" and other "social" investments.[269]

Writing for Columbia Law School's blog, *Blue Sky*, columnist Neil Whoriskey describes the problem:

> ISS and Glass Lewis have arrogated to themselves the power to make law, promulgating a civil code of astounding breadth and detail, ruling over decisions on board composition, director qualifications, term limits, majority voting standards, executive compensation, capital structure, poison pills, staggered boards, the advisability of mergers, spin-offs and recapitalizations, and, increasingly, ESG policies ranging from animal welfare to climate change, diversity, data security and political activities. They enforce this civil code by advising their clients, institutional investors with huge, varied and increasingly concentrated holdings across the economy, to vote against proposals or against directors

---

3   Italian dictator Benito Mussolini founded the first fascist party as a politically more marketable alternative to Communism. Instead of seizing and nationalizing businesses as the Communists did, fascists allowed companies to remain private in a partnership arrangement, with government as the senior partner, so it could dictate corporate activities, achieving the same goals without seizing the companies outright. Fascism and Communism are distinctions without a difference.

if any aspect of the new civil code is disobeyed. The vote of these clients is often decisive, and the implications of the votes—especially when considered in the aggregate—have far-reaching consequences for the operation and performance of U.S. public corporations.[270]

The Evil Eye

Americans are an independent, innovative, and self-reliant people. Indeed, the history of America is one of overcoming obstacles and adapting in the face of new challenges. From Eli Whitney to Thomas Edison, from the ENIAC[4] to the iPad, America's is a history of adaptation and innovation. We are not unique. Humans everywhere are capable of overcoming seemingly insurmountable problems, and have demonstrated so, time and again. Left to their own devices, people can adapt to uncertainty and thrive in the most inhospitable places.

But America is the only country in modern history to codify that spirit in the foundation of government. And that structure has allowed America herself to confront challenges within and without: from the Civil War to civil rights, from Pearl Harbor to Normandy, from 9/11 to Abbottabad, Americans accept challenges, take risks, adapt, and *win*, often at brutal cost.

This structure has provided the fertile ground that has grown the most affluent society in history. The world economy floats on American affluence, and America has become a beacon of hope to people from all corners of the globe, who clamor to get in.

Yet, since the dawn of time, there has always been a malevolent undercurrent, a dark side of human nature that despises success. It is called envy. And throughout history, envious people have sought to undermine and subvert the best in us. Unwilling or unable to perform on an equal par, they seek instead to pull the world down to their level.

---

[4]   The Electronic Numerical Integrator and Calculator, what is generally believed to be the first computer was built between 1943 and 1945, although it may have been preceded by Britain's Colossus, used to break German codes during WWII. See: http://www.computersciencelab.com/ComputerHistory/HistoryPt4.htm.

The late Dr. Jack Wheeler called it the "Evil Eye" and described how primitive cultures are shot through with it:[271]

> Among the Yanomamo and other tribes deep in the Amazon rain forests still adhering to the ancient hunting-gathering lifestyle practiced by our Paleolithic ancestors, it is an accepted practice that when a woman gives birth, she tearfully proclaims her child to be ugly.... She does this in order to ward off the envious black magic of the Evil Eye, the *Mal Ojo*, that would be directed at her by her fellow tribespeople if they knew how happy she was with her beautiful baby.

> The fundamental reason why certain cultures remain static and never evolve...is the overwhelming extent to which the lives of the people within them are dominated by envy and envy avoidance: as anthropologists call it, the envy barrier.

Any effort to progress in those societies is sabotaged by the group. Wheeler quoted sociologist Helmut Schoeck, who describes it as:

> A self-pitying inclination to contemplate another's superiority or advantages, combined with a vague belief in his being the cause of one's own deprivation.... Whereas the socialist believes himself robbed by the employer, just as the politician in a developing country believes himself robbed by the industrial countries, so primitive man believes himself robbed by his neighbor, the latter having succeeded by black magic in spiriting away to his own fields, part of the former's harvest.[272]

Wheeler concluded:

> The three great political pathologies of the 20th century are all religions of envy: Nazism, preaching race envy toward "rich, exploitative Jews"; Communism,

preaching class envy toward the "rich, exploitative bourgeoisie"; and Moslem terrorism, preaching culture envy toward the "rich, exploitative West."[273]

All people are vulnerable to envy and greed. But our founders' inspiration gave us a system that would allow full expression of the best within us, implicitly recognizing that it could deliver the freedom and prosperity that all desire—"if you can keep it," as Benjamin Franklin quipped.[274]

How transparently hypocritical that Communist propagandists envision a future world of selfless purity while promising prospective converts a bounty of spoils from the "selfish" rich. Is it any wonder that all their "workers' paradises" without exception devolve into ruthless, parasitic kleptocracies unable or unwilling to even feed their own?[5]

Yet that's what the Left wants for us. Their entire edifice has been built on the primitive emotion of envy. They have become a poisonous spear, thrust deep into the heart of America's spirit, and today threaten our very way of life.

What happens when an organization whose core beliefs eschew any and all morality gets the keys to the kingdom? What happens when an organization whose credo is "the ends justify the means" is given access to 20 percent of the US economy through the federal budget? Add to the mix the knowledge that this organization's overriding goal is to entrench itself in power in order to leech its host country dry, and what do you have? You have a prescription for rampant corruption, chaos, and societal disintegration.

But that fact doesn't sit well with the Left. They know it's true. So how then, can they make it appear otherwise? Lately, it actually *has become true in America*. But that is not the result of free market capitalism. It is the result of deliberate, cumulative actions by the Democratic

---

[5] An incredible description of the failure of Soviet agriculture was provided by Russian economist Yuri Maltsev at a Mises forum, May 14, 2011. See: Yuri N. Maltsev, *What Soviet Agriculture Teaches Us*, May 14, 2011, speech presented at Agricultural Subsidies: Down on the DC Farm forum, Mises Institute, Indianapolis, IN, https://mises.org/podcasts/agricultural-subsidies-down-dc-farm/what-soviet-agriculture-teaches-us. Maltsev refers skeptics to another film, *The Soviet Story*, www.sovietstory.com.

Party and its allies in finance and business, who have sought to sabotage our economy while making themselves rich.

Those actions turned their claim into a self-fulfilling prophecy. The rich Democrats do indeed keep getting richer, while the rest of us get poorer, because unlike free market capitalism, where you must produce something worthy of your fare, Democrats steal from us to achieve their wealth.

Connecticut Democratic senator Chris Murphy recently admitted that Democrats can't win on policy alone. He said that they had to go back to the tried-and-true divide and conquer method of vilifying capitalism. "Democrats cannot win if we just talk about programs," he said. "We need to tell a story—about how the concentration and [sic] wealth & power is ruining America."[275]

In other words, "the rich get richer while the poor get poorer." The magazine he read to draw this conclusion? *Jacobin* magazine. The Jacobins were the first Communists, who led the French Revolution and decapitated tens of thousands of people. Only Communists and their sympathizers read this rag. Frances Fox Piven was interviewed by *Jacobin* in 2020, spouting her revolutionary drivel.[276] They're all on the same page.

It is the assertion of this book that the Left is a single massive organism dedicated to its own longevity. It builds a wall of misinformation that justifies policies, philosophies, and movements that cause chaos, corruption, and societal breakdown while providing pretext for a small core of parasitic gangsters to insinuate themselves into positions of power. Once ensconced, they direct vast wealth to themselves at public expense while working to further destroy the societal institutions that stand in the way of their complete control.

There has always been corruption in politics. There have always been political payoffs, pork barrel spending, and logrolling. But this is a new form of corruption. Premeditated and strategic, it serves the Left for a number of reasons:

1. It destroys market economics and replaces it with crony Socialism, often misleadingly called "crony capitalism," where political

overlords choose winners and losers in business. Obama called it "public private partnerships." As noted earlier, the correct word for it is fascism.[277]

2. It channels tax dollars illegally or unethically to political allies, making them stronger and more capable while robbing taxpayers and pauperizing opponents.

3. It undermines the rule of law. Law loses its legitimacy, making a nation ungovernable except through edict backed by force, i.e., despotism.

4. It hinders our ability to fight the Left, because many political leaders who are not part of the conspiracy are nonetheless compromised by its corrupting influences. Others are intimidated by it.

5. It's a great way for leftists to make a bunch of money.

This began in earnest decades ago but took a nasty turn under the presidency of Bill Clinton.

Subprime Mortgage Manufactured Crisis

If you listen to former president Obama, all of the economic woes suffered during his presidency resulted from George W. Bush's mishandling of the economy. According to Obama and the Democrats, Bush presided over a period of lax financial regulation and ill-considered economic policy that led to the mortgage crisis, the 2008 financial meltdown, and subsequent recession. Bush made the situation so bad that despite an unprecedented $1 trillion "stimulus" and countless "bailouts," we still haven't recovered. While it is true that President Bush was in office when all this came to a head, its genesis was decades earlier, and much, if not all, of it can be laid at the Democrats' feet.

In 1977, President Jimmy Carter signed the Community Reinvestment Act (CRA). A group of Chicago housing activists[278] successfully lobbied for the law, charging that banks had engaged in a form of lending discrimination called "redlining," that is, denoting racial and ethnic zones on a map with a red line—mostly in urban areas—indicating where loans would supposedly be denied or limited regardless of the creditworthiness of residents.[279] The CRA required banks to discontinue the redlining practice and expand mortgage loan offerings to minorities and less creditworthy customers.

It was actually government regulation that instituted redlining. In the 1930s, the Federal Housing Administration began *requiring* banks to redline in order to receive FHA loan guarantees. These FHA guidelines—another titanic failure of the liberals' New Deal—were developed by President Franklin D. Roosevelt's administration and contributed mightily to urban decay for decades afterward. These rules were revoked in 1968.[280]

Activists have studiously overlooked this fact in their vilification of banks. Since the CRA's passage, a number of studies have been conducted by the Richmond Federal Reserve Bank. They found no evidence of redlining to support activists' claims and that market demand and economic risk factors played the major part in determining the quantity of mortgage loans in a given area.[281]

This is what one would expect, based on market economics. Banks are in business to earn a profit, and denying loans to creditworthy customers based on their race or any other reason is bad for business. This is why the South needed segregation laws to maintain segregation. This is why South Africa needed apartheid. Such race-based barriers restrict the free enterprise that would occur in their absence and require government intervention to maintain them. Redlining should be laid at the feet of government—liberal big government—not the private market, but the agitators won't admit it.

With passage of the CRA, ACORN and other activist groups got in the housing business. They began pushing banks to offer high-risk mortgage loans to low-income borrowers. ACORN and some of the others used the tried-and-true NWRO method of confrontational agitation, angrily occupying bank lobbies, disrupting business, terrifying customers, and demonstrating on the lawns of bank executives, always with the implicit threat of violence to them and their families.

The Center for Community Change (CCC), a far-left activist group, was instrumental in getting the CRA passed. In *Architects of*

Ruin, Peter Schweizer writes of the CCC's involvement in the "$4 trillion shakedown":

> As it fought to weaken banking standards, the organization was heavily funded by the Fannie Mae Foundation, the Rockefeller Foundation, the Carnegie corporation, and the Woods Foundation of Chicago [where Obama cut his teeth].... Labor unions, such as the United Mine Workers, United Autoworkers, Service Employees International, and Amalgamated Clothing and Textile Workers Union became involved in a national campaign to shakedown banks. And civil rights organizations such as the NAACP and the Southern Christian Leadership Conference joined Jesse Jackson in the cause. National activists such as Ralph Nader also mobilized their supporters.[282]

When changes to the CRA were being considered by Congress in 1991 and again in 1995, ACORN activists occupied hearing rooms. In 1995, five of the activists, including ACORN president Maude Hurd, were arrested.[283] Following Republicans' congressional election victory in 1994, the new majority in Congress attempted to roll back the CRA law. The House Banking Subcommittee chairman, then representative Marge Roukema (R-NJ), feared that the CRA was lowering underwriting standards and turning into a *de facto* quota system for mortgage loans.[284] But Democrats in Congress, in collusion with ACORN activists and the Clinton White House, prevented Republicans from enacting any reforms and instead began aggressively expanding the program through regulatory changes.[285]

Franklin Raines, then vice chairman of the Federal National Mortgage Association (Fannie Mae), a so-called government-sponsored enterprise (GSE),[6] later testified before Congress that in 1994, Fannie Mae launched a program to invest $1 trillion to serve ten million under-served families by the end of 2000.[286] This included low- and mod-erate-income families, minorities, new Americans (i.e., immigrants, including illegals), residents of central cities and rural areas, and people with special housing needs. Having reached that goal, in early 2000, he committed *another $2 trillion* for the next ten years.[287]

Clinton housing secretary Andrew Cuomo (later NY governor Cuomo), acknowledged that it would increase mortgage lending risk but said it was worth the effort.[288] To make this palatable to lenders and investors, Fannie Mae and Freddie Mac (Federal Home Loan Mortgage Corporation) were pressured by the Clinton administration and con-gressional Democrats to underwrite the risk.[289] The predictable bubble and burst soon followed.

Let's reiterate that. Democrats committed American taxpayers to underwriting the risk for a total of *$3 trillion in subprime mortgages targeted directly at the Democrats' voting demographic*, fully aware that they were generating enormous risk.

ACORN itself made millions of dollars pushing so-called NINJA (No Income, No Job, No Assets) loans. The Clinton administration gave ACORN and similar groups oversight responsibility in evaluating bank compliance to his expanded CRA regulations. This allowed ACORN to shake down banks under the threat of poor report cards, creating what amounted to a protection racket. Some companies would agree to underwrite ACORN projects or simply donate to the group. For exam-ple, J.P. Morgan donated hundreds of thousands of dollars to ACORN to avoid hold-ups on a planned merger with Chase Manhattan Bank.[290]

There were countless examples like these, and radical leftist groups continue to get a share whenever the DOJ shakes down a company. Under Obama, the DOJ sued banks over the subprime mortgages banks

---

[6]   GSEs are private corporations with public purposes created by Congress to reduce the cost of capital to certain buyers. Fannie Mae, Freddie Mac, and Sallie Mae (Student Loan Marketing Association) are probably the best-known examples. Their loan guarantees are assumed to be backed by the federal government, and as such, they have no viable competitor in the private market.

were forced to underwrite by the Clinton administration. Settlements were in the billions of dollars. Much went to radical Left organizations.

President Trump ended that practice in 2017. In 2022, Biden attorney general Merrick Garland started it up again. The Heritage Foundation explains:

> The Justice Department sues a company, seeking billions of dollars in damages. The company realizes that defending the suit will be expensive, time-consuming and burdensome. Plus, there's no guarantee of success.
>
> That's when the Justice Department makes the company an offer they can't refuse. If the company agrees to pay money to one or more third-party advocacy groups on an approved list, DOJ will settle the case, often for a fraction of the original amount demanded, and often with two-for-one credit for each dollar donated to the favored group.[291]

Garland was met with harsh reactions from GOP members of Congress, who demanded he stop, but it is doubtful he listened.[292] That can create a big war chest for the Left. In 2021 alone, the DOJ collected $5.6 billion in settlements.[293] Environmental groups are really excited about it. The Sidley law firm announced: "DOJ's 'return to normal' aligns with the current administration's focus on environmental justice initiatives in communities of color, low-income communities, and tribal communities."[294]

The "return to normal" means restoration of the corruption that the bad old Trump administration ended in 2017. Beneficiaries will likely include Sidley—an influential Democrat law firm—the Natural Resources Defense Council, and other leftist environmental groups that make a practice of suing for the settlement. This will be fun for the DOJ Environment and Natural Resources Division (ENRD), which has its own Office of Environmental Justice.[295] Yet another way to pay off Democrat voters.

But it's not the only way. In 2023, Garland bragged that he had secured over $107 million in relief for "communities of color," after receiving more settlements from banks the DOJ accused of "redlining."[296] As explained earlier, redlining was ended in 1968 and was never a bank priority. It was foisted on them by the FHA. Yet that was the fraudulent pretext used to force banks to make subprime mortgage loans during the 1990s that caused the 2008 recession. And here they are doing it *again*!

Leftists claim that conservatives unfairly treated the CRA as a scapegoat for the mortgage crisis. They also claim that groups like ACORN contributed only marginally to the mortgage market meltdown—that the true culprit was unregulated Wall Street greed. This is categorically false. When the government—through Fannie Mae and Freddie Mac—agreed to underwrite investment risk by purchasing high-risk mortgages, the entire risk suddenly became the responsibility of US taxpayers. Banks and investment companies could now write mortgages to anyone with no downside risk. A recent article in the *Wall Street Journal* explains:

> Enter Fannie and Freddie. They don't make loans. Instead, they buy them from lenders, package them into securities, and sell those to investors. They promise to make investors whole when mortgages default. In other words, they take the credit risk.[297]

This is called privatizing the return and socializing the risk. There is nothing related to "free market capitalism" or "Wall Street greed" about this. It is essentially government welfare policy executed on the government's behalf by lending institutions. In the run-up to the subprime mortgage crisis, banks and investment houses implicitly understood the government was guaranteeing the risk. When the crisis exploded, that guarantee became explicit.

But even this misses the point. The CRA and resulting subprime mortgage lending pushed by groups like ACORN completely changed the paradigm. ACORN actually helped write the 1992 law that mandated Fannie Mae and Freddie Mac participation in the subprime market. According to a *Wall Street Journal* report:

> The watershed moment was the 1992 Federal Housing Enterprises Financial Safety and Soundness Act, also known as the GSE Act. To comply with that law's "affordable housing" requirements, Fannie Mae and Freddie Mac would acquire more than $6 trillion of single-family loans over the next 16 years.[298]

At the start of the financial crisis, there were twenty-seven million subprime mortgages valued at over $4.5 trillion; that *represented approximately half of all mortgages outstanding. Of this total, over 70 percent, valued at $2.7 trillion,* were owned by Fannie Mae, Freddie Mac, FHA, and other government programs.[299] The rest were held by the Democrat-connected, systemically corrupt Countrywide Financial—which held about $500 billion in bad mortgages—and other investment companies.[300] The GSEs played a central role in the crisis as evident in the chart below. Fannie Mae and Freddie Mac's investment in mortgages literally exploded, starting in the 1990s when the Clinton administration began pushing banks to originate more subprime loans.

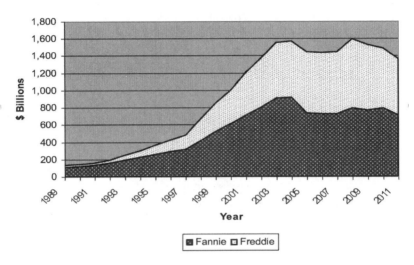

Fannie Mae & Freddie Mac - Total Mortgage Assets Held for Investment

Source: Federal Housing Finance Agency: 2011 Report to Congress; Tables 5 and 14.

Former representative Barney Frank (D-MA) sat on the House Banking Committee, which has oversight responsibility for Fannie Mae. He lobbied Fannie Mae to get a job for his live-in boyfriend, Herb Moses.[301] Moses worked for Fannie Mae from 1991 to 1998, the entire time he was living with Rep. Frank, and developed many of Fannie's affordable housing programs.[302] Moses broke up with Frank about the same time he quit Fannie Mae. Maybe he had outlived his usefulness in more ways than one.

For his part, Frank boisterously denied there was any problem in the subprime mortgage market until the meltdown actually occurred; then he belligerently blamed Republicans.[303] Meanwhile, he and other key Democrats, including Senate Banking Committee chairman Chris Dodd (D-CT) and then senator Barack Obama, received hundreds of thousands in campaign contributions from Fannie and Freddie. Though he only served part of one term in the Senate, Obama was one of the top recipients.[304]

Franklin Raines became Fannie Mae CEO in 1999. He left in 2004 after being accused of "cooking Fannie's books," inflating earnings by billions to earn a $90 million bonus. The Office of Federal Housing Enterprise Oversight (OFHEO) initially sought $115 million in returned bonuses and a $100 million penalty from three Fannie Mae officials, including Raines, but ultimately settled for $3 million that was paid by Fannie's executive insurance policy.[305]

Fannie Mae itself was required to pay $400 million. So the company gets tagged, but those responsible run free. Sound familiar? As long as they're Democrats, that is. As Weather Underground terrorist Bill Ayers once said, "Guilty as hell, free as a bird...." Former president Obama considered Raines for an economic advisor post but was forced to deny it when news of Raines's Fannie Mae scandal emerged.[306]

In 2007, the National Community Reinvestment Coalition (NCRC), an umbrella organization for community activist organizations including ACORN, bragged that between 1997 and 2007, banks had made commitments to make $4.5 trillion in CRA loans at their behest.[307] The evidence suggests they're right, but their complicity in engineering the collapse of the housing market has never been properly investigated.

To add insult to injury, these and other groups were the recipients of as much as $200 million as part of settlements with Citibank and Bank of America, and likely J.P. Morgan, for misrepresenting the risks of mortgage-backed securities.[308] The National Council of La Raza (now called UnidosUS), an illegal alien advocacy group, received $2 million.[309]

These securities were comprised of those same toxic mortgages the Department of Justice under Bill Clinton *forced* banks to make— Clinton even bragged about shaking banks down for that $1 trillion in loans that Raines later reported to Congress.[310] And they are the same securities Fannie Mae and Freddie Mac were *forced* to underwrite with the connivance of the Democrats.

Who are the true criminals here?

It became a regular pattern under Obama. An investigation by the House Judiciary and House Financial Services Committee found that the Obama Justice Department had "engaged in a pattern or practice of systematically subverting Congress' budget authority by using settlements from financial institutions to funnel money to left-wing activist groups."[311]

The other factors blamed for the crisis, for example, deregulation and the use of mortgage derivatives, had little actual impact. For example, the 1999 Gramm–Leach–Bliley Act partially repealed the 1930s-era Glass–Steagall Act by allowing banks to affiliate with securities firms. But banks didn't get into trouble for this reason.

Glass–Steagall always allowed mortgage lending, and high-risk mortgages demanded by the leftist administration of Bill Clinton were the source of the problem. Likewise, loans of all varieties have been securitized into derivatives for decades with no federal government underwriting. The problem was not with mortgage-backed securities; it was with the subprime mortgages themselves—a direct consequence of Democrat meddling in the mortgage market—and the government's promise to guarantee the loans.[312]

This is an apt example of how leftists institutionalize the crisis strategy. Sound lending principles became discredited secondary considerations replaced by non-market social policy goals. It was the key change that sowed the seeds of the financial meltdown.

In September 2008, Fannie Mae and Freddie Mac came under the conservatorship of the newly created Federal Housing Finance Agency. At the time, the two GSEs held $3.7 trillion in mortgage-backed securities. The subprime mortgage crisis caused the "Great Recession," the worst recession since the Great Depression. It was Cloward–Piven reinvented to crash the economy.

Obama 2.0

The Biden administration is little more than an extension of the Obama years, with Obama and his cabal of Communists still firmly steering the ship. Obama told the *New York Times* that about 90 percent of Biden's staff are former Obama White House aides.[313] He said that Biden and his crew are "essentially finishing the job," Obama started.[314] And Biden really is finishing the job. He is finishing the United States.

The Obama administration was a warm-up for what we see today, and many of his policies were trial runs of even larger, more destructive versions now being pushed on America by Biden and the congressional Democrats.

In 2009, Obama and congressional Democrats enacted the American Recovery and Reinvestment Act (ARRA), a supposed "economic stimulus" that largely went to state governments and unions, along with an $80 billion "green energy" initiative that stimulated no one but Obama's political supporters.[315] The so-called "shovel ready" projects that would send us all back to work were estimated to comprise only about 5 percent of the original stimulus monies. Even that proved to be an exaggeration. Obama joked about it in 2011, saying, "Shovel-ready was not as shovel-ready as we expected."[316]

The secret goal of the stimulus was to carry out Obama's political agenda.[317] The bill was originally crafted by Obama's presidential transition staff and congressional Democrats almost as soon as he was elected.[318] It recommended a Recovery Accountability and Transparency Board (with the apt acronym, RAT) to oversee disbursement of stimulus money and, incredibly, gave RAT power to block investigations of RAT's activities by inspectors general.[319] The multiple subsequent "green jobs" and other "stimulus" scandals demonstrated why the "most transparent administration in history" needed RAT. Haven't we heard that the Biden administration is the "most transparent administration in history" too? The apple doesn't fall far from the tree.

Until Biden, the ARRA was the largest single Keynesian stimulus program since the 1930s. And that wasn't all. There was the $100 billion auto bailout, endless unemployment benefit extensions, and the $26 billion teacher bailout, to name but a few. But none of this improved the job market. During the Obama administration, for the first time since 1948, the labor force stopped growing. Labor force participation reached its lowest point at any time since 1978. Some cited the aging population as the cause, but more elderly were working than ten years before. Most blamed the recession.[320] Obama proposed an additional $447 billion "jobs" bill in 2011, which fortunately never passed.

During the Obama administration, the crisis strategy metastasized into an epidemic of chaos.[321] His repeated unconstitutional actions, countless scandals, political payoffs, endless conspicuously ostentatious vacations, misuse of government property, and defiance of enacted law was an assault on American values. He also kicked off the border crisis. More about that later.

But it has gotten multiple times worse since Biden took office. Successive massive spending bills have risen national debt to $34 trillion, or about 140 percent of GDP. This exceeds the debt-to-GDP ratio during the height of World War II—126 percent—the only other time in history the debt/GDP ratio was so high. The postwar economy grew us out of record high debt, but if Democrats remain at the helm in 2024, there will be no similar economic growth to pull us out of this mess. Quite the opposite.

In 2020, President Trump boosted government spending by almost 50 percent with the $2.2 trillion CARES Act in response to the COVID shutdowns. This should have been a one-time increase, but Biden used COVID as an excuse to spend another $1.9 trillion in 2021 with his "American Rescue Plan," even though $1 trillion from the CARES Act had not yet been spent.[322]

Biden's "rescue" plan mostly rescued Democrats, including $90 billion to bail out union pension funds, $200 billion to welfare, and $362 billion to bail out mostly Democrat states and counties. This included $100 million to communities like Beverly Hills, Palm Beach, the Hamptons, Greenwich, CT, Cambridge, MA, and other bastions of liberal wealth.[323] Only about 5 percent of the bill was actually for COVID-related expenditures. And as mentioned earlier, the extension of enhanced unemployment compensation kept people out of work.[324]

Next, Biden introduced his "infrastructure" bill. Once again, a lot of spending on unrelated things. You will be happy to know that all cars built after 2025 will be required to include a "kill switch" that passively monitors your driving to determine whether or not you are "impaired," then shuts down the car if it determines you are. What would that mean if your car decided to quit on you in a sub-zero snow storm—or in any location at any time? What if the device malfunctions? You could be stranded anywhere. It's also an open system hackers could exploit.[325]

Even worse is Biden's mandate that 56 percent of new vehicles purchased by model year 2032 must be EVs.[326] This is actually a war on privately owned vehicles. The Left is intent on banishing them for good, as the UN's Maurice Strong, WEF chairman Klaus Schwab, and others have articulated. What better way than mandate the destruction of the market for gas-powered cars and force the much more expensive and unreliable EVs on private citizens. And remember, forcing reliance on electricity for fuel reduces your independence because electricity is distributed by government-regulated energy monopolies. It could suddenly be shut down for any number of reasons.

Finally, Biden proposed the "Inflation Reduction Act" under the mindless presumption that printing $740 billion more money would somehow reduce inflation. Once again, this is a joke of a bill, but the joke is on us. In reality, this new bill:

- Raises $570 billion in taxes, approximately $4,500 per household.[327]
- Provides corporate subsidies of $510 billion or more.[328]
- Gives the IRS $80 billion, $46 billion of which will go to increased enforcement. Look out for audits![329]
- Showers $369 billion onto "Green New Deal" programs,[330] an unprecedented amount; and we can guess whose pocket it will wind up in.

The bill includes a $27 billion EPA-run "climate bank," a slush fund that will doubtless finance all kinds of leftist attacks on energy. It also includes a $250 billion Energy Department loan guarantee program, just like Obama's corrupt $80 billion "Green Energy" program but three times larger.[331] Furthermore, no surprise, prices have remained high and will likely get worse as this bill impacts the economy. So far, as of this writing, since Biden took office:[332]

- Inflation is up more than 18 percent.

- The cost of groceries for Americans has increased 20 percent.
- Gasoline prices are 50 percent higher.[333]
- Natural gas prices are up 30 percent.
- Real wages have declined.[334]
- Mortgage rates were down 32 percent under Trump. They are up 140 percent under Biden.[335]

But not to be deterred, Joe Biden had, as of this writing, just floated a new budget bill of $7.3 trillion. That amounts to spending $57,000 per household, rising to $60,000 in 2026.[336] Are you getting your money's worth? The House GOP leadership called the spending "reckless... Biden's budget doesn't just miss the mark—it is a roadmap to accelerate America's decline."[337] Exactly, and that's the point.

Obama Columbia University classmate Wayne Allyn Root told anyone who would listen: "I've been saying it since he was elected in 2008, [Obama's] goal is the Cloward and Piven plan we learned at Columbia University—you've got to bankrupt your opposition and you've got to bankrupt the United States of America. You've got to bankrupt it with debts, entitlements and spending. And it's all happening in front of our very eyes."[338] And Biden has turbocharged the strategy. The late political commentator Jack Wheeler warned:

> Our country is faced with an impending economic catastrophe, a Second Great Depression. It is being brought about on purpose by a political party that cares only for keeping and expanding its power, and looks upon prosperity as a threat to that power.[339]

The Left's crisis strategies must be viewed in military terms. They are pincer movements, attacking us from all sides: economic, military, cultural, and rhetorical. The goal is our destruction. *You must understand this.* There is no recovering from what they intend. The Left has no legitimacy. Their issues are never the issue. Their one issue is always revolution—which we now understand to mean gaining absolute power and wealth, all at our cost.

WEAPONIZING THE POOR:
THE WAR ON BLACK AMERICA

*"I'll have those niggers voting Democratic
for the next 200 years."*
—President Lyndon B. Johnson

The Cloward–Piven Strategy was designed to create crises that would eventually drive people into the streets after *"intensifying the evils and miseries of the people until at last their patience was exhausted..."* as Nechayev had advocated. With each new agenda, Cloward and Piven's true goal was always to find a means to institutionalize their orchestrated anarchy, and poor people were the instruments.

As described earlier, Richard Cloward's ideas inspired President Lyndon Johnson's Great Society—a massive increase in entitlements that have since become the greatest single expenditure of the federal government, consuming about 50 percent of total federal government spending. With vote fraud, strategic corruption, open borders, and every other crisis strategy in operation today, it is not an exaggeration to say that their ideas may ultimately be credited with the demise of this country. Although, we also recognize that their "contributions" are little more than a modern application of the Left's catastrophism plans that originated with Nechayev.

While Democratic politicians justify the burgeoning welfare state as reflecting compassion for the "poor and oppressed," President Johnson's cynical statement quoted above reflects the reality. That Johnson harbored such feelings is beyond question. In meetings with Democrats, he frequently used the n-word pejorative. On March 13, 1965, he met at the White House with Alabama governor George Wallace and his top aide, Seymore Trammell, regarding racial violence then ongoing in the South. Trammell related to his son what Johnson said at the meeting. Please forgive the language:

> Now you boys, you gotta get your G--damned asses back down to Alabama and make those G--damned niggers act right and calm the hell down! I am G--damned tired of hearing 'bout those G--damned niggers on the G--damned news every night! …You boys got it lucky. Hell George, all the hell you got is those G--damned niggers throwing rocks and tot'in signs! Hell, here, I had to get the Secret Service to put-up double thick bullet proof glass to the White House windows cause these G--damned niggers and hippies up here are shootin' bullets at me and my wife and 2 little girls are scared to death! I hate those G--damned niggers and hippies.[340]

With less contempt, but nonetheless plainly stating one of their motives for executing the crisis strategy, Cloward and Piven explained that by enabling welfare beneficiaries to receive every benefit available to them, the favor would be repaid at the polls.

It is for this reason that Cloward and Piven's ideas inspired Johnson's Great Society. And it worked. In 1960, 58 percent of black voters were Democrats, 22 percent were Republicans, and 20 percent were independents. By 1968, 92 percent were Democrats, 5 percent were independent, and only 3 percent were Republicans.[341] Until Trump came along, black voting patterns had not changed appreciably. Trump garnered 6 percent of the black vote in 2016 and 12 percent in 2020. Today his support could be as high as 20 percent or more.[342]

But President Johnson had only expanded on Depression-era New Deal domestic welfare programs started by President Franklin Delano Roosevelt. Prior to the Great Depression, many blacks were registered Republicans—the party of Lincoln. FDR's New Deal initiated a wholesale black migration to the Democratic Party, despite some of FDR's discriminatory policies, like the aforementioned redlining.[343]

It is no coincidence that, as president, Barack Obama claimed inspiration from FDR. For just like Johnson, FDR's domestic policies, which doubled peacetime federal spending,[344] were designed to deliver virtually permanent Democrat majorities in Congress.

The Democratic Party has capitalized on an entirely unearned reputation for "compassion," because the Democrats brought the New Deal and Johnson's Great Society. And while the 1964 Civil Rights Act was signed by President Johnson, it could not have passed without significant GOP support. Democrats enjoyed a 67–33 majority in the Senate, but only forty-six voted for its passage. Twenty-seven of thirty-three Republicans voted for the bill. And this succeeded only after an extensive sixty-day filibuster by Senate Democrats.[345]

Both the New Deal and the Great Society programs radically increased the federal government's intervention in the market by introducing welfare at the federal level. Those federal programs that were supposedly developed to help bring blacks out of poverty—welfare, affirmative action, preferences in hiring, and so forth—carry two implicit assumptions: (1) that without such help, blacks can't make it; and (2) such policies are necessary to overcome the widespread racism that infects society as a whole. Neither assumption is true, but the Left would have you believe it.

In *City Journal*, columnist Sol Stern observed, "[T]his explosion of the welfare rolls only helped to create a culture of family disintegration and dependency in inner-city neighborhoods, with rampant illegitimacy, crime, school failure, drug abuse, non-work, and poverty among a fast-growing underclass."[346]

That was *the goal*.

Communist Influence in the Black Community

The Left has been at war with the black community for over one hundred years. It has been an ongoing, relentless campaign of vilification, marginalization, subversion, and vicious attacks designed to inflame hate, division, and rage while making sure poor blacks find it increasingly difficult to get ahead. For many blacks, this forms the impression of a "white supremacist" class intent on oppressing them. And in fact, there is a (mostly) white supremacist class doing just that. They are called Democrats.

Meanwhile, for whites and others without an agenda but who *are* prejudiced, the sorry state of many black communities is simply confirmation of their preexisting biases that the black race is somehow inferior. Even many African blacks look down on America's black community as being inferior. As black African commentator Phrankleen noted, "Africans perceive African-Americans as lazy, as they are bums, as they are dangerous people not to associate with."[347]

Now Phrankleen was making the point that this was perception rather than reality, because in reality, he said that if you look into Africa, you can find communities with the same problems.[348] But even this misses the point. Coming from centuries of slavery, American blacks made a remarkable recovery. A great deal of this progress can be attributed to the legendary work of one man, Booker T. Washington.

In his foreword to Washington's autobiography, *Up from Slavery*, author and columnist Mychal Massie calls it, "the deeply moving, riveting account of a man's life—a man who was born into slavery and who entered freedom as bereft of education as he was in the knowledge of the proper use of silverware. And yet by the time of his passing, he had dined with the titans of his era, world leaders, and presidents. Had he been born a half-century later, he would have been named Dr. Martin Luther King."[349]

Reflecting on the America of the day, Washington said:

> Then, when we rid ourselves of prejudice, or racial feeling, and look facts in the face, we must acknowledge

that, notwithstanding the cruelty and moral wrong of slavery, the ten million Negroes inhabiting this country, who themselves or whose ancestors went through the school of American slavery, are in a stronger and more hopeful condition materially, intellectually, morally and religiously than is true of an equal number of black people in any other portion of the globe. This is so to such an extent that Negroes in this country, who themselves or whose forefathers went through the school of slavery, are constantly returning to Africa as missionaries to enlighten those who remained in the fatherland. This I say, not to justify slavery. On the other hand, I condemn it as an institution, as we all know in America it was established for selfish and financial reasons, and not from a missionary motive—but to call attention to a fact, and to show how Providence often uses men and institutions to accomplish a purpose."[350]

Washington recognized that while racism still existed, he saw America for the land of opportunity it was and strove to help his fellow blacks attain the skills and training to succeed. He also recognized that despite racist attitudes remaining following the Civil War, he had received significant, even dispositive help and widespread encouragement from many whites who shared his desire to see the black man rise from slavery to become successfully integrated into American society.

But something changed in the early twentieth century. From the beginning, the Communist Party sought to recruit blacks into its cause. Radicals like W. E. B. Du Bois became the predominant symbol of Black leadership. Instead of championing the great strides made by Blacks under the leadership of Booker T. Washington, Du Bois and his fellow leftists instigated the early stages of what has become the grievance industry.

William Edward Burghardt Du Bois was a prominent black author, activist, and teacher. He was raised a free man from a family in the mostly white town of Great Barrington, Massachusetts, went to an integrated public school, and had his college tuition paid by members of Great Barrington's First Congregational Church.[351]

Du Bois believed capitalism was inherently racist. He did take justifiable stands against the mistreatment of blacks that were more common at the time. But Du Bois and company focused not so much on building the skills and abilities of blacks as Washington had but on endeavoring to see the white Western superstructure destroyed.

Du Bois vilified and slandered Washington, just like the Left does to its enemies today. Leftist cancel culture has been around for a long time. As Lenin said a century ago, "We must be ready to employ trickery, deceit, law-breaking, withholding and concealing truth.... We can and must write in a language which sows among the masses hate, revulsion, and scorn towards those who disagree with us."[352]

Du Bois joined the Socialist Party in 1911 and, despite disputes with the party, spent most of his adult life working alongside Socialist and Communist Party members until he officially joined the Communist Party USA (CPUSA) later in life. He helped found the National Association for the Advancement of Colored People (NAACP) in 1909. He was the only black of the original executive staff. The rest were white Socialists. Francis X. Gannon, author of *The Biographical Dictionary of the Left*, writes:

> The formation of the NAACP was urged by the leading radicals of the era including Jane Addams, John Dewey, William Lloyd Garrison, John Haynes Holmes, Lincoln Steffens, Brand Whitlock, Lillian Wald, Rabbi Stephen Wise, and Ray Stannard Baker. Among the first officials of the NAACP were more radicals including: Mary White Ovington, Oswald Garrison Vilard, Walter E. Sachs, John Milholland, Frances Blascoer, and William English Walling.
>
> Other radicals were among the first NAACP members: Florence Kelly, William Pickens, James W. Johnson, Charles E. Russell, and E. R. A. Seligman. (Many of these individuals were already or would soon become

enrolled in the newly formed Intercollegiate Socialist Society, which later became the League for Industrial Democracy, and, within a few years, they were prominent in various pacifist groups, including the Fellowship of Reconciliation and the American Civil Liberties Union. The NAACP gave them one more vantage point—agitation for Negroes' equality—from which they could promote Socialism and other facets of radicalism.)[353]

Communist influences were evident early on. The American Fund for Public Service, also known as the Garland Fund for its founder, Charles Garland, funded far-left causes and groups. It was a major contributor to the NAACP.[354] Early NAACP officer Moorfield Storey, a left-wing lawyer and former president of the American Bar Association, joined the Garland Fund after its 1922 formation, along with CPUSA co-founder Benjamin Gitlow, CPUSA leader William Z. Foster, CPUSA chairwoman Elizabeth Gurley Flynn, Socialist Norman Thomas, ACLU founder Roger Baldwin, and numerous other Communists and Socialists.

By the way, regarding the ACLU, Roger Baldwin, himself an anarchist, later said, "I don't regret being part of the communist tactic. I knew what I was doing. I was not an innocent liberal. I wanted what the communists wanted and I traveled the United Front road to get it. Communism is good."[355]

The ACLU's founders included the aforementioned Communist party leader Elizabeth Gurley Flynn, Socialist leader Norman Thomas, and Alice Smedley, later a Soviet agent.[356] The ACLU's job has never been to promote civil liberties. Instead it has become a main instigator of the Manufactured Crisis strategy. It has been at the forefront of the legal battle to destroy our nation from day one, including: attacks on Christianity and Judaism; access to pornography for all ages, including pedophilia; free and easy abortion; removing prayer from schools and all aspects of public life; undermining military good order, morale, and discipline, and making it ever more difficult to enforce our laws.

Two other white NAACP members, the pro-Socialist Jane Addams and pro-Soviet National Education Association director John Dewey, were also instrumental in organizing the ACLU, as was CPUSA leader William Z. Foster.[357]

Former black Communist Foster Williams Jr. testified before Congress in 1954 regarding Communist subversion within the black community. He said:

> The Communist Party has a very despicable policy in regard to the American Negro. They tell him they are the only organization that is trying to help the Negro advance in obtaining all of his democratic rights that are justifiably his. Many Negroes, for a short period of time, believe this, but once you actually join the Communist Party and begin to work with them, you see how the Communist Party very sneakily manipulates the Negro people for their own purposes. The NAACP has had this trouble in the past…. The Communist Party is not interested in the welfare of the Negro, but simply takes these cases up to make propaganda.[358]

Du Bois officially joined the CPUSA in 1961, telling then party boss Gus Hall, "Communism will triumph. I want to help bring that day."[359] But he had visited and supported the Soviet Union and Communist China for many years before.

By 1922, the Communist International had ordered American Communists to exploit blacks in a manner that would threaten "the peace and security of the United States."[360] As a result, "In its early history, the NAACP proved to be a natural attraction for Communists. Du Bois, the real leader of the organization, 'hailed the Russian Revolution of 1917,' and he traveled to the Soviet Union in 1926 and 1936. He especially liked 'the racial attitudes of the Communists.'"[361] His visit to the USSR inspired him to call the Soviet system "the most hopeful vehicle for the world."[362]

In 1934, he was forced out of the NAACP. As told in *The Biographical Dictionary of the Left*, "Du Bois' views, so overtly compatible with the Communists' plans for a segregated Negro America, were an embarrassment to the NAACP which, of necessity, had to depend upon financial and other support from white America. And, in 1934, Du Bois separated from the NAACP. (He returned ten years later but within four years he left the NAACP permanently and devoted his energies full-time working for Communist projects.)"[363]

Despite the NAACP's discomfort at Du Bois's public support for Communism, in practice, the organization remained well within the Communist orbit. The late black author George Schuyler described those influences:

> [T]he Association [NAACP] was playing patsy with the forces of the Left…. As the Communists, crypto Communists and fellow travelers moved in on the New Deal and took charge, the NAACP was more and more affected. The indefatigable Walter F. White, NAACP executive secretary, was weekly in Washington cultivating white power which was often Red. Then the New York Communist organizers, Manning Johnson and Leonard Patterson, traveled to Washington, contacted the Red faculty members at Howard University, and "sold" them on organizing an activist National Negro Congress (NNC). Among the first suckered into it was the NAACP's executive secretary. This committed the Association to supporting an outfit tailored originally by the Communist Party of the U.S.A. to destroy it.[364]

Manning Johnson was a hardcore Communist who later repented and went on to write *Color, Communism and Common Sense*.[365] A true believer at first, he came to realize that the Communists intended to use American blacks as the cannon fodder for their upcoming revolution. He said the NAACP was "a vehicle of the Communist Party designed to overthrow the government of the United States."[366]

According to *The Biographical Dictionary of the Left*: "There could be no doubt that the NAACP was of particular interest to the Communist

Party. At the fourth national convention of the Workers (Communist) Party in 1925, the comrades were told that it was 'permissible and necessary for selected Communists...to enter its [the NAACP's] conventions and to make proposals calculated to enlighten the Negro masses under its influence as to the nature and necessity of the class struggle, the identity of their exploiters.'"[367]

The CPUSA actually had orders to build what became known as the "Black Belt," a grouping of contiguous majority black southern counties that would become a wholly controlled separate state. There was, however, little enthusiasm for such an effort among blacks.[368]

In 1952, Du Bois took a job teaching Marxism at the Communist Party's Jefferson School of Social Science in New York City.[369] In 1954, he explicitly expressed his beliefs:

> The authorities at the Jefferson School never, never in any way dictated the content or orientation of my teaching. They of course knew, or if asked I would have told them of my interest in the philosophy of Karl Marx; of the fact that I am a Socialist in my theoretical teaching; that I have visited the Soviet Union, Czechoslovakia, Poland and China and followed their development with the greatest sympathy and interest.[370]

Now, the "authorities at the Jefferson School" were all Communists, as the school was a program of the CPUSA, so Du Bois could certainly expect academic freedom to teach Marxism. It would have been very different, however, if he had promoted capitalism—but then he wouldn't have taken a job there in the first place. It is important to note that during his career as a college professor, he taught at Harvard, Yale, Wellesley, Smith, Vassar, Bryn Mawr, Princeton, Columbia, Cornell, CUNY, Chicago, and fourteen state universities. Many people believe that Marxism taught in universities is a recent phenomenon.[371] But that is far from the truth.

Despite its strong history of promoting civil rights for blacks, the NAACP has allied itself all along with Communists and Communist causes. This includes Soviet agent Paul Robeson, Communist Langston

Hughes, SPLC leader Julian Bond, Supreme Court Justice Felix Frankfurter, whom has been characterized as an "unreconstructed Bolshevik," and many more.[372] The NAACP helped found the Progressive Citizens of America—closely allied with the CPUSA—which launched the campaign of Henry Wallace to run for president. The late Supreme Court Justice Thurgood Marshall was the NAACP's chief counsel. He also worked on the board of the National Lawyers Guild, a Communist front group, as well as the similarly disposed International Judicial Association.[373]

In a brief on the *Brown v. Board of Education* case, Marshall wrote against racial preferences to suggest that the NAACP supported color-blind justice: "Distinctions by race are so evil, so arbitrary and invidious that a state, bound to defend the equal protection of the laws must not invoke them in any public sphere."[374]

But as a Supreme Court justice, however, Marshall told a different story. "You [white] guys have been practicing discrimination for years. Now it's our turn," he said.[375] Today, the NAACP is a full-fledged member of the hard Left. It supports:[376]

- Black Lives Matter
- Suing Trump as a J6 "insurrection" conspirator
- Diverse and inclusive hiring and promotion
- Cancelling student debt
- $15 federal minimum wage
- Removing police from schools
- Emptying jails
- Forced low-income suburban housing projects
- Opposing all voter integrity laws as voter "suppression"
- Environmental and climate "justice"
- Income redistribution (they call it "Economic Equity")
- Single-payer socialized healthcare
- Gun control

Black Lives Matter is a loosely knit organization with many independent groups. A leader of the Rhode Island BLM even claims to support Donald Trump.[377] However, its founders, Patrisse Cullors,

Alicia Garza, and Opal Tometi, all worked for organizations under the Liberation Road umbrella. Formerly known as Freedom Road Socialist Organization (FRSO), Liberation Road is a Communist organization that evolved from the Maoist New Communist Party. In his book *Blood Money*, Peter Schweizer describes how BLM activists were actively trained and radicalized by an elite unit of the People's Liberation Army working out of China's Houston consulate before it was shut down.[378]

And what was the result of all that? The BLM/Antifa/Liberation Road George Floyd "mostly peaceful" riots caused twenty-eight deaths, over two thousand injuries to police with thirteen shot and nine hit by cars, ninety-seven police vehicles torched, 2,300 cases of looting, businesses destroyed, sixteen thousand arrests, and billions of dollars in damages—most of which fell on the black community![379] Cloward and Piven got their riot after all.

Here is another observation. A writer at *American Thinker* observed that the "excess" number of blacks killed after BLM began its legacy of rioting and murder (11,005) exceeded all blacks lynched over eighty-six years, between 1882 and 1968 (3,446).[380] He defined the number of murders over the 2014 base year as "excess murders." And while 2014 represented a historic low, if you averaged the deaths over the previous fifteen years, the assertion would still hold, because throughout those years, murders of blacks were at a historic low. They did not begin to go up again until 2014, when rioting over the police killing of Michael Brown and calls to "defund the police" began, culminating in the unprecedented George Floyd riots of 2020.

Deneen Borelli, the author of *Blacklash: How Obama and the Left are Driving Americans to the Government Plantation*, has said of the NAACP: "As a black conservative, I've been attacked for communicating my values of individual liberty and economic opportunity for all Americans.... Sadly, this once venerable civil rights organization has morphed into a political arm of the progressive movement, and it reserves its advocacy for left-wing causes and individuals."[381]

In truth, the NAACP has always been radical, just more openly so today. Since its birth, the NAACP's main publication has been appropriately titled "The Crisis."

The Welfare Trap

Inflation-adjusted welfare spending has gone up over 1,900 percent since President Johnson's War on Poverty began in 1965 and today is near an all-time high, only eclipsed by the two COVID years.[382] Since its inception, the War on Poverty has cost over $37 trillion after correcting for inflation.[383] This is over four times the total cost of all wars going back to our nation's founding—$8.4 trillion in inflation-adjusted dollars.[384] But have we made a dent in poverty? No, things just keep getting worse.

That is deliberate. Keeping the poor on welfare, dependent and helpless, serves the Democrats' purposes. What would happen to their franchise if those people suddenly found themselves financially independent? Adding ever more people to the welfare rolls also increases the government's financial burden, pushing it ever closer to collapse. Self-reliance and independence do not. Remember: it was Cloward and Piven's overriding goal to enrage the poor. Happy, prosperous people would never serve the revolution.

Currently, some one hundred different federal programs spread across thirteen agencies and departments offer cash or in-kind benefits for individual welfare recipients, targeted groups, and communities.[385] This includes cash, food, housing, medical care, social services, job training, community development funds, energy needs, and education. Including Medicaid, over ninety million people receive some kind of means-tested welfare. Some seventy million also participate in one or more of the other programs.[386]

In 2023, the federal government spent $1.2 trillion on welfare.[387] State and local governments added another $0.7 trillion more.[388] As of 2023, welfare spending at the federal, state, and local levels stood at 6.9 percent of GDP. By comparison, 2023 defense spending was $1.1 trillion—4.3 percent of GDP. Despite this skyrocketing spending, figure 1 below shows that America's official poverty rate has remained relatively constant since 1967, hovering between 11 and 15 percent.[389] In 2022, there were 37.9 million people in poverty, and the poverty rate was 11.5 percent.

Figure 1

Welfare spending versus poverty rate, 1967–2021

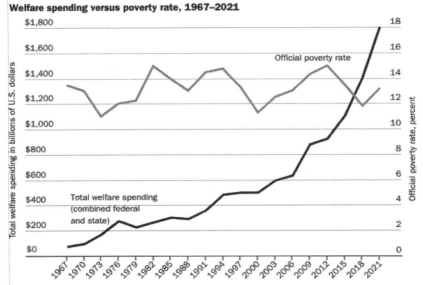

Sources: U.S. Census Bureau, Number in Poverty and Poverty Rate: 1959 to 2020 § (2021); Michael D. Tanner, "What's Missing in the War on Poverty?," Commentary, Cato Institute, January 23, 2019; Rachel Sheffield and Robert Rector, "The War on Poverty after 50 Years," Poverty and Inequality, Heritage Foundation, September 15, 2014; "Budget Digest: CBO Report on Federal Spending for Anti-poverty Programs," Budget Digests, House Budget Committee, June 24, 2019; and "Public Welfare Expenditures," State and Local Backgrounders, Urban Institute, March 20, 2022.

How can this be? Well, for one thing, the Census Bureau counts only cash welfare in determining the percentage of the population under the poverty line. As of 2024, a family of four is considered to be in poverty if household income is $31,200 per year or less. For a single person, it is $15,060.[390] But when you add in the dollar value of non-cash benefits like food stamps, Medicaid, education, and other benefits, the income equivalent is much higher. When calculated this way, a study by the Cato Institute estimated that the actual poverty rate may be less than 3 percent.[391] A better representation of the situation may therefore be in figure 2 below.

Figure 2

Welfare spending versus Meyer-Sullivan poverty rate, 1967–2018

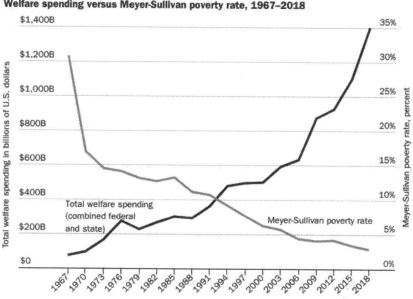

Sources: U.S. Census Bureau, Number in Poverty and Poverty Rate: 1959 to 2020 § (2021); Bruce D. Meyer and James X. Sullivan, "Winning the War: Poverty from the Great Society to the Great Recession," no. w18718, National Bureau of Economic Research, 2013; and Bruce D. Meyer and James X. Sullivan, "Annual Report on U.S. Consumption Poverty: 2018," American Enterprise Institute, October 18, 2019.

Cato states that "most of our efforts have been focused on making poverty less miserable, by making sure that people who are poor have food, shelter, medical care, and other necessities."[392] In other words, our welfare system is lousy at getting people out of poverty but instead makes living in poverty easier. And that is the real problem.

The *Economist* magazine observed, "If reducing poverty amounts to just ushering Americans to a somewhat less meagre existence, it may be a worthwhile endeavour but it is hardly satisfying. The objective, of course, should be a system that encourages people to work their way out of penury."[393] But, as we have been showing, that is the last thing the Left wants.

And the Left knows what they are doing. People are risk averse. It is one of the most basic tenets of economics. In the job market, most of us build confidence in our skills only slowly and dare not risk career moves that may jeopardize what we have already achieved once we have established ourselves and become reasonably comfortable. This is why so many people remain in the same job for decades, despite having talents, abilities, and skills that could carry them much further. It is also why entrepreneurs are compensated so well. They have a single skill that is indeed rare: the willingness to take risks. And the compensation for those risks is called *profits*. Without profits, there would be no economy, as Communist nations quickly learn.

People living at or near poverty start out with numerous disadvantages that make them even more risk averse. They have few skills and few examples of success within the community on which to model their work ethic. And while it is certainly possible to work one's way out of poverty, as examples like Dr. Ben Carson and Supreme Court judge Clarence Thomas aptly prove, most will wind up working low-skilled jobs and progress slowly, if at all. And they are further incentivized to stay there given the current welfare system.

With the plethora of entitlement programs available, it is even tempting to forego the risk and uncertainty of the job market and simply accept the dole. This is especially true in today's world, where the prevailing culture justifies the entitlement mindset, even though it entrenches a lifestyle that offers a bleak future. Once accustomed to privation, one can become content with even marginal improvement, and modern welfare offers much more than that.

While some members of society may actually need a safety net, the vast majority of people using welfare today are perfectly capable of supporting themselves—or would be if the open spigot of government benefits had not disabled them. Rational people intuitively understand that open-ended welfare for the able-bodied is wrong for the following reasons:

- The more time spent on the dole, bad habits become entrenched while good ones fall into disuse.
- Job skills are lost with time away from productive work.
- Opportunities to learn new job skills and improve existing ones are missed.

- Opportunities to network with other employees and to establish the work track record necessary to advance are lost.
- Accepting welfare when it isn't needed corrupts one's soul because you are taking from another without giving anything in return. But one's conscience becomes calloused with each passing day on the dole.
- This moral corruption encourages other negative behaviors, like drug use or "double dipping" by working in the underground economy.
- Working in the underground economy further corrupts the soul because it usually involves some form of illegal activity: dealing drugs, prostitution, or even just continuing to accept welfare illegally while gainfully employed.
- All of this is legitimized by a liberal culture that excuses bad behavior and justifies welfare as rightful compensation for oppressed classes.

So what has been the result? A deeply entrenched, dysfunctional underclass seething with resentments. And blacks were targeted directly. As described earlier, the Cloward–Piven crisis strategy's "solution" to poverty was a guaranteed annual income for all Americans. In 1970, the target guarantee was a minimum of $5,500 per year for a family of four, up to $10,000. In today's dollars, that would mean about $44,000 to $80,000.[394] Broken down by race, median income in 2022 was as follows:

Median Household Income: 2022	
All races/ethnicities	$74,580
Asian	$108,700
White, not Hispanic	$81,060
Hispanic (any race)	$62,800
Black	$52,860

Source: US Census Bureau: Income in the United States: 2022.

Now consider, if the guaranteed annual income minimum was $44,000, people at the low end of the income scale could collect at least that amount on an ongoing basis. How many would work? How many would start working under the table? The crisis strategy destroys incentives and corrupts those who want to work. Welfare has already destroyed the inner city by encouraging crime, drug use, and prostitution, problems that were much less evident before Johnson's so-called Great Society began.

Federal welfare spending totaled $1.2 trillion in 2023. If we added the guaranteed income, it would cost an additional $3 trillion, assuming it were guaranteed to the lowest income quintile.[7] And as discussed earlier, the guaranteed income *would not* replace those other programs already in operation; it would be added to them. Replacing the old system would seem the rational thing to do, because its supposed purpose was to provide a basic, livable income. But remember, the true goal is to crash the whole system.

The Left knows as well as we do that a guaranteed annual income policy is unsustainable, and if codified in law, would assure that even the federal government would eventually collapse under its own weight. They could just sit back and watch. Indeed, despite the Left's failure to overtly enact a comprehensive guaranteed income, they have largely accomplished it through the back door. Added together, when considering the cash value of the many various welfare benefits available, it approaches today's median family income level. In some locations, it goes far beyond that.

The Illinois Policy Institute published a report in 2015 describing how much a working single-parent household with two children could receive in welfare benefits in Chicago and surrounding counties. For example, a single mother working a job earning between $8.50 and $12 per hour could receive benefits giving her a combined income equivalent to $76,000 per year. If she accepted a job earning a higher hourly wage, she would lose her benefits, creating what has been called the "welfare cliff." To earn back what she was receiving in benefits, she would have to

---

[7]   To facilitate study, economists divide the population into five equal sized groups called quintiles, measured from the lowest income group to the highest.

find a job earning $38 per hour.[395] Is there any incentive to grow? While these benefits may provide for this family's basic needs, the wage earner will likely never seek her full potential given the risk versus reward. Welfare essentially traps recipients at the low end of the income scale.

In 2019, 99.1 million people took one or more kinds of welfare.[396] And welfare is not a problem among blacks alone. See the table below. In absolute numbers, there are twice as many whites on welfare as blacks. As of 2022, the composition of welfare recipients is 38.8 percent whites, 39.8 percent blacks, 15.7 percent Hispanic, and 6.7 percent Asians and others.[397] The key statistic, however, is the percent of the total relevant population in poverty. In 2022, 17.1 percent of the black population was in poverty. Hispanics were close at 16.9 percent but currently may well be exceeding the black rate with the mass invasion of illegal aliens. As it stands right now, one of every two immigrant households uses at least one form of welfare, while 30 percent of native-born citizens receive welfare.[398]

People in Poverty & Receiving Welfare by Race & Hispanic Origin, 2022

	Population (Thous.)	In Poverty (Thous.)	% Total Population	% of Poverty Population	% of Welfare Population
White non-Hispanic	193,200	16,690	8.6%	44.0%	38.8%
Black non-Hispanic	44,520	7,626	17.1%	20.1%	39.8%
Hispanic	63,800	10,780	16.9%	28.4%	15.7%
Asian	21,590	1,866	8.6%	4.9%	2.4%
Other	6,990	958	13.7%	2.5%	3.3%
Total	330,100	37,920	11.5%	100.0%	100.0%

Sources: US Census Bureau: Poverty in the United States 2022; Gitnux.org Welfare Recipient Statistics, https://gitnux.org/welfare-recipient-statistics/.

Yet this does not often make the news. In focusing almost exclusively on blacks, our left-wing media displays its bias as much by what it does not report as by what it does. It is difficult to characterize whites as being a privileged class when 16.6 million live in poverty. Only by pretending white poverty doesn't exist can media hype the "white privilege" narrative. But do these people manifest any different behavior than minorities on welfare? No. Whites on the dole are subject to the same dynamic, the same disincentives, and have the same problems as a result. Rural communities, once visualized by the peaceful Mayberry image of *The Andy Griffith Show*, today face an epidemic of crime, drug abuse, and overdose deaths.[399]

Out-of-control budgets, work disincentive effects, and a languishing economy are not the only consequences of a burgeoning welfare state. As welfare programs expand, and oversight becomes more difficult, criminals take advantage of the system. A big food stamp fraud case was uncovered in Georgia in 2014. Fifty-four defendants were charged with laundering $18 million in food stamp and Women, Infants, and Children (WIC) food vouchers by illegally purchasing them at a discount for cash from beneficiaries then reimbursing themselves through a network of convenience stores they owned.[400] But this was small change.

In 2022, forty-seven Somalis in Minneapolis, Minnesota, were charged with pocketing $250 million in pandemic relief funds that were supposed to pay for a federal child nutrition program. A tax-exempt "nonprofit" organization called *Feeding Our Future* wildly exaggerated the number of people it served, then would file for reimbursement based on the inflated numbers. They created shell companies to make it appear their client base had expanded.[401]

This, too, is a drop in the bucket, however. The federal government tracks "payment integrity" for various welfare programs. These "improper" payments cost taxpayers billions every year. In the Medicaid program for example, overpayments ran between $5 and $12 billion between 2016 and 2020. In 2021 and 2022 however, overpayments were $98 billion and $80 billion respectively.[402] This is going to skyrocket over the next few years with the wave of illegal aliens flooding the border.

During President Obama's terms, the number of Americans receiving food stamps—now called the Supplemental Nutrition Assistance

Program (SNAP)—more than doubled between 2008 and 2013, reaching a record high in 2013 of 47.6 million. It declined slightly for the next two years and plummeted during the Trump presidency by almost 20 percent between 2016 and 2019. It increased slightly in 2020, the first year of the pandemic, and has risen throughout the Biden years. Costs under Biden have increased to record highs, however. Between 2020 and 2023, program costs increased by 43 percent—the result of inflation. Yet another consequence of Biden mismanagement. In 2023, total outlays for the SNAP program were $113 billion. The average monthly benefit per person was $211.66, so a family of four could receive over $800 per month.[403]

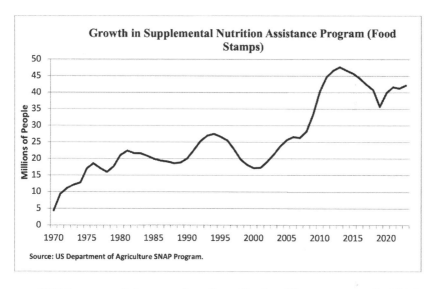

Growth in Supplemental Nutrition Assistance Program (Food Stamps)

Source: US Department of Agriculture SNAP Program.

SNAP is one of the most heavily utilized welfare programs. In 2020, 39.9 million people used SNAP, while 37.2 million people were in poverty, a utilization rate of 107 percent. This is because people are eligible for SNAP benefits at incomes up to 130 percent of the poverty level. SNAP usage remains higher among blacks than other groups, as shown in the table.

Although the number of Hispanic recipients is equal to blacks, they are a lower percent of the overall Hispanic population. But Hispanics are catching up. These data are from 2020, the latest available. Given the seismic shift in populations with some ten million Latino illegal aliens flooding our borders, Hispanics are likely to become the new blacks in terms of welfare usage—another break the bank strategy. As it stands, as of 2020, 23.3 percent of blacks use SNAP compared with 7.7 percent for whites and 16.5 percent for Hispanics.

Food Stamp (SNAP) Recipients 2020

	Recipients (Millions)[8]	% Total Recipients	Total 2020 Population	% Recipients to Total Population
White non-Hispanic	14.9	39.8%	193.9	7.7%
Black	10.1	27.0%	43.2	23.3%
Hispanic	10.1	27.0%	61.4	16.5%
Asian and Other	3.9	10.4%	34.3	11.3%

Census Survey of Income and Program Participation (SIPP) Detailed Program Receipt Tables: 2020.[404]

And that is not all. A nationwide study of ten thousand individuals conducted by the Center for Human Resource Research at Ohio State University found a strong linkage between food stamp use and obesity.[405] The USDA has similarly found that food stamp usage contributed to obesity among non-elderly women—almost 30 percent of SNAP beneficiaries.[406] *Americans are not starving*, as the Left would have you believe. If anything, they are eating too much, and of the wrong things.

Cash welfare comes primarily in the form of Temporary Assistance for Needy Families (TANF) and Supplemental Security Income (SSI). Of the 37.9 million people in poverty in 2022, about 2.4 million, or 6.3 percent, availed themselves of TANF on a monthly basis. It cost about $31.3 billion, split evenly between a federal block grant of $16.5 billion and state Maintenance of Effort (MOE) dollars.[407] While Hispanics were 37.3 percent of TANF recipients, Blacks and Hispanics participated in TANF at close to identical rates as a percentage of their relative population: 1.5 percent.

---

[8]   Totals may not add due to rounding.

TANF Recipients 2022

	Recipients (Thousands)	% Total Recipients	Total Pop. (Millions)	% Recipients to Total Pop.
White non-Hispanic	606	25.5%	193.9	0.3%
Black	635	28.8%	43.2	1.5%
Hispanic	937	37.3%	61.4	1.5%
Asian and Other	136	7.3%	34.3	0.4%

Source: Health and Human Services, Administration for Children and Families.[408]

Supplemental Security Income is a larger program, but it specifically targets the aged and disabled. The latest data with this level of detail are for 2020. A greater percentage of the black population utilizes SSI than other groups. Again, these are 2020 data. The huge influx of illegals may see a commensurate increase in utilization by Hispanics. Illegal aliens are barred from legally obtaining SSI, but it is a program fraught with fraud.[409] In 2022, the government spent $65 billion on SSI. The average monthly benefit in 2024 was $943 for an individual and $1,415 for a couple.[410]

SSI Recipients 2020

	Recipients (Millions)	% Total Recipients	Total 2020 Pop.	% Recipients to Total Pop.
White non-Hispanic	4.0	47.1%	193.9	2.1%
Black	2.2	25.5%	43.2	5.1%
Hispanic	1.7	19.6%	61.4	2.7%
Asian and Other	0.9	10.7%	34.3	2.7%

Source: Survey of Income and Program Participation (SIPP) Detailed Program Receipt Tables: 2020.

By far, the largest welfare programs are Medicaid and the Children's Health Insurance Program (CHIP). In 2021, 82,301,771 people were enrolled, 25 percent of the US population, at a cost of $756.2 billion.[411] Broken down by race and ethnic origin, the latest data available are from 2021.[412] Table 4 shows that as a percent of their total population, blacks utilize Medicaid at over twice the rate of whites (37.9 percent versus 16.5 percent) but in this case are exceeded by Hispanics (40.1 percent), likely the result of rapidly increasing illegal immigration.[413] The ten-million-plus illegal aliens who have arrived in the past few years almost guarantee that, since some states have already begun offering Medicaid to illegals and more will likely follow suit.[414] Yet another angle of attack within the crisis strategy.

Medicaid/CHIP Recipients 2021

	Recipients (Millions)	% Total Recipients	Total 2021 Pop.	% Recipients to Total Pop.
White non-Hispanic	32.5	39.50%	196.8	16.5%
Black	15.9	19.30%	41.9	37.9%
Hispanic	25.1	30.50%	62.6	40.1%
Asian and Other	8.8	10.70%	30.6	28.8%
Total	82.3	100%	331.9	24.8%

Source: Census Bureau. Statista 2023: Distribution of Medicaid/CHIP enrollees in the US in 2021.

No matter how you cut it, welfare is a big expense. Of the top four federal government spending categories, welfare costs the most.

Top Federal Spending Categories 2023

	$ Trillions	% Total
Welfare	$1.45	15.3%
Medicare & Social Security	$1.35	14.3%
National Defense	$1.19	12.6%
Education	$1.12	11.8%
All Other	$4.38	46.1%
Total	$9.49	100.0%

Source: USGovernmentSpending.com.

Both taxpayers and recipients know who is footing the bill, so taxpayers get resentful while welfare recipients get defensive. Enter the Left. Because welfare has become associated in the public mind with inner-city blacks, the Left deliberately misinterprets any expression of taxpayer frustration or anger toward the welfare system as racism. This "racist" narrative serves many purposes:

1. It helps promote the Left's ongoing theme that America is "racist," "sexist," and so forth.

2. It intimidates taxpayers from complaining too much. Indeed, Republicans are labeled "racist" precisely because the GOP is identified with efforts to reform or abolish welfare.

3. It provides positive reinforcement to those who express support for the program, rewarding them for being "compassionate," thereby elevating them in status above those supposedly hateful, intolerant people who want the poor to work.

4. It reinforces minorities' perceptions that they live in a "racist" society. With media focused intently on their problems and hyping "racist," "white privileged" America's attitude toward them, minorities are literally bathed in resentments.

5. It allows minorities to rationalize their situation by blaming others, making it more difficult for them to confront the real problem.

6. The whole thing provides the Left the pretext for the next big ask: reparations. One more nail in the Cloward–Piven coffin.

Blacks have indeed suffered disproportionately. Any number of statistics bears out the ruinous effects of liberal policies on American blacks. While overall unemployment rates have come down somewhat from their 2009 recession highs, black unemployment rates remain extremely high—double that of most other groups.

Unemployment Rates and Age Q4: 2023

		Age	
	All	16–19	20 & Over
White, non-Hispanic	5.3	18.1	4.7
Black, non-Hispanic	11.7	33.7	10.8
Asian	4.5	12.9	4.3
Hispanic	7.3	25.1	6.4

Source: Current Population Survey, US Bureau of Labor Statistics. Table E-16.

Prior to the Great Society, black labor force participation compared favorably with whites. The late, great George Mason University economist Walter Williams, himself a black, wrote:

> From 1900 to 1954, blacks were more active than whites in the labor market. Until about 1960, black male labor force participation in every age group was equal to or greater than that of whites. During that period, black teen unemployment was roughly equal to or less than white teen unemployment. As early as 1900, the duration of black unemployment was 15 percent shorter than that of whites; today it's about 30 percent longer.[415]

Williams cited government policy, particularly the minimum wage, which "makes hiring low-skilled workers a losing economic proposition. In 1950, only 50 percent of jobs were covered by the minimum wage law," he writes. "That meant the minimum wage didn't have today's unemployment effect. Today nearly 100 percent are covered."

He also cites the Davis–Bacon Act, which requires union-level wages in government construction projects. Both the minimum wage and Davis–Bacon were created to support unions, which were being undermined by non-union, and in many cases minority, businesses. The Biden administration attempted to raise the Davis–Bacon minimum wage to over $15 through an executive order—without the authority to do so. Thankfully, that was slapped down by the courts.[416] According to Williams, Davis–Bacon was written:

> …for the express purposes of excluding blacks from government-financed or -assisted construction projects. Labor unions have a long history of discrimination against blacks. Frederick Douglass wrote about this in "The Tyranny, Folly, and Wickedness of Labor Unions," and Booker T. Washington did so in "The Negro and the Labor Unions." To the detriment of their constituents, black politicians give support to labor laws pushed by unions and white liberal organizations.[417]

Williams's assertions are backed by the following charts. The first chart below illustrates the labor force participation rate of blacks twenty years and older over time. This is a measure of the percentage of the relevant employment-age population in the labor force, whether working or not. Since 1972, the black labor force participation rate has been on an almost continual downward slide. It began a modest upward path during the Trump years and following COVID has made something of a comeback. Whether or not this continues will depend on the policies pursued in Washington.

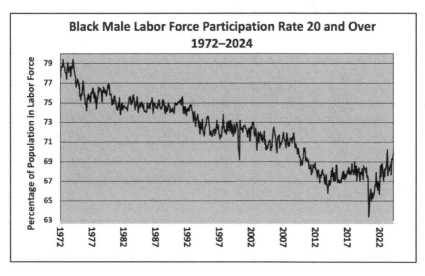

Source: FRED Labor Force Participation Rate Twenty Years and Over, Black or African American Men, Percent, Monthly, Seasonally Adjusted.[418]

Black male employment has also been on a long-term downward trend. Between 1972 and 2013, black employment declined from 73.6 percent of the black male population to 63.5 percent, a 14 percent drop. During the Trump years, it recovered a few percentage points but then dropped off precipitously during COVID. Black female employment, meanwhile, shot up 30 percent between 1972 and 1999, which explains some of the drop-off in male employment. But then the female rate began a downward slide, mirroring the males—bottoming out in 2013. The female rate also recovered during the Trump years but fell off again during COVID.

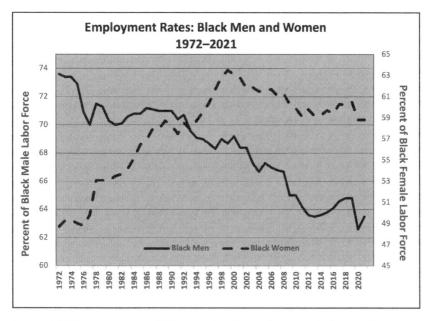

Source: LFPR by sex, race, and Hispanic ethnicity, 1948+ Women's Bureau, Department of Labor.[419]

The gulf between black and white unemployment rates over time is evident in the graph below. While both rates cycle with business activity, the difference between the two is substantial and the changes more dramatic for blacks. You can see the reductions in unemployment that occurred when President Reagan was elected in 1982, a downward trend in unemployment for both blacks and whites that bottomed out around 1990. The unemployment rate shot up during the recession following the subprime mortgage meltdown.

It is indeed ironic that President Obama should be the one who presides over that disaster, for it was the strategies of Cloward and Piven, and Obama's ACORN friends, that caused it. Finally, unemployment rates plunged under President Trump, bottoming out in November 2019 at 4.9 percent, the lowest rate for black male unemployment on record. The same was true for black women, who obtained the lowest unemployment rate in August 2019 of 4.2 percent.[420]

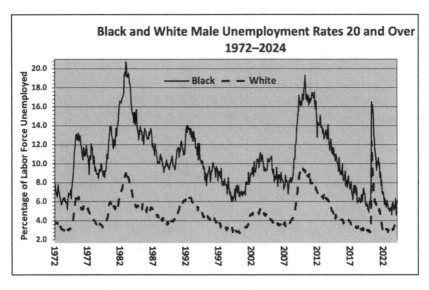

Sources: FRED Unemployment Rate—Twenty Years and Over, Black and White Men.[421]

Breakdown of the Black Family

So why are blacks so closely associated with welfare? The media pounds away the message that black poverty is directly related to America's racism. But as Walter Williams pointed out, African Americans actually fared better economically during the earlier period in history when discrimination was much more widespread. The Left manufactured extreme poverty by destroying incentives to work. It also destroyed the greatest source of stability and strength in the black community: the nuclear black family. This occurred as part of the Left's overall campaign to undermine traditional Christian morality and as the result of adverse incentives built into welfare.

As early as 1965, Daniel Patrick Moynihan, then an assistant secretary of labor in the Lyndon Johnson administration, warned of the decay of the nuclear black family and the impacts it was having in black communities. In a seminal report titled "The Negro Family: The Case For National Action," he wrote:

> The fundamental problem, in which this is most clearly
> the case, is that of family structure. The evidence—not

final, but powerfully persuasive—is that the Negro family in the urban ghettos is crumbling. A middle-class group has managed to save itself, but for vast numbers of the unskilled, poorly educated city working class the fabric of conventional social relationships has all but disintegrated.[422]

For his efforts, he was savaged by the Left and continues to be savaged to this day, despite being dead for over twenty years. Johnson, who initially liked the report, later had it suppressed—perhaps because he knew his "Great Society" was at least partially responsible. But the report was prophetic. Recently, it has enjoyed a resurgence of interest among thinking Americans (that excludes the Left, of course) and with good reason. Family is key to curing both poverty and crime. And this is true for everyone. A report titled, *What Can the Federal Government Do to Decrease Crime and Revitalize Communities?* by the Department of Justice found that in fatherless homes there were:[423]

- 63 percent of youth suicides
- 90 percent of all homeless and runaway youths
- 85 percent of all children that exhibit behavioral disorders
- 71 percent of all high school dropouts
- 70 percent of juveniles in state-operated institutions
- 75 percent of adolescent patients in substance abuse centers

Walter Williams has correctly said, "The welfare state has done to black Americans what slavery couldn't do... And that is to destroy the black family."[424]

After Johnson's Great Society launched, welfare administrators overlooking the various welfare programs began policing black neighborhoods. In most cases, welfare was only offered to single parents, usually the mother. So when the father was discovered living in the house, he was forcibly removed. As described by Harvard professor Paul Peterson:

"[S]ome programs actively discouraged marriage," because "welfare assistance went to mothers so long as no male was boarding in the household…. Marriage to an employed male, even one earning the minimum wage, placed at risk a mother's economic well-being." Infamous "man in the house" rules meant that welfare workers would randomly appear in homes to check and see if the mother was accurately reporting her family-status.[425]

The "man in the house" rule primarily focused on "substitute fathers," that is, men who lived with women collecting welfare but who were not the husband or father to the kids. However, some programs required the husband to be absent for the mother to collect benefits. These rules were enforced specifically on black mothers and included midnight raids where "Black men and boys were often dragged from homes in the middle of the night for no reason."[426]

From the 1800s to the 1950s, more black women were married than whites. With the advent of welfare, and especially the "man-in-the-house" rule, that began changing.[427] The percentage of births to unwed mothers of all races as of 2021, the latest data available as of this writing, stands at 40 percent, that is, almost four out of every ten babies are born to unmarried women. The white rate, historically less than 5 percent, now stands at 27.5 percent. The rate for Hispanic mothers is higher, 53.2 percent.

By far, the greatest percentage of out-of-wedlock births is among black women. While that rate has always been higher than for whites, rates for both blacks and whites had been relatively stable from the 1930s into the 1950s. Beginning in 1952, the black rate began to increase. By the time Moynihan wrote his report, the percentage of children born to unwed black mothers had doubled from its historical average, and that looked like a lot. When Johnson's War on Poverty kicked in, however, it exploded, rising to about 70 percent in the 1990s, and hasn't declined since. Today, 70.1 percent of black children are born to unwed mothers.[428]

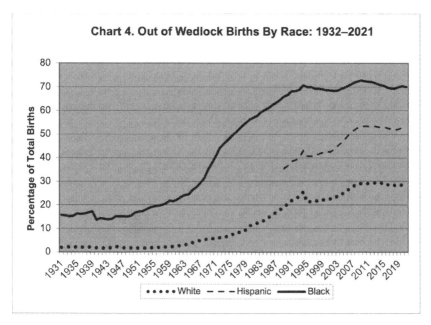

Chart 4. Out of Wedlock Births By Race: 1932–2021

Sources: National Vital Statistics Reports, the National Center for Health Statistics, US Census, and other government sources.

There is a direct correlation between poverty, crime, and single-parent households. Politically incorrect as it is to say so, children *need* both parents. Married families are much less likely to face poverty than unmarried families. And this is true across race and education levels. In a study published in 2012, Heritage Foundation poverty and welfare expert Robert Rector found:

- Among non-Hispanic white married couples, the poverty rate was 3.2 percent, while the rate for non-married white families was seven times higher at 22.0 percent.

- Among Hispanic married families, the poverty rate was 13.2 percent, while the poverty rate among non-married families was three times higher at 37.9 percent.

- Among black married couples, the poverty rate was 7.0 percent, while the rate for non-married black families was seven times higher at 35.6 percent.[429]

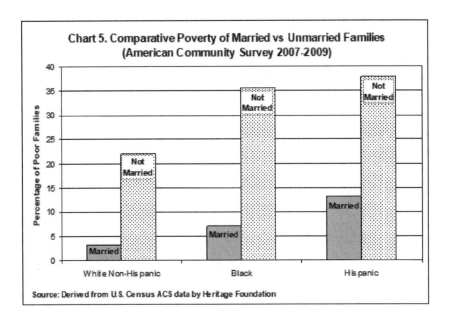

Chart 5. Comparative Poverty of Married vs Unmarried Families (American Community Survey 2007-2009)

Source: Derived from U.S. Census ACS data by Heritage Foundation

These statistics hold, even if the father is present. According to a Princeton University study quoted by Heritage, approximately 50 percent of fathers are cohabiting with the mother when these children are born. But these are less committed relationships. Two-thirds break up within five years. Meanwhile, 80 percent of married couples are still married five years later.[430]

Children from single-parent households are also more likely to get into trouble. Rector reported they were:

- more than twice as likely to be arrested for a juvenile crime;
- twice as likely to be treated for emotional and behavioral problems;
- roughly twice as likely to be suspended or expelled from school; and
- a third more likely to drop out before completing high school.[431]

This may at least partially explain the dramatic increase in crime rates in the twentieth century. Single parenting took off in the 1960s. Approximately twenty years later, crime rates skyrocketed. This is aptly illustrated in the chart below. It shows the percentage of out-of-wedlock births plotted against the US incarceration rate (prisoners/one hundred thousand population) lagged twenty years. When the data are lined up this way, incarceration closely tracks birth rates.

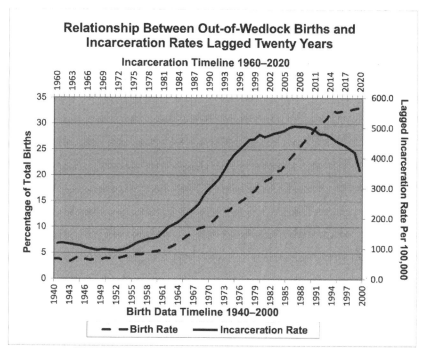

Relationship Between Out-of-Wedlock Births and Incarceration Rates Lagged Twenty Years

Sources: Incarceration rates: Sourcebook of Criminal Justice Statistics, University at Albany; birth statistics: National Vital Statistics Reports.

These incarceration data are not broken out by race. The chart below shows the relationship between black births and incarceration twenty years later. As noted earlier, black out-of-wedlock birth rates dwarf those of all other racial demographics. Some twenty years after unwed birth rates took off among blacks, black crime rates went through the roof. While always higher than whites, black incarceration rates were relatively low for the better part of the last century. In 1926, the white incarceration rate for prisoners in federal and state institutions was 36 per 100,000 of the white population. The black rate was 106 per 100,000 of blacks.[432] Today, the white rate stands at 222 per 100,000, an increase of 517 percent. However, the black rate is now 1,186 per 100,000, an increase of over 1,000 percent.[433]

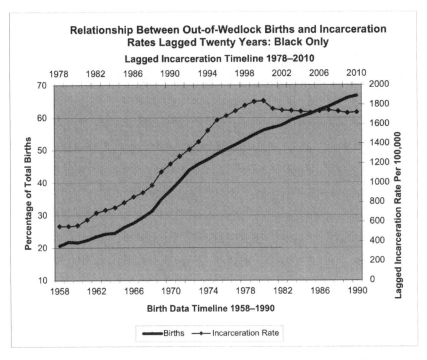

Relationship Between Out-of-Wedlock Births and Incarceration Rates Lagged Twenty Years: Black Only

Source: Incarceration Data National Prisoner Statistics 1978–2011; birth statistics: National Vital Statistics Reports.

However, while out-of-wedlock birth rates have remained high, incarceration rates have declined dramatically for over a decade. This is true for all racial and ethnic groups as shown in the table below. This is the result of the prison reform movement. Sentencing guidelines have been reduced, and fewer people are being incarcerated. And while criminal activity declined over some of those years, with the advent of anti-police activism that started in the Obama years and accelerated following the George Floyd riots and the election of pro-criminal district attorneys, crime has again skyrocketed. The Left turned prison "reform" into just another crisis strategy. Woke DAs are allowing criminals of all types, including murderers, to go free, and some have murdered again.

Incarceration Rates by Race and Ethnic Origin (Per 100,000 Population)

	White	Black	Hispanic	Asian	Others[9]
2010	311	2,044	992	139	1,457
2011	303	1,960	976	137	1,363
2012	296	1,866	939	132	1,277
2013	295	1,818	935	126	1,160
2014	290	1,749	903	125	1,232
2015	281	1,659	871	124	1,172
2016	275	1,599	866	122	1,152
2017	272	1,543	837	118	1,183
2018	268	1,488	804	116	1,165
2019	263	1,436	763	111	1,175
2020	224	1,238	641	93	1,030
2021	222	1,186	619	90	1,004

Source: Office of Justice Programs, National Prisoner Statistics 2020–21.

Many factors determine levels of crime and incarceration. There was, for example, a huge explosion in prison construction in the 1980s, which also provided space for "tough on crime" policies. But those policies were a response to soaring crime rates. And of course, the rampant increase in drug use is responsible in large part. But the increased use of drugs is itself a reflection on the breakdown of the nuclear family, especially among blacks. And as discussed earlier, *this was a deliberate policy instigated by the Democrats.* There seems little doubt that the many changes in our society wrought by the radical Left in the 1960s began showing heavy impacts as the next generation came of age.

Black former Louisiana state senator Elbert Guillory made history in 2013 when he switched from being a lifelong Democrat to the

---

[9]   Others include American Indians, Alaska Natives and Pacific Islanders.

Republican Party. He explained his decision in an interview with the Daily Caller's Ginni Thomas:

> Democrat policies over the last thirty years, forty years, have created a government plantation, and we are all, most of the folks in my community, are dependent, and on that plantation, held there by these little government handouts. And it has destroyed very much of what we were....
>
> There was an old expression.... A person would say, 'You are working like a black man.' That was one of the highest compliments that could have been paid to someone. It meant that you were really producing, you're really working, you're sweating, you're giving it your all. Not anymore. That concept and that phrase have both passed from the American consciousness....
>
> *The left is only concerned with one thing, control, and they disguise this control as 'charity.' Programs such as welfare, food stamps. These programs were not designed to lift black Americans out of poverty. They were always intended as a mechanism for politicians to control the black community. The idea that blacks, or anyone for that matter, need the government to get ahead in life is despicable.* (Emphasis added.)
>
> And more important, this idea is a failure. Our communities are just as poor as they have always been; our schools continue to fail children. Our prisons are filled with young black men who should be at home, being fathers. Our self-initiative and self-reliance have been sacrificed in exchange for allegiance to our overseers who control us by making us dependent upon them.[434]

Rush Limbaugh's former call screener, James Golden, who is black, agrees. Known to Rush listeners as "Snerdley," Golden was with Rush thirty years before Rush's passing, and he considers his time with Rush "the greatest professional blessing he could ever imagine." He says that liberals have hurt blacks specifically by pushing for the minimum wage:

> Most black people don't understand that, cause they're not taught, in school, economics, because most economics are taught by liberals and they don't teach the truth about this. But the hardest hit anytime the minimum wages go up, are black young men looking for jobs....[435]

He is exactly right. Golden cites the "good old days," when most black families were headed by both parents, most blacks were employed, and black crime was much lower than it is today. Unfortunately, he says, the "good old days" were the days of segregation. Desegregation and the civil rights movement should have made things better, instead, he says, "What liberalism has done to black communities, is horrific."[436]

The results have been devastating. Minority crime, especially Black crime, is off the charts. And who does most of this crime fall on? Their fellow blacks, because most crimes are committed where the criminals live, and with few exceptions, that means in black neighborhoods. The murder rate among blacks today, which is largely black-on-black, is similar to the rates in some of the most violent third-world nations. No other racial or ethnic group comes close.

Firearms Homicide Numbers and Rates Per 100,000 by Race and Ethnicity: 2022

	Total	Rate
White, non-Hispanic	3,825	2.0
Black, non-Hispanic	11,565	27.5
American Indian/Alaska Native	224	9.3
Asian/Pacific Islander	233	1.1
Hispanic	3,500	5.5
Total	19,637	5.9

Source: Centers for Disease Control and Prevention.[437]

And the frequent, heartrending stories of innocent, usually black, children killed in gang shootings is an inevitable consequence. One story in particular captures the impact of both the violence and the blame shifting that is the direct result of the Left's provocation tactics.

On December 30, 2018, in Houston, Texas, seven-year-old Jazmine Barnes was killed in a drive-by shooting while in the car with her family on their way to Walmart. Witnesses described a white man with blue eyes wearing a hoodie. Online activist Shaun King tweeted, "URGENT. ALL HANDS ON DECK. A 40 y/o white man w/ a beard in a red pickup truck pulled up on 7 y/o Jazmine Barnes and her family near a Houston @Walmartand shot and killed her and injured others."[438]

In a case of mistaken identity, a composite sketch looking remarkably like Robert Cantrell was released by the sheriff's office. Cantrell had been arrested and jailed the same day as the shooting and was driving a red pickup. It was originally categorized as a hate crime. But a few days later, two black men were arrested and charged with the murder. One admitted being the driver of the shooter's car, and the pistol used in the shooting was recovered at his house.[439] Cantrell had probably just been driving by as the shooting occurred and was mistakenly assumed to be the shooter.

Meanwhile, Cantrell's family continued to face death threats. One Facebook post on his niece's page said, "Someone is going to rape, torture and murder the women and children in your family."[440] Cantrell, who had remained in jail since that day for other charges, hanged himself in July.

In this hyped atmosphere of mistrust and enflamed hatred, it is impossible to imagine that Democrats are ignorant enough to be unaware of what they have done. An examination of what has happened to blacks since Johnson's expansion of the welfare state, not to mention the deepening crisis in inner cities, almost entirely run by Democrats, proves it.

The "defund the police" agenda is another case in point. The Left screams about police brutality, but most people in poor communities do not want the police defunded. They know firsthand how bad it is, even with the police doing their jobs. But almost all big cities are run by Democrats, left-wing Democrats—most of whom are black. So the Left prevails, and the police back off. The immediate result is skyrocketing crime. Police have gone through endless trainings, consent decrees with the Department of Justice, regular turnover in police commissioners, and everything else but simply allowing the police to do their jobs.

And it is all based on a lie: that police brutality is a common thing. No doubt there are bad cops but no more than in any other profession. When it comes to dealing with blacks, the statistics tell a different story. While blacks comprise only 13 percent of the population, they are responsible for almost 40 percent of police officers feloniously killed in the line of duty.

Officers Feloniously Killed - by Assailant Race

	Officer	# of Assailants				% of Assailants			
	Deaths	White	Black	Other	Unk	White	Black	Other	Unk
2004	57	27	34	0	0	44%	56%	0%	0%
2005	55	36	20	0	0	64%	36%	0%	0%
2006	48	25	29	0	3	44%	51%	0%	5%
2007	58	35	26	4	1	53%	39%	6%	2%
2008	41	20	21	1	0	48%	50%	2%	0%
2009	48	24	17	0	0	59%	41%	0%	0%
2010	55	32	39	6	3	40%	49%	8%	4%
2011	72	44	28	3	1	58%	37%	4%	1%
2012	49	32	17	2	0	63%	33%	4%	0%
2013	28	15	12	0	1	54%	43%	0%	4%
2014	59	43	14	2	0	73%	24%	3%	0%
2015	37	18	18	1	0	49%	49%	3%	0%
2016	56	33	17	1	5	59%	30%	2%	9%
2017	43	26	16	1	0	60%	37%	2%	0%
2018	57	33	23	1	0	58%	40%	2%	0%
2019	48	28	15	1	5	57%	31%	2%	10%
2020	43	16	13	1	13	37%	30%	2%	30%
2021	67	21	11	0	35	31%	16%	0%	52%
2022	61	15	6	0	30	29%	12%	0%	59%
Total	982	523	376	24	97	53%	38%	2%	10%

Source: FBI UCR: Law Enforcement Officers Feloniously Killed 2004-2022

The same can be said of interracial violence. The mass media focuses like a laser every time a black becomes a victim of violence by a white. When a black commits violence on a white, it is rarely newsworthy. The chart below plots interracial violent crimes committed between blacks, whites, and Hispanics from 2017 through 2022.

Over the six years measured, blacks committed almost three million violent crimes against whites. Whites, on the other hand, committed 468,000 violent crimes against blacks—a ratio of over six to one. When you extract murder data only, blacks commit 2.2 times more murders of whites than whites do black, and for these data, Hispanic whites are included. This is consistent over time. For example, from 2010 to 2019, blacks murdered 4,870 whites, and the yearly total varied from a low of 409 in 2013 to a high of 576 in 2017.[441] Whites killed 2,196 blacks over the same period, ranging from a low of 187 in 2014 to a high of 264 in

2017.[442] Considering the fact that blacks represent about 13 percent of the US population, the level of interracial violent crime perpetrated by blacks is literally off the charts. Nothing else compares.

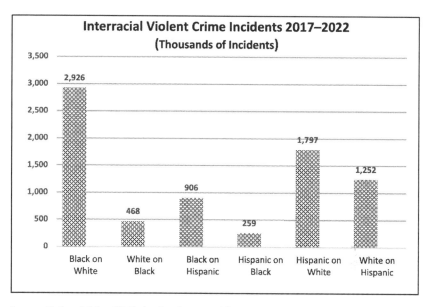

Source: National Crime Victimization Survey, Table 13, 2017–2022.

And despite blacks committing the majority of violent crimes, police kill many more whites each year in the line of duty than they do blacks. Here it is in black and white. Yet despite this proof, MSNBC, Newsweek, and other media hyped a report with the headline, "Black people are still killed by police at a higher rate than other groups."[443] No, they aren't. Whoever wrote that report did not have the proper stats. MSNBC cited the *Washington Post* as the source for the statistics. How about just looking up the actual published numbers? They claimed that blacks accounted for 27 percent of those killed by police in 2021 while they are only 13 percent of the population. No, actually, from the table below, blacks accounted for about 8 percent of the total killed by cops on average, with little variation year-to-year. Whites were double that amount.

People Killed by Police by Race and Ethnicity (2017 - 2023)								
	2017	2018	2019	2020	2021	2022	2023	Total
White	458	459	424	459	446	458	425	3,129
% Total	15%	15%	14%	15%	15%	14%	13%	15%
Black	222	228	251	243	233	222	229	1,628
% Total	7%	8%	8%	8%	8%	7%	7%	8%
Hispanic	180	167	168	171	136	180	133	1,135
% Total	6%	6%	6%	6%	4%	6%	4%	5%
Other	44	41	42	27	25	22	29	230
% Total	1%	1%	1%	1%	1%	1%	1%	1%
Unknown	77	88	114	120	208	341	347	1,295
% Total	3%	3%	4%	4%	7%	11%	11%	6%
Total	2,998	3,001	3,018	3,040	3,069	3,245	3,186	21,557

Source: People shot to death by US police 2017–2024, by race, Statista.[444]

This is all the direct result of the Left's long-range divide and conquer strategy. The have so marginalized the black community while pointing the finger at whites, this is what we get. Ghetto blacks not only feel entitled to whatever the system can give them, they feel entitled to commit criminal acts at will against the "white supremacist" hierarchy. If they want to attack someone, they should attack Democrats, *of any color*, because they are the true oppressors.

And this all goes back to the question: Why are things so bad in black communities? The crisis strategy, with the deliberate targeting of the nuclear black family, aided and abetted by a public school system that indoctrinates instead of teaching, gives young people few options. A life of crime begins to look like the only way out.

I served on the board of a Baltimore charter school years ago. Parents were literally desperate to get their kids in. Why? Because the school simply taught what all schools used to: reading, writing, math, science—unpolluted by today's radical Left "woke" agenda.

Deliberately Sabotaging Reform

The Left uses income redistribution, special legal protections for favored groups, and other unethical activities to purchase reliable, captive voting blocs, misinform the public, destroy political opponents, and channel both taxpayer and private, tax-exempt funds into rigging the entire system for Democrats. Ultimately, they seek to inflame, not pacify, divisions in society. And many, if not most, of those divisions would not exist without leftist activism. Their strategy invariably includes:

- A definable "victim" group that allows Democrats to seize the moral high ground in the victims' defense—for example, minorities, gays, illegal aliens, women, and the latest, transgenders.

- Victimhood status, and for the poor, a weary familiarity with criminal activity, all reinforced by leftist propaganda, gives victim classes a sense of entitlement that facilitates unethical and/or illegal activities that advance the Left's cause—for example, vote fraud, which is endemic in inner cities.

- The Left's assertion that law is simply an expression of "the imperialist, white supremacist, capitalist patriarchy,"[445] which further engenders contempt and disregard for the law. The most recent example of this is the epidemic spike in smash-and-grab store invasions and the unprecedented increase in ambush-style unprovoked attacks on police.

- Victimhood used as pretext for funding government programs that use tax dollars to cement policies in place, institutionalizing victimhood and building reliable voting constituencies who will now have a vested interest in their victim status.

- Encouraging an entitlement mindset and extensive financial incentives that cultivate government dependency, stripping victim classes of morality, dignity, and self-reliance. This encourages destructive activity—drugs, crime, prostitution, and unwed pregnancy—and further entrenches government support programs that require constantly increased funding.

- Sucking wealth from the private sector through taxes, regulation, and legal offensives that support and advance the victims' cause to build the Left's power, while sapping private resources to weaken opposition and gradually destroy private enterprise.

- Working to automate the process, using government and government-funded nonprofits to carry out the Left's policies at taxpayer expense, allowing radicals to focus on new initiatives. Automatic voter registration is but one example.
- Constant propaganda and misinformation in education, media, and Hollywood to inflame victim class hatred for traditional America, preventing the poor from seeing the true cause of their predicament, and guaranteeing the Left a ground army for revolution when the inevitable collapse occurs.

Victimhood policies have created cottage industries of tax-exempt groups that survive on government grants, essentially using tax dollars to employ and enrich leftists and to finance their war against America while further entrenching a taxpayer-supported army of reliable Democrat voters. And the number of such organizations has skyrocketed over the past thirty years. If you recall, in 1973, Cloward and Piven inspired creation of the Office of Economic Opportunity, which created thousands of tax-exempt groups, all government funded to serve the radical Left. This got the ball rolling.

In 1991, there were about five hundred thousand such tax-exempt, so-called "nonprofit charitable" organizations. As of 2022, that number had grown 187 percent to almost 1.5 million.[446] As then, today virtually all are left-leaning, some very left, and they receive money from foundations and government bureaucracies dominated by the Left.

Furthermore, they are nonprofit only in the technical legal sense as dictated in tax codes. Top executives often earn salaries commensurate with corporate executives, and retained earnings can measure in the tens or even hundreds of millions. The Southern Poverty Law Center, for example, had net assets of $689 million as of January 2023, some of which is squirrelled away in offshore accounts.[447]

The GOP-controlled US House of Representatives is investigating the misuse of these tax-exempt organizations.[448] We touched on that in the vote fraud chapter. This has been a long time coming; 501(c)(3) organizations are supposed to be nonpartisan and cannot fund political activities. However, in practice, most do and have for decades. Some of these organizations also accept funds from foreign donors who use them as a sort of money-laundering operation to influence US elections. You can be sure that if the Democrats win a majority in Congress in 2024, they will shut down this investigation overnight.

Soros's Open Society Foundations are responsible for funding some of the Left's most destructive activities, for example, underwriting the campaigns of anti-law enforcement district attorneys like George Gascon in Los Angeles and Larry Krasner in Philadelphia. Who suffers the most when criminals are given a free pass? Since many are black, their fellow blacks suffer the most. Do you believe these DAs are unaware of that? They do it deliberately, to *increase "the evils and miseries of the people."*

The Soros foundations' tax-exempt status should be revoked, and they, along with many other foundations, should have their assets seized and forfeited under the Racketeer Influenced Corrupt Organizations (RICO) laws. Their goal is to destroy our nation. As Soros himself said, "The main obstacle to a stable and just world order is the United States,"[449] and he has made it his life's mission to see America collapse. A saner nation would label his activities as treason, and he would be in jail for life.

Compassion for the poor, and the policies promoted under its pretext, are simply a reliable vehicle for accomplishing the Left's ultimate goal: complete Communist takeover of society and the power and wealth that comes with it. They care about *nothing* else. Democrats—today almost indistinguishable from the Communist Party—demonstrate their contempt for blacks every single day by relentlessly pushing these destructive policies. The evidence is right in front of our faces. And as this manuscript has shown, among themselves the Left have been very open about their plans.

To see how important this strategy is to Democrats, one only need observe the fate of welfare reform. It was a major Republican victory in 1996 when the Personal Responsibility and Work Opportunity Reconciliation Act (PRWORA) was signed into law by President Clinton. Despite claims that he favored welfare reform, Clinton had vetoed two earlier Republican bills but feared vetoing the popular measure again in an election year.[450]

What happened? According to the Brookings Institution, a very liberal DC think tank, "it worked." Following are some of the results Brookings cited, taken largely verbatim:[451]

- Welfare caseloads began declining in the spring of 1994 and increased after PRWORA was enacted in 1996.
- Between 1994 and 2004, the caseload declined an unprecedented 60 percent.
- Since 1996, more than forty separate studies have shown that 60 percent of adults leaving welfare are employed.
- Between 1993 and 2000, the percentage of low-income, single mothers with a job grew from 58 percent to nearly 75 percent, an increase of almost 30 percent.
- Employment among never-married mothers, the most disadvantaged and least-educated subgroup of single mothers, went from 44 to 66 percent—an unprecedented 50 percent increase.
- In 1993, earnings accounted for about 30 percent of the income of low-income, mother-headed families while welfare payments accounted for nearly 55 percent. By 2000, this pattern had reversed: earnings had leaped by an astounding 136 percent to constitute almost 57 percent of income while welfare income had plummeted by nearly half to constitute only about 23 percent of income.
- Between 1994 and 2000, child poverty fell every year and reached levels not seen since 1978. By 2000, the poverty rate of black children was the lowest it had ever been.

Read that last bullet again: *By 2000, the poverty rate of black children was the lowest it had ever been.* Heritage's Robert Rector threw in a few more observations about the success of reform:

- Prior to work-based welfare reform in the 1990s, marriage was rapidly disappearing; single women have the most abortions; less marriage led to more abortions.

- After welfare reform, the steady, rapid collapse in marriage abruptly halted; the non-marital teen pregnancy and abortion rates plummeted.
- Work-based welfare reform produced a dramatic drop in dependence and the single-parent poverty rate while leading to 9.8 million fewer abortions.[452]

No doubt you never heard about these successes from the mass media, but you probably haven't heard the following either. President Obama essentially abolished welfare reform, first with changes buried in the 2009 "stimulus" bill,[453] and again in 2012, when he quietly *and illegally* ordered regulatory changes that effectively wiped that law off the books.[454]

Obama went out of his way to sabotage that reform because it threatened the entire agenda. It seems baffling that anyone would want to undermine success for people who so much need it. But then you remember the agenda. They *do not want* people happy and successful. They want them dependent and angry.

The Left throws out another bogus straw man argument to justify federal welfare programs. They claim that if government welfare benefits vanished tomorrow, "the poor" would be helpless. This is categorically false. Throughout life, almost all of us need a hand up at one time or another. For this reason, some form of welfare has always existed. Before the federal government got into the welfare business in the 1930s, it was provided primarily by churches, other charitable organizations, and state and local governments.

Charitable organizations and state and local governments have limited funds, so welfare was provided only to those who genuinely needed it, was more closely monitored, and was almost always temporary. Furthermore, because it was locally focused on the individual, agencies were better able to tailor assistance on a case-by-case basis.

This was a much better arrangement and why many argue that federally sponsored welfare is unconstitutional. As James Madison stated in 1794: "The government of the United States is a definite government, confined to specified objects. It is not like the state governments, whose powers are more general. Charity is no part of the legislative duty of the government...."[455]

Because it was limited, able-bodied people accepting welfare knew they would have to find a job at some point and set themselves to this task. There was also a stigma against accepting the dole. So while people could find help when genuinely in need, this system maintained the ethic of work and self-reliance. Modern welfare has destroyed that. In fact, as described earlier, eliminating the stigma associated with welfare was one of Cloward and Piven's chief concerns.

When the federal government became involved, it usurped the role formerly taken by churches and other charitable organizations. This move alone weakened those organizations, and the increased taxes took monies that otherwise might have been tithed or donated to charity. As the church's role in society and the monies available to it have diminished, the moral backbone of our society has deteriorated. This was another planned consequence of the crisis strategy.

From the 1930s to the 1990s, Democrats controlled both houses of Congress for all but a few years and continued to rule from below, even after Republicans managed to seize control in 1994, because virtually the entire bureaucracy is controlled by the Left. With virtually unbroken power, Democrats have literally turned the organs of government into a vast vote buying machinery, making entire demographics government-dependent, reliable democratic voters, while blithely ignoring the devastating crime and cultural evisceration such policies have left in their wake. This was *a premeditated plan*, as described by the Democrats themselves.

Through ACORN, Cloward and Piven were able to apply the crisis strategy to welfare, voting, and housing. But whether or not they were personally involved, every single agenda pursued by the Left today is an application of the crisis strategy; and open borders—conducted in flagrant violation of federal law—is the most damaging form inflicted on our nation yet.

It has been especially devastating to the inner-city black community, as illegal aliens now replace blacks as the Democrats' favored recipients of government largesse, and illegals start businesses that undermine established black businesses. They can do this because as illegals, they don't bother to obey tax and employment laws. This is especially true in cities, where officials turn a blind eye. But corporations throughout America see the benefit of illegal immigration as well, because the pool of low-skilled labor drives the overall price of that labor down. And who suffers the most? The American poor and working classes.

While the federal government is not doling out benefits to illegals to any great extent *yet*, in many cases, states and cities are. In New York for example, Governor Hochul quietly made a rule change that allows illegals to obtain benefits through the state Safety Net Assistance program. Hochul has set aside $4.3 billion to handle New York's so-called "migrant" crisis.[456] And while NYC's Mayor Adams decries the "immigrant crisis" the city is facing, the city offers welfare benefits to those "regardless of immigration status" and now provides these same illegals with prepaid debit cards.[457]

So why would Adams talk out of both sides of his mouth? Because the Democrats don't want the migrants to leave—they just want help paying for them. The massive influx of illegal aliens is mostly headed to cities, and those are mostly run by Democrats. Democrats want them for two related reasons: (1) to inflate the Democrat vote—in cities, this is easier to accomplish through vote fraud and passing local laws allowing illegals to vote; suburban and rural communities tend to be more conservative, and vote fraud is more difficult to accomplish—and (2) to replace the black vote, which is becoming less and less reliable as blacks realize how seriously they've been mistreated by Democrats. This was well summarized in a *Tablet* magazine article:

> Between the inauguration of Bill Clinton in 1993 and that of Joe Biden in 2021, the Democratic Party morphed into a new party of elite, college-educated white professionals, Black Americans, and mostly Hispanic immigrants concentrated in a few big cities in a few populous states like California and New York. Many Democrats have called this new, big-city political machine "the coalition of the ascendant," confident

that the growth in the share of nonwhite voters fed by immigration, combined with increasing social liberalism, will lead to inevitable one-party rule by a hegemonic Democratic Party.

In reality, however, the Democratic Party is an alliance of interests threatened with long-term demographic decline—declining industries, declining states, declining cities, declining churches and nonprofits. These civic downtrodden have united around the hope that they can reverse the unpopularity of their offerings among U.S.-born Americans by importing new citizens en masse.[458]

And lying in the rubble is Black America.

SURGE THE BORDER

*I would in fact make sure that there is, we
immediately surge the border. All those people seeking
asylum. They deserve to be heard. That's who we
are. We're a nation that says if you want to flee,
and you're fleeing oppression, you should come.*[459]

—Joe Biden

This chapter can almost write itself. Of all the Cloward–Piven strategies to date, this is the deadliest. When this author published *The Red-Green Axis 2.0* in 2019, a book describing in detail the problems with immigration and refugee resettlement, migrant caravans were already surging the border.[460] We had warning from the 2015 migrant invasion from Africa and the Middle East that reshaped Western Europe and skyrocketed Islamic terrorism throughout. Note that none of the Eastern European nations or Russia had a single problem. They shut their doors tight. No one called them "racists," "Islamophobes," or "xenophobes." Why is that?

But Western European leaders did nothing to stop the migrant waves. Many facilitated it, especially German chancellor Angela Merkel. Most people are unaware that Merkel, while born in West Germany in 1954, moved with her family to East Germany shortly thereafter and grew up there. At age fourteen, Merkel joined the Free German Youth (in German: Freie Deutsche Jugend or FDJ), which was the official German Communist Youth organization, and became a committed Marxist-Leninist. While attending college, she became the FDJ Secretary for Agitation and Propaganda.[461]

When the Wall fell, Merkel, like many other Communists, infiltrated freely into West Germany and insinuated herself into the conservative Christian Democratic Union party. She became German chancellor Helmut Kohl's personal protégé, but when his CDU became embroiled in a campaign donations scandal, she turned on him and demanded his resignation, seeing it as an opportunity to take his place. He said, "I bought my killer. I put the snake on my arm."[462]

When the mass migration started in 2015, Merkel threw open the German border, allowing in hundreds of thousands of migrants. And while the German people at first welcomed them, very quickly most German polls became strongly opposed to this open-borders policy. But Merkel ignored them and left the borders open. What followed was a horror show of terrorism, gang rapes, and other crimes.

This was not a one-off. It has been a longstanding plan of the Comintern to use immigration to facilitate the movement of "communist political armies" to target countries. This was described in a 1956 pamphlet written by Col. Archibald Roosevelt, son of Teddy Roosevelt. The pamphlet was titled "Conquest via Immigration." He says, "The International Labor Defense, as the American section of the International Red Aid, was organized in 1925 to facilitate immigration of communist agents and to fight deportation of red aliens already here."[463]

Ten years later, the International Labor Defense (ILD) had grown to 225,000 members with 800 branches nationwide. In 1932, the Comintern publication INPRECORR reported that the International Red Aid umbrella organization had a total membership of 11.5 million people, but the ILD was of critical importance. In its effort to covertly infiltrate America with Communist political armies, it advocated:

> [C]omplete right of asylum for all emigrants who have
> been compelled to leave their own country for political
> or economic reasons; that they should not be expelled

or extradited; they shall be allowed to enter all countries without documents or visas; they shall be given
identification papers valid in all countries; unrestricted
right to stay in any country; full right to work and to
relief in case of unemployment; immediate cancellation
of all expulsion and extradition orders; the release of
all arrested emigrants, and finally the right to take part
in the political and trade union life in the country in
which they have found asylum.

Does that not describe what we hear from Democrats every day
now? Today, the Biden administration is carrying out these wishes in
ways even the most optimistic Communist would never dream of. And
it is because the Democrat Party is fully invested, knowingly or otherwise, in the Communist plan. Now add to that the fentanyl overdose
epidemic, the criminals being released from Venezuelan jails and committing crimes here, the child sex trafficking, and the illegal population's
increasingly strident demands for every kind of service, and you get a
true picture of the multi-front war against America being facilitated by
the open-borders agenda.

And this is just from the open borders enabled by our own government. There is no doubt that this is all part of the international Communist plan. For example, the House Select Committee on the CCP
has found that the Chinese government:[464]

- Directly subsidizes the manufacturing and export of illicit fentanyl materials and other synthetic narcotics through tax rebates.
- Gave monetary grants and awards to companies openly trafficking illicit fentanyl materials and other synthetic narcotics.
- Holds ownership interest in several PRC companies tied to
  drug trafficking.
- Strategically and economically benefits from the fentanyl crisis.

Furthermore, when asked by US law enforcement for assistance,
instead the Chinese communists alert fentanyl traffickers that they are
being targeted. It should be clear now why the Comintern placed so

much emphasis on immigration. We are literally being overwhelmed with crisis after crisis.

The 2015 migrant crisis in Europe presented in shocking relief that most Western European leaders were not on the side of their people but were instead part of the global elite who are doing everything they can to marginalize and oppress their native citizens, while accommodating every whim of these new, and often overtly hostile, "immigrants."

Bad as it was, the European invasion was a trial run. The crisis we are facing here in America is many magnitudes worse. In March 2024, Fox News host Jason Chaffetz interviewed former Trump national security advisor Ambassador Robert O'Brien. O'Brian said the concerns over the border were keeping him up at night:

> Jason, this does not end well. We've got two PLA divisions' worth of Chinese males; like thirty thousand military-aged males from China have come in. Untold numbers of Jihadis and Iranian activists—Hezbollah, Hamas operatives. Something bad's going to happen, and it's because of the wide-open border. It's a terrifying situation. As a national security advisor, it's keeping me up at night....[465]

The ambassador has it right. China expert Gordon Chang reported that Communist China is installing the infrastructure needed to launch an attack within the US. Chinese migrants posted videos on X showing them shooting rifles and pistols. He described rituals Chinese military men perform. He also reported the discovery of a secret Chinese bio-weapon lab in a town near Fresno, California. Authorities discovered at least twenty pathogens, including Ebola, and one thousand mice bioengineered to spread disease.[466] Chang believes there are more labs like it. Chang quoted retired Air Force general Blaine Holt, who said:

> Tens of thousands of military-age men have come across our border and are now in America, organized by group and nationality. Among them are terrorist and state actors, in particular, members of the People's Liberation

Army of China. As we speak, these actors are training, making plans and obtaining weapons, watching our patterns, and learning our vulnerabilities.[467]

The border crisis is almost too severe to contemplate, and it is difficult to believe that any American leader would want to visit this on their citizens. But that is the agenda, because they are literally working for our enemies:

- ten million illegal aliens since Biden opened the border;
- terrorists, criminals, and thousands of military-aged men;
- current number of illegals in the US between thirty and fifty million;
- Biden administration now flying migrants directly into the US;
- enough fentanyl has been confiscated to kill every American many times over;
- epidemic child sex trafficking at the border;
- Biden administration working with Mexican cartels to facilitate the flood;
- Biden administration, numerous nonprofits colluding with multiple UN agencies to facilitate the mass invasion;
- Democrats counting on Census reapportionment counting illegals to gain multiple new seats in Congress;
- 59 percent of non-citizens, which includes illegal aliens, use welfare.

Senator Marco Rubio reported in March 2024 that the FBI had confirmed a smuggling ring existed that imports people with ties to ISIS terrorists into the US.[468] Since 2021, the Border Patrol has arrested 331 illegals on the terrorist watch list. But there are about 1.8 million "gotaways," that is, people the Customs and Border Protection didn't catch. And those are the ones we know about.[469] Most looking to take advantage of our border for economic reasons just turn themselves in. Why do the gotaways try to get away?

In March 2024, every Senate Democrat voted against an amendment attached to the consolidated appropriations bill. The amendment would have removed illegal aliens from the Census count in reapportionment.[470] Elon Musk sent out a tweet about it:

> Most Americans do not know that the U.S. census currently counts, for purposes of voting power, all people in a district, regardless of citizenship! Senate Democrats just voted unanimously to defeat an amendment that would have stopped counting illegals for congressional seat apportionment and electoral college (presidential) votes. Since illegals are mostly in Democrat states, both the House and the Presidential vote are shifted ~5% to the left, which is enough to change the entire balance of power! This is a major reason why the Biden administration is ushering in record levels of illegals and doing so few deportations.[471]

Democrats are not even trying to hide their agenda anymore. The Biden administration is lawlessly flying hundreds of thousands of migrants in from their home countries, sparing them the effort of walking. Senator Bill Hagerty introduced an amendment to end that. Every single Senate Democrat voted against it.[472] As described in the vote fraud chapter, Biden is enabling this by abusing immigration parole, which is supposed to grant legal entry to a small number of people in trying circumstances on an individual basis. Instead we are getting millions.

The Biden administration is also doing all it can to pile illegal alien "migrants" into the pipeline to become citizens, abusing the various legal pathways to immigration. Upon taking office, the Biden administration raised the annual refugee allowance from President Trump's 15,000 to 62,500 for fiscal year 2021, promising to rase the cap to 125,000 in FY 2022.[473] The cap has been 125,000 every year since, allowing a total of 437,500 through FY 2024. He will set it again by the same amount in September for FY 2025. If not reversed, that will mean a total of 562,500.

Biden has also granted or renewed Temporary Protected Status for illegal aliens from South Sudan, Burma, Somalia, Syria, Venezuela, Yemen, and Haiti. TPS allows aliens fleeing war or natural disaster to remain in the US temporarily, supposedly until the crisis is over. However, TPS gets renewed repeatedly, keeping anyone from those countries here indefinitely. TPS for El Salvador, for example, has been in force since 2001. The Trump administration revoked this longstanding TPS for El Salvador, Honduras, Nepal, and Nicaragua. However, in 2023, DHS secretary Alejandro Mayorkas announced that the Department of Homeland Security had reversed every single one.[474] As of March 29, 2024, 1,187,230 illegal aliens currently in the US are eligible for TPS.[475]

So with these three actions alone, Biden has virtually guaranteed legal permanent resident status, with eventual citizenship, to over three million illegal aliens. By the end of 2024, that number will be substantially higher.

Finally, as described in the vote fraud chapter, many of the illegals flooding the border will likely vote because a provision in existing law allows them to get away with it if they believed they were legal citizens. No doubt they are being told that by Democratic politicians and the many left-wing groups assisting the illegal migration.

Meanwhile, the costs of managing the illegal alien invasion have skyrocketed. The US House Committee on Homeland Security has estimated the cost at $451 billion. Much of this goes to cover healthcare.[476] States are swamped with overwhelming costs, and some hospitals may be forced to close their doors. Illinois expects to spend almost $1 billion in 2024, up from $768 million in 2023.[477] Leaders in Democrat-run states do not help. In California, for example, a new law will cover healthcare costs for all illegals in the state, at an estimated cost of between $3 and $6 billion.[478]

Illegals and refugees bring innumerable diseases, many of which were heretofore thought to be extremely rare or wiped out entirely. This includes polio, measles, chicken pox, chagas, malaria, and even leprosy.[479] Does the Biden administration care about this? No more than Obama did in 2014, when illegal alien minors imported Enterovirus D68—rare in the US but more common in Central and South America—which overwhelmed hospital emergency rooms, and paralyzed and killed American children.[480]

The War on White America

When the Left sees this subchapter title, they will take the title out of context and use it to triumphantly point to the "racist" author who believes conspiracy theories about "white genocide" and such nonsense. There *really is* a war against white America, but remember, you don't have to be white to be "White." You simply have to be a person who believes in our Constitution and shares the Judeo-Christian values that were responsible for making our nation the greatest, most welcoming, and most prosperous in the world. You can be Jewish, black, Hispanic, Asian, Indian, or a lily-white WASP; it really doesn't matter.

So, there is indeed a war against white America in that sense. There is also a war against white men, straight men and women, Asians, conservative gays, and more. The list is pretty long when you get right down to it. And while there is a hellacious war against blacks as described in the "Weaponizing the Poor" chapter, if blacks were the majority in America, and all our historical roles and experiences were reversed, the Left would be openly vilifying blacks as "black supremacists," and whites would be the "poor, oppressed underclass."

The truth is, the Left is at war with pretty much everyone. Because it is not race or ethnic origin being targeted. It is the America we know and love. And *that* is being targeted not because it is flawed or because we have "white privilege" (another divide and conquer strategy brought to us by American Communists, by the way),[481] but precisely because it is the source of our strength. It goes back to the entire motive of the Left: power and wealth, *our* power and *our* wealth. And it is truly a spiritual war between the forces of darkness and light. When Joe Biden declared Easter Sunday 2024 to be the "Transgender Day of Visibility," he at once blatantly renounced the Catholicism he ridiculously claims to believe and made a mockery of Christian values and beliefs. But there really is a war against white America for two related reasons: (1) more whites than any other group vote Republican, and (2) whites are the largest repository of societal knowledge and understanding of the US Constitution and our Judeo-Christian values. Both must be defeated for the Left to achieve absolute power.

Caravans, Cash, Crime, and Chaos

We are funding our own demise. Currently, there are dozens of UN and other government agencies as well as numerous private, tax-exempt organizations assisting the migrant caravans flooding our borders. Blaze Media named eight of them:[482]

- The International Organization for Migration (IOM)
- The American Red Cross
- The United Nations International Children's Emergency Fund (UNICEF)
- The Hebrew Immigrant Aid Society
- The European Union
- Doctors Without Borders
- The United Nations High Commissioner for Refugees (UNHCR)
- The Norwegian Refugee Council

But actually, there are 248 non-governmental organizations (NGOs) assisting in the migration and numerous UN-related agencies. By the UN's own report, in addition to IOM, UNICEF, and UNHCR, it includes the World Health Organization (WHO), the UN Population Fund (UNFPA), and the World Food Programme (WFP), in collaboration with the Pan American Health Organization (PAHO) and the Oxford Committee for Famine Relief (OXFAM), an umbrella of twenty-one British NGOs.[483] The UN has budgeted $1.7 billion in 2024 to assist some three million from seventeen countries, of which 624,000 "in-transit" migrants will receive $372 million in cash.[484]

And while all these government agencies and nonprofits enable the mass caravans with billions of tax and tax-exempt foundation dollars, the main overseers are transnational criminal organizations (TCOs) that facilitate much of the travel and cross-border operations. It has become a $13 billion business—excluding drug trafficking. Smuggling fees range from $2,000 to $40,000, according to a report by the *New York Times*.[485] So is the cash that's being given to the migrants just being laundered through the migrants to go into the cartels' pockets?

US Representative Chip Roy has proposed legislation removing funding from those organizations that receive tax dollars. That would be every organization listed except maybe the Norwegian Refugee Council. Probably the biggest reason the Left has been so successful to date is that they rig it so that we wind up paying. They need to be divested of their war chest.

That is especially true of the UN. The United States is by far the largest single contributor to the UN budget, characteristically paying about 20 percent annually. That was over $18 billion in 2022.[486] Despite that fact, or maybe because of it, the UN has been able to work against American interests since its founding.

Most people are unaware that the UN Charter was written by Alger Hiss, an American State Department employee and one of the most notorious traitors in our nation's history. Following its completion, he traveled to the Soviet Union, where he received an award for his work.[487] Apparently no one noticed.

The Left claims that "immigrants" commit less crime than American citizens. Of course, they don't distinguish between illegal aliens, the correct legal term for the "migrants" entering the US illegally, and people who have migrated to the US legally. But there is indeed a difference. Illegal aliens commit many violent crimes, and some countries, like Venezuela, are deliberately sending their worst, as Cuban leader Fidel Castro did with the Mariel Boatlift in 1980.[488]

Texas makes pains to positively identify criminal *illegal* versus legal aliens. Many states, and the federal government, do not. There is likely an ideological reason for that. The Left does not like to be embarrassed by the truth, and most government officials working in that area are to the political left. Below is a table documenting the lifetime of violent crimes committed by 333,000 illegal aliens incarcerated in Texas between 2011 and 2024. This includes a total of 771,000 charges and 329,000 convictions.

Texas Illegal Alien Lifetime Arrests and Convictions (Incarcerated 2011-2024)

	Arrests	Convictions
Homicide	3,490	1,923
Kidnapping	1,866	623
Rape & Other Sex Offenses	23,571	12,386
Drugs	95,100	45,134
Robbery	7,631	4,429
Assault	94,962	37,788

Source: Texas Department of Public Safety.[489]

When these kinds of statistics surface, the open-borders lobby quickly jumps in, claiming that illegal aliens commit fewer crimes than Americans do. It is a straw man argument, of course. If there were strong border controls, none of these crimes would have been committed. Those thousands of bereaved families whose sons, daughters, husbands, or wives were murdered by illegals could have lived their lives without the crushing grief of losing a loved one. Ask them if they care whether or not illegal aliens murder more people than American citizens. With a secure border, few, if any, of those people would have died, or been kidnapped, or raped, or robbed, or anything else. But according to the Left's twisted logic, it's okay just so long as these people aren't as bad as US citizens.

But let's look at Arizona and just evaluate the really nasty crimes. The table below shows those incarcerated for various crimes in February 2024, the latest data as of this writing. Aliens committed 11.4 percent of those, including almost 15 percent of all kidnappings and over 23 percent of child molestation cases. And while we do not know the illegal alien population in Arizona, it seems clear that aliens commit a huge proportion of violent crimes in the state.

Arizona Incarceration Statistics February 2024

	AZ Corrections		
Charge	Total	Aliens	% Total
Kidnapping	985	147	14.9%
Homicide/Murder	3,939	397	10.1%
Rape & Other Sex Offenses	3,384	406	12.0%
Child Molestation	1,110	260	23.4%
Total	9,418	1,210	11.4%

Source: Arizona Dept. of Corrections; Corrections at a Glance, 2/24.

There are countless anecdotes of illegal aliens repeatedly committing crimes with little permanent resolution. For example, in early April 2024, one Fermin Garcia-Gutierrez was arrested for murder in the northern border town of Hamilton, Ohio. He had been arrested eleven times previously, charged with twenty different crimes, including domestic violence, weapon possession and use, and drunk driving. He was deported eight times. He was a gang member with at least seven different assumed names and three separate birthdays.

The sheriff said his border county of Butler, Ohio, has detained one thousand illegal aliens since 2021 at a cost of $4 million. While he would not disclose Gutierrez's victim's name, the sheriff said he would be alive were it not for our current leadership. "Our border is broken," he said. And, pointing to pictures of Joe Biden, DHS chief Alejandro Mayorkas, and Mexican president Andres Manuel Lopez Obrador, he added, "These individuals are the cause of it."[490]

Illegal immigration has been causing chaos in cities for decades. But problems are increasing exponentially. A few years ago, the author analyzed the cost to public education of dealing with disparate cultures from across the globe. This included a trip throughout New England to discuss these issues with school administrators and local leaders.

This is not a new statistic, but there are over four hundred languages spoken in US public schools today.[491] Courts, first responders, teachers, and the community must deal with languages from every corner of the globe, including many unknown languages like Kirundi (from Burundi), Dzongkha (from Bhutan), Cushitic (spoken in parts of Kenya, Tanzania, and Sudan), Amharic (from Ethiopia), and other heretofore unknown dialects. Some of the Central American illegal alien minors resettled throughout the United States under the Unaccompanied Alien Children (UAC) program speak heretofore unknown remote highland village dialects.

K–12 English language learner (ELL) public school programs are overwhelmed as education budgets explode to handle the influx. For example, the following is a list of languages spoken by students in Portland, Oregon, public schools: Akan, Albanian, Amharic, Arabic, Bengali, Bosnian, Bulgarian, Burmese, Cambodian, Canjobal, Cantonese, Cebuano, Chamorro, Chuukese, Creole, Czech, Danish, Dinka, Dutch, non-standard English, Ewe, Farsi, Fijian, Filipino, French, Fulbe, German, Guatemalan, Hebrew, Hindi, Hmong, Island Carib, Italian, Japanese, Kannada, Karen, Khmer, Kinyarwanda, Kirundi, Korean, Kurdish, Lao, Lingala, Mandarin, Marshallese, Mayan, Mien, Nepali, Oromo, Palauan, Pashto, Persian, Pohnpeian, Portuguese, Romanian, Russian, Saho, Sango, Spanish, Somali, Sonsorolese, Swahili, Tagalog, Tamil, Telugu, Thai, Tibetan, Tigrinya, Tongan, Turkish, Ukrainian, Urdu, Vietnamese, Visayan, and more—over eighty-five languages in all.[492]

ELL classes frequently have no instructors knowledgeable on the numerous languages. Some school districts are being sued for not providing needed instruction to such students. For example, in 2015, the ACLU won a case against the state of California for not adequately providing such instruction. The Obama Justice Department joined the suit despite the fact that the federal government is largely to blame for this mess.

The following table provides a list of school districts around the nation showing the size of their ELL programs and the number of languages spoken by students trying to learn English:

English Language Learners in K-12 U.S. Public Schools				
	Languages Spoken	% Student Body	# Students ELL	Total
Amarillo, TX	75	15.2%	5,041	33,066
Anchorage, AK	99	13.0%	6,200	47,692
Buffalo, NY	84	10.5%	3,895	37,000
Chicago, IL	99	18.7%	67,664	361,314
Denver, CO	124	37.0%	33,650	87,398
Des Moines, IA	100	20.6%	6,800	32,500
Federal Way, WA	120	30.9%	7,141	23,075
Lewiston, ME	35	28.1%	1,547	5,503
Lincoln, NE	125	7.5%	3,000	40,000
Manchester, NH	76	11.2%	1,968	17,500
Minneapolis, MN	90	21.6%	7,800	36,093
Nashville, TN	120	29.8%	25,300	85,000
Omaha, NE	76	14.0%	7,000	50,000
Philadelphia, PA	100	10.6%	13,800	130,000
Portland, ME	58	24.8%	1,719	6,940
Portland, OR	85	7.8%	3,798	48,459
Sioux Falls, SD	90	9.8%	2,350	24,000
Worchester, MA	80	34.4%	8,717	25,306
U.S. Overall	>400	9%	4,813,693	53,700,000

Sources: State and local public education records, research studies and news stories

Much of that is due to refugee resettlement as opposed to illegal immigration, but it is all part of the same agenda. That is, to bring in so many diverse cultures that American culture and society becomes diluted to the point that it simply disappears. Costs of managing these diverse languages and the number of students needing ELL have skyrocketed. For example, in 2001, approximately five thousand Somalis and other refugee immigrants migrated from Georgia to Lewiston, Maine, following the discovery that Maine was one of the most generous welfare states in the nation. As a result, Lewiston's ELL budget has increased over 4,000 percent since the year 2000.[493] In FY 2017–18, Lewiston's ELL budget was $16,601,113, adding $3,048 per student cost, over and above the basic cost for students in Lewiston schools.[494] Eighty-six percent of Lewiston's 5,655 students are poor or very poor, making them eligible for reduced-cost or free school lunch.

The influx of people from Islamic countries, primarily through refugee resettlement, has added its own kind of problems. Many Muslims practice "Sharia" or Islamic law, much of which directly contradicts US law. Some would like to see Sharia become the law of the land, and of course there are leftist jurists who uphold that, another dimension of the crisis strategy. For example, one New Jersey judge permitted a Muslim man to get away with beating and raping his wife, because, the judge explained, "The court believes that he was operating under his belief that it is, as the husband, his desire to have sex when and whether he wanted to, was something that was consistent with his practices and it was something that was not prohibited."[495]

The ruling was fortunately overturned, with the appeals court specifically noting that the judge based his ruling on the defendant's religious beliefs, not on the law. In this, the appeals court ruled that "the judge was mistaken."[496] It is absurd, however, that there are judges out there who would make such a ruling in the first place.

The influx of Muslims to America has created a second problem loosely associated with the first: terrorism. Over the past thirty years, there have been numerous mass shootings, bombings, and other killings conducted by Muslim men. The recent anti-Israel protests in the wake of October 7, 2023, have brought to light the depth of anti-Semitic hatred felt by both Muslims and the Left toward Israel, our most trusted Middle East ally, and all people of the Jewish faith. It is reminiscent of pre-war Nazi Germany.

And the tax-exempt organizations paid by the federal government to resettle refugees do not help. They resettle Sunni Muslims next to Shia Muslims, with predictable results. They also resettle Muslims and Christians from the same home country, for example Syria, in the same neighborhoods, where the Muslims continue to oppress Christians, as they did in the old country. Somalia is a nation of clans, which in Somalia act a lot like street gangs. They are dumped in US cities side-by-side, and we suffer the resulting chaos. Is this deliberate, or just sheer careless stupidity by the resettlement organizations? I would say it is a combination of both.

But things are getting intolerably worse, as floods of immigrants with no place to go overwhelm our ability to deal with them. It is Cloward and Piven on steroids. And of course, the Democrats are going out of their way to encourage it. With the combination of anti-police prosecutors and radical Left legislators coming up with new giveaways every day, states—especially sanctuary states—act as magnets for illegals and especially criminal illegals. And it seems that California's Democratic leaders are doing everything possible to bring the entire state crashing down on their own heads. It's almost inexplicable. One bill proposed in the California legislature in March 2024 would expand legal services to criminal illegal aliens, including the ability for the alien to resist deportation. Assemblywoman Kate Sanchez of California stated:

> It would give hardworking taxpayer dollars to fund and expand a program that would allow criminals, illegal alien criminals that have been convicted, to stay in California. Not only that, it would expand it to those across the United States with…the intent to come to California to live.[497]

Former president Obama actually deliberately instigated the first waves of Central American migrants. During his time in office, Obama tried to redefine the term "refugee" to enable migrants seeking better economic conditions to emigrate as refugees—thereby circumventing the long, arduous process to immigrate legally. He created something called the Central American Minors (CAM) program, which allowed minors to obtain refugee status under certain conditions and fly directly to the US. Trump ended the program, but Biden restarted it.

But Obama wanted much more than that. The US State Department worked behind the scenes in Guatemala to help Claudia Paz y Paz, a Communist guerrilla sympathizer, become Guatemala's attorney general in 2010. Her father was a leader of the Castro-supported Rebel Armed Forces (FAR) during Guatemala's thirty-six-year civil war. FAR assassinated US Ambassador John Gordon Mein in 1968 and Germany's ambassador to Guatemala, Karl von Spreti, two years later.[498]

The guerrilla groups were still active in a small corner of the country but had been largely neutralized. When Paz y Paz took over, she reclassified these Communist guerrillas as "civil rights" groups and gave them free rein throughout the countryside. These militias were enthusiastically supported by the Obama administration.[499] Guerrilla activities dramatically increased, spreading like cancer throughout the countryside. They made life a literal hell, terrorizing the people and attacking any economic development projects that would reduce rural poverty. They gave the peasants a choice: work for us or don't work.[500]

At the same time, immigration and refugee resettlement nonprofits began talking about the poor conditions and high crime faced by Central Americans. In 2012, Obama created the Deferred Action for Childhood Arrivals (DACA) program that allowed illegal alien minors who came to the US to remain in America indefinitely. He tried the same thing with the Deferred Action for Parents of Americans (DAPA) program, but that was struck down in court. So facing a stick in Guatemala, migrants saw the carrot Obama was dangling and began the trek north, assisted by open-borders NGOs.

Shortly after that, waves of illegal aliens began hitting our border. In 2011, the Border Patrol apprehended only 4,321 Central American minors. That number increased to 68,541 in 2014.[501] A disproportionate number came from Guatemala. In 2016, Obama's last year in office, Customs and Border Protection apprehended 563,204 illegal aliens, and it has not stopped since. The migrant caravans swamping our borders were instigated by Guatemalan Communists, in collusion with the Obama administration and assisted by tax-exempt and taxpayer-funded open-borders groups. *This entire effort was a premeditated campaign by the Obama administration.*

Demographics Is Destiny

America is being undermined by a tidal wave of immigration. It has been going on since Ted Kennedy's Immigration and Naturalization Act of 1965 was enacted, and that changed the face of immigration by opening it up to every nation in the world. But it really took off under President Obama, and we have all witnessed what has happened since.

Federal agencies collaborate with multinational entities to bring in people from all over the world under a universe of immigration programs, while so-called "volunteer agencies" (VOLAGs) and hundreds of small tax-exempt organizations are remunerated handsomely with taxpayer dollars to resettle and assist illegal aliens, refugees, asylum seekers, and other similar groups. It has turned into a multibillion-dollar industry.

The Democrat Left and its establishment enablers in the business community and GOP have engaged in a long-term project to change America by changing its people. The Left seeks power above all else, and while we all debate the wisdom of this or that policy, and businesses benefit from cheap foreign labor—both legal and illegal—the Left has gradually been importing enough people to permanently change voting demographics in its favor.

It is indisputable that this is the primary goal of open-borders policies and the reason the Left so fanatically fought President Trump on all aspects of immigration. Following the 2018 midterm elections, members of Democracy Alliance—a secretive group of billionaire leftist funders, including George Soros and oil magnate Tom Steyer—met in Washington, DC, to discuss how demographic changes impacted the election in their favor and what they must do to capitalize on them for 2020.[502] But this was not the first time. Prior to the 2008 election, Democrat insiders John Podesta, Andrew Stern, and Anna Burger wrote a secret memo to these same billionaire leftists. As stated in the memo:

> **Ensure that Demographics is Destiny.** An "emerging progressive majority" is a realistic possibility in terms of demographic and voting patterns. But it is incomplete in terms of organizing and political work. Women, communities of color, and highly educated professionals are core parts of the progressive coalition. Nationally, and in key battleground states, their influence is growing. Latinos and young voters are quickly solidifying in this

coalition as well. But many of these voters are new to the process. All of these groups—in addition to working class voters and independents picked up in 2006—will require significant long-term engagement in order to keep them reliably on our side.[503]

This goal was publicly repeated in a 2009 speech by Socialist labor leader Eliseo Medina, at the time one of the most influential open-borders advocates in the US. Assuming the oft-repeated low-ball estimate of about twelve million illegals in the US, Medina said:

> We in the last election had the largest turnout of Latino voters in our history. And everything tells us these voters fully intend on becoming engaged into elections in the future.... Number one: if we are to expect this electorate to win, the progressive community needs to solidly be on the side of immigrants. Let us solidify and expand the progressive coalition for the future.... Number two, we reform the immigration laws, it puts 12 million on the path to citizenship and eventually voters. Can you imagine if we have even the same ratio [as Obama got] two out of three, if we had 8 million new voters that care about our issues and would be voting, we would create a governing coalition for the long-term, not just for an election cycle.[504]

So what is the illegal alien population in the US? The Census Bureau and most immigration think tanks, even conservative ones, stuck doggedly to the estimate of about ten to twelve million illegals, even with the Obama-instigated border surges starting in 2012 and continuing through the Trump administration.[505] The latest revision by the conservative Federation for American Immigration Reform (FAIR) brings it up to about sixteen million.[506] The liberal Pew Research inexplicably finds that the number went up by a mere three hundred thousand between 2019 and 2021 and now stands at 10.5 million.[507] This is absurd.

In 2005, Bear Stearns estimated the illegal alien population at roughly twenty million based on telltale evidence like increases in remittances to foreign countries, school enrollments, and use of social services among border states. This was a much more credible estimate.[508] A 2018 report by three Ivy League scholars estimated the current illegal alien population in the US at 22.1 million, with an upward boundary of thirty million.[509] Since then, that number has been augmented by well over ten million. For the four fiscal years that Joe Biden has been in office, the total is 10,147,015, and for just FY 2024 so far, there have been over 2.2 million.[510]

But well before Biden, Obama's DHS was printing thirty-four million green cards and work permits to accommodate what he called "executive amnesty."[511] Why would they need that many? So a low-ball estimate today is thirty million illegals, but it could be as many as forty or fifty million. Either way, that would be enough to fundamentally transform America into the Democrats' fantasy Communist paradise.

This agenda is decades old. Until the border surges, it was primarily through legal immigration. Every year since the 1980s, the US government has allowed approximately one million immigrants to become legal permanent residents (LPR) in the United States. In FY 2022, we imported 1,018,349.[512] While advocates will say we need these people to supplement a shrinking labor force, in 2022 only 270,000, about 25 percent of LPRs, immigrated for employment reasons. And this is more than average. Typically, it has been closer to 15 percent. Most of the others usually arrive under family reunification programs. For the most part we are *not* importing people for employment reasons. A *sane* legal immigration policy would allow in only those needed to cover shortfalls in critical employment fields, approximately 160,000 on average since 2013.[513]

Additionally, among those obtaining permanent resident status are people from countries very unfriendly to the US, including hundreds of thousands from Muslim majority and Communist countries. Of the latter, the most significant is the People's Republic of China. About 857,000 Chinese nationals received LPR status between 2010 and 2022, over seventy thousand annually, and another six hundred thousand immigrated from 2000 to 2009.[514] Given the conditions in many of those nations, you can be confident that some do represent a threat of terrorism, espionage, sabotage, influence operations, or all of the above.

California, for example, has become a haven for Chinese espionage. Many of the Chinese nationals awarded immigrant and non-immigrant visas have actually turned out to be spies. In one case, Chinese intelligence officers working out of China's San Francisco Consulate bussed in between six thousand and eight thousand Chinese students in California on (J) visas (for scholars, professors, and exchange visitors) to disrupt an anti-Chinese government rally in San Francisco held by members of the Chinese Falun Gong religious group, Tibetan and Uighur dissidents, and others.[515]

The Chinese Communists have been infiltrating the US with spies for fifty years. Currently, there are approximately twenty-five thousand Chinese spies in the US; five thousand of these came in after 2012 as students, businessmen, or immigrants. According to national defense expert Bill Gertz, another eighteen thousand Americans of various ethnic groups, including Chinese, have been recruited by Chinese intelligence. So, we're looking at the possibility of over forty thousand Chinese espionage agents and spies in the US.[516]

The annual influx of seventy thousand Chinese provides a large pool of recruits for specific operations, like the San Francisco protest, or for other nefarious purposes. While some may come here for legitimate reasons and no doubt find American freedom preferable to the oppressive Communist state, every one of the millions of Chinese who emigrated from the PRC over the last twenty-plus years are potential spies or saboteurs. Chinese intelligence knows who they are and where they are, and they can be called on at any time, whether they like it or not. US-based Chinese intelligence operatives threaten to retaliate against relatives still in China if they don't comply.[517]

And now, with the border wide open, young Chinese men of military age and bearing are flooding in by the thousands. As Ambassador O'Brien warned, this cannot end well. With all the demands for open borders and supposed "compassion" toward illegal aliens, migrants, and legal immigrants, one never asks why China and Russia don't share this compassion. Why don't these open-border advocates ever demand China and Russia open their borders, since so many are openly sympathetic to Communism and Communist causes? We know why, of course.

In 2016, President Trump tried to maintain his border promises upon election but was stymied by Democrats and members of his own party as well. As the result of partisan judicial intervention, overcrowded holding facilities, and a defiant bureaucracy still seeded with many Obama holdovers, the Trump administration was forced to continue Obama administration "catch and release" policies.[518] Illegal aliens were transported by air and bus from facilities along the border to undisclosed locations within the US, accompanied by personnel from the Department of Health and Human Services, which oversees the Unaccompanied Alien Children (UAC) program.[519] So this burgeoning, secretive open-borders agenda was even being facilitated under Trump by the federal government, with your tax dollars.

Elon Musk recently tweeted, "This is actually happening!" a retweet of a tweet from @WesternLensman with the heading "WATCH: The Democrat Open Borders Plan to Entrench Single-Party Rule Explained in Under Two Minutes."[520]

1. Flood the country with untold millions of illegals by land, sea, and air from all over the world, enough to eclipse the populations of thirty-six individual US states.

2. Prioritize the needs of these millions of non-citizens over the needs of American citizens, with free flights, busses, hotels, meals, and phones, ensuring their loyalty to the political party that imported them.

3. Keep them in the country at all costs, even when they commit violent crime like murder and rape. Attack the language used to attack the criminals, as opposed to the criminals themselves. Slander critics as racists.

4. Ensure their privileges are made irrevocable with city and state sanctuary laws that act as population magnets. Codify permanent status and ensure non-cooperation with ICE.

5. Count the non-citizens in the census that will determine congressional apportionment in the House of Representatives. As of now, that would equal thirteen extra congressional districts, a tremendous amount of electoral power.
6. Wage a massive, heavily funded lawfare campaign to change state voting laws that legalize mass mail-in ballots—no signature verification and no proof of citizenship requirements, making it nearly impossible to prove voter fraud.
7. Lock in the permanent voting majority with campaign promises of lavish benefits and permanent privileges, enshrining generational fealty to the Democrat Party.
8. Win elections.
9. Entrenched single-party rule has been achieved.

This tweet perfectly summarizes everything this book is proving. But every time you think it couldn't get worse, leave it to the Left. It can always get worse, at least until their ultimate goal is accomplished. Obama-appointed US district judge Sharon Johnson Coleman ruled on March 8, 2024, that Heriberto Carbajal-Flores, an illegal alien with no right to carry a gun, had his rights violated when he was arrested for possession of a gun and ammunition.

Carbajal-Flores's legal team argued that he had a clean record in the US and only carried the firearm to protect himself and his property. Coleman wrote in her decision:

> The government argues that Carbajal-Flores is a noncitizen who is unlawfully present in this country. The court notes, however, that Carbajal-Flores has never been convicted of a felony, a violent crime, or a crime involving the use of a weapon. Even in the present case, Carbajal-Flores contends that he received and used the handgun solely for self-protection and protection of property during a time of documented civil unrest in the Spring of 2020.[521]

While one might have sympathy with Carbajal-Flores, given all that has been happening, illegal aliens do not have the same rights as US citizens. Judicially awarding them rights undermines our tripartite system of government and the rule-of-law, as this judge, and certainly the defense attorneys, must know. It has severely skewed the Supreme Court *Bruen* decision, where it argued that the right to keep and bear arms "is consistent with this nation's historical tradition of firearm regulation." Subsequent decisions by lower courts will be used to further undermine that decision.

This opens the door for every illegal coming to the US to feel entitled to carry firearms. Some of the Chinese nationals already do, apparently. And since illegals have publicly stated their desire to wreak havoc in America, this does a great job of facilitating the Left's agenda to make America an ungovernable anarchy. That in turn will give them the pretext they have been seeking for decades to abolish the Second Amendment and seize the firearms of legal citizens.

Federal legislation, which includes amnesty, has been proposed repeatedly since 2001 but has not passed yet. The Democrats are relentless. Given amnesty, the population of illegals already here is enough to create a one-party nation in the US for the foreseeable future. In the 2020 elections, 66 percent of Hispanics voted Democrat.[522] Vast demographic changes have occurred throughout our nation as a direct result of the wave of both legal and illegal immigration. The 2020 election showed many Republicans in previously safe seats winning by razor-thin margins. Of course, that implies that illegals had a profound impact.

For example, deep-red Texas may not remain so for long. The table below shows the radical demographic changes that have occurred in the Lone Star State since 1980. Texas is now a minority majority state. The Hispanic population has increased over 300 percent since 1980 and currently exceeds that of whites, who were 65.7 percent of the population in 1980 but now comprise only 39.8 percent of the population.

Texas Population 1980 to 2022

	White	Hispanic	Black	Other	Total
1980	9,350,297	2,985,824	1,692,562	200,508	14,229,191
%Total	65.7%	21.0%	11.9%	1.4%	100.0%
1990	10,291,680	4,339,905	1,976,360	378,565	16,986,510
%Total	60.6%	25.5%	11.6%	2.2%	100.0%
2000	11,074,716	6,669,666	2,364,255	743,183	20,851,820
% Total	53.1%	32.0%	11.3%	3.6%	100.0%
2022	12,140,314	12,262,327	4,087,442	2,013,218	30,503,301
% Total	39.8%	40.2%	13.4%	6.6%	100.0%

Source: Census Bureau.

The primary factors keeping Texas red are (1) low turnout among Hispanics and other minorities and (2) a large proportion of illegal aliens, only some of whom attempt to vote. Although it must be added that the more established Hispanics in Texas tend to vote Republican more than elsewhere. The "other" category has almost quadrupled since 2000. Under former president Obama, Texas surpassed California as the largest refugee resettlement state, which was no doubt deliberate, but many more categories of minority whose immigration status is not specified make up the "other" numbers.

Democrats have been engaged in a full-throated effort to register low-turnout minorities and immigrants in Texas for years and even try to register non-citizens, including pre-checking the US citizen box on voter registrations and urging non-citizens to vote. Some have voted.[523]

California's rapid descent into third-world status is also explained by the next table. The white population has actually declined as increasing taxes, regulation, rampant homelessness, and the massive increase in illegal aliens and their associated costs have driven them out in a dramatic example of "white flight." Whites now comprise only 34.7 percent of the total population. Because of the illegal population, California is now home to 30 percent of the nation's homeless.[524] California Democrats have created their own crisis strategy by making the state a magnet for illegals.

California Population 1980 to 2023

	White	Hispanic	Black	Other	Total
1980	15,763,992	4,544,331	1,783,810	1,575,769	23,667,902
%Total	66.6%	19.2%	7.5%	6.7%	100.0%
1990	17,029,126	7,687,938	2,092,446	2,950,511	29,760,021
%Total	57.2%	25.8%	7.0%	9.9%	100.0%
2000	15,816,790	10,966,556	2,181,926	4,906,376	33,871,648
%Total	46.7%	32.4%	6.4%	14.5%	100.0%
2023	13,383,496	15,543,369	2,506,995	7,135,293	38,569,153
%Total	34.7%	40.3%	6.5%	18.5%	100.0%

Source: Census Bureau.

The state currently faces an unrecoverable combined state and local debt of $1.6 trillion or about $125,000 per household. Not to be deterred, Governor Newsom wants to add another $6 billion for "the homeless."[525] The illegal alien population literally mires the state in intractable problems that the liberal political establishment meets with ever more deficit spending.

Despite these facts, former California governor Jerry Brown made it worse by declaring California a sanctuary state and signed numerous bills protecting illegal aliens, including violent felons, from being removed by Immigration and Customs Enforcement (ICE). He called opponents of his actions "low-life politicians."[526]

It was not always so. When the Vietnam War ended and some 130,000 Vietnamese refugees were granted asylum in the US by President Gerald Ford, then governor Jerry Brown—yes, the same one—vigorously opposed Vietnamese refugees coming to his state. Why? Brown said he had too many Hispanics already, too many on welfare, and too much unemployment. "There is something a little strange about saying, 'Let's bring in 500,000 more people' when we can't take care of the 1 million [Californians] out of work," he said.[527]

Brown even tried to prevent aircraft carrying Vietnamese refugees from landing at Travis Air Force Base. According to an NPR report, "They didn't want these people."[528]

Brown was joined in this protest by his then secretary of Health and Welfare, Mario Obledo. Obledo co-founded the Mexican American Legal Defense and Education Fund (MALDEF), one of the most virulent open-borders organizations. In 1998, Obledo said, "California is going to be a Hispanic state and anyone who doesn't like it should leave. If they [whites] don't like Mexicans, they ought to go back to Europe."[529]

And they call the rest of us "racists."

Many other prominent Democrats supported Brown and Obledo, including Joe Biden, who tried to stall refugee legislation in Congress. Liberal New York representative Elizabeth Holtzman said that "some of her constituents felt that the same assistance and compassion was not being shown to the elderly, unemployed and poor in this country."[530]

Why did Democrats so adamantly oppose refugee resettlement then? Because *those* refugees were fleeing Communism. And it is a certain bet Democrats thought the Vietnamese—many of whom fought alongside US forces in the Vietnam War—would be more likely to vote Republican. When Joe Biden finally did support refugee resettlement legislation in 1980, it was when the emphasis on saving victims of Communism was no longer part of the goal, and in fact, the refugee resettlement bill flipped the emphasis from refugees fleeing Communism to welcome radicals fleeing their home countries to avoid arrest.

UCLA professor Marcelo Suárez-Orozco has said, "Where L.A. goes is where the rest of the state goes and where the rest of the country goes. We announce, demographically speaking, the future for the rest of the country."[531]

He is right. These demographic changes are occurring all over the nation as shown below and will guarantee that "demographics is destiny" if nothing changes. The Left will get its "permanent progressive majority," and the US will become the last domino to fall in the international Communist quest for world domination. It will throw our nation and the world into a depth of darkness from which it may never return.

US Population 1980 to 2023

	White	Hispanic	Black	Other	Total
1980	180,256,103	14,608,673	26,104,285	5,576,744	226,545,805
%Total	79.6%	6.4%	11.5%	2.5%	100.0%
1990	188,128,296	22,354,059	29,216,293	9,011,225	248,709,873
%Total	75.6%	9.0%	11.7%	3.6%	100.0%
2000	194,552,774	35,305,818	33,947,837	17,615,477	281,421,906
%Total	69.1%	12.5%	12.1%	6.3%	100.0%
2023	197,264,873	63,968,745	45,548,426	28,132,851	334,914,895
%Total	58.9%	19.1%	13.6%	8.4%	100.0%

Source: Census Bureau.

However, there may be a silver lining. The Left aways overplays its hand. That is because they really are lunatics. They have been getting away with everything, so their agenda just gets wilder and wilder—utterly unglued from reality. Sooner or later, it starts dawning on people, even those the Democrats are hoping will deliver their "permanent progressive majority," that their policies are just too extreme. As described by Michael Lind in *Tablet*:

> Unfortunately for the Democratic Party's pro-mass-immigration coalition of the declining, many immigrants and their children are deserting both the party and the cities and states that it rules. Having counted on Hispanic immigrants and their descendants to compensate for the exodus of the white working class, Democrats were shocked in December 2023 by a Reuters/Ipsos poll that showed Hispanics favoring Trump over Biden by 38% to 37%. An even more recent *USA Today* and Suffolk University poll has Trump leading Biden among Hispanic voters 39%-34%. Trump's share of the national Hispanic vote rose from 28% in 2016 to 36% in 2020. In Texas, ground zero of America's immigration crisis, the number of

Hispanics who identify as Democrats fell from 63% in 2019 to 54% in 2022.[532]

Lind neglected to mention the black vote. But this is a major reason Democrats support open borders. They know their support among blacks is also declining, though not as dramatically as working-class whites. Considering what the Democrats have done to black America, it is surprising it took so long. According to one poll, Trump now enjoys support from 17 percent of blacks, double the support he received in 2016, and that year was a recent record.[533] According to a *New York Times*/Siena poll, Trump's support among blacks is 23 percent.[534] That is a seismic change.

MAKING TAXPAYERS A MINORITY

Hence a wise general makes a point of foraging on the enemy. One cartload of the enemy's provisions is equivalent to twenty of one's own, and likewise a single picul of his provender is equivalent to twenty from one's own store.

—Sun Tzu

The "progressive" income tax was supposedly created to make it "fairer" for low-income people, but as with all things the Left does, this is a smoke screen. We are all painfully familiar with the Left's class warfare rhetoric. The "rich" don't pay their fair share, they claim. Democrats raise this issue all the time. Left-wing pundits ceaselessly repeat the mantra. In 2012, then vice president Joe Biden added his annoying voice to the chorus, saying that he wanted a tax code where "everyone, and I mean *everyone*, has skin in the game and no one gets played for a sucker."[535] He has made similar statements many times since. Meanwhile, a Congressional Research Service report shows he may owe up to $500,000 in taxes he avoided by improperly classifying income.[536]

Actually, the "rich" have much more skin in the game than anyone else, and more and more, they are looking like the real suckers. The following table never gets play in the mainstream media. You will see immediately why.

Table 8. Distribution of Income Taxes Paid—2021

	Adjusted Gross Income ($ bil.)	Income Taxes Paid ($ bil.)	Group's Share of Total AGI	Group's Share of Income Taxes
All Taxpayers	$14,742.2	$2,193.2	100.0%	100.0%
Top 1%	$3,872.4	$1,004.1	26.3%	45.8%
Top 5%	$6,182.2	$1,439.7	42.0%	65.6%
Top 10%	$7,745.5	$1,662.6	52.6%	75.8%
Top 25%	$10,613.6	$1,956.9	72.1%	89.2%
Top 50%	$13,191.2	$2,141.9	89.2%	97.7%
Bottom 50%	$1,531.0	$51.2	10.4%	2.3%

Source: Tax Foundation.[537]

These are the latest data available. While the top 1 percent of tax-payers earned 26.3 percent of all adjusted gross income in the US in 2021, they pay almost half of the total tax bill. The top 10 percent pay 76 percent of the tax bill, and the top 25 percent pay almost 90 percent. In fact, the top 50 percent of American taxpayers pay 98 percent of all income taxes. The bottom half pay almost nothing, and within those income brackets, many get tax credits in excess of what they pay, so in some cases, they effectively have negative income tax rates. This, by the way, is a back door form of the guaranteed income advocated by Cloward and Piven.

Now, the Democrats will respond that even the poorest workers pay the payroll tax. But this is a straw man argument. The payroll tax funds Social Security, a retirement program, not an entitlement. Those taxes will become a benefit when those workers retire. And there are already many redistributive elements built into Social Security that dispropor-tionately benefit lower income retirees. But the Left has been trying to abolish the payroll tax for lower income people as well.

The Left also makes another false argument. What's the difference, they ask, between them wanting to provide more government benefits to their voting demographic and Republicans rewarding their voting demographic by cutting taxes? There is one very fundamental difference: the Left is confiscating tax revenues paid by income earners and redistributing it to those who didn't earn it, and they continually look to find new beneficiaries—for example, illegal aliens—to expand the voting base they otherwise could not obtain legitimately. Cutting taxes, on the other hand, just returns income to its rightful owners. Tax cuts don't take away anything from anyone. They put the money back where it belongs, and by the way, where it will do the most good for the economy. Don't let the Left get away with that argument.

The Left has worked for years to increase the percentage of taxes paid by those in the upper income brackets while eliminating taxes to those in lower brackets. It is another divide and conquer strategy. When Democrats charge that "the rich aren't paying their fair share," as Joe Biden repeatedly has, it provokes envy and animosity from the poor, who have bought into the Left's phony argument that the "rich" have been keeping them down.

It also angers taxpayers, who resent being falsely accused of not paying enough. They pay *a lot*, and for the most part aren't even "rich." The top 25 percent for example, represent those earning $94,440 per year or more. The threshold for the top 50 percent is a mere $46,637 per year. Only the top 10 percent and above are earning $169,800 or more, and even that is not really big money for a family of four these days, especially when you consider that their after-tax income will be on average about 20 percent less.[538]

But the Democrats' real objective with this class warfare tactic is to push taxpayers into the minority, with those paying no taxes in the majority.[539] This is apparent from the chart below, which shows changes in the income tax burden on the bottom 50 percent over the past three decades. The Democrats have been able to gradually lower the tax rate for the lower half to almost zero while pushing the rate on the top 50 percent close to 100 percent. Yes, they have had help from feckless

Republicans, who cringe when Democrats accuse them of pandering to the "greedy rich." The Party of Stupid keeps showing its colors.

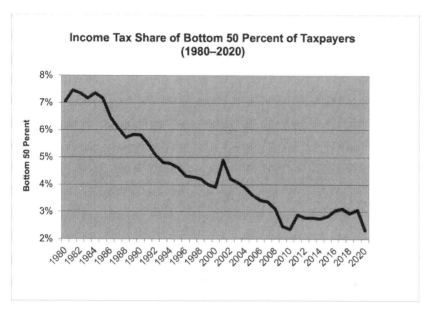

Source: Internal Revenue Service.

If Democrats can get over 50 percent of income earners paying no taxes, taxpayers will become effectively disenfranchised. They will be a captive minority, working to support the tax-free majority, who will have a strong vested interest in voting Democrat to keep things that way. It is yet another way Democrats seek to enslave America. Apparently, they haven't really changed much from the old days. Their slave state mentality has just taken a different form.

But even this is just an intermediate stage. As a shrinking taxpayer base is increasingly squeezed for ever more revenue, while a growing legion of welfare recipients survive on the proceeds, the economy will move inexorably toward crisis and collapse.

Today, as our economy continues to languish, Obama's disastrous economic policies are driving more and more people out of the labor force. The welfare rolls are exploding as poverty spreads to the general population. The civilian labor force grew continuously from 1948 to

2008 at about 1 percent per year on average. Since 2008, it has been essentially flat, growing seven-tenths of 1 percent since its prior peak in October 2008. This flat line is dramatized in the chart below, which shows labor force data since 2000.

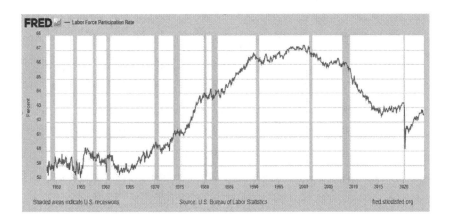

The employment/population ratio in the next chart   shows   the alarming downward trend in employment relative to the overall population. In the 1970s and 1980s, both baby boomer employment and increased labor force participation by women boosted this ratio. With baby boomers retiring, and women working less, this ratio was on a downward trend, but it has been greatly exacerbated by the 2008 recession and the actions the Obama administration has taken since, with many people leaving the labor force for lack of employment opportunities.

Civilian Employment Population Ratio

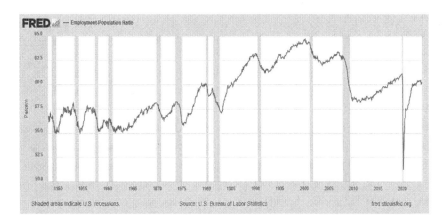

Full-time private sector employment is the best measure of our economic health. While approximately 17 percent of the labor force works part-time, it makes up a small percentage of total income generated. Approximately 160.8 million people were employed full-time as of February 2024, according to the Bureau of Labor Statistics. This includes 21.1 million federal, state, and municipal employees and 139.7 million employed in the private economy.[540] Government does not produce income. Individuals employed in the productive, private economy pay the salaries of government employees and all government programs through taxes and debt (which is merely future taxes). So the burden of government falls almost entirely on this group. In 2023, government spending at all levels totaled $9.5 trillion.[541] That translates to $68,000 per full-time private sector worker. Total national debt in 2023 was an estimated $36.4 trillion, is over 130 percent of GDP, and translates to over $260,000 per private sector employee.[542]

Under the enormous strains of spending, taxation, and regulation, it is obvious that the monstrous, growing cancer of government cannot be sustained by this diminishing private sector. President Biden has weaponized government spending, and his administration seeks to do still more. His efforts, however, have been assisted by a multi-front, decades-long offensive using welfare to enslave minorities and a nonstop campaign of racist propaganda to keep them seething with resentments and feeling entitled to more.

Other Democratic politicians and pundits hype this narrative. For example, following the Ferguson, Missouri, police shooting of Michael Brown, a Troy, New York, Democratic city councilwoman claimed in an internet comment that she thought police behavior was "leading to rounding up and executing of us as a people...." She asked, "Does America want to have a race war? Or we being baited [sic] for a systematic change in how Blacks are dealt with in this country?"[543] According to John Tedesco, Troy chief of police, her activism and that of other local race-baiters has prevented Troy police from aggressively combating a recent increase in homicides.[544]

The continuing crisis has enflamed passions to a fever pitch. Our nation is like a tinder box just waiting for the match. It remains to be seen if the poor's "burden" becomes so heavy, our nation collapses under its own weight, or if, as Cloward and Piven hoped, the fever of resentments gets so hot, it ignites a blazing revolution. Perhaps both will occur. In the stifling calm before the storm, we can hear Nechayev's *Catechism* echoing from the past:

> The Society [of revolutionary conspirators] has no aim other than the complete liberation and happiness of the masses.... Convinced that...the achievement of this happiness can only come about as a result of an all-destroying popular revolt, the Society will use all its resources and energy toward increasing and intensifying the evils and miseries of the people until at last their patience is exhausted and they are driven to a general uprising.

The Left has weaponized the poor. The issue is never the issue.

WHY DO THEY DO IT?

*A socialist America would be the greatest
calamity for the future of mankind.*
—Milovan Djilas, Yugoslavian dissident
and former vice president of Yugoslavia

There is nothing new under the sun. Mature adults understand this intuitively. While we make amazing technological advances every day, human beings are, and have always been, human, that is, imperfect. We are not gods and can never be. But since the dawn of time, there have always been people whose ambitions, egos—and occasionally, talent—drive them to believe that they possess some unique insight or mighty ability that sets them apart. This conceit can be traced as far back as the early Greek philosophers and doubtless to the beginning of human history.[545] It is the temptation for all time, the ego trip of all ego trips, that "ye shall be as gods" (Gen. 3:5 KJV).

This temptation's most recent expression, Communism, or today's euphemism, "progressivism," or even "wokeism," has increasingly infected Western society for over 150 years. This is the mind of the progressive. He sees himself as the messianic savior of the world. Before Communism was ever imposed in the real world, the true believers could always indulge themselves in the fantasy of what their ideal Communist world would look like. And no one could dissuade them from this fantasy, because it is exceedingly difficult to discredit an idea that has never been tried, even if its folly is obvious to others.

Revolutionary Catechism author Sergey Nechayev justified his agenda based on fantasies of a revolutionary future, but there was no practical, real-world experience with Communism yet to spoil his delusions. Today's progressives have no such excuse. The complete failure of Socialist systems is indisputable, whether measured by real world or even Socialist standards. It produces misery, inequality, injustice, and unmatched economic and environmental calamity.

The late Yugoslavian dissident Milovan Djilas, who went on to become vice president of Yugoslavia, said as far back as 1988, "Communism (or 'socialism') as a *realistic* blueprint for running human society is nonsense and dangerous nonsense at that. 70 years of Communist history make it incumbent upon us to record this simple conclusion as a fact and a warning."[546]

Yet many Americans, mostly youthful idealists, continue to genuinely believe that Socialism can work. Having spent his life under the shadow of Communism in a "Socialist" nation of the East Bloc, Djilas knew better. He gave a lecture at Princeton University in 1968, and his observations reveal how ignorant American university students were— even at an Ivy League school like Princeton. They are doubtless even more ignorant today:

> In 1968 I was asked to meet a group of leftist students at Princeton University. The unrest on American campuses was riding high. The students assured me that within four years the USA would be "socialist." American socialism, they said, would of course be different— it would be a developed kind of socialism, without censorship, without repression, without a bankrupt economy, and so on. This put me on my guard."

Djilas told students:

> "I don't really believe that the USA will be socialist by 1972," I said. "In any case, I very much hope that it will

not be." "How can you say that," the students asked. "Because," I answered, "a socialist America would be the greatest calamity for the future of mankind. America is a rich and advanced country, and it has the means and the skills to build what would appear to be a working model of 'socialism.' If it did, a socialist USA would send a false message to the rest of the world that there is such a thing as good and workable socialism, whereas there isn't."[547]

Yet the Left has become, if anything, shriller, more demanding, and more self-righteous. They are driven by a galling sense of superiority. They know better and can defy the verdict of history because people as smart as they are weren't around when Russia, China, Vietnam, Cambodia, North Korea, Ethiopia, Angola, Zimbabwe, Zambia, Congo, Nicaragua, Cuba, Venezuela, and others went Red. All those countries just did it wrong. American leftists are certainly smarter than *that*.

As young idealists, living well in affluent, capitalist America, it is all theoretical, so they can indulge their fantasies while promoting this destructive agenda with impunity—all while living large in our market economy. For these people, ignorance is literally a blessing, for if they soberly analyzed their ego-driven beliefs, they would be embarrassed.

We have lost any remaining shred of innocence about the nature of our government and political class. Under Obama and Biden, we have seen lawmakers directly defy our objections and pass sweeping legislation that threatens to fundamentally restructure our society. With countless spending bills, we have witnessed national debt grow to historic proportions. We have watched in stunned silence as the Biden administration legislates by executive order.

Meanwhile, our foreign policy has unleashed chaos across the globe and made us the laughingstock of the world. Add the endless list of scandals that grows daily as some new outrage is unearthed. While all this occurs, Congress and the national media stand idly by. This is no accident. The Left is relentlessly pursuing Nechayev's destructive ambition aimed at "*increasing and intensifying the evils and miseries of the people until at last their patience is exhausted....*"

This has been a jarring revelation for many Americans. As the extreme nature of the Democrat agenda has become more obvious, people who never cared about politics have taken to the streets. People who wouldn't dream of speaking ill of anyone have been seen at town hall meetings pounding their fists and shouting in protest. This includes the young, middle aged, and even the elderly, using walkers, canes, and crutches—people of all colors and backgrounds. What is their answer? We are all domestic terrorists! Especially those damned Catholics!

Government has been encroaching on our lives for decades, but when first Barack Obama, and now Biden, came along, it exploded. Discussing the gradual expansion of government used to be a largely academic exercise, the sole preserve of people interested in politics, but as the size and scope of government ballooned, Americans began to experience firsthand the awesome, terrible power of government to crush civil society by crowding out the private sector and curtailing individual rights, civil liberties, and economic freedoms. In large swaths of society, it has begun to sink in that however much you may try to ignore government, government never ignores you.

But none of this information satisfactorily answers one key, nagging question. *Why?* Why do they do this? What is the endgame? Everywhere and always, the Left's honest answer—in those rare instances when they are willing to be honest—is that Socialist fantasy future, *the revolution.*

Soberly analyzed, however, *this answer is inane.* It is entirely inadequate. For Socialism, sooner or later, everywhere and always, *kills.* It destroys. It cannot do otherwise. Socialism is an ideology that forces society to feed on itself, taking from the economy until there is nothing left to take. As the late former British prime minister Margaret Thatcher once said, "Socialist governments traditionally do make a financial mess. They always run out of other people's money."[548]

Admittedly, Socialist policies can seem harmless enough when first introduced. In a nation with an otherwise healthy economy, Socialism's destructive nature is temporarily masked. Buoyed by affluence, the nation can initially withstand some Socialism, digesting pieces of it for a while. The US and western Europe provide good examples of economies that can thrive to an extent *despite* some anti-market, Socialist policies.

But Socialism is like a python that slowly squeezes the life out of its prey. It creeps ever more into mainstream policymaking, and new Socialist-inspired programs become the order of the day, along with the taxes and regulation that necessarily accompany them. With each new failure, the answer is always more government and more money. The economy becomes moribund and slowly creaks to a halt. There are fundamental economic reasons for this, but it is really very simple: you can't get something for nothing.

If free market policies are not instituted to turn things around, i.e., lower taxes, loosened regulation, and reduced government spending—as President Trump did in his first four years—eventually, the whole monstrosity collapses on itself. Remember, this is the plan Cloward and Piven articulated. It is happening today, and we can see it coming. Even those Scandinavian countries always touted as models of Socialism have gotten by, as the late P. J. O'Rourke quipped, "through the novel expedient of not practicing it."[10] Ultimately, Socialism fails. Always. It has to, for it advocates an economic system based entirely on false premises. And in Communist countries, the victims can be counted in the millions.

But we still haven't answered the key question: Why? Why do they go through such trouble, only to construct an untenable economic system that pauperizes the country and savages those very people they claim to represent? If the economy crashes, they suffer too, don't they? Are they insane? For such a well-organized lot, a movement dedicated for 150 years to overthrowing the existing order, you'd think they'd have an endgame. Even radical organizer Saul Alinsky said, "The price of a successful attack is a constructive alternative."

Who on earth are these people? Are they "useful idiots," as Soviet leader Vladimir Lenin reputedly called them—people whose misguided

---

[10]   P. J. O'Rourke, *Eat the Rich*. In truth, these countries are more socialized, with, for example, a government-run medical system, but they are more and more feeling the negative effects as the adverse incentives such policies create work their way through the system. But these problems go largely unreported by the press.

compassion, egotism, and vanity have tricked them into believing they are forging a liberating utopia for the "oppressed of the earth"? Are they blind fanatics, so obsessed with their agenda that they will work against their own interests to see it to fruition? Are they arrogant, hypocritical elitists who think their ideas are so beneficial to society that they should get special dispensation and don't have to abide by their own oppressive edicts? Are they vengeful sociopaths, more interested in destruction than their own futures? Are they power-mad despots, lusting for absolute control, or are they merely seedy, corrupt thugs who see a fortune to be made in seizing the levers of power?

The simple answer is, "Yes."

All of the above are true. However, the key thing to understand is that it is no accident. The Left must be seen as a single amorphous organism with many operating parts, nominally independent but ultimately moving in the same direction toward the same end. Like a giant amoeba, one segment may move one way and a second another, but the whole organism moves slowly forward as one, and when prey is detected, all come together to encircle it. And every member of the Left has a part to play in this drama, wittingly or otherwise. Every single progressive who ever lived, every single true believer who risked reputation, jail, even life for this cause was ultimately in the service of an evil that has utilized these people for its own malevolent purposes.

POLITICAL PONEROLOGY: THE FOUNTAIN OF EVIL

Most analyses of Marxism-Leninism are philosophical exercises conducted in the intellectual stratosphere. This approach has a limited utility, but is based on a deeply flawed premise: that Marxism-Leninism is a form of high theory, rather than an operational code for a new-style mafia, far more interested in finding a rationale for seizing or wielding power than in liberating "prisoners of starvation" or the "wretched of the earth."[549]
—John P. Roche, advisor to JFK and Lyndon Johnson

onerology is the study of evil. The term comes from the New Testament Greek word *poneros*, which means great evil, corruption, especially moral corruption, or a "wicked one," i.e., Satan.[550] Polish psychologist Andrew M. Lobaczewski coined the term. Following the imposition of Communism in Eastern Europe, he collaborated secretly with a small group of Polish, Hungarian, and Czechoslovakian scientists who observed and studied the Communist leaders in an effort to understand the totalitarianism that confronted them. The secret police watched these scientists closely, and one of them died under suspicious circumstances.

The Polish Communist leaders were Lobaczewski's petri dish and were highly mistrustful of him. In 1968, he threw the first edition of his manuscript in a furnace minutes before the secret police came to search his residence. The second edition was given to an American tourist who promised to take it to the Vatican, but it simply disappeared. He emigrated to America in 1977 after a Radio Free Europe correspondent he had shared some of his ideas with denounced him to authorities. He was given the option of jail or exile. He chose the latter and left Poland for New York with nothing. Polish secret police alerted the Communist network in New York, and they prevented him from finding any meaningful work in his field. He got a job as a laborer and wrote his book at night.

He completed the book in 1984, *Political Ponerology: The Science of Evil, Psychopathy, and the Origins of Totalitarianism.*[551] However, publishers refused to take it. He even approached fellow Pole, Zbigniew Brzezinski, President Carter's former national security advisor (and father to that horror, *Morning Joe* co-host, Mika Brzezinski). Brzezinski blew him off. In Lobaczewski's own words, "he strangled the matter."[552] He was finally able to publish the book in 2006, one year before his death. It is an absolutely brilliant dissection of the totalitarian impulse.

In it, he argues that radical political ideologies, whether fascism, Communism, or anarchism, are not the drivers of totalitarian systems but rather simply the window dressing that attracts and allows ambitious psychopaths to insinuate themselves into positions of power and wealth.

That is the true goal of totalitarians everywhere: *power and wealth.* But it is never the earned kind. It is stolen, taken by people with extreme psychological disorders, literal psychopaths, who have convinced themselves that they are entitled and are willing to commit—even enjoy committing—mass murder to get their way. And the individual revolutionaries attracted to these violent ideologies are themselves so untrustworthy, unethical, and driven, only the worst of them rise to the top in this cesspool of monsters. I describe them as "Jeffrey Dahmers in Tweeds." Tucker Carlson's recent interview with Vladimir Putin was utterly pointless for this reason. Putin is a murdering sociopath. You can't trust a word he says.

In the foreword to Lobaczewski's book, Dr. Michael Rectenwald summarizes one of his insights:

> Lobaczewski explains that totalitarian ideology operates on two levels; the terms of the original ideology are taken at face value by true believers, while the party insiders substitute secondary meanings for the same terms, and normal people are subjected to gaslighting. Only the cognoscenti, the psychopaths, know and understand the secondary meanings. They recognize that actions purportedly undertaken on behalf of "the workers" translate into the domination of the party and state on behalf of the psychopaths themselves. The truth is the opposite of what the party insiders claim to be the case, and they know it. Political Ponerology thus explains the origin of "doublespeak," which [George] Orwell portrays so well [in his novel, *1984*].[553]

The things happening in today's American society can only be described as evil. While one political party promotes open borders, the floods of people and drugs are literally killing us. The fentanyl-driven overdose epidemic is taking over one hundred thousand lives per year, while criminal aliens commit murder and other crimes. Every single illegal alien who has committed murder in the US had an accomplice: the Democratic Party. Joe Biden and all those others promoting open borders are accessories to murder. Likewise, the epidemic of overdose deaths can be laid at their feet.

Child trafficking threatens to become a bigger business than drug trafficking, and the mutilation and gender confusion of children being inflicted by the radical LGBTQ/transgender movement is literally barbaric. And consider the reaction to COVID, where the use of proven remedies like ivermectin and hydroxychloroquine were suppressed to the point where pharmacies would refuse to fulfill doctor prescriptions.

Some doctors who urged their use were banned from hospitals and even lost their licenses. Unheard of.

Meanwhile, anyone forced into the hospital was likely to die from the treatment, while family members were barred from even seeing them. Perhaps the most insane was NY governor Andrew Cuomo's order forcing elderly COVID patients back into retirement homes, thereby spreading the disease to the most vulnerable. At least six thousand died as a result.[554]

COVID pandemic policies, including the economic shutdowns, school closings, epidemic misinformation, and other COVID insanity, have been blamed for a spike in suicides in recent years. But there is much more to that. Suicides have been increasing for decades. Suicides among those aged ten to twenty-four increased 62 percent between 2007 and 2021, while from 2001 to 2007 there was no appreciable increase.[555] Suicide death rates among youths twelve to seventeen increased 47.7 percent from 2011 to 2021, and the rate for all demographic groups increased 24.9 percent.[556]

Suicides among military and former military members are at the highest rates ever and increased radically over the past five years. As of 2021, 30,177 military members had committed suicide since 9/11, over four times the number killed in combat during the same period![557] For the entire population, suicides reached their highest numbers ever in 2022.[558]

And consider the J6 prisoners accused of "insurrection." The treatment they are receiving in jail sounds like something out of medieval times. They are denied water, given unhealthy food, placed in solitary confinement, prevented from spending time outside, and even denied showers. Clothes sent out for cleaning are returned to them soiled with feces and urine, toilets don't work, and prison guards have been accused of beatings and even rape. It is reminiscent of jails in North Korea or the treatment of US POWs during the Vietnam War.

All this while Congress twiddles its thumbs, and media remains in stony silence. It's an indescribable outrage—while a year's worth of rioting, murder, and billions in destruction and theft by Antifa/BLM groups during the phony George Floyd "mostly peaceful protests" go uncommented and unaddressed. That was *true* insurrection.

This is but a partial description of the misery and uncertainty resulting from the astronomically rising chaos, division, and insanity being inflicted on American society today. Is betrayal by our leaders at the heart of so much depression among service members—who have watched friends die because of leadership incompetence or worse?

After twenty years in Afghanistan and over four thousand American deaths, the Biden administration abandoned that nation without warning, leaving thousands of US citizens, visa holders, and other US supporters stranded to be hunted down and killed by the Taliban. His administration even prevented others from attempting their rescue. At the same time, we abandoned Bagram Airfield in the middle of the night without even telling the Afghan leadership and left billions worth of military equipment to the Taliban. Getting thirteen military members killed at Karzai Airport was just icing on the cake. It is so horrific, it is difficult to actually believe. Our active-duty force is the smallest since 1940, and military recruitment is at record lows.[559] What a surprise. Who wants to join a military when its leaders are trying to kill you!

Human depravity seems to have sunk to a new low in America, but it is not new. As we have seen, it was a big part of the critical theorists' plan to "make the West so corrupt it stinks." And while they were at it, totalitarian regimes of the Nazis and Communists were giving us an object lesson in just how low governments could go—murdering their own citizens wholesale. We all know about Hitler's crimes but don't hear so much about the Communists. Is that simply an oversight, or because Communists are still doing it, and many people are actually cheering them on?

When Lenin's Bolsheviks took over Russia after the October 1917 coup, the depravity of their ideology could not be denied. Of course, it is still denied by true believers because they are addicted to their seductive fantasy. But true believers, Lenin's useful idiots, are merely tools—no longer the force behind the Communist movement, which is utterly corrupted and drunk with the power delivered into its hands.

And there it is: *the issue is never the issue*; the issue is always power. And power always has a byproduct: the opportunity for unearned wealth in the form of plunder. The true motive of the world "progressive" movement is power and plunder. We saw hints of that in Karl Marx's personal greed and lust for power, but it has since been proved again and again each time some unfortunate nation falls under the spell of Communism. But it is even worse than that. "Progressive" ideologies were invented by and to serve the ambitions of literal psychopaths.

What Is a Communist?

But isn't this all academic? Didn't Communism collapse in 1991? No, in fact, it didn't. It did not collapse, because *it has never existed*. Our collective understanding of Communism, Socialism, and progressivism is so far off the mark, we need to be rapidly re-schooled so our nation does not suffer the fate of so many others before it.

When the Soviet Union, the first full-fledged Communist state, emerged in 1917, it quickly became apparent that the leaders cared not a whit for the needs of the "proletariat," the "peasants," or anyone else except themselves and were willing to commit mass murder on an unprecedented scale to prove it.

Lenin decided that anyone not with him was against him, and everyone and anyone against him had to die.[560] Felix Dzerzhinsky (who came to be known as "Bloody Felix"), the founder of Lenin's dreaded Cheka,[11] initiated the Red Terror, a systematic campaign of official, state-sponsored terrorism and mass murder. Defenders of Lenin's killers like to claim the Red Terror was only instituted following an attempt on Lenin's life. While the Red Terror did not become official policy until September 5, 1918, following an attempt on Lenin's life by Fanny Kaplan, a Socialist revolutionary, in fact, it had begun almost immediately following Lenin's ascension to power the previous year.[561]

---

[11] Soviet Secret Police. "Cheka" was slang for VChK, the Russian acronym for the KGB's progenitor, the Soviet Extraordinary Commission for Combating Counterrevolution, Speculation and Sabotage. Though the KGB domestic operation has now been renamed the FSB, Russians still call it the *Cheka*.

In either case, it is a pretty thin reed on which to justify genocide. For perspective, the "oppressive" czarist regime the Bolsheviks sought to overthrow had put to death a total of 3,932 civilians for political activities between 1825 and 1917. Almost all of these were executed for insurrection between 1905 and 1908 following the 1905 Russian Revolution.[562] The death of Czar Alexander II in 1881 at the hands of one of Sergey Nechayev's revolutionary co-conspirators did not instigate any mass killings. Two of the conspirators committed suicide, one died in the explosion that killed the czar, and five of the eight living conspirators were hanged. The sixth, a pregnant woman, was to be sentenced to hard labor, but both she and the child died shortly after its birth. The seventh received twenty years, and the last, Vera Figner, remained at large and assassinated General Mayor Strelnikov in 1884. She served twenty years for that murder.[563]

Lenin's Communists executed more people in the first four months of his rule than czarist Russia had in the previous one hundred years.[564] Although official Cheka records claim 8,500 deaths in the first year, there were likely many more victims. Historians believe one hundred thousand or more were killed between 1918 and 1920, the years of the Red Terror.[565]

In addition to the terror campaign, disease and starvation were rampant. People living in cities fled or died. Moscow's population dropped 50 percent.[566] So many people left the cities in search of food that only one-third of the industrial workforce remained.[567] The mass migration was described as a human wave crossing the nation in search of food. The ensuing bloodbath of the following decades surpassed anything seen in history up to that time—and vastly outnumbered Hitler's body count. They were not liberating the oppressed of the earth; they were liberating the oppressed *from* the earth, delivering them to their maker way ahead of schedule.

And lest anyone rationalize that the Communists were just "breaking a few eggs to make an omelet,"[12] the Cheka did not merely execute its victims; it systematically carried out horrifying torture on a scale never seen before. Methods included: officially sanctioned rapes and beatings, gouging out eyes, scalping, sawing off joints, skinning alive, rolling naked victims in nail-studded barrels, pouring molten wax on the face, and other grisly innovations. One involved placing a rat inside a steel tube that was then closed at one end while the other end was placed against the victim's stomach. The tube was then heated and the rat escaped by gnawing through the victim.

Another involved walking prisoners, naked, into the streets of frigid Russian winters and dousing them with water until they turned into statues of ice. White Russian officers were lashed to boards and slowly fed into furnaces or boiling water. Priests were given communion with molten lead. Amputations, sexual mutilations, disemboweling, and other torture often preceded killing to maximize pain. Psychological terror included severe isolation, sleep deprivation, threats against relatives, and mock executions.[568]

It became apparent relatively quickly that Russia had fallen victim to a massive, deadly, ruthless, parasitic organism. No one was spared. All property, all wealth fell into Communist hands. Lenin began the process of preemptively labeling and exterminating entire classes of people, as Nechayev had specified in *Catechism*. Anyone suspected of merely having the potential to challenge Communist authority was rounded up and shot. Lenin stated: "We can't expect to get anywhere unless we resort to terrorism: speculators [anyone opposing the regime] must be shot on the spot."[569] Dzerzhinsky stated their intentions plainly in a 1918 interview:

> [The society and the press] think of the struggle with counterrevolution and speculation on the level of

---

[12] Although generally attributed to Stalin, the slogan had already been around for a while. But it was used by the Communists to rationalize their slaughter. *New York Times* reporter and Stalin apologist Walter Duranty supposedly loved to repeat the phrase regarding Stalin's mass murder, but it has also been attributed to Lazar Kaganovich, Stalin's enforcer. See: "Russia: Stalin's Omelette," *Time*, October 24, 1932.

normal state existence and for that reason they scream of courts, of guarantees, of inquiry, of investigations, etc. We have nothing in common with the military revolutionary tribunal. We represent in ourselves organized terror—this must be said very clearly.[570]

Those "oppressed of the earth," the beloved proletariat that Karl Marx had called "stupid boys, rogues, asses," were ground up in Lenin's genocide machine in record numbers. So Lenin was indeed a Marxist, at least in the sense that he shared Marx's contempt for those he was claiming to save. But Lenin was not a Communist; at least, not in the sense in which the word is usually understood.

But Lenin was indeed a Communist in the correct sense of the term. So then, what is Communism and what is a Communist? As with Socialism, one must distinguish between the *perception* and the *reality* of Communism. Let's look at some dictionary definitions:

> *Oxford English Dictionary*: a political theory derived from Karl Marx, advocating class war and leading to a society in which all property is publicly owned and each person works and is paid according to their abilities and needs.[571]

> The Free Dictionary: A theoretical economic system characterized by the collective ownership of property and by the organization of labor for the common advantage of all members.[572]

> *Merriam-Webster*: a way of organizing a society in which the government owns the things that are used to make and transport products (such as land, oil, factories, ships, etc.) and there is no privately owned property.[573]

> Dictionary.com: a theory or system of social organization based on the holding of all property in common, actual ownership being ascribed to the community as a whole or to the state.[574]

Note that these are the primary definitions representing Western culture's most common understanding of what the word means. Observe that some suggest a positive, even beneficial system. For example, the Free Dictionary claims Communism works "for the common advantage of all members." Wow! What have we been missing? *Oxford* claims, "Each person works and is paid according to their abilities and needs." Wow again! Wouldn't that be nice? Of course Marx never said that. He said, "*From* each according to his abilities, *to* each according to his needs." Marx was talking about confiscation of property, not voluntary charity. The other two definitions are blandly neutral.

There are secondary definitions that more closely approximate the reality of Communist systems, for example, *Merriam-Webster*'s alternatives include, "2. *b*: a totalitarian system of government in which a single authoritarian party controls state-owned means of production."[575] The primary definitions, however, often implicitly or explicitly pay tribute to the Left's delusional fantasies of Communist utopia—a testament to how deeply misperceptions of Communism have become entrenched in our society.

In the foreword to Igor Shafarevich's seminal work, *The Socialist Phenomenon*, Aleksandr I. Solzhenitsyn wrote, "The doctrines of socialism seethe with contradictions, its theories are at constant odds with its practice, yet due to a powerful *instinct*—also laid bare by Shafarevich—these contradictions do not in the least hinder the unending propaganda of socialism. *Indeed, no precise, distinct form of socialism even exists*; instead there is only a vague, rosy notion of something noble and good, of equality, communal ownership, and justice: the advent of these things will bring instant euphoria and a social order beyond reproach." (Emphasis added.)[576]

The reality of Socialism, i.e., *Communism*, is completely different. Wholesale confiscation of private property, barbaric mass murder, and torture are features of every single Communist country in the world. It is *doctrine*. A small cabal of leaders dictate policy in a smothering totalitarian dictatorship. Press is strictly controlled, and individual freedom is nonexistent except for those at the very top.

It turns out that Communism in practice is not a political doctrine based on Marxist economics at all but rather a system of strategies that capitalize on secular man's conceited aspirations to fix the world. Only secular man is attracted to this because truly religious people understand that it is not within humankind's capabilities to fix the world and would not be our job in any event. That job is reserved for God. Man's job is to apply his God-given talents to contribute to the world, but to think he can or should try to play God is laughable.

It is a titanic con game that enables a group of ambitious, unscrupulous, barbaric psychopaths to insinuate themselves into positions of power under the pretext of seeking "social justice for the poor and oppressed." Once entrenched, they rule ruthlessly for their own gain. Communism is gangsterism clothed in counterfeit morality.

Indeed, in the classic *Nomenklatura: The Soviet Ruling Class*, author Michael Voslensky writes, "Leninism, unlike Marxism, is not a theory or hypothesis, but a strategy and tactics for the seizure of power decked out in Marxist slogans."[577]

He adds, "True, it makes extensive use of quotations from the works of Marx and Engels, and employs Marxist terminology and some of Marx's ideas that suit its propaganda purposes. At the same time, it passes over in silence a whole series of Marxist principles, and some of his works are actually banned."[578]

Communist leaders are thus not "Communist" in the theoretical sense at all; they are simply pathological criminals who have discovered a very effective mechanism for power and control. But in fact, this is the true definition of Communism. Even Lenin knew it. In 1910, well before the revolution, he wrote, "'Our doctrine'—said Engels, referring to himself and his famous friend [Karl Marx]—'is not a dogma, but *a guide to action.*' This classical statement stresses with remarkable force and expressiveness that aspect of Marxism which is very often lost sight of." (Emphasis added.)[579]

Lenin was more interested in power and blood lust, but all subsequent Communist leaders have proven themselves just as interested in plunder—the motive of despots since the dawn of time, but with a twist. Its implementation requires the ambitions of sociopaths, willing, even eager, to commit mass murder. At its heart, this totalitarian impulse is pure evil.

Political ponerology is what we are confronting today—pure, satanic evil, delivered through the power and machinations of the political Left. We must see it for what it is. Call it wokeism, Socialism, "progressivism," or even Communism. All wind up in the same place: totalitarianism. If it succeeds in America, the world will awaken to a nightmare of unprecedented proportions that will require a miraculous act of God to overcome.

DEI AND THE
WEAPONIZATION OF CULTURE

*When misguided public opinion honors what is
despicable and despises what is honorable, punishes
virtue and rewards vice, encourages what is harmful
and discourages what is useful, applauds falsehood
and smothers truth under indifference or insult,
a nation turns its back on progress and can be
restored only by the terrible lessons of catastrophe.*
—French economist Frederic Bastiat

Michelle Obama recently tweeted: "@Beyonce you are a record-breaker and history-maker. With *Cowboy Carter*, you have changed the game once again by helping redefine a music genre and transform our culture. I am so proud of you!"[580]
So with Taylor Swift and Miley Cyrus, traditional country western music accelerated its slide into debauchery. Now Beyonce is trying to break into that brand, and Michelle's reference to redefining and transforming "cowboy culture" no doubt means taking the "racist," "misogynistic," traditionally conservative genre and turning it toward the degenerate, leftist popular culture, preoccupied with sex and obsessed

with "diversity," "equity," and "inclusion." It is all part of the "fundamental transformation" of society former president Obama referred to.

The Socialist concept of redistribution is captured in Marx's phrase "from each according to his ability to each according to his need." This is popularly perceived to mean income redistribution from rich to poor, with the imagined endpoint being perfect equality of incomes across society. This never happens, of course. In Socialist and Communist countries, it simply means that government determines the distribution of income, with the predictably massive corruption, theft, and misallocation of resources that occurs when despotic bureaucrats, rather than markets, make the decision. Whereas the self-deluded utopian dreamers can always fantasize a perfect world fixed by Socialism in the abstract, in practice, it always devolves into a kleptocracy. In fact, kleptocracy is and always has been the true objective.

Diversity, equity, and inclusion (DEI) prioritizes the advancement of targeted minority groups, parsed out by color, ethnicity, sexual orientation, or whatever other classification, over individual qualifications. DEI programs are now mainstream throughout our culture in corporations, schools and colleges, and entertainment. In a very extreme recent example, the FAA announced it was launching an aggressive effort to hire people that "include hearing, vision, missing extremities, partial paralysis, complete paralysis, epilepsy, severe intellectual disability, psychiatric disability and dwarfism."

Under normal circumstances, it might seem admirable to find work for such people. But this announcement came shortly after a door blew off a Boeing 737 Max 9 in midflight, forcing the aircraft to return to land. No one was injured, but it raised the issue of declining standards in all fields as concerns over DEI replace competence as a hiring standard.

Elon Musk tweeted, "Just had a conversation with some smart people could not believe this is happening."[581]

Actor James Woods tweeted, "Compassion is one thing, common sense another. At 35,000 feet, I'll opt for common sense."[582]

While there is nothing wrong with creating a jobs program for people with special needs, DEI standards are replacing competence in virtually all hiring decisions. And as the priorities shift, they develop their own momentum. This could indeed be the consequence for Boeing, which has been cited for an increasing number of safety issues.[583]

But the near assassination of President Trump is perhaps the most eye-popping example of just how dangerous DEI can be—literally a national security risk. The Secret Service director, Kim Cheatle—reportedly pushed for confirmation by Jill Biden—was clearly not up to the job.[584] In videos taken at the event, two of the female agents detailed to protect Trump were very short. One appeared overweight and out of shape, and struggled to holster her pistol. She looked more frightened than concerned with the task at hand. It must be said, however, that the poor planning and inadequate staffing for the Trump campaign could have also been politically motivated, as Cheatle made her contempt for Trump well-known. So it's difficult to decide in her case what is worse, partisan corruption that would deliberately minimize protection surrounding candidate Trump, or the appointment of a person clearly not up to the job.

DEI is nothing more than cultural Marxism, or more accurately, Critical Theory. It is based on the presumption that America is racist, white supremacist, imperialist, and the like and must be replaced. But this is entirely false. America is the most diverse, welcoming, and inclusive society in the world. And despite everything the Left does to weaken it, it thrives. People from all cultures and walks of life are free to follow their ambitions and are only stymied by the roadblocks the Left erects to prevent it.

You have heard the phrase, "A rising tide lifts all boats." But it is more accurate to say that America raises the level for all boats. Anyone can come here and make it if they are willing to work. The free market removes barriers to achievement. People in other cultures battle with each other because in most places, they do not have this freedom.

But here, your abilities can be recognized and all benefit. The desire to prosper overcomes longstanding prejudices and cultural barriers, because the strongest human instinct is that of survival, and when working with someone else, whatever their background, improves your prospects for survival and prosperity, you recognize it is more important and willingly engage.

Government is required to prevent people from integrating. Segregation in the South and apartheid in South Africa were maintained by laws. And it was economic pressure, as much as anything else, that caused those laws to crumble. Writing in *EconLib*, Thomas W. Hazlett states:

> The now-defunct apartheid system of South Africa presented a fascinating instance of interest-group competition for political advantage. In light of the extreme human rights abuses stemming from apartheid, it is remarkable that so little attention has been paid to the economic foundations of that torturous social structure. The conventional view is that apartheid was devised by affluent whites to suppress poor blacks. In fact, the system sprang from class warfare and was largely the creation of white workers struggling against both the black majority and white capitalists. Apartheid was born in the political victory of radical white trade unions over both of their rivals. In short, this cruelly oppressive economic system was socialism with a racist face.[585]

And how could the labor unions manage that? By creating a monopoly backed by government force.

Few understand that the Left's strategy is to apply redistribution universally, including based on minority or ethnic status, immigration status (e.g., to favor illegals), age, sex, sexual orientation, or any combination of these factors, also subdivided by geography within a town, city, county, state, region, or even between countries. The countries on the short end of the stick are without exception those of the West.

The Left is expert at creating new victim classes that are parsed into ever more diverse identity groups who develop a financial interest in promoting that identity. For example, sex change operations are now being promoted as a civil right, which will add further to the burgeoning costs of healthcare. The dark blue states of California, Maryland, Connecticut, and Massachusetts have enacted "transgender bathroom" laws, which allow K–12 children to choose which bathroom to use and which sports to participate in based on their self-determined sexual identity.[586]

Parents are confronted with tuition increases at some universities to accommodate the construction of transgender bathrooms, as well as the added costs of entire departments devoted to "gender identity" or LGBT studies. It should be added that students who enroll in such majors receive degrees that have little practical value other than to teach the same subject somewhere else—i.e., to spread propaganda. And in addition to paying higher taxes and direct service costs, we all support these movements with our routine purchases. For example, Campuspride.org, an LGBT campus advocacy group, receives financial support from Google, the SPLC, Starbucks, and others.[587]

This all has a number of benefits that serve the Left's agenda. Resources, land, and people can only be redistributed through the power of government, with ever-increasing amounts of wealth taken from taxpayers who earn their incomes from the private sector. This constant bleeding pushes working Americans toward penury and the economy toward crisis and collapse.

Because tax revenues are limited, available resources shrink with each new program, so each favored demographic must battle ever harder to maintain its share, putting us increasingly at war with ourselves. As the Left finds new demographics to reward, it creates ever more divisions within society, building animosity among all these groups until at some point, society must collapse into anarchy or civil war.

This is yet another reason the Left constantly seeks to enflame racial divisions as it did with the Trayvon Martin, Michael Brown, George Floyd, and other cases. For example, shortly after the Michael Brown shooting, Teaching for Change, an activist group that pushes radical education themes in public school, began promoting a lesson plan for the 2014–15 school year titled "Teaching about Ferguson" that hits all the Left's favorite mantras—racism, social justice, police brutality, oppression, and so forth—and even includes references to the Black Panthers' 1966 "10 Point Plan" and the teachings of Malcolm X.[588] Libs of TikTok reported one example of the terrible consequences:

In Hazelwood East High School, the district who won a DEI award in 2022 and the school where students beat a girl who's now in critical condition, just 5% of students are proficient in Math and just 21% in reading.[589]

There are countless similar examples. As the perceived benefactor of all these disparate groups, the Left expands its power and influence, and the entire political class is increasingly sucked into its orbit: join or become irrelevant. This partially explains the otherwise inexplicable support illegal alien amnesty is receiving among some quarters within the Republican Party. The GOP also gets a lot of money from corporate America—which is happy to replace American workers with foreigners, whether legal or illegal—that will work for half the price.

Those who protest are usually the ones who are paying the bills or who see the increasing balkanization of society as the threat it is. We are isolated and attacked as "racists," "sexists," "homophobes," "xenophobes," and so on—threatened to stony silence while this burgeoning parasite feeds off our decaying body politic. Using their growing political clout, the Left has further tightened the noose by passing "hate crimes" legislation that can make such criticism an actionable offense. In some other countries, it already is.[590]

Harry Potter author J. K. Rowling said she was willing to go to jail to defend her right to call men, men and women, women.[591] This was in reaction to the extreme criticism she received for objecting to a news report referring to a biological male as a woman simply because he is a cross-dresser using a female name.

"I'm so sick of this sh*t. This is not a woman," Rowling exclaimed in a tweet.[592] The twenty-six-year-old man, who goes by the name Scarlet Blake, was sentenced to life for killing another man. He will serve his time in an all-male prison. Four months earlier, he posted a video on social media of himself killing a cat then putting it in a blender. This is a truly sick person.

Rowling justifiably believes the trans movement is dangerous. "I can only say that I've thought about it deeply and hard and long. And I've listened, I promise, to the other side," she said. "And I believe, absolutely, that there is something dangerous about this movement, and it must be challenged."[593]

There have been five mass shootings since 2018 where the shooter identified as trans or "nonbinary."[594] The media claims this is not a trend, but it certainly looks like one. Is there any surprise that these mentally ill people are becoming more common when doctors are aggressively promoting sex reassignment to children, and teachers are pushing gender confusion to kids as young as kindergarteners? A Connecticut woman was recently sued by her school board for asking to see the materials they were teaching her kindergarten child.

In a recent video, Dr. Wallace Wong, a psychologist representing the World Professional Association for Transgender Health (WPATH), claimed that three-year-old children "knew their authentic self" better than their parents.[595] WPATH's "underlying principles" claim conversion therapies for children are harmful. Yet Dr. Wong encouraged a Canadian girl he began counseling in fifth grade to begin testosterone treatment in seventh grade, without her father's permission or knowledge.[596]

Her father, Robert Hoogland, became the target of an extended legal battle over his daughter when courts ordered him not to speak about the situation or attempt to detransition her. He spent two months of a six-month sentence in jail for defying the courts but finally won his right to speak out in 2023. However, he has not seen his daughter since 2019. He said the trans ideology and the Canadian legal system "destroys families and it destroyed mine. I'm hoping one day, when my child realizes, when she possibly detransitions—I'm waiting. I'm waiting with open arms for that day."[597] Hoogland was featured in the Matt Walsh documentary, *What Is a Woman?*

There are endless horrific stories of children being taken from their homes because parents don't want them to "transition." A good example is the Montana case of Jennifer Kolstad, a troubled girl who at fourteen was removed from her home by Child Protective Services because her parents refused to let her "transition." GOP governor Greg Gianforte agreed with CPS, despite a Montana law banning such surgeries. The *Daily Mail* reported, "On January 19, the couple lost custody of their daughter to CPS, who said that allowing Jennifer to be transgender is 'in her therapeutic interest' and that her parents are 'not following recommended therapy.'"[598]

Since Montana does not allow this, CPS moved her to a Wyoming facility for a month, where she was treated like a boy and addressed as "Leo," her preferred name. Ultimately, she will be moved to Canada to live with her biological mother, where presumably she will get the chemicals and surgery unavailable in Montana. Her birth mother abandoned her when she was very young. This woman was described by Jennifer and her sister as "uncaring, abusive and 'crazy.'"[599] So is this really in her best interest?

Polls have shown that most Americans disapprove of any kind of surgery, drugs, or behavioral changes for minors considering sex change operations, just as most disapprove of biological men competing in women's sports and laws allowing men to use women's restrooms. Some state legislatures are coming around to banning these things, but you can count on Democrat states to do just the opposite.

Colleges and corporations are falling into line with the radical Left's agenda as more and more of them create "diversity, equity, and inclusion" programs and offices. A 2024 study by Adam Andrzejewski's Open the Books found that the University of Virginia's DEI program costs $20 million per year, with salaries and benefits for top employees of $500,000 or more.[600] The program employs approximately 235 people. Following, reprinted with the permission of Open the Books, is a chart showing compensation for the top ten UVA DEI employees. For comparison, Virginia governor Glenn Younkin earns $175,000 annually.

UVA'S HIGHEST PAID DEI STAFF

NAME	TITLE	PAY	EST. TAXPAYER COST PAY + BENEFITS
MARTIN N. DAVIDSON	Senior Associate Dean & Global Chief Diversity Officer	$451,800	$587,340
KEVIN G. McDONALD	VP For DEI & Community Partnerships	$401,465	$521,905
TRACY M. DOWNS	Chief Diversity & Community Engagement Officer & Prof. of Urology	$312,000	$405,600
MARK STEVEN CARTWRIGHT	Senior Dir. of Procurement & Supplier Diversity Services	$224,375	$291,688
MEARA M. HABASHI	Associate Dean For DEI School of Engineering & Applied Science	$212,749	$276,574
KEISHA JOHN	Associate Dean For Diversity & Inclusion	$202,674	$268,476
RACHEL SPRAKER	Asst. VP For Equity & Inclusive Excellence	$186,800	$242,840
CHRISTIE JULIEN	Senior Asst. Dean, DEI	$177,700	$231,010
KIERAH BARNES	Dir. of Advanced Practice Diversity & Development	$172,000	$223,600
MARK CHRISTOPHER JEFFERSON	Asst. Dean for Community Engagement & Equity	$166,260	$216,138

Source: UVA FOIA

☑ LEARN MORE AT OPENTHEBOOKS.COM

California is now providing cash to kids to indoctrinate them into far-left radicalism. In the *Liberty Sentinel*, Alex Newman writes:

> Government schools in California are offering children large sums of taxpayer money to become social-justice warriors through a far-left extremist group that has been accused of anti-Semitism, sparking alarm among critics about how "education" has become cover for indoctrinating students and turning them into revolutionaries.

> The explosive scandal, first reported by *The Free Press*, was revealed thanks to contracts showing that Long Beach Unified School District gave $2 million to "Californians for Justice." The funding was used to offer $1,400 "stipends" to about 100 children in exchange for becoming radical activists. Other districts in the state are also involved.

The organization involved brags online about how it is a "youth-powered organization fighting for racial justice." In reality, it is a taxpayer-funded and taxpayer-powered outfit that is bilking taxpayers and using it to buy "youth activists" ready to promote an extreme left-wing agenda backed by politicians and their allies.[601]

California's Stanford University now has 177 or more DEI employees, according to a new report by Christoper Rufo.[602] These bureaucrats are not limited to overseeing humanities departments either. There are forty-six overseeing Stanford's medical school, the largest number in any department. Their physics department boasts an "Equity and Inclusion Strategic Plan" that will direct priorities and poison effectiveness of the entire program:

> The plan details actions in six areas: Department Climate and Policies, Undergraduate, Graduate, Postdoctoral Fellow & Research Associates, Faculty, and Staff. For each area, we have formulated key goals and their desired five-year outcome, with specific strategies to achieve each of those key goals.[603]

That is how this malevolent agenda is injected into our culture: with a lot of money. But while this highlights the problem, it also provides the solution. It is within the power of each state government to stop funding such things. Florida governor Ron DeSantis signed a law banning funding for DEI programs at Florida universities in May 2023.

As a result, in March 2024, the University of Florida closed its DEI program and ended funding for all related contractors.[604] Texas governor Greg Abbott signed a similar law shortly thereafter, forcing the University of Texas at Austin to shutter its DEI program. In Austin, the university even had a glossary of terms like "wimmin," a deliberate misspelling of "women," to avoid having to spell "men."[605]

Some of the other Florida state-funded universities have ended DEI and similar programs; for example, the University of North Florida closed its LGBTQ+ and Women's Centers in February 2024. In some instances, however, it appears that the changes may be nominal. Florida University's associate dean of diversity, inclusion, and global affairs in the College of Nursing is now the associate dean of community engagement and global affairs. Other deans have simply dropped the DEI title and are now just listed as deans.[606] So it is imperative not only that these activities be defunded but that the people committed to promoting such destructive ideologies be replaced by people who simply want our children educated.

Newman concluded his article by describing an interview he had with former Newsmax and One America News host Emerald Robinson.[607] As a White House correspondent, she was warned by others not to ask the Biden administration tough questions, lest it threaten her career. But Newman correctly said that people such as herself had to speak out to let the truth be heard.[608] Alex asked Emerald what motivates journalists to so regularly lie to the public. Her answer was on the money, summarized here:

- About 30 percent are "kind of dumb." They are the sheep. Controlled.
- About 30 percent are pure activists. They are Communists, they are Marxists, and they are pushing a Marxist agenda from the Marxist, globalist elite. They consider themselves "in the club."
- About 30 percent are "dangerously ambitious." They want to get ahead and will say or do anything to satisfy that ambition. They also like being accepted by the media elite—being invited to parties, being well spoken of, and not being cancelled.
- The rest are either just "stragglers" who don't care or those who do care but are very afraid.

She concluded by saying that there were only a few willing to speak out but that their voices are beginning to be heard. The corporate media lost so much credibility during the COVID pandemic that more and more people are seeking reliable sources. Unfortunately, now the media is trying to censor that.[609]

We all must realize that DEI is yet another Trojan Horse operation, introduced under the mantle of "compassion" and "fairness." It is really yet another crisis strategy, the purpose of which is to undermine and fracture our society. It is an asymmetrical form of warfare. The lie is obvious. DEI was developed by the Left and is imposed by the Left, those same people who espouse the superiority of the Communist model of society. Yet those "superior" models of government, best exemplified by Communist China and Russia, have no such programs. In fact, they militantly demonstrate the exact opposite.

AGENDA 2030:
ESG, SOCIAL CREDIT,
AND THE WAR ON CAPITALISM

You will own nothing and be happy.
—World Economic Forum

The World Economic Forum (WEF) held its 2024 annual meeting on January 15–19 in Davos, Switzerland. Attendees included political leaders such as Ukraine's Volodymyr Zelensky, Chinese premier Li Qiang, US secretary of state Antony Blinken, newly elected Argentine president Javier Milei, "Climate Czar" John Kerry,[13] and many others—in all, almost three thousand corporate and political leaders from 120 nations.

Prior to the 2023 meeting, WEF chairman Klaus Schwab declared 2023 the year of "polycrisis," saying, "Economic, environmental, social, and geopolitical crises are converging and conflating, creating an extremely versatile and uncertain future."[610]

---

[13] Note: Kerry resigned this position at the end of January 2024, to be replaced by Clinton insider John Podesta.

He was pretty prescient. That year, a WEF poll of 1,200 world business and political leaders found that among their top concerns were "energy inflation, food and security crises," with cost-of-living increases the top immediate concern.[611]

The year 2023 was indeed one of polycrisis. In fact, we have been in polycrisis since Biden took the helm. But despite his worries, Schwab had announced just a few months prior that fuel prices—a major driver of inflation—*weren't anywhere near high enough*. He wants to see gasoline prices *higher by multiples* in order to "safeguard democracy."[612]

Now for 2024's confab, the theme was "rebuilding trust." One has to laugh. The leftist elite, of which Schwab is a prominent member, have created all the crises he was talking about, *on purpose*. But not to worry, Schwab thinks that "rebuilding trust" means getting rid of all us "extremists," with you-know-who as the chief agitator. In *Davos 2024: Rebuilding Trust in the Future*, Schwab wrote:[613]

> Increasing division, heightened hostility and a surge in conflicts are defining the current global landscape. The perpetual need for crisis management is depleting the crucial human energy that could otherwise be channeled into shaping a more optimistic future.

Very true. All instigated by Joe Biden, Klaus Schwab, and their allies in the Left.

> Despite facing serious crises in the past, the current wave of pessimism is unprecedented. And unlike the past, the power and presence of global media and communications technology today means that every challenge and setback is amplified, further magnifying the sense of doom and gloom.

Again, very true. All instigated by people like Klaus Schwab and his media allies.

> After an era that lifted a billion people out of poverty and improved living standards everywhere, the anxiety

about losing control over what lies ahead is pushing people towards embracing extreme ideologies and the leaders who champion them.

Ahh, there it is: "extreme ideologies and the leaders who champion them." And who could that be? Not Joe Biden, certainly. Of course it is Donald Trump and the MAGAs. We are domestic terrorists. And all this out of the mouth of a man who keeps a bust of Communist leader Vladimir Lenin prominently displayed on the bookcase in his office.

But it is true. America did lift a billion people out of poverty, despite the efforts of Joe Biden, Barack Obama, Bill Clinton, Klaus Schwab, and all the other creatures inhabiting the caves of the vindictive, ambitious, and utterly unethical Left. Will Hild, executive director of Consumers' Research, responded to Schwab's sophomoric post, "The only thing World Economic Forum can do to rebuild trust is to repudiate their aims of lowering living standards for the entire world, except for themselves."[614]

Even better was the speech by Argentine president Javier Milei. It was a barn burner:

> Today I am here to tell you that the West is in danger; it is in danger because those who are supposed to defend the values of the West find themselves co-opted by a vision of the world that—inexorably—leads to socialism, and consequently to poverty.
>
> Unfortunately, in recent decades, motivated by some bien-pensant desires to help others, and others by the desire to belong to a privileged caste, the main leaders of the Western world have abandoned the model of freedom for different versions of what we call *collectivism*.[615]

He went on to describe how free market capitalism had raised the world's living standard and brought more people out of poverty than any other system. Socialism, he explained, was everywhere and always a failure. His speech before this crowd, whose leaders espouse Socialism, was as provocative as the speech President Trump made before this same group in 2020 when he said, "America will never be a socialist country."[616]

Prominent among discussions, as always at WEF forums, was the ever-present threat of "catastrophic climate change." Schwab claims the answer will require an unprecedented level of "public-private cooperation." So once again, we hear Schwab and Company advocating fascism, this time to combat "climate change."

Sustainability, ESG, and Social Credit Scores

Sustainability has become a household word. We see it on product labels and hear it discussed in relation to everything from electrical generation to financial investments. Most people remain unaware, however, of its origin, true nature, or the goals pursued under this seemingly innocuous word.

"Sustainable development" was first articulated in 1987 in "Our Common Future," a paper produced by the UN World Commission on Environment and Development.[617] What came to be called the Brundtland Commission was led by Gro Harlem Brundtland, Socialist International leader and former prime minister of Norway.[618] As derived from the commission report, the UN defines "sustainable development" as "development that meets the needs of the present without compromising the ability of future generations to meet its own needs."[619] To accomplish this, Brundtland stated that it constituted "a global agenda for change."[620]

Other luminaries on the Brundtland Commission included UN heavyweight Maurice Strong (more about him later); William Ruckelshaus, first head of the US Environmental Protection Agency (the only American); and luminaries from such enlightened states as Zimbabwe, Communist China, Russia, Algeria, Saudi Arabia, and Cote d'Ivoire.

Sustainable development is found at the intersection of the three "Es" of economy, environment, and (social) equity. It implies government restraint of economic growth to limit the depletion of natural resources over time and prevent anthropogenic climate change while redistributing resources to achieve "equity"—i.e., Socialism.

Figure 1. Sustainable Development. Source: FutureLearn.com, https://www.futurelearn.com/info/courses/sustainability-society-and-you/0/steps/4618.

This Socialist aspect of "sustainability" was emphasized throughout the Brundtland Report. For example, on page 22, point 70, it states, "Many essential human needs can be met only through goods and services provided by industry, and the shift to sustainable development must be powered by a continuing flow of wealth from industry."[621]

Origins of Sustainability

Like most, if not all, left-wing agendas, the sustainable development concept has been with us a long time. Developed slowly, stealthily, and thus largely unnoticed, the ideas began to take shape in the late 1960s, when Sweden proposed a conference to discuss man's interaction with the environment. The outcome was the 1972 United Nations Conference on the Human Environment, which included 109 recommendations and a three-part action plan.[622] Maurice Strong was asked by UN secretary-general U Thant to organize and lead this conference.[623]

Later, at the 1976 UN Conference on Human Settlements in Vancouver, British Columbia, participants discussed how humans could and should be redistributed throughout the world. Maurice Strong had a hand in this one too, asking Barbara Ward, whom he had made founding director of the International Institute for Environment and Development, to get involved. She wrote a book titled *The Home of Man*, which became the theme for the conference.[624]

Ward, who became prominent in her own right, was an early champion of sustainability and spoke openly of redistributing resources from rich to poor nations.[625] She demanded that the wealthy nations donate a minimum of 1 percent of GDP to the poorer nations. This became one of the UN's asks at the UN Conference on Environment and Development, the "Earth Summit," held in Rio de Janeiro, Brazil, in June 1992. The follow-on Millennium Development Project initially called for "developed countries" to donate 0.7 percent of GDP every year. Predictably, now the UN says that's not enough.[626]

The 1976 conference envisioned redistributing not only wealth but also land, resources, and populations worldwide, not as a matter of individual choice but of UN-crafted policy. This is also one of the excuses for the invasion of US borders occurring today, which is being facilitated directly by the UN.[627]

The conference report states, "Human settlement policies can be powerful tools for the more equitable distribution of income and opportunities." Furthermore:

> Human settlements policies should aim to improve the condition of human settlements particularly by promoting a more equitable distribution of the benefits of development among regions; and making such benefits and public services equally accessible to all groups.[628]

The conference discussed the world in terms of "regions" rather than nations, an implicit nod to the notion of world government. Of course, "equity" is one of the three Es of sustainability. Documents from the 1976 conference make clear that the UN believes the government should be deciding where and how everyone in the country lives. In particular, the section on land use makes explicit that UN planners seek to abolish private property:

> Land, because of its unique nature and the crucial role it plays in human settlements, cannot be treated as an ordinary asset, controlled by individuals and subject to the pressures and inefficiencies of the market. Private land ownership is also a principal instrument of accumulation and concentration of wealth and therefore contributes to social injustice; if unchecked, it may become a major obstacle in the planning and implementation of development schemes. *Social justice, urban renewal and development, the provision of decent dwellings-and healthy conditions for the people can only be achieved if land is used in the interests of society as a whole.* (Emphasis added.)[629]

The UN justified these measures based on expectations about population growth, various environmental policies, and of course, "social justice." These three concerns later morphed into the three "pillars" of the UN sustainability concept: environment, economy, and social equity. It is merely Socialism repackaged.

Maurice Strong headed the 1992 Earth Summit, where the first set of "sustainability" goals were articulated in a document titled "Agenda 21."[630] The document summarized that "Agenda 21 is a comprehensive plan of action to be taken globally, nationally and locally by organizations of the United Nations System, Governments, and Major Groups in every area in which human impacts on the environment [sic]."[631]

A total of 178 governments signed on, including the United States under President George H. W. Bush's signature. The Democrat-controlled US House of Representatives passed Concurrent Resolution 353, which states "that the United States should assume a strong leadership role in implementing the decisions made at the Earth Summit by developing a national strategy to implement Agenda 21 and other Earth Summit agreements."

The resolution called for:

> Adoption of a national strategy for environmentally sustainable development, based on an extensive process of nationwide consultations with all interested organizations and individuals; (2) the Government encouraging and facilitating means for adopting individual Agenda 21 plans of action, including the establishment of local, county, State, business, and other boards and commissions for achieving sustainable development; (3) the President establishing an effective mechanism to plan, initiate, and coordinate U.S. policy for implementing Agenda 21; and (4) policies being formulated for foreign policy and assistance to help developing countries and for domestic actions to assure appropriate action to implement Agenda 21.[632]

The US Senate did not ratify Agenda 21 or vote on H.Con.Res. 353, but President Bill Clinton signed Executive Order 12852, creating the President's Council on Sustainable Development, which operated until 1999, building structures throughout government and promoting the same for city, county, and state governments throughout the US—where offices of sustainability are now the rule.

Agenda 21 also advanced in the US to a great degree because "sustainability" concepts were insinuated early on into the American Planning Association's (APA) guidelines—used almost universally by planning and zoning boards throughout the US. Today the APA Foundation is committed to "help steward the next generation of planners and help create more equitable, sustainable, and prosperous communities."[633]

Agenda 21 was rebranded in 2015 as Agenda 2030, with seventeen sustainable development goals (SDG).[634] It is an all-encompassing prescription for regulating every aspect of human activity on a global scale under the pretext of "sustainable development." The WEF openly promotes Agenda 2030 as the ultimate goal of sustainable development.

A few recognizable sustainability concepts are "smart growth," "walkable communities," "15-minute neighborhoods," "20-minute neighborhoods," "strong communities," "strong cities," or "strong towns." All seek to cram people into housing projects with all amenities within walking distance—dispensing with the need for automobiles. As the WEF now advertises, "You will own nothing and be happy."[635]

While the supposed benefits of these developments are widely promoted, *the true purposes are to abolish private autos, reduce or eliminate private property, and push people back into cities.* This is both because cities are losing revenues as people flee high crime and taxes, and because the UN-endorsed Wildlands Project (now called the Wildlands Network) seeks to return major swaths of America now occupied by suburban single-family homes and rural farms to the wild.

It should be mentioned that the Wildlands Network was founded by the late Dave Foreman, co-founder of the ecoterrorist group *Earth First!* Foreman pioneered using tree spikes to protest logging. Spiking caused deadly accidents, including a young man who had parts of his face ripped off.[636] Foreman paid nothing for his many acts of terrorism, despite being investigated by the FBI. He was an intimate partner in the development of the sustainability agenda until his death in 2022. Foreman has said:

> We must make this an insecure and inhospitable place for capitalists and their projects. We must reclaim the roads and plowed land, halt dam constructions, tear down existing dams, free shackled rivers and return to wilderness millions of acres of previously settled land.[637]

And:

> Phasing out the human race will solve every problem on earth, social and environmental.... The optimum human population of earth is zero.[638]

The "sustainability" concept was introduced to the investing world in 2006 with the UN publication "Principles for Responsible Investment" (PRI), which advocated investments that incorporated environmental, social, and governance (ESG) concepts.[639] Once again, the three

Es of sustainability, but government has replaced the E of economy, making the governmental role explicit.

PRI is directly tied to Agenda 2030. Citing the UN-mandated SDGs, Acuity Knowledge Partners, an investment advisory group, calls "sustainable finance" a "new frontier" toward investment banking that is "environmentally and socially sustainable."[640] Increasingly, investment companies have been arm-twisted to adopt ESG "sustainability" concepts in making investment decisions. In 2006, sixty-three investment companies signed on. [641] As of 2021, over four thousand PRI signatory companies held assets totaling $120 trillion under management.[642]

Numerous organizations now pursue the UN's notion of sustainability. This includes large and influential organizations explicitly involved in promoting Agenda 2030, such as the WEF, investment firm BlackRock, and thousands of smaller ones. BlackRock partners with Climate Action 100+, which includes numerous corporations, other investment funds, and nonprofits controlling $60 trillion in assets.[643]

At the November 2022 G20 Summit in Bali, Indonesia, member countries including the US signed the Bali Declaration, which acknowledges support of the UN sustainable development goals:

> We met in Bali on 15–16 November 2022, at a time of unparalleled multidimensional crises. We have experienced the devastation brought by the Covid-19 pandemic, and other challenges including climate change, which has caused economic downturn, increased poverty, slowed global recovery, *and hindered the achievement of the Sustainable Development Goals.* (Emphasis added.)[644]

The 2023 G20 Summit was held in New Delhi, India, in September. The 2023 Leaders' Declaration included such subjects as a "Green Development Pact for a Sustainable Future," "Implementing Clean, Sustainable, Just, Affordable & Inclusive Energy Transitions," and "Gender Equality and Empowering All Women and Girls," with subsets like, "Driving Gender Inclusive Climate Action." [645]

What on earth is "gender inclusive climate action?" And how will they reconcile "empowering all women and girls," with the Left's effort to redefine what a woman is, who can participate in women's sports, use women's bathrooms, and so forth? Answer: they cannot and will not, because what they publicize as their intent is not their intent. The intent is frustration, confusion, chaos, and ultimately, cultural homicide. In poker, a "tell" is a gesture or expression that gives away your hand. The "tell" here is that none of this garbage is being considered by Communist China or Russia, or for that matter any of the former Eastern Bloc countries. They don't even pretend to go along with it. The insanity is targeted wholly on the West.

Like many of the leftist agendas, once "sustainability" caught on, it grew and metastasized. Sustainability now includes dozens of "social equity" concepts, social credit scores, and the WEF's "reinventing" capitalism—calling it "stakeholder capitalism." It is also behind the movement to abolish all carbon fuels and gasoline-powered autos.

First articulated in a 1973 Davos manifesto, stakeholder capitalism directs corporate profits to underwrite the Left's wish list of woke agendas.[646] It not only violates corporate responsibilities to shareholders but also subtly undermines private property rights by providing benefits to many "stakeholders" that have no ownership in the relevant stocks. KPMG has stated:

> KPMG ESG solutions are both holistic and practical. We'll guide your teams to drive sustainable innovation across your business and help you gain a competitive edge. With deep expertise across critical issues— including decarbonization, reporting, sustainable finance and DEI (diversity, equity and inclusion)— we'll help you create the right blueprint for integrating ESG. A blueprint that simplifies your strategy, guides its full implementation and lets you take the lead on ESG...because how you grow matters.[647]

KPMG has an entire department devoted to directing its clients into an ESG model. Its "ESG Maturity Assessment" makes clear that results of that assessment will become public knowledge—an implicit form of social credit scoring that will pressure any company foolish enough to complete the assessment to comply with WEF dictates. Cheryl Chumley of the *Washington Times* wrote:

> Under a WEF-imagined stakeholder system, banks wouldn't lend to businesses that don't comply with, say, climate change policies or, say, vaccination mandates. Investors wouldn't invest if the WEF didn't approve. Insurers wouldn't insure—governments wouldn't permit—developers wouldn't develop—builders wouldn't build—and so forth and so on. The government, through partners and friends in business, would be the behind-the-scenes' strings puller. And better believe this: The only businesses that would fit into this new government-run system would be the leftists.[648]

In 2020, the WEF reported that "120 of the world's largest companies" had created what they called Stakeholder Capitalism Metrics.[649] By 2023, it had actually added only 17 more companies, and only 55 of the 137 had been reporting for the past two years.[650] Maybe the enthusiasm for stakeholder capitalism is overrated?

BlackRock is the most aggressive promoter of sustainable development. It is getting pushback about its support for stakeholder capitalism at the expense of its investors.[651] CEO Larry Fink has faced pressures to resign.[652] In June 2023, he stated he would he would stop using the term "ESG" because he claims it had been mischaracterized.[653] But it does not appear to be a substantive change.

In March 2024, Texas pulled $8.5 billion from BlackRock over its destructive ESG investment policies that threated the financial viability of Texas's Permanent School Fund.[654] Other GOP-led states are taking similar action, pulling pension dollars and other state investments from BlackRock because of its ESG policies.

The state of Florida removed $2 billion from BlackRock control in 2022. Florida's chief financial officer Jimmy Patronis said, "When you consider how much responsibility [CEO Larry] Fink has, when he's got trillions of dollars, in trying to influence politics, and those dollars aren't his. They belong to first responders, they belong to retirees, they belong to those trying to set up a future with peace of mind.... I put BlackRock in the same category as what Budweiser has been dealing with Bud Light. They have forgotten who their customer is, and now they step into politics and have gotten themselves in a real pickle."[655]

Will Hild of Consumers' Research sees things getting better. "I would say we're in the early innings of this fight against ESG.... But consumers and American citizens should feel very empowered about just the changes that have been made in a short period of time."[656]

According to Charity Support, for 2023, the top nine nonprofits promoting sustainability concepts were:

- Environmental Working Group
- Union of Concerned Scientists
- Earthjustice
- Natural Resources Defense Council
- Environmental Defense Fund
- Friends of the Earth
- The Nature Conservancy
- Rainforest Alliance
- Conservation International

If you donate to any of these, stop. But as we have seen, that is just the tip of the iceberg. The entire society has become infected with this misplaced agenda. MIT even offers a professional certificate program for "sustainability." Many colleges now offer a bachelor's degree in sustainability.[657]

The World Bank digital ID for sustainable development is also a component of the Agenda 2030 goals. McKinsey Global Institute calls the digital ID "a key to inclusive growth":

> Digital identification, or "digital ID," can be authenticated unambiguously through a digital channel, unlocking access to banking, government benefits, education, and many other critical services. The risks and

potential for misuse of digital ID are real and deserve careful attention. When well-designed, digital ID not only enables civic and social empowerment, but also makes possible real and inclusive economic gains—a less well understood aspect of the technology.[658]

McKinsey acknowledges that digital IDs could be abused and that a successful digital ID program must be guided by the rule of law. But whose law? China and many other nations recognize no law and use social credit scores to control and persecute their people. To imagine that the UN would respect individual rights would require ignoring practically everything the UN does. The United States appears to be following suit as more and more government corruption and incompetence is discovered at every level. Imposing digital ID on everyone in the world would put everyone under the control of increasingly despotic governments.

The idea of using digital IDs as vaccine passports was also discussed at G20 meetings. The 2022 declaration included a section promoting "digital solutions and non-digital solutions, including proof of vaccinations…as part of the efforts to strengthen prevention and response to future pandemics, that should capitalize and build on the success of the existing standards and digital COVID-19 certificates."[659]

The 2023 declaration included a section on developing digital currencies and implied development of a digital ID managed by the World Health Organization. The language is deliberately vague, and earlier in 2024 the WHO sought to obtain an "ambitious, legally binding" agreement on pandemic responses by May 2024.[660] Fortunately it failed, despite support from the Biden administration, but officials are undaunted, saying they hope to get a deal "within the next year or two."[661] Truly frightening. This is another decision point, because under a Trump administration, this nonsense will be dead in the water. If a Democrat wins the White House, it will be very much alive. Do you want the WHO using a digital ID to decide your healthcare?

Bad Economics

The Green New Deal advocates claim to want net-zero carbon emissions. This imperils the economy of the world. The steps the Biden administration has already taken have pushed the US toward recession and inflation not seen since the early 1980s. These kinds of policies will destroy the economy well before any transition to a carbon-free world could be developed—but they aren't really looking for that anyway. The entire global warming narrative is yet another excuse for the grifters of the Left to steal our money. More on that later.

But even if you take it at face value, the UN notion of sustainability displays a profound misunderstanding of the most basic economics. The UN's "sustainable" development concept requires government control over the economy because it assumes that private markets will simply use resources to exhaustion—never bothering to find substitutes when resources become scarce.

This is a common misperception among the Left. A good example is the history of whaling. Whales were hunted largely for the oil used in oil lamps and for other purposes. As demand for whale oil grew, some species of whales were pushed to near extinction. Whale oil became increasingly expensive as a result. The whales were saved by the "robber baron" John D. Rockefeller, founder of Standard Oil, and those who followed him.[662] Petroleum-produced kerosine rapidly replaced whale oil as a much less expensive, safer, and more versatile substitute. Edison's electric light later replaced kerosine.

This type of automatic market response happens over and over again, but only because the market can quickly react to shortages to find profitable alternatives. The price mechanism guarantees that as a resource becomes less plentiful, its price goes up, prompting entrepreneurs to find less expensive alternatives. Market forces also disrupt monopolies because the price mechanism motivates people to find cheaper alternatives to a monopoly-priced product. The only way monopolies last for any appreciable time is if they are protected or created by government. Yet government control of everything is the UN mantra.

The UN approach to population control is similar, accepting Dr. Paul Ehrlich's doomsday book *The Population Bomb* as gospel.[663] But Ehrlich has been proven wrong over and over again. Populations adjust to differing pressures. Western nations have reduced population growth to replacement rates, and some are experiencing negative growth rates.

Ironically, while it continues to advocate Ehrlich's prophesies of doom, the UN has said immigration is needed to *increase the populations* of target countries with a shrinking workforce. You've heard the term "replacement migration," supposedly a far-right "conspiracy theory." As usual, the Left is lying. *Replacement migration is a UN program.*[664] And the UN is at the heart of the massive border invasion, seeing that we get replacement migration whether we want it or not!

The sustainable development approach is the tired and false assumption that economics is a zero-sum game. We discussed this in an earlier chapter. On a global scale, is it "unfair" that the US consumes 25 percent of the world's resources but has less than 5 percent of the world's population? According to the sustainability crowd, America is greedy and should cut consumption so the rest of the world can get an equitable share. Yet if the US were foolish enough to follow this prescription, what would happen? Would other countries jump in to purchase the goods and materials we didn't? No. The world economy would suddenly see markets for its products vanish, and the global economy would collapse overnight.

The US produces about 25 percent of the world's output. The truth is that the US *exchanges* monetary wealth and other resources with the rest of the world to accomplish this. Reducing US GDP to 5 percent of the world's output would represent an 80 percent cut in our purchases from the rest of the world. For perspective, US GDP declined 29 percent during the Great Depression, which pushed the world into economic collapse and World War II.[665] An 80 percent contraction of GDP would create a worldwide depression of unimaginable proportions.

But the Left sees this as an opportunity. Following the 2009 recession, real GDP fell 4.3 percent.[666] Then secretary of state John Kerry claimed that the decline in economic activity reduced greenhouse gas emissions by 6 percent. He wanted to see a 20 percent reduction, which would require a GDP decline of about 15 percent—a recession three times as bad as it was. He said:

> Let me emphasize something very strongly as we begin this discussion. The United States has already this year alone achieved a 6 percent reduction in emissions simply because of the downturn in the economy, so we are effectively saying we need to go another 14 percent.[667]

You simply cannot make this stuff up. Unemployment went to 10 percent during that recession. If Kerry had his way, unemployment may have exceeded 20 percent—near Great Depression levels. At the 2023 WEF Davos meeting, Kerry described what is needed to fight climate change:

> Well, the lesson I've learned in the last year—I learned it as secretary of state and it has since been reinforced in spades, is money, money, money, money, money, money, money.[668]

An article in the *Stanford Social Innovation Review* states, "Estimates of how much money is needed for an energy transition away from fossil fuels over the next three decades range from $100 trillion to $150 trillion."[669] For perspective, the entire world economy is approximately $94 trillion.[670] Meanwhile, according to Climate Action 100+, if nothing is done, and global temperature increases 4°C (one estimate of many, based on the flawed models of the UN Intergovernmental Panel on Climate Change),[671] global economic costs will total $23 trillion by 2080.[672] Has anyone really been doing his homework?

According to the *Review*, which advocates eliminating the fossil fuel industry entirely, the transition would create "massive dislocations," including the loss of eight million jobs in the industry by 2050 with multiples of that in downstream industries. It would also require major adjustments in how business is conducted worldwide. Most of these disruptions would of necessity be handled by government spending to provide retraining and other benefits. Some state economies—such as

West Virginia, Texas, Oklahoma, Louisiana, North Dakota, and others—would be "devastated," and recovery would require massive government intervention to lessen the impact.[673]

That is a best-case scenario. Spending multiples of the trillions already being spent by the US on the Green New Deal and other wasteful projects with the associated inflation and debt would send the US into third-world hyperinflation and economic collapse—never mind the massive amounts of graft and corruption likely to accompany the spending. But haven't we quoted them over and over saying that it is what they want?

Who Was Maurice Strong?

Maurice (pronounced "Morris") Strong, a Canadian who became wealthy in the oil industry, was probably the most influential driver behind the entire sustainability agenda. Though his name is not well known outside of UN circles, he practically invented "sustainability" and was behind much of the UN-driven environmental movement. His roles included:

- secretary-general, UN Conference on the Human Environment (1972 Stockholm conference)
- founding executive director, UN Environment Programme (UNEP)
- foundation director, World Economic Forum
- co-chairman, Council of the World Economic Forum
- senior advisor to UN secretary-general Kofi Annan
- senior advisor to World Bank president James Wolfensohn
- commissioner, World Commission on Environment and Development
- secretary-general, UN Conference on Environment and Development (UNCED)
- chairman, the Earth Council
- commissioner, Commission on Global Governance
- member, Club of Rome
- board member, United Nations Foundation

- board member, International Institute for Sustainable Development
- chairman, World Resources Institute

These are but a few of Strong's activities. He died in 2015, but his influence remains. In an obituary on the World Economic Forum website, WEF founder Klaus Schwab described Strong as his mentor and credited him with elevating the WEF to the prominence it enjoys today:

> He deeply incorporated the World Economic Forum's mission of improving the state of the world into everything he did. He was a great visionary, always ahead of our times in his thinking. He was my mentor since the creation of the Forum: a great friend; an indispensable advisor; and, for many years, a member of our Foundation Board. Without him, the Forum would not have achieved its present significance.[674]

Another tribute called him "the founding giant of the global environment movement."[675] This is important because Strong made no bones about his radicalism. He described himself as "a socialist in ideology, a capitalist in methodology."[676] And many of his views are becoming mainstream political narratives. For example, he said in a 1991 UNCED report:

> Current lifestyles and consumption patterns of the affluent middle class—involving high meat intake, consumption of large amounts of frozen and convenience foods, ownership of motor vehicles, golf courses, small electric appliances, home and work place air-conditioning, and suburban housing are not sustainable. A shift is necessary toward lifestyles less geared to environmentally damaging consumption patterns.[677]

Eat bugs anyone? Strong went even further. In the 1992 pamphlet "Stockholm to Rio: A Journey Down a Generation," he suggested that nations would have to surrender sovereignty to global dictates:

The concept of national sovereignty has been an immutable, indeed sacred, principle of international relations. It is a principle which will yield only slowly and reluctantly to the new imperatives of global environmental cooperation. *It is simply not feasible for sovereignty to be exercised unilaterally by individual nation states, however powerful. The global community must be assured of environmental security.* (Emphasis added.)[678]

In a 1990 interview, Strong discussed an idea for a novel he had.[679] He tells the reporter:

The World Economic Forum convenes in Davos, Switzerland. Over a thousand CEOs, prime ministers, finance ministers, and leading academics gather in February to attend meetings and set economic agendas for the year ahead. With this as a setting, he then asked:

What if a small group of these world leaders were to conclude that the principle risk to the earth comes from the actions of the rich countries?... *So, in order to save the planet, the group decides: isn't the only hope for the planet that the industrialized civilizations collapse? Isn't it our responsibility to bring that about?* (Emphasis added.)

He continued:

This group of world leaders form a secret society to bring about an economic collapse. It's February. They're all at Davos. These aren't terrorists. They're world leaders. They've positioned themselves in the world's commodity and stock markets. They've engineered, using their access to stock exchanges and computers and gold supplies, a panic. Then they prevent the world's stock markets from closing.... The markets can't close. The rich countries...[Strong makes a slight motion with his fingers as if he were flipping a cigarette out the window.]

The reporter recognizes that this is not mere fantasy, writing: "I sit there spellbound. This is not any ordinary storyteller. This is Maurice Strong. He knows these world leaders. He is, in fact, co-chairman of Council of the World Economic Forum. He sits at the fulcrum of power. He is in a position to *do it*."[680]

Strong tells him, "I probably shouldn't be saying things like this."[681]

Some of these quotes have been falsely attributed to George Soros, but make no mistake, Soros agrees with all of them. At the WEF meeting in 2018, Soros said: "Clearly, I consider the Trump administration a danger to the world. But I regard it as a purely temporary phenomenon that will disappear in 2020."[682] Given his deep involvement in electing radical DAs and secretaries of state, and everything else vote fraud, maybe he knew something.

Maurice Strong was instrumental in founding, advising, or supporting numerous organizations, and he joined the boards of many, among them:[683]

- Aspen Institute
- Bretton Woods Committee
- Commission on Global Governance
- Earth Charter
- International Institute for Environment and Development
- International Institute for Sustainable Development
- International Union for the Conservation of Nature
- Rockefeller Foundation
- University for Peace
- World Wildlife Fund
- World Economic Forum
- World Resources Institute

The Great Reset

The WEF has not suggested the world should collapse, but Klaus Schwab has repeatedly stated his call for global governance in one form or another, using crises to justify its need. In 2020, he used the pandemic to advocate for a "Great Reset" of capitalism. Citing what he claimed was a looming depression following the COVID lockdowns, he said:

> To achieve a better outcome, the world must act jointly and swiftly to revamp all aspects of our societies and economies, from education to social contracts and working conditions. Every country, from the United States to China, must participate, and every industry, from oil and gas to tech, must be transformed. In short, we need a "Great Reset" of capitalism.[684]

With that, the WEF launched the Great Reset.[685] It has aptly been called "communist capitalism."[686]

While they have been working assiduously to achieve the Great Reset through all the means discussed in this book, they have not yet succeeded, though they are well on the way. But some form of crisis, be it "climate change," the pandemic, or whatever, has been the vehicle to urge the UN agenda on the world. This year is no different. In 2023, WEF members predicted a "catastrophic global cyber attack" likely to occur in the next two years.[687] "This is a global threat, and it calls for a global response and enhanced and coordinated action," said Jürgen Stock, INTERPOL secretary-general.[688]

Will this be another unforced error or manufactured crisis, like the global COVID shutdown the WEF advocated? A large-scale cyberattack is indeed a possibility, given the state of world hostilities. But the question is, who would carry it out? It would likely be a UN member nation, and we can probably guess who—e.g., China, Russia, North Korea, or Iran. And yet Klaus Schwab has expressed his admiration for the "Chinese model" as the government of the future.[689]

Practically everything Maurice Strong stated about our future, both in his fantasy book idea and on his very public platforms, has been incorporated in the WEF agenda one way or another. For example, while Klaus Schwab never actually said we will eat insects and like it or that we'll own nothing and be happy, it is not a "conspiracy theory" as the Left would have you believe. The WEF did post articles saying all these things.

One piece is titled, "Why We Need to Give Insects the Role They Deserve in Our Food Systems."[690] NPR obliged with an article titled, "Your Ancestors Probably Ate Insects. So What's Bugging You?"[691] And we will eat less meat if Klaus has his way. In 2016, the WEF posted an article and an embedded Facebook video predicting how life will be in 2030. These are the exact words from the video:[692]

> "You will own nothing and be happy."

> "Whatever you want you'll rent, and it will be delivered by drone."

> "The US won't be the world's leading superpower."

> "A handful of countries will dominate."

> "You'll eat much less meat."

> "A billion people will be displaced by climate change."

> "We'll have to do a better job of welcoming and integrating refugees."

> "There will be a global price on carbon; This will help make fossil fuels history."

The video also mentioned future tech, like 3-D printing of human organs and travel to Mars to keep things interesting. But the WEF will have no hand in those things. Its role is strictly political and dedicated to UN Agenda 2030. Who will be the "handful of countries who dominate"? If the US loses world dominance, our enemies—those with the military power to do so—will take its place. So we will have China, which gave us the pandemic, and Russia, which gave us the war in Ukraine, and a few more thugs overseeing things. Strong would approve.

Sustainability, when seen in the proper light, is the opposite of what it seems. Sustainable development, like everything based on a Socialist model, is *not* sustainable. It creates shortages and other calamities that will indeed force the world into a great reset that could make the Great Depression look trivial by comparison. But the leaders at Davos and the UN seem unfazed by this danger and are determined to move forward regardless. It is the tip of the spear for those advocating a one-world, Socialist government—the true endgame.

SAVE THE PLANET:
KILL EVERYTHING

One of the saddest lessons of history is this: If we've been bamboozled long enough, we tend to reject any evidence of the bamboozle. We're no longer interested in finding out the truth. The bamboozle has captured us. It's simply too painful to acknowledge, even to ourselves, that we've been taken. Once you give a charlatan power over you, you almost never get it back.

—Astronomer Carl Sagan

n November 1974, *The Guardian* published an article with this breathless conclusion: "The facts have emerged, in recent years and months, from research into ice ages of the past. They imply that *the threat of a new ice age must now stand alongside nuclear war as a likely source of wholesale death and misery for mankind.*" (Emphasis added.)[693] Two years earlier, Walter Cronkite had reported on the same thing.[694] Today we are supposedly being threatened by end-of-the-world catastrophic global warming.

What are we supposed to believe? Carl Sagan's quote describes exactly where America, and indeed the entire Western world, finds itself today. We have been lied to so persistently, so overwhelmingly, so convincingly, that the lie has worked its way into almost every aspect of our lives. Virtually every institution of society—industry, finance, government, the education establishment, news media, and entertainment—has been saturated in the lie and has turned its attention to promoting as well as underwriting its alleged "cost." And they are just warming up.

Do you believe them? Do you believe that sex is not biology but a "choice" over fifty or so competing "genders"? Do you believe that children should be encouraged to have sex change operations without parental consent or knowledge? If surgery is required to change one's sex, how is it merely a choice? Do you believe that endless government spending can reduce inflation, as the name of President Biden's $740 billion Inflation Reduction Act implies? (It's now assessed to actually cost $1.2 trillion.)[695]

Do you believe that America is the most racist country that ever existed, or that learning Critical Race Theory is more important for our children than reading, writing, and arithmetic? Do you believe that "our borders are secure," as Homeland Security secretary Alejandro Mayorkas has assured us on many occasions? Is "climate change" threatening the imminent destruction of the earth?

The Left wants us to believe all of that is true, and anyone who questions any of it is vilified, cancelled, fired from longstanding employment and sometimes threatened with death. Momentarily ignoring these threats, is there really any reason to believe any of what they say? Well, let's look at that, because we are rushing to implement a massive change in how we produce energy, that most critical sector that fuels the modern age.

In his book, *Fake Invisible Catastrophes and Threats of Doom*, Dr. Patrick Moore, Greenpeace co-founder and founding director of the CO2 Coalition based in Washington, DC, writes:

> You have heard the news on climate change that says human-caused emissions of carbon dioxide are going to make the world too hot for life. So now as you drive down the highway in your SUV, you are afraid

that you are killing your grandchildren by doing so. As this makes you feel guilty and accountable, you vow to send a hefty donation to Greenpeace, or any of the other hundreds of "charities," selling you this narrative. It is a very effective strategy on their part, as stirring a combination of fear and guilt is the most powerful motivator to get people to open their wallets in an effort to help avoid this alleged disaster. And all this inevitable doom due to an invisible gas that is essential for life and even now is only 0.0415 percent of the atmosphere.[696]

Carbon Is Not a Poison

Carbon is not a poison. The basic fact rarely heard among the climate fanatics is that *carbon is the basis for all life on earth*. And the carbon source utilized is the carbon dioxide (CO_2) taken from the atmosphere. *Plants require carbon dioxide to survive. Carbon dioxide is plant food.* Plants take it in from the atmosphere and, using the energy of the sun, combine it with water (H_2O) to make various sugars in a process called photosynthesis. All sugars bear multiples of the basic formula CH_2O. That is one carbon atom (C), two hydrogen atoms (H), and one oxygen atom (O). In its most basic formula, the chemical reaction can be expressed:

$$CO_2 + H_2O + \text{sunlight} \rightarrow CH_2O + O_2$$

The sugar actually produced in this process is glucose, $C6H12O6$, which is then used as plant food. Animals then eat the greens and fruit produced, and the "waste" product released into the air from this chemical reaction is the oxygen (O_2) we breathe. Carbon dioxide is essential to life on earth, and it comprises a mere 0.04 percent of the atmosphere.

Dr. Moore is one of the few scientists talking about this. It was the focus of a Prager University video, where he said:

> All life is carbon-based. And the carbon for all that life originates from carbon dioxide in the atmosphere. All of the carbon in the fossil fuels we are burning for energy today, was once in the atmosphere as carbon dioxide, before it was consumed by plankton in the sea and plants on land. Coal, oil and natural gas are the remains of those plankton and plants, that have been transformed by heat and pressure deep in the earth's crust. In other words, fossil fuels are 100 percent organic and were produced with solar energy.... If there were no carbon dioxide in the earth's atmosphere, the earth would be a dead planet, period. Talk about catastrophic climate change. Take away CO_2 and you'd have it. And yet the U.S. Environmental Protection Agency has deemed this essential ingredient for life a pollutant.[697]

In an interview with Conversations that Matter, Dr. Moore explained that, if anything, we need more carbon dioxide in the atmosphere, not less.[698] Famed Princeton physicist Dr. William Happer agrees. He says that we are actually experiencing a "carbon drought, and that more CO_2 in the atmosphere would be a good thing."[699]

Dr. Moore says he left Greenpeace when it went from being humanitarian to being "anti-human, basically, and saying that humans are the enemy of the earth."[700] He called the climate agenda "a huge convergence of interests among the elites, that is driving the political agenda today."[701] Dr. Moore stated that "oil has produced our longevity, our prosperity and our personal freedom.... Is that evil?" he asks. "Apparently so."[702]

"The world will end in 12 years!" screamed Alexandria Ocasio-Cortez in 2019.[703] What do you tell children who come home from school after being told that by their teacher? Why do homework? Why even bother with school?

Five years on since that lunatic outburst, we haven't seen any evidence of the world ending. But if anything, the hysterics have become even more insane. In January 2023 at the World Economic Forum meeting in Davos, Switzerland, Al Gore said:

> We're still putting 162 million tons [of greenhouse gas] into [the atmosphere] every single day and the accumulated amount is now trapping as much extra heat as would be released by 600,000 Hiroshima-class atomic bombs exploding every single day on the earth.... That's what's boiling the oceans, creating these atmospheric rivers, and the rain bombs, and sucking the moisture out of the land, and creating the droughts, and melting the ice and raising the sea level, and causing these waves of climate refugees.[704]

Climate refugees? Where? Six hundred thousand Hiroshima-class bombs every day? Where? Boiling the oceans? Are we supposed to believe such lunacy? Al Gore has been wrong on all of his predictions since beginning his crusade following publication of his 2006 book and movie, *An Inconvenient Truth*.

His famous graph purporting to show a direct relationship between CO_2 and global warming conveniently leaves out the fact that historical increases in CO_2 came between two hundred and one thousand years *after* global temperatures increased. And this has been revealed by polar ice core analysis.[705] That detail is not visible on the graph because data covering six hundred thousand years is crammed into a small graph.

So how are we to conclude that CO_2 is the villain here? Either Gore and his researchers were grossly incompetent, or they were flagrantly lying. In either case, this fact alone is enough to dismiss *An Inconvenient Truth* for the nonsense it is. The number of other errors in the book is too long to list here, but has Al ever gotten rich! He has managed to amass a $300 million net worth.[706] And no, he did not invent the internet.

But there is much more. Below is a chart tracking temperature and CO2 levels over a much longer period in earth's history, reprinted with permission from Dr. Moore's book.

Geological Timescale: Concentration of CO2 and Temperature Fluctuations

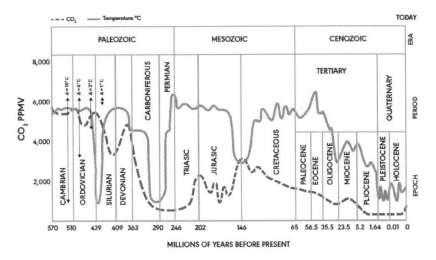

Source: Patrick Moore, *Fake Invisible Catastrophes and Threats of Doom.*

The graph suggests no correlation between rising temperatures and rising CO2 levels. Indeed, Moore states:

> The fundamental question is whether or not the claim that carbon dioxide is the "control knob" of global temperature is valid. The chart shows very clearly that CO2 and temperature are out of sync more often than they are in sync. This does not support the claim that there is a strong cause-effect relationship between CO2 and temperature over the long-term history of the Earth; in fact, it rules against this conclusion. We are being told that the correlation between carbon dioxide and

temperature both rising concurrently over that past 170 years, out of 570 million years of Earth's history, proves a cause-effect relationship. It does not, and the historical record indicates the opposite....

The simultaneous rise of carbon dioxide and temperature over the last 170 years in no way supports a strong cause-effect relationship, in fact it is sufficient to reject that conclusion.

But like petulant children, Al Gore's cronies have become even more shrill. The Left is demanding that something must be done *right now* to avoid catastrophic climate change. In early March, the *New York Times* cited a recent report by the UN Intergovernmental Panel on Climate Change (IPCC), with the headline, "Climate Change Is Speeding Toward Catastrophe," and reads, "Earth is likely to cross a critical threshold for global warming within the next decade, and nations will need to make an immediate and drastic shift away from fossil fuels to prevent the planet from overheating dangerously beyond that level...."[707] Commenting on the report, UN secretary-general António Guterres said:

The climate time bomb is ticking. But today's IPCC report is a how-to guide to defuse the climate time bomb. It is a survival guide for humanity....

This report is a clarion call to massively fast-track climate efforts by every country and every sector and on every time frame. In short, our world needs climate action on all fronts, everything, everywhere, all at once.[708]

One would think this should be cause for genuine alarm. However, note the IPCC website has a disclaimer. It says: "IPCC endeavors to ensure, but cannot and does not guarantee the accuracy, accessibility, integrity and timeliness of the information available on its Website."[709] How many websites have a disclaimer regarding supposed "facts," the accuracy of which cannot be guaranteed? Yet "immediate and drastic" changes to the entire world economy are necessary?

In 2021, *The Guardian* blared this headline: "Equivalent of Covid emissions drop needed every two years."[710] The article claims, "Carbon dioxide emissions must fall by the equivalent of a global lockdown roughly every two years for the next decade for the world to keep within safe limits of global heating, research has shown."

Marc Morano of Climate Depot writes:[711]

> A prescient government-funded report by five universities in the United Kingdom (Cambridge, Imperial College, Oxford, Bath, Nottingham, and Strathclyde) titled Absolute Zero, released in November 2019, envisions what a society locked down for the sake of the climate would look like. "Stop doing anything that causes emissions regardless of its energy source.... Stop eating beef and lamb.... Either use 60% fewer cars or they will be 60% the size," urged the report, funded by the United Kingdom's Engineering and Physical Sciences Research Council. By 2050, "All remaining airports close.... All shipping declines to zero." According to the report's executive summary, there is no choice but to follow this draconian path because it is "the law."

> Canadian banker Mark Carney, a climate advisor to both UK prime minister Boris Johnson and Canadian prime minister Justin Trudeau, has a plan to financially lockdown businesses that don't adhere to the dictates of the climate agenda. "Carney's Brave New World will be one of severely constrained choice, less flying, less meat, more inconvenience, and more poverty: 'Assets will be stranded, used gasoline-powered cars will be unsaleable, inefficient properties will be unrentable,' he promises," wrote Peter Foster, columnist for the National Post and the author of Why We Bite the Invisible Hand: The Psychology of Anti-Capitalism.

The agenda's objectives are in fact already being enforced, not primarily by legislation but by the application of non-governmental—that is, non-democratic—pressure on the corporate sector via the ever-expanding dictates of ESG (environmental, social, and corporate governance) and by 'sustainable finance,' which is designed to starve non-compliant companies of funds, thus rendering them, as Carney puts it, 'climate roadkill.' What ESG actually represents is corporate ideological compulsion. It is a key instrument of 'stakeholder capitalism.'

So you will own nothing, eat bugs, and be happy. We covered ESG earlier. Pensioners, as well as investment funds, are already paying the price for ESG. The following Bloomberg chart shows what losers these funds are when compared to the S&P 500 index:

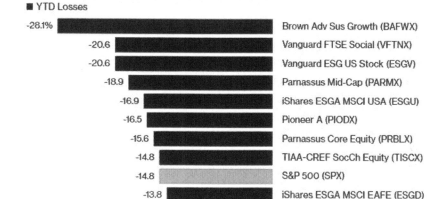

Large ESG Funds Mixed vs S&P 500 in 2022

Majority in top 10 by assets underperformed index

■ YTD Losses

-28.1%	Brown Adv Sus Growth (BAFWX)
-20.6	Vanguard FTSE Social (VFTNX)
-20.6	Vanguard ESG US Stock (ESGV)
-18.9	Parnassus Mid-Cap (PARMX)
-16.9	iShares ESGA MSCI USA (ESGU)
-16.5	Pioneer A (PIODX)
-15.6	Parnassus Core Equity (PRBLX)
-14.8	TIAA-CREF SocCh Equity (TISCX)
-14.8	S&P 500 (SPX)
-13.8	iShares ESGA MSCI EAFE (ESGD)
-13.0	TIAA-CREF Core Im Bond (TSBIX)

Source: Bloomberg
Note: Data measures total return, through Dec. 5

Recall that former Biden climate czar John Kerry was enthusiastic back in 2009 when the recession caused a 6 percent reduction in greenhouse gas emissions. Kerry wanted to see a 20 percent reduction, which would have required a recession almost four times worse. Successive COVID lockdowns described in *The Guardian* would be magnitudes worse and literally destroy the world economy, as COVID almost did.

And while these people are setting off alarm bells about the dangers of rising CO2 levels, energy secretary Jennifer Granholm stated publicly that we could learn some lessons from Communist China about their investments in "clean energy."[712] China has the worst carbon footprint by far of any nation in the world and is rapidly building *new coal-burning power plants equal to existing US capacity.*[713] China's investment in "green energy" is in building the massively polluting lithium batteries they will sell to us but never use themselves. Granholm's statement is simply bizarre for its tone-deaf ignorance or more likely deliberate dishonesty.

With the Paris Climate Agreement, we are on the hook to spend trillions of dollars. And what will this do to the American economy? A report published in 2017 through the US Chamber of Commerce estimated a cost of $3 trillion to the economy, with 6.5 million jobs lost by 2040 and a reduction in household income of $7,000 per year. Furthermore, because of "leakage," i.e., the transfer of production to other countries that will continue to use fossil fuels as we lessen output to meet climate targets, this shift will neutralize any reduction in carbon emissions.[714] Finally, China and Russia, two of the largest greenhouse gas emitters, will not do anything. Just for your edification, in 2023, China emitted over twice the CO2 of the US. India ranked third and Russia, fourth.[715] In other words, the entire effort would be useless.

The Greatest Heist in World History

Why are the global elites of the World Economic Forum, the United Nations, and the world's "progressives" pursuing this blatantly insane agenda with such abandon? As the saying goes, *follow the money*. Therein lies the reason for the ever more strident calls for action on "catastrophic climate change."

Czechoslovakia's famous leader Václav Klaus has called global warming a religion whose motivating ambition is greed and power. In a 2009 Fox News interview, he said:

> We'll be the victims of irrational ideology. They will try to dictate to us how to live, what to do, how to behave. What to eat, travel, and what my children should have. This is something that we who lived in the communist era for most of our lives—we still feel very strongly about.... Some of them are really just rent seekers who hope to get some money either for their businesses or for their countries.[716]

When a con man wants your money, he tries to rush you into a panicked decision before you have time to think. The trillions they want to spend on "the Green New Deal," will wind up in their pockets. As with virtually everything the Left does, such spending certainly will allow the rich leftists to get richer while the rest of us get poorer.

Former president Obama's $80 billion green energy program was a trial run for the greatest heist in world history: the claim of cataclysmic anthropogenic global warming. It was small compared to the monies already enacted under the Biden administration, but it provided a window into the true motive.

In his best-selling book *Throw Them All Out*, author Peter Schweizer compiled a partial list of Democrat financial supporters who donated a total of $457,834 to either Barack Obama's 2008 presidential campaign or to the Democratic Party. Companies run or invested in by these insiders subsequently received US Department of Energy (DOE) grants and loans for $11.3 billion—a payoff rate of twenty-five thousand to one.[717]

Obama appointed former bundlers and campaign managers to run the DOE loan office. These people had solicited donations directly from individuals who later received loans.[718] Sometimes those loan officers even arranged loans for their own companies. Obama mega-fundraiser Sanjay Wagle became the Obama administration's "renewable energy grants advisor." Wagle's company, VantagePoint Capital Partners, subsequently received federal loan guarantees.[719]

Another big green winner in Obama's spending spree was Arvia Few, who promised to raise $50,000 to $100,000 for his 2012 reelection campaign. Her husband, Jason Few, at the time was executive vice president at NRG Energy, which received a $1.2 billion Energy Department loan to construct a solar farm in California.[720] In all, Obama's friends, donors, and bundlers' total take was almost $19 billion.

There are more loans and other politically connected beneficiaries not mentioned here. The complete list would likely fill a book. What followed this $80 billion boondoggle was twenty-seven failures costing taxpayers at least $8 billion. It spurred 1,900 investigations and about six hundred convictions. And while the media has long since moved on, things are just warming up.

In one of his first acts as president, Joe Biden signed Executive Order 13990, which ordered all agencies to review any relevant regulation promulgated under President Donald Trump and rescinded those actions that enabled our nation to become energy independent for the first time since the 1970s. Following a lawsuit by many Republican-led states, a federal judge recently blocked implementation of Executive Order 13990.[721]

But they have not relented. Secretary of the Navy Carlos Del Toro remarked that "I have made climate one of my top priorities since the first day I came into office."[722] All federal agencies have been enlisted in pushing this agenda as a top priority. The end-of-the-world prediction by Rep. Alexandria Ocasio-Cortez (D-NY) is now the basis for public policy, and the Biden administration has taken it to heart. The hilariously misnamed Inflation Reduction Act (IRA) and so-called infrastructure bill both include many elements of AOC's multitrillion-dollar Green New Deal.

The Congressional Budget Office (CBO) estimated that Biden's IRA includes $370 billion to transition the US economy away from carbon-based energy. However, the CBO often wildly underestimates costs, as with its estimate for Obamacare.[723] The actual cost of Biden's IRA will likely be closer to $1.2 trillion, according to Goldman Sachs.[724]

In any event, the IRA includes many tax credits for wind energy. The Renewable Energy Production Tax Credit, for example, provides a tax credit of 2.6 cents per kilowatt-hour (kwh) for ten years.[725] This significantly cuts the direct cost of wind energy to consumers, which still far exceeds the cost of traditional energy sources. A recent study by the Institute for Energy Research found that the cost per kwh for existing coal, natural gas, nuclear, and hydroelectric plants was significantly less than the cost for new wind and solar plants: coal ($0.041), gas ($0.036), nuclear ($0.033), hydroelectric ($0.038), new wind ($0.09), and new solar ($0.089).[726]

Offshore wind is extremely expensive. Constructing massive towers miles out to sea in deep water, with long cables to deliver electricity to the shore, requires a huge infrastructure investment. According to a Manhattan Institute report, the Energy Information Administration has estimated that the levelized cost of offshore wind (the lifetime cost when all investment factors are included) ranges from $0.102 to $0.155 per kwh, with an average of $0.122 per kwh for wind farms operational in 2025.[727] Supposedly, costs will decline in the future, but the Manhattan report is skeptical that it will decline as much as forecast.

That skepticism is warranted. The massive turbines being planned are as high as 853 feet, with turbine blades longer than a football field. Construction of these behemoths at sea requires special ships, of which there are only twelve at present out of a total fleet of thirty-two. Rental costs for the smaller ships are $180,000 per day, and purchase price is $100 million or more. Claire Richer, director of federal affairs at American Clean Power Association, says, "It's pretty insane."[728]

It is truly insane. According to the International Energy Agency, offshore wind currently provides 0.3 percent of world energy needs. That is expected to increase fifteen times by 2040. In other words, for spending multiple trillions over decades to create an industry that would never, ever have even been contemplated without massive government subsidies, by 2040, offshore wind will contribute just 4.5 percent of energy needs.[729]

Offshore wind turbines present hazards to shipping and aircraft, face threats from heavy weather, and incur astronomical maintenance and repair costs.[730] Wind turbines may also have serious consequences for the environment. Wind turbines kill over one million birds per year according to the American Bird Conservancy, although others are quick to point out that cats and cell towers kill more.[731] Grim comfort.

Fishermen along the East Coast are afraid these wind farms will destroy their way of life, calling it "a matter of survival." They have partnered with industry associations and others to sue multiple federal agencies, which they claim authorized these wind farms illegally.[732]

Some environmental groups have also expressed concern that offshore wind farms and construction of windfarms are disrupting marine life and may be responsible for the unusual number of whales dying recently.[733] Amid this growing concern, the Save Right Whales Coalition has produced a report detailing conflicts of interest in that offshore wind companies have made extensive payments to many environmental organizations.[734] These include:

- Woods Hole Oceanographic Institution. Net assets of $385.7 million as of 2019.[735] Accepted $500,000 from Orsted Wind around 2018 and has supported offshore wind since.
- New England Aquarium Corporation. Net assets of $55.4 million as of 2019.[736] Received donations from three separate offshore wind companies—Vineyard Wind, Bay State Wind, and Equinor—between 2018 and 2020. Now supports offshore wind.
- Environmental League of Massachusetts. Net assets of $1.5 million as of 2019.[737] Received $5,000 to $9,000 from Vineyard Wind in 2020. Has supported offshore wind since 2010.
- National Fish and Wildlife Foundation. Net assets of $243.5 million as of 2020.[738] Has received $100,000 to $499,999 from Avangrid Renewables and Apex Clean Energy in 2019 and 2020. Apex has promised to donate $1,000 per megawatt of its commercial generating capacity. The foundation is silent on offshore wind.
- National Audubon Society. Net assets of $585.2 million as of 2021.[739] Has received monies indirectly from the Avangrid

Foundation, associated with Avangrid Renewables, a large wind and solar firm. Audubon supports wind.[740]

- The World Wildlife Fund. Net assets of $375 million as of 2019. Received undisclosed donations from Orsted in 2019. WWF supports offshore wind.
- Other recipients include The Nature Conservancy, the Wetlands Institute, Blue Planet Strategies, Maryland Coastal Bays, Assateague Coastal Trust, and others.

In fact, all of the usual media suspects are now singing the same tune. The headlines blare that whales dying from wind turbine noise is just a hoax. And who are the people peddling this fake news? Donald Trump and conservatives, of course![741]

US Wind is building a major wind farm off the coast of Maryland. In late 2021, it announced "partnerships" with three Maryland organizations to which it pledged $250,000: $100,000 to the Maryland Coastal Bays Program, $100,000 to the Delaware Center for the Inland Bays, and $50,000 to the Assateague Coastal Trust Coast Kids program.[742]

Mainstream journalists are also being paid to promote wind and other "green" energy. AP bragged that it had received $8 million from philanthropists to hire over twenty "journalists" specifically to cover "climate" issues.[743] Foundations donating this money included the William and Flora Hewlett Foundation, the Howard Hughes Medical Institute, Quadrivium, the Rockefeller Foundation, and the Walton Family Foundation.

Finally, some radical environmental groups have been supported by hostile foreign governments. The Sierra Club, the Natural Resources Defense Council (NRDC), and the League of Conservation Voters received a total of $23 million indirectly from Russia to fight hydraulic fracking, according to a report by the Environmental Policy Alliance.[744]

Fracking helped make America energy independent for the first time in decades under President Trump. The resulting decline in oil prices hurt the Russian economy, so this is one of the ways they fought back. The money was donated through the Sea Change Foundation, which received the $23 million through Klein Ltd. Klein is a Bermuda-based shell corporation that acted as a passthrough for funds donated by Russian organizations.

The NRDC, which has strong influence on the Biden administration, also has direct ties to the Communist Chinese government.[745] NRDC employees have worked in China since the 1990s, some directly for the Communist government, and Biden's first climate czar, Gina McCarthy, was formerly the NRDC president.

Another organization with ties to China is the Rocky Mountain Institute, which was behind Biden's proposal to ban gas stoves. Rocky Mountain received $750,000 from the Biden administration to develop "charging corridors" for electric vehicles in California.[746] With the trillions of dollars at stake for these energy companies and their political supporters, it is not surprising that they would enlist the help of environmental groups and attempt to buy off local communities, many of which are now starting to protest these massive, dubious projects.[747]

The point to all this is that so-called clean energy is neither clean nor marketable without substantial government subsidies, loan guarantees, and mandates. But the potential windfall to those who support it, including the companies that will temporarily make money (until the subsidies run out), is impossible to resist.

Remember the "green jobs" Obama promised? Supposedly 125,000 people would be retrained for these jobs after losing their jobs in traditional energy businesses. Less than half, about fifty-three thousand, were actually trained, and only eight thousand got jobs. As economist Steve Moore points out:

> After more than $100 billion spent on the first Green New Deal, by 2016 only about 1 percent American energy was coming from solar energy. Less than 2 percent of cars on the road were electric vehicles—even with the government offering thousands of dollars of cash rebates to buy the vehicles.[748]

How the Green Graft Works: One Example

The state of Maryland had a unique opportunity to fix Chesapeake Bay pollution in 2011—supposedly the big concern among Maryland's elite—but instead, it squandered the chance by focusing on pet ideological projects and wasteful boondoggles for then governor Martin O'Malley's political pals.

The Chicago-based Exelon Corp. was planning a merger with Maryland's Constellation Energy. Exelon owns the one-hundred-year-old Conowingo Dam, which needs dredging. Every time a big storm comes along, the dam spills massive amounts of sediment and nutrients into the bay, smothering the oyster beds, now almost nonexistent in the upper bay. The Conowingo is the greatest single source of bay pollution, dwarfing all others.[749]

To obtain approval for the merger, Exelon agreed to pay the state $1 billion—no analysis of merger benefits or costs, just a big payoff. If O'Malley were truly interested in the environment, he would have demanded Exelon spent some of the $1 billion cleaning up the Conowingo. But none, *zero*, was requested to address the sedimentation problem. Instead, O'Malley showered that $1 billion on green projects that, just like Obama's program, guaranteed lots of green for the governor's friends but saddled Marylanders with expensive, unsustainable, green energy.

There was a proposed $89–$157 million for a new power plant fueled by chicken excrement. The idea was a favorite of O'Malley buddy and Attorney General Doug Gansler. As of 2021, when Gansler geared up for a second run for governor, he was still talking about it, but that's all it was: talk.[750] What happened to the money?

Given that they agreed to this billion-dollar payment, Exelon wasn't interested in talking about dredging. Governor Larry Hogan suggested a $250 million dredging project in 2015, with most of the cost absorbed by Exelon.[751] They weren't buying. O'Malley missed a genuine opportunity to "Save the Bay" by using part of that $1 billion he extorted to dredge. But he had better things to do with it.

About the same time, O'Malley's chief of staff and boyhood friend, Michael Enright,[752] quit his job to take a position as managing director of Beowulf Energy, a firm looking to capture leasing rights for the off-shore wind project then being contemplated. Enright's move paid off almost immediately. In early 2011, Beowulf formed Maryland Solar, LLC, and won expedited approval for constructing a wind farm in two months, a process that usually takes two years.[753]

By July, Maryland Solar had its license and leasing rights to build the state's then largest solar energy farm on 250 acres owned by the Maryland Correctional Institute (MCI) near Hagerstown, Maryland.[754] It was the only bidder for the lease, which is supposed to be a competitive process. The cost of this project was $70 million and would power up to 2,700 homes, 0.1 percent of Maryland's 2.3 million residences.[755] This $70 million project would supplant current capacity, already adequate to handle new demand, so it was totally unnecessary.

Maryland Solar was to receive a $24 million subsidy from the federal government. But here's the real kicker. The firm also secured a buyer for 100 percent of its electricity output once the facility was complete. FirstEnergy, a company that merged with Allegheny Power in February 2011, proudly announced its commitment to purchase all the output for twenty years and pay the state $460,000 to lease the property for that period. FirstEnergy did this to fulfill "its renewable energy commitment pursuant to the negotiated settlement between FirstEnergy and the State as a condition of its merger with Allegheny Power."[756]

Governor O'Malley secured commitments from FirstEnergy to do this as part of the merger agreement. Maryland Solar did not even have a website, and when this story broke, Beowulf Energy's site said "coming soon."

FirstEnergy stated, "The agreement provides the Maryland Solar project the source of guaranteed revenue necessary to obtain financing for its construction."[757] In other words, without Governor O'Malley's scheme forcing FirstEnergy to buy expensive solar power, the entire enterprise could never find anyone foolish enough to invest in it.

While the solar project bragged about adding 125 temporary construction jobs in Maryland, long-term labor costs are low as inmates at

MCI provide routine maintenance. US taxpayers and Maryland citizens will be forced to cross-subsidize this boondoggle through higher taxes and electrical rates. Commenting on the fact that his friend put this whole deal together, O'Malley saw nothing wrong and merely commented, "Given the strides that this project will make to achieving our renewable energy portfolio, I only wish Mr. Enright had joined the private sector earlier rather than later."[758]

It's amazing what you can do in the private sector when friends in government guarantee your success. Mr. Enright is no longer associated with the operation, very likely having cashed out early on. Maryland Solar is now called Arevon. This is a prime example of fascism at work.

Despite O'Malley's ambition to become known for green policies, he, his cronies, the state legislature, and the entire radical environmental movement they support seem to be much more concerned with the kind of green you can shove in your pockets. His flagrant disregard for the existential threat posed by Conowingo sediment and preoccupation with "green" energy boondoggles belie a stunning hypocrisy and systemic institutional corruption. The real-world consequences are further hemorrhaging of Maryland taxpayer dollars and continued environmental calamity that will delay if not doom the prospects for the Chesapeake Bay's recovery. Today, solar and wind farms saturate the Maryland countryside, and county after county is battling further solar development:

> Across Maryland, as clean energy advocates and the solar industry work to meet the state's ambitious mandate of having at least 14.5 percent of the state's energy produced by solar power by 2030, counties are battling what they see as an infringement of their longstanding control over land use and zoning.[759]

The most recent opposition comes from Prince George's County, whose residents don't want the large, unsightly development in their backyard.[760] In 2023, the Carroll County Commissioners voted to ban all further solar farm development on county farmland.[761] As of December 2023, 187 companies were dealing with solar. Collectively, solar puts out 2,054 megawatts, providing a mere 6.32 percent of Maryland's energy needs. [762] Counties are similarly resisting the development of new wind farms, both in rural counties and offshore. This is a welcome development.

Net Zero Is Unattainable

One of the Biden administration's stated goals is to "deploy 30 gigawatts of offshore wind energy by 2030 and achieve a net-zero carbon economy by 2050." [763] As already pointed out, this will only increase offshore wind's contribution to 4.5 percent, and then only with massive government spending, loan guarantees, and mandates because green energy, especially offshore wind, is not profitable.

Biden's Inflation Reduction Act has turbocharged the agenda, already well under way. But that is a drop in the bucket compared to a full implementation of the Green New Deal, estimated to cost between $51 and $93 trillion. [764]

But could "net zero" be achieved, even with the spending envisioned by the Green New Deal? Non-carbon energy comes from four main sources: solar, wind, nuclear, and hydroelectric. (There is also a modest amount of geothermal and hydrogen.) Existing hydroelectric dams in the US are already being dismantled at an unprecedented rate, so constructing new ones will be unlikely. [765] We are left with solar, wind, and nuclear. Ignoring the fact that the Left will rabidly oppose new nuclear plants, it is literally not possible to construct enough "clean" energy plants, including nuclear, to achieve net zero by 2050 or even much further out. [766]

First, one must construct enough wind, solar, and nuclear plants to replace all fossil fuel plants. Then one must construct enough to generate electricity for the switch to electric vehicles, ships, and aircraft. Finally, if carbon-based fuels like coal and oil cannot be used in industry, steel mills, for example, will need to rely entirely on electric power to replace blast furnaces, which usually use coal. It's been compared to "using a toaster's electric wires to melt steel…instead of using a coal furnace." [767] Entirely new equipment will need to be invented to make this possible. Sweden has a pilot program using hydrogen in place of coal it hopes to bring to market by 2026, but it faces many hurdles, not least of which is cost.[768]

To manage this change, total energy output will have to approximately double.[769] According to analysis by Donn Dears, author of *Net-Zero Carbon: The Climate Policy Destroying America*, to achieve net zero by 2050, the US would need to build 995,141 new 2.5-megawatt (MW) wind turbines (35,551 units annually), 881 new nuclear plants (thirty-one annually), and 3,918,996 MW of new solar production (139,954 MW annually).[770]

For comparison, since 2000, the maximum annual construction of each kind of power plant is one nuclear plant, 5,680 2.5 MW wind turbines, and 21,500 MW of solar. This does not include production of storage batteries, essential for wind and solar. Another analysis conducted for Australia found that achieving net zero by 2050 in that nation alone would require:

- 354 new wind turbines installed every month, or *11.8 every day*, until 2050, at a cost of $476 billion;
- eighteen thousand solar rooftop systems together with sixty-seven solar farms installed every month at a total cost of $326 billion;
- carbon offsets for irreplaceable fossil fuel burning equipment: seventeen billion trees/year, ultimately covering 50 percent of Australia's arable land;
- a total cost of $1.13 trillion.[771]

This is insanity. So much so, that it is almost impossible to believe any legislator would support it. But green speaks louder than reality for politicians, so-called "environmentalists," and businesspeople.

The Geological Survey of Finland conducted an exhaustively detailed one-thousand-page study of requirements to transition the US, European Union, and People's Republic of China to net zero.[772] Included was an analysis of the number and weight of lithium batteries needed to replace diesel freight locomotives with electric motors. The analysis found that each locomotive would require a battery weighing

281.9 metric tons, and that battery could drive a standard freight load for 14.4 hours. It estimated a total of 104,894 locomotives, with battery needs totaling 29.6 million metric tons (104,894 × 281.9 metric tons = 29.6 million metric tons). That's 32.6 million standard tons.[773] Total global production of lithium in 2021 was 130,000 tons, and estimated global reserves are ninety-eight million tons.[774]

Lithium demand from electric vehicle (EV) cars, ships, or planes would dwarf requirements for locomotives.[775] Examine the table below. It is reproduced from the Finnish study, which estimates that cars, trucks, busses, and motorcycles would need 282.6 million metric tons (311.5 million standard tons) of lithium-ion batteries.

Size of Required Electrical Vehicle Fleet for the Global System

Vehicle Class	Number of Self Propelled Vehicles in 2018 Global Fleet	Total km driven by class in 2018 Global Fleet	Electrical power to be generated, assuming a 10% loss in transmission between power station and charging point	Estimated Summed for Vehicle Class Battery Capacity to be Manufactured	Total Mass of Li-Ion batteries
	(number)	(km)	(kWh)	(kWh)	(tonne)
Transit Bus + Refuse Truck + Paratransit Shuttle + Delivery Truck + School Bus	29,002,253	8.03E+11	1.60E+12	5.98E+09	25,988,541
Light Truck/Van + Light-Duty Vehicle	601,327,324	7.89E+12	2.99E+12	2.53E+10	110,181,094
Passenger Car	695,160,429	5.40E+12	1.55E+12	3.25E+10	141,450,035
Motorcycle	62,109,261	1.60E+11	2.65E+10	1.34E+09	4,968,741
Total	1,387,599,267	1.43E+13	6.1584E+12	6.5188E+10	2.83E+08
	1.39 billion vehicles	14.25 trillion km travelled in 2018	6 158.4 TWh power generated to charge batteries	65.19 TWh of Batteries	Total Li-Ion battery mass 282.6 million tonnes

Source: Table 26.4. *Assessment of the Extra Capacity Required of Alternative Energy Electrical Power Systems to Completely Replace Fossil Fuels*, Geological Survey of Finland.

Data from the Finland geological survey reproduced in the table below shows the US requirement alone for alternative energy production to meet net zero goals between 2023 and 2050. The world requirement is off the charts and doesn't even account for essential growth in emerging economies. Besides, we cannot control what the rest of the world does. China, for example, is pointedly ignoring the move to alternative fuels, although they are only too happy to be our primary source for lithium.

Number of Additional Non–Fossil Fuel Power Stations to Phase Out Fossil Fuels in the United States

Power Generation System	United States non-fossil fuel electricity production in 2018 (Appendix B & BP Statistics 2019) (kWh)	2018 ratio percent of non-fossil fuel electrical power systems in United States (%)	Expanded extra required annual capacity to phase out fossil fuels (kWh)	Power Produced by a Single Average Plant in 2018 (kWh)	Estimated number of required additional new power plants of average size to phase out fossil fuels (number)
Nuclear	8.50E+11	52.77%	4.36E+12	1.28E+10	341
Hydroelectric	2.89E+11	17.93%	1.48E+12	1.33E+09	1,118
Wind	2.78E+11	17.25%	1.43E+12	8.12E+07	17,549
Solar PV	9.71E+10	6.03%	4.99E+11	3.30E+07	15,088
Other Renewable	9.70E+10	6.02%	4.98E+11	7.70E+07	6,470

Source: Table 26.12. *Assessment of the Extra Capacity Required of Alternative Energy Electrical Power Systems to Completely Replace Fossil Fuels*, Geological Survey of Finland.

Thus, based on current average output and size of energy plants, to transition entirely away from fossil fuels, the US would need to build *forty-seven* solar farms, *fifty-four* wind farms, *one* nuclear power plant, *three* hydroelectric dams, and *twenty* geothermal, tidal, or biowaste plants *per month until 2050*.[776]

And this assumes the greens will allow nuclear and hydroelectric, which they will not. The absurdity of this agenda is beyond dispute. In the real world, as the Finnish study relates, "the incubation time for the construction of a new power plant can range between two to five years (or 20 years for a nuclear plant)."[777]

A small bit of good news: the Biden administration had planned to install 3,400 large ocean wind turbines off the New Jersey coast, but delays and cost overruns forced two of three projects to be abandoned. Meanwhile, a group concerned about the wind farm's potential harm to the endangered right whale have tried to stop it. Legislators are calling for a halt on further development, and the Government Accountability Office will be conducting an investigation into the industry.[778]

The feds claim the wind farm would "adversely affect" the whales but do no permanent damage. How do they know this? What *is* killing the whales? And a sampling of mainstream media posts shows an amazing uniformity. They include the same "adversely affect" line and "no long-term damage." If we didn't know they were in it for the money also, we might be tempted to believe them.

The global warming fanatics are forcing energy firms to invest in losing technologies while abandoning existing successful, inexpensive, readily available, *and clean* sources. (Remember, CO_2 is not a pollutant.) The multiple billions of dollars already invested in cleaning up coal will be wasted as more and more coal plants go offline—unable to meet ever more restrictive greenhouse gas regulations.

Our vast conventional energy infrastructure will be slowly abandoned as companies driven by subsidies and mandates build more solar, wind, and other non-economical alternative energy facilities. Energy costs will skyrocket, crippling the economy, and when government subsidies run out, as they surely must, the entire green energy infrastructure will collapse, just as it did under President Obama's green energy program. But there will be nothing to fall back upon because we have left our carbon-based energy infrastructure fallow. Without reliable energy, our nation will be crippled. *Our nation, indeed the world, requires abundant, cheap, reliable energy.*

By imposing this new, expensive, inefficient energy regime, the Left is forcing consumers to pay much higher utility bills while opening the spigots of government spending once again to finance an unsustainable activity. Furthermore, to compete, companies are forced to invest in the political market rather than their own markets and products. The Left is *incentivizing corruption*, luring private companies away from free market capitalism to crony Socialism (aka *fascism*), and literally threatening the continued viability of our market economy, our standard of living, and perhaps even our survival. The global warming activists will destroy it all if we let them.

The Left is a death cult.

JANUARY 6 WAS NOT AN "INSURRECTION"

I've been indicted more times than Alphonse Capone.
—Donald Trump

The events of January 6, 2021, had all the hallmarks of a classic Communist influence operation. Everything from the fake "bombs" found at the RNC and DNC headquarters to the way the J6 protest unfolded was planned in advance by Democrat leaders with the likely assistance of the FBI and other, unknown people.

Most of the violent actors, or at least the ones who initiated violence, were leftist plants. There are photos of Antifa types donning MAGA apparel before heading to the barricades and confronting police. That is not to say that Trump protesters did not get involved. Some were definitely goaded into it, because there was plenty of anger over the very questionable loss of the 2020 election. Some members of the Proud Boys have pled guilty and apparently were there to mix it up.

But the media even gaslighted this. Reports of the sentencing of Proud Boys leader Enrique Tarrio referred to the Proud Boys as a "neo-facist group" that "became a force in mainstream Republican circles."[779] The Proud Boys aren't neofascists, and certainly were not "a force in mainstream Republican circles." The Proud Boys were simply a group that liked to meet force against Antifa/BLM force.

Those groups, if any, should be called the "neofascists" because it was always they who provoked violence. That is Antifa's entire reason for being. And while J6 protesters, especially groups like the Proud Boys and the Oath Keepers, got the book thrown at them, the violent and deadly George Floyd rioters have gotten off in most cases with a slap on the wrist. They were the true insurrectionists. Reports also repeated the lie that it was "violent chaos fueled by Trump's lies about the election that helped inspire right-wing extremists like the Proud Boys and the Oath Keepers."[780]

No, it was the reality that the Democrats used every device at their disposal to cheat in the election, as intimately detailed in the vote fraud chapter, that fueled their anger—not that it justified violence. But most people were at the Capitol on January 6 simply to do what President Trump had told them to do, peacefully protest. "I know that everyone here will soon be marching over to the Capitol building to peacefully and patriotically make your voices heard,"[781] he said.

The media ignores that statement as well, and chooses to take it out of context, focusing on another part of the speech where Trump said, "We fight like hell. We fight like hell." What he actually said was:

> And again, most people would stand there at 9 o'clock in the evening and say I want to thank you very much, and they go off to some other life. But I said something's wrong here, something is really wrong, can have happened.

> And we fight. We fight like hell. And if you don't fight like hell, you're not going to have a country anymore.

> Our exciting adventures and boldest endeavors have not yet begun. My fellow Americans, for our movement, for our children, and for our beloved country.

And I say this despite all that's happened. The best is yet to come.

So we're going to, we're going to walk down Pennsylvania Avenue. I love Pennsylvania Avenue. And we're going to the Capitol, and we're going to try and give.[782]

Taken in context, does this sound like he was telling the crowd to riot at the Capitol? No, he was making a statement about the ongoing fight we need to engage in to defeat the lunatic Left. Reuters, which used to be a relatively balanced news source, basically reinvented what Trump said:

The chaos unfolded after Trump—who before the election refused to commit to a peaceful transfer of power if he lost—addressed thousands of supporters near the White House and told them to march on the Capitol to express their anger at the voting process. He told his supporters to pressure their elected officials to reject the results, urging them "to fight."[783]

That's not what he said, and it is not how he said it. But this is how we are being gaslighted by the media. The Reuters article cited here also attempts to debunk claims that there were Antifa members among the crowd provoking violence. They referenced numerous photos of Jacob Chansley, the so-called QAnon Shaman, who was incorrectly identified at first. But there were many other photos that neither Reuters nor anyone else has answered for.

What follows borrows generously from an eyewitness account by J. Michael Waller, senior analyst for strategy at the Center for Security Policy, former CIA operative, and author of the bestselling book *Big Intel*. Waller is a seasoned analyst who has attended many protests and received training from professional agitators in his youth, so he knows what to look for. Waller was at the Capitol on January 6 and made these observations (emphases in the original):[784]

1. **Plainclothes militants.** Militant, aggressive men in Donald Trump and MAGA gear at a front police line at the base of the temporary presidential inaugural platform;
2. **Agents-provocateurs.** Scattered groups of men exhorting the marchers to gather closely and tightly toward the center of the outside of the Capitol building and prevent them from leaving;
3. **Fake Trump protesters.** A few young men wearing Trump or MAGA hats backwards and who did not fit in with the rest of the crowd in terms of their actions and demeanor, whom I presumed to be Antifa or other leftist agitators; and
4. **Disciplined, uniformed column of attackers.** A column of organized, disciplined men, wearing similar but not identical camouflage uniforms and black gear, some with helmets and GoPro cameras or wearing subdued Punisher skull patches.

Waller said the first, second, and fourth group engaged in violence. He added that unlike the crowd, which was generally happy and care-free, the people in all four of these groups looked totally out of place. They appeared sullen and angry, and most wore face masks. The fake Trump protesters in group three "walked, often hands in pockets, in clusters of perhaps four to six with at least one of them frequently look-ing behind. These outliers group looked like trouble. I presumed that these **fake Trump protesters** were Antifa or something similar," he said. But he did not witness group three engage in any violence.

Another group, he said, "also stood out. While many marchers wore military camouflage shirts, jackets, or pants of various patterns and states of wear and in all shapes and sizes, here and there one would see people of a different type: Wiry young men in good physical condition dressed neatly in what looked like newer camouflage uniforms with black gear, subdued patches including Punisher skulls, and helmets.... They showed tidiness and discipline.... Unlike others in old military clothes who tended to be affable and talkative, these sullen men seemed not to speak to anyone at all."[785]

Trump supporters usually do not wear helmets, because they do not intend to be violent. This group would later become an attacking force.

Waller said, "All of these cells or groups stood out from the very large crowd by their behavior and overall demeanor. However, they did not all appear at the same time. Not until the very end did it become apparent there was a prearranged plan to storm the Capitol building, and to manipulate the unsuspecting crowd as cover and as a follow-on force."[786]

Waller said that a large portion of the crowd was funneled into a small area that was difficult to retreat from. The violent group confronting police at the barriers was at the very front, but many behind them wanted to leave. The police started throwing canisters of tear gas at them. They tried to retreat. Waller's narrative continues:[787]

> Then, a loud, bellowing shout from behind: "Forward! Do not retreat! Forward!"
>
> Retreat? Nobody was retreating. They were trying to escape the tear gas. But the man kept yelling not to "retreat," as if this were a military operation. In a powerful voice he exhorted the crowd to remain on the plaza and not to disperse on the lawn or depart down the steps to the footpath. Thousands more people continued pouring in from Constitution Avenue.
>
> Then two other men, standing across from one another on the high granite curbs on either side of the footpath, bellowed variations of, "Forward! Don't you dare retreat!" Some made direct eye contact at people and pointed directly at them, as if trying to psyche them to submit.
>
> A third man standing on a chair, also shouting "Forward," reached down to grab me by the shoulder and barked, "Don't retreat! Get back up there!" It wasn't an expression of enthusiasm or solidarity; it sounded like a military order. And it wasn't from a wild kid; this guy was probably in his 50s. He looked furious with me.

What did he care what I did? What difference would the departure of ten or even a hundred of us make, with so many more surging in. The furious man crouched down and yelled in my face: "We're going into the Capitol!" I ignored him, broke away, and worked my way down the steps....

What the barking men were doing didn't hit me later when we found out about the attack: They appeared to be part of an organized cell of agents-provocateurs to corral people as an unwitting follow-on force behind the plainclothes militants tussling with police—but who, we would later learn, were actually breaking into the Capitol beneath the Great Rotunda to storm Congress. It was just before 3 o'clock.

These agents-provocateurs placed hundreds of unsuspecting supporters of the president in physical danger. They attempted to block exits for people seeking to escape tear gas. They endangered vulnerable people, including children, the frail, and the elderly. They funneled and pushed hundreds if not thousands of innocent people into a crush toward the Capitol. They did so with the goal of forcing those people into a confrontation with federal police defending Congress.

Capitol police began hurling tear gas grenades into the crowd, even though the crowd was not violent, and it was impossible for them to retreat. It seemed to Waller that the police were trying to provoke the crowd. This was suggested much later as well, when video surfaced of police throwing a rubber ball grenade, which disperses tear gas, rubber balls, or both. It caught one person on fire. Police regulations require First Amendment protesters be warned three times before using such equipment. Police gave no warning.[788]

Waller concluded by saying, "The deadly riot at the US Capitol bore the markings of an organized operation planned well in advance of the January 6 joint session of Congress."[789]

In testimony before the US Senate, Jill Sanborn, FBI assistant director for counterterrorism, agreed with Waller's assessment.[790] Former Capitol police chief Steven Sund also acknowledged in testimony that they expected Antifa to be there:

> The assessment indicated that members of the Proud Boys, white supremacist groups, Antifa, and other extremist groups were expected to participate in the January 6th event and that they may be inclined to become violent.[791]

These reflections came a short time after the riot. But since then, much more has come out that confirms this presumption.

The entire "insurrection" narrative is based on a lie. In order for the Democrats to claim President Trump agitated for a violent "insurrection," they would first have to explain how that would help him. It was the last thing he wanted. Trump planned to use the Electoral Count Act of 1887 to legally challenge the electors of seven states. Under the law, the president of the senate, Mike Pence, could legally make that determination. So the last thing Trump wanted was a riot or any kind of violence that would spoil his plans. So there was no insurrection.[792]

Trump was well within the law to use this device. And under the "ok for me but not for thee" category, the Democrats had used that very same tactic (unsuccessfully) against George W. Bush in 2004. Trump made no secret of his plan. The Democrats knew about it and so could not have thought he would provoke violence. He even tried to tweet Capitol protesters to stop when he heard the Capitol had been breached.[793]

But you can see how the Democrats have used it. The Fourteenth Amendment disqualifies anyone for public office who participated in "insurrection" or aided and abetted anyone who did. So of course, three Democrat states used that excuse to try to remove Trump from the presidential ballot for 2024. Fortunately, they got slapped down. But they could conceivably have used it against any political candidate who was in any way involved in January 6, or "aided and abetted" anyone who was, to bar thousands of Republicans from running for any office under the thinnest of pretexts.[794] And this tactic once again reveals the two-tiered justice system we are currently living with. Kamala Harris set up a fund to help Antifa/BLM members arrested for rioting during the George Floyd protests. That is certainly "aiding and abetting" insurrectionists. But don't expect Kamala to be barred from future office because of it.

But Trump didn't give them an insurrection. So they created one instead. This entire fiasco was a setup.

The former Capitol Police commander who evacuated the House and Senate following the breach of the Capitol says, "J6 was not an insurrection, but not many people would listen."[795] Officer Tarik Johnson evacuated the Capitol after waiting for then assistant chief Yogananda Pittman, another diversity hire, to give him the green light. She ignored him, so finally, he just went ahead and did it without her permission. He said she was just sitting in the command post, watching it all unfold on CCTV, but kept ignoring his requests. He reported her to Vermont Democratic senator Patrick Leahy (a big mistake), and one hour later, he was put on leave, told not to speak to anyone, and told to stay in his house every weekday from 8 a.m. to 4 p.m. until he left the department—seventeen months later.[796]

In an interview with Tucker Carlson, Representative Clay Higgins, a former police officer himself, laid it all out. Following were facts he said *we know*:[797]

- There were "well over two hundred" FBI agents embedded within the J6 protester crowd, inside and outside the building.
- FBI agents infiltrated the online Trump community months before J6.
- Online FBI infiltrators seeded the idea, "Using language that incited behavior that could go the wrong way..." suggesting protesters do "something more."
- FBI agents dressed as Trump supporters were inside the Capitol and waved protesters in.

- The FBI "tricked" local police to participate in this entrapment that they had been planning for ten months.
- Government officials literally lured Trump supporters into the Capitol on J6.

Rep. Higgins called it "a conspiracy in our government at the highest level to set the stage for a compromised election cycle in 2020, *and then* the actions that took place on J4, 5, and 6. *And then*, the criminal investigation, arrest and prosecution the Americans they were able to entrap…." The objective, he said, was to destroy the entire MAGA movement by destroying the reputation of the movement.[798]

Rep. Higgins said: "On the inside, you had FBI assets dressed as Trump supporters who knew their way around the Capitol before the doors open. Or else how are you going to get around the Capitol?"

He made the point that the Capitol is like a maze, and it's virtually impossible to find, for example, the House Speaker's office, without guidance. The FBI lured protesters to those locations that would make the worst case. "They were setting the stage for arrest and prosecution," he said.

No such attention was ever paid to any of the deadly Antifa/BLM riots that occurred during 2020. Those truly were acts of insurrection, as the leftists themselves proudly boast. And whereas those rioters received legal assistance financed by public figures like Kamala Harris, J6 prisoners have received little help, had bond revoked, and have languished in prison for years in some cases, for misdemeanor crimes like trespassing. One small bright spot: one hundred J6 defendants are suing the Capitol Police for the brutal treatment they received at the hands of police on January 6.

The unfortunate Ashli Babbitt was another victim of this two-tiered justice system. Despite her efforts to break into the Capitol, the Capitol policeman who shot her, Michael Byrd, had no reason to do so. She was unarmed, and police officers were standing right next to her as she tried to break in. She could have been stopped right there. Instead, she was given no warning and likely did not even see Officer Byrd.

Just previous to that, she had prevented another person from breaking in.[799] As a former policeman, Rep. Higgins said that shooting was entirely unjustified. But instead of being disciplined, Officer Byrd was celebrated. Higgins said if it had been him, Babbit would have been arrested, handcuffed, and told to sit it out.[800]

We have been summarily denied the truth about what happened on January 6. But the truth always leaks out, sooner or later. Hopefully House Majority Leader Johnson will release the full digital files of everything they have, to expose the true insurrectionists for who they are. It could determine the outcome of the 2024 election.

AN INTERNATIONAL CONSPIRACY

*I want you people here to organize and
keep organizing until you are able to
overthrow the damned rotten capitalistic
government of this country.*
—Leon Trotsky, Bolshevik leader of the
Soviet Red Army, to NYC Communists

The anti-Israel, pro-Hamas protests and riots that have wracked American college campuses since the October 7, 2023 Hamas terror attack on Israel have been funded by America's radical Left foundations, but also the Iranian Revolutionary Guard Corps, (IRGC). This was revealed in a letter written by the IRGC's deputy commander-in-chief. Note carefully what he says, because the target is not specifically Israel, but to create utter chaos using Israel's very justifiable counterattacks on Hamas as pretext:

> This…is the announcement of a collective movement aimed at disrupting the public order in Europe, USA, Australia and Asia all under the pretext of supporting Palestinians. *This is a political movement intended to cause as much chaos and instability as possible, which are the exact goals of the Islamic Republic of Iran.* The regime

of the Islamic Republic has on multiple occasions stated clearly that their goal is to destroy the modern society and build a global Islamic state. (Emphasis added.)[801]

The fanatical anti-Semitism demonstrated at these protests almost defies description. Students chant "Death to Israel" and scream at Jewish students, "Go back to the ovens." But this isn't even new. Students have been protesting this way for years.[802] After decades of hearing about the Nazi Holocaust, it seems incomprehensible that leftist students would be speaking this way, especially since they almost daily accuse the rest of us of being Nazis. But in fact, that is the entire point. Their true goal is to create blind chaos, turning reality on its head. And they are aided and abetted by our enemies abroad.

Another May 2024 article revealed that some of the organizers behind the anti-Israel protests were trained for years by Communist Cuba.[803] Once again, we are presented with the hard evidence: These protests are agenda-driven, and activists are drilled in the methods of protest. They only need a pretext. And you can be sure they had advanced warning of the Hamas attack.

The American Left was not incubated in a tube. The "Seeds of Crisis" chapter described how the international Communist movement, led at the time by the Soviet Union, first established a firm foothold within the American educational establishment in the 1930s through the Frankfurt School based at Columbia Teachers College. But the international connections preceded that by decades.

Communism, Socialism, and anarchism had become increasingly popular among radicals starting with the publication of Karl Marx's *Communist Manifesto* in 1848. The First International, also called the International Workingmen's Association, was founded in 1864. Karl Marx became its leader. It was organized into national factions of Socialists, anarchists, and labor leaders but split in 1873 over rivalries between Marxists and anarchists.[804]

The Second International was founded in Paris, France, in 1889. It was a loose organization of Socialist national labor and political party leaders. By 1912, it had about nine million Socialist and Social

Democratic Party members in the US, Canada, Japan, and all European nations. While it claimed to seek resolutions to war by peaceful means, in 1907, it adopted a resolution co-written by Vladimir Lenin where "the International pledged its member parties in belligerent countries to *use the social and economic crisis brought about by war to promote social revolution.*" (Emphasis added.)[805] Lenin knew the value of crisis strategies even then.

While the international movements of the radical Left were gaining steam, they really had no national foundation from which to solidify their strength. That changed with the establishment of the Soviet Union with the Bolshevik takeover of Russia in 1917. The Third International, which came to be known as the Communist International or Comintern, was founded in the Soviet Union in 1919. Lenin quickly turned it into a centrally controlled organ by which he could wield power over the Communist parties of the world. All moderates were expelled.[806]

The Communist Party USA (CPUSA) was established that same year, which gave the Communist movement a more centralized base from which to operate in America. But it is critical to understand that almost from the beginning, most CPUSA activities were financed and directed by Moscow. The CPUSA is not an organization of people who just believe in Communism; it is a fifth column within the United States working to overthrow our country. Every single Communist living within the United States should be tried as an enemy agent and expelled, imprisoned, or executed for treason.

The Chinese and Russian consulates spread all over the United States are there for two primary reasons: (1) to contact, recruit, pay, and direct American spies to do their dirty work, including the CPUSA and others under their employ, and (2) to engage in theft of intellectual property and state and corporate secrets. There is no logical reason for them to remain open. They should be shuttered immediately and their members expelled.

The hand of international Communism has become increasingly visible over the past few years. Some American and European politicians and global elitists see Communist China as a friend and even role model. Communist Chinese influence peddling has become blatant.

Joe Biden and his family have received millions of dollars from foreign governments and shady individuals associated with them—at least $36 million from Communist China alone, as documented in Peter Schweizer's books, *Red-Handed*, and his latest, *Blood Money*.

Joe Biden has been very circumspect about our fentanyl epidemic. It comes from Communist China and has been sent here with the complicity of the Chinese government as one of China's unrestricted warfare strategies to undermine, corrupt, and demoralize the US. According to *Blood Money*, the Bidens received $5 million from Ye Jianming, a business partner of a former Chinese triad leader known as the "White Wolf." White Wolf's triad, the United Bamboo Gang, has a direct relationship with the Mexican Sinaloa cartel and according to Schweizer, has made the cartel into the "King of Fentanyl." Top Chinese leaders call the White Wolf, "Big Brother."[807]

Meanwhile, China has been purchasing large tracts of land, some near sensitive US military bases. But not only China—Russia, North Korea, and Iran have purchased land also.[808] Collectively, they own four hundred thousand acres of US farmland as of 2021.[809] While currently representing only about 1 percent of foreign-owned land in the US, these are our enemies. They should not own one acre. The second largest foreign US landowner is Chen Tianqiao, a Chinese national, who owns 198,000 acres of timberland in Oregon.[810]

Will that land become one of the home bases for the thousands of Chinese military-aged men crossing the border? In 2023, Customs and Border Protection reported encountering thirty-seven thousand Chinese nationals crossing the southern border.[811] Another twenty-one thousand have come across so far in fiscal year 2024.[812] Are they simply looking for a better life, or are they part of a plan to wreak havoc here at some point? As described earlier, they don't have a choice. If the Chinese government wants them to engage in nefarious acts, they will do so.

But more importantly, many are likely members of military special forces. The Russian Spetsnaz are highly trained special operators whose job it is to infiltrate a target country and wreak havoc—create multiple crises—to weaken our defenses and distract military and first responders in advance of military invasion or some other major offensive. China has a similar unit designed for the same purpose and almost certainly has infiltrated members of those units.

On the domestic side, a seemingly benign nonprofit is the State Legislative Leaders Foundation (SLLF). It describes itself as:

> A nonpartisan, nonprofit organization dedicated to professional development for our nation's current and future state legislative leaders. Our constituency includes Speakers of the House, Senate Presidents, Majority Leaders, Minority Leaders, and Leaders Pro Tempore. And through our *Emerging Leaders Program*, we offer mentoring to first- and second-term legislators who have been identified by their peers as future leaders.[813]

In fact, it has nominally partnered with the Chinese People's Association for Friendship with Foreign Countries (CPAFFC), a front for the Chinese Communist Party. In 2015, Hunter Biden's business partners lobbied the Obama administration to approve this partnership.[814] Obama supported the idea, and it was made official following a September 2015 meeting in Washington, DC, with Chinese leader Xi Jinping. The Chinese government published a list of the agreements made. Point 39 reads:

> To enhance sub-national exchanges and cooperation between China and the U.S., the Chinese People's Association for Friendship with Foreign Countries and the U.S. State Legislative Leaders Foundation reached consensus on establishing the China-U.S. Sub-national Legislatures Exchange Mechanism, and plan to co-host the First China-U.S. Sub-national Legislatures Cooperation Forum in 2016.[815]

The SLLF brags a long list of state legislators from both political parties. The June 2024 Conference of State Majority Leaders lists the host as South Carolina GOP state senate majority leader, Shane

Massey.[816] The website does not list its board of directors, but its most recent IRS filing lists Connecticut State Senate President Pro Tempore Martin Looney as its board chairman and GOP Wisconsin Assembly Speaker Robin Vos as vice chairman.[817]

Looney is a far-left legislator in office since 1993.[818] Vos is a long-serving conservative GOP state assembly leader. In an interview with Speaker Vos on April 9, 2024, he said that the SLLF had not had contact with CPAFFC or anyone in China since 2017.[819]

That may be true; however, in December 2015, the SLLF website proudly announced: "SLLF and the Chinese People's Association for Friendship with Foreign Countries sign historic pact."[820] It came to our attention after a March 2024 article on Breitbart calling out Speaker Vos for this relationship.[821] The announcement references the agreement Obama and Xi made in 2015, stating in part:

> We are honored to represent the USA in this important new initiative.
>
> Over the upcoming months and years, SLLF and CPAFFC will be convening a series of educational programs in China and here in the USA focusing on a variety of critical public policy issues of mutual importance to both nations and in a larger sense, to the world. As with all SLLF programs, our goal will be to inform the debate by providing key political and business leaders in both nations with objective, factual and relevant information on the many issues and concerns that require our shared commitment. Equally important, this new partnership heralds the establishment of a new framework for advancing communication, cooperation and friendship between our nations.
>
> We look forward with great anticipation to the many opportunities this partnership affords all parties to advance the cause of peaceful coexistence and lay the

foundation for lasting friendships built on trust and mutual respect.[822]

In June 2016, a forum held in Honolulu, Hawaii, was co-hosted by CPAFFC and the SLLF. The Chinese Embassy announcement said the forum "aims to implement one of the important outcomes of President Xi Jinping's state visit to the US, and to promote the exchanges and cooperation between the sub-national legislatures of China and the US.... The delegates of both sides had in-depth discussions on how to promote tourism cooperation through legislation, strengthen the part-nership between Chinese provinces and the US states, create a business friendly environment, etc."[823]

This was in 2016, so it is unclear how much interaction occurred between the SLLF and China subsequently, but an SLLF retrospective ("SLLF at Fifty: Looking Forward to Fifty More!") dated December 9, 2022, states, "As the first decade of the century came to a close, SLLF began a relationship with China, conducting programs across that vast nation and bringing Chinese leaders to the US, and even ventured into South and Central America with programs in Mexico and Argentina."[824]

According to the SLLF website, in 2023, SLLF legislative leaders from California and Tennessee attended the UN-sponsored COP 28 climate change conference in Dubai, United Arab Emirates, to discuss "subnational collaboration addressing climate change between the United States and China."[825]

Again, while Speaker Vos may be correct in saying that Wisconsin delegates have not been involved with China since 2017, it seems clear that the SLLF finds collaboration, or at least interaction, with China to be beneficial. And that will always play to China's advantage.

Ironically, in July 2022, the Biden administration—the last ones you'd expect—put out a warning that the SLLF Hunter Biden and com-pany had lobbied for was vulnerable to Chinese Communist influence operations.[826]

Given all the recent concerns over Chinese ownership of American lands, a bill proposed in the state assembly in 2024 sought to outlaw any purchases of Wisconsin farm or forestry property by "a foreign adversary."[827] Speaker Vos said he favors this bill, but it has no teeth because federal treaty obligations dictate what they can or cannot do. He said he would support federal legislation that abrogated the treaty, which would allow such laws to be upheld.

The bill was referred to the state Committee on Agriculture. Opponents say he could have asked it be put to the floor for a vote. Current law, as well as the state constitution, does not bar "alien" ownership of land as long as they are US residents but limits foreign ownership of non-farm or non-forestry property to 640 acres. Furthermore, it prohibits foreigners from owning any farm or forest property, except "whose rights to hold larger quantities of land are secured by treaty."[828]

Unrelated to this, but relevant to ongoing Chinese influence operations against the US, on October 11, 2023, officials from the Department of Energy met secretly in China with Sun Ying, president of the China Construction Technology Company, a state-owned company. Sun Ying is a dedicated member of the Chinese Communist Party. They had a total of four meetings and offered to give Chinese scientists access to technology developed by the Lawrence Berkeley Laboratory and other high-tech labs.

This became public through a letter sent by Senator John Barrasso, ranking member on the Energy and Natural Resources Committee, to energy secretary Jennifer Granholm. He listed the many ways this was a bad idea, characterizing the meeting as "misguided interactions."[829] He was being too generous. Granholm, like Biden, knows exactly what she is doing. That agreement would open some of our most sensitive research facilities to Chinese Communist spies.

We discussed some of China's involvement in the George Floyd riots earlier, but Russia was involved as well. A post by Kyle Shideler of the Center for Security Policy described the activities of Aleksandr Viktorovich Ionov, allegedly an agent of Russia's Federal Security Service. Ionov was indicted in August 2022, accused of coordinating with three American radical black organizations: the Florida-based Uhuru Movement, also called the African People's Socialist Party; the Black Hammer Party of Atlanta, Georgia; and California-based Yes California. The FBI considers these groups "instruments of the Russian Government."

While Shideler described the interactions as relatively minor, he thought it unlikely they would warrant such close FBI attention unless there was much more going on.[830]

Russia is involved in another little-known influence operation. It was uncovered and extensively documented by author and filmmaker Trevor Loudon.[831] Alexander Dugin, a Russian with close ties to Russian leader Vladimir Putin, created a political party called the National Bolsheviks. The idea was to get people like Richard Spencer, the organizer of the Unite the Right rally in Charlottesville, Virginia, in 2017, and individuals of the radical Left, to join forces and overthrow the corrupt West. Spencer would become an early enthusiast, and his wife is actually Dugin's English translator.[832] Another follower of the National Bolsheviks was Brenton Tarrant, the Christchurch, New Zealand, shooter who massacred fifty-one people at a mosque in 2019. His backpack and weapons were all stamped with the National Bolshevik logo, and his "manifesto" reflected that ideology, essentially a marriage of Nazis and Communists against the West.[833]

Now Dugin has come up with an offshoot: MAGA Communists.[834] It would be funny except some people are actually buying into it. One of these MAGA Communists, Jackson Hinkle, tweeted a photo of himself walking next to Putin with the statement: "I am a Christian Communist American Patriot, and I stand with Putin!"[835]

Dugin tries to make a case for a system that rejects both anti-Communism and anti-fascism, as if this suggests a marriage between the Right and the Left.[836] He calls it "multipolarity." The true goal, however, is "sowing deep political divisions within the United States and Europe, exploiting existing tensions to foment civil unrest and chaos."[837]

This merging of ideologies, Dugin says, should agree that capitalism is bad, while rejecting the atheism of Communism. Therefore, all peoples should unite against the corrupt West, led by Russia, China, and Iran.[838] But really, it is just a clever reframing of the perennial Communist narrative, which is that the West is imperialist and corrupt and sees itself as "unipolar," that is, the rightful world ruler based on Western values. He somehow manages to conflate that with globalism, which the MAGA Communists should, of course, reject.

But fascism and Nazism are not right-wing. Like Communism, both are every bit Socialist, that is, based on government control of the economy. As described earlier in this text, at their heart, they are all based on *totalitarian* impulses. Richard Spencer, who claimed to have created the term "alt-right," is not right-wing at all. And it is the Communists who see themselves as the rightful, singular rulers of the world.

Even more laughable is the idea that Putin and the Communists oppose globalism. The United Nations was created by the Left to provide the international Communist movement with a base of operations to move toward one-world government. Globalism is just another world for Socialism, as laid out explicitly by the UN in Agenda 2030. And Socialism is simply the slow road to Communism.

Loudon calls it "a scam used to turn people against the West by fomenting civil war and unrest in Europe and the United States so that Russia, China, Iran, and their allies can achieve world dominance."[839] But some conservatives have been taken in by the absurd notion that Putin is somehow a "Christian." It is a profoundly ignorant proposition. And one can only hope that MAGA Communism doesn't become widespread. In any case, Communists' depth of penetration into all institutions of government and culture is an existential threat to America's survival. We must recognize that.

WHAT IS TO BE DONE?

If you're going through hell, keep going.
—Winston Churchill

That is the title of a tract by Lenin describing what they had to do to advance their "revolution." This book has described in detail the agenda that evolved. But now comes the important part. What can we, what should we do to stop them? Is it too late?

We are witnessing the Communist takeover of America right now in real time. We are on the precipice of a disaster that will transcend national boundaries. It seems baffling that the Communists should be so intent on killing the goose with the golden eggs that they don't seem to contemplate what happens afterward. Killing America will kill the biggest market in the world, one on which all other nations rely for their own prosperity, either directly or indirectly.

Communism didn't fail after seventy years. Communist economies fell overnight, almost as soon as the Communists took power. And that is true in every single Communist country in the world. The dirty secret of Communism is that it has survived this long on Western largesse, either through investments and loans or trade. The Chinese economy would collapse without our markets. As always, the Communists have been hell bent on "revolution" but are so obsessed with destruction, they can't see the endpoint.

But that doesn't mean it'll be any better for us—no, just as bad or worse. The envy-borne vitriolic hatred for the US will be borne on our backs. I don't think people are prepared for the kind of barbarity Communists willingly inflict on their defeated foes. This is why this book devoted some time to describing how it played out in Russia following the coup that installed the Soviets. We will face as bad or worse.

That is why the upcoming 2024 election is the most important election in our history, because if Kamala Harris or another "Democrat" is elected, our nation won't last another four years. So at this point it is important to contrast the four years of misery we have suffered under Biden and the Democrats with the four years under the first Trump presidency. Even if you don't believe we are headed for disaster if the Democrats win the 2024 presidential election, you should at least recognize we had it much better under Trump. Economist Steve Moore put together a short pamphlet comparing the Trump years versus the Biden years that is summarized on the last page. That summary is reproduced below:[840]

- Americans' median family income rose by $6,500 under Trump, and has fallen $6,000 under Biden
- Inflation averaged 2% under Trump, 6% under Biden
- Unemployment rates and poverty for minorities hit all-time lows under Trump
- In 2 years, Biden increased the national debt by $10 trillion (2021–2030)
- Mortgage rates are currently twice as high as when Trump left office
- America energy independent under Trump, while Biden dismantles American energy
- Trump is the only president since 2009 to have had a net negative impact on the cost of federal regulation
- Mortgage rates have seen unprecedented spikes as the Biden administration tries to curb hyperinflation
- Biden has slashed American oil production by millions of barrels, and has bled strategic petroleum reserves

- Gas prices are $1 higher on average than when Trump left office
- 2 of 3 Americans rated the economy "good" or "great" under Trump, less than 1 in 3 rate the economy "good" or "great" under Biden
- Border secure under Trump, record high illegal immigration under Biden

The inflation rate described in the list above is the commonly used "less food and energy" index. But food and energy are major expenditures in every budget. If those items were included, the difference in inflation rates would be much more pronounced, especially given the deliberate trashing of our energy sector by the Biden crew and resulting spike in prices. So just look at the gas price chart below. The only reason prices have come down at all under Biden is because he has emptied the strategic petroleum reserves and accepted Russian oil to make the Democrats look better in the run-up to the election. They have made it perfectly clear, however, as described in my Save the Planet chapter, that their true goal is to abolish carbon fuels. Wouldn't you rather see us energy independent again, with gas prices in the $2.00 range rather than $3.50 or higher? If the Democrats win, gas prices will skyrocket until the carbon fuel energy sector implodes, then you will be forced to use electric cars. That's if you are even allowed to use privately owned vehicles at all, because they plan to abolish those next. Under Trump, none of that will happen.

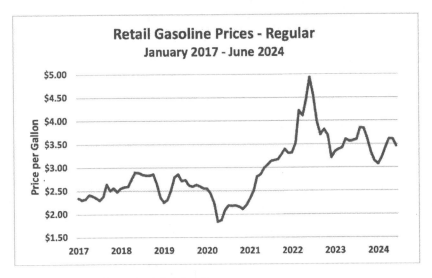

Source: US Energy Information Administration

Food inflation has also been off the charts, as you all know. But nothing beats a visual. Examine the chart below. And note that the graph shows percentage changes, not price levels, so while the chart slopes downward in the latter part of 2022, just remember that these are further increases following the spike that started in 2021. Prices are now 22 percent higher than when Biden took office. They have not come down; prices are just increasing at slower rates. Under President Trump, food inflation followed the slow 2 percent growth in overall prices we enjoyed under Trump. Food inflation rates under Biden, on the other hand, have not been seen since the Carter presidency.

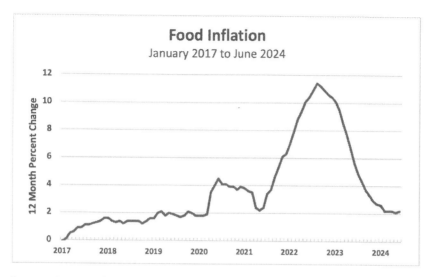

Food Inflation
January 2017 to June 2024

Source: US Bureau of Labor Statistics, Consumer Price Index, Food in US Cities Avg., monthly

On the blog, *The Burning Platform*, author Justin Smith published a piece on April 5, 2024, titled, "America Is Hurtling Toward a Full Blown Hot Civil War."[841] While I do not subscribe to the notion that such an end is unavoidable, things do not look well for our future. Following are selected passages from this emotionally powerful piece:

> It never ceases to amaze me at how little so many people in this country have done to train their minds to critically analyze information. They have eyes to see and ears to see, and yet, somehow the truth of any major issue still seems to evade them, or they simply refuse to recognize the truth with it standing right in front of them, slapping them in the face....
>
> But never in my wildest imagination did I expect to see every single government institution corrupted to its very core and heavily infiltrated by men and women seeking to destroy traditional America—to "transform America"—and bring great harm to all Americans in the process, as evil was called "good" and good was

called "evil," turning the world upside down as foretold in Isaiah 5:20, as we all witnessed in 2020, driven by the Democratic Party Communists and fascists and globalists of the country, for the most part....

The heavy infiltration of Illegal Aliens from many foreign countries that are unfriendly or outright enemies of America is one more dynamic and issue of concern for all who love America, since they will certainly come down on the side which is trying to destroy America. No one should be oblivious to the fact that various "sleeper cells" of Hamas and Hezbollah have been in America for several decades now. Taken in conjunction with thousands of military aged Chinese men entering the country illegally the coming chaos will be Biblical in proportion to anything we have witnessed in all American history....

All good and decent Americans, who can still remember what America used to be or who have been well taught from childhood and know what a great nation—an exceptional nation—She has been in years gone by, will soon be forced to fight against enemies-from-within and foreign enemies supported by the World Economic Forum and the United Nations, so that our friends, families and communities can survive this period and freedom and liberty shall not perish in our land. And as we fight, we must pray and hope that our side emerges victoriously from the din and cacophony of the conflagration and chaos, in order that we may purge the land of those who hate America and restore Her to a land that truly understands what "equality under the law" actually means, to be governed in a manner that actually defends and protects the Inalienable God-given Rights for all, restoring America as something better than She has been in a long, long time.

This is the war that lays ahead of us, looming just over the horizon, and our very lives and the lives of our loved ones depend on our success. The death of America as She has stood is guaranteed, unless liberty-minded patriots rise from the ashes of the next civil war. That is the reality and the future we now must face.

There is much more in that piece, essentially a summary of this book. And the border invasion in particular is likely to turn violent. I do believe that one of the Biden administration plans is to use these "military age" migrants to launch attacks throughout our nation, to give the Democrat "president" the pretext to declare martial law and suspend the Constitution, thereby enabling them to seize privately owned firearms and cancel or postpone the election. That is my prediction, and I hope I am wrong.

But to expect "liberty-minded patriots" to organize and fight, as in with guns, is a fantasy. The FBI has already shown its method of infiltrating and compromising "liberty-minded" groups by instigating the "insurrection" on J6. Doubtless that intelligence operation is ongoing. Felix Dzerzhinsky would be proud. It's unfortunate that the FBI doesn't seem to show that kind of interest with Antifa and other left-wing terrorist groups. The FBI does use that tactic against those with jihadi ambitions by entrapping foolish men with promises of weapons and support, then arresting them when they try to launch an attack. It's a good way to inflate the arrest numbers. But with real jihadis, they have shown themselves to be incompetent or worse, as with the Boston marathon bombers and the jihadi attack against the Muhammad Art Exhibit in Garland, Texas. The FBI agent who infiltrated that group may have helped provoke it. At best he did nothing to stop it.[842]

But I am not advocating preparation for civil war. I have reproduced these passages to underscore the precarious position we find ourselves in. If you didn't get that by reading my book, I haven't done my job. What we must do, and are doing to some extent already, is create fertile ground for liberty and free-market affluence to flourish in those states where liberty-minded leaders can make it happen. Florida is the best example to date, but there are many more. We are creating what has been called a "parallel society" that will compete with the Left and blossom in those states as the Democrat-controlled states become more and more dysfunctional.

This can be accomplished on a macro as well as a micro level. For example, we have all heard about public figures and companies that have been "de-platformed" because of beliefs or activities that offend the Left. If social credit scores gain prominence, they will try to force us into compliance by denying us access to banks and other services when our politically incorrect activities and purchases are identified.

This can be stopped by passing laws at the federal and state level to stop them. But only if we elect the right people. The Tennessee governor signed legislation passed in spring 2024 that outlaws "de-banking," that is, denying credit or banking services to people or businesses the Left objects to. The law specifically "prohibits financial institutions and insurers from denying or canceling services to a person, or otherwise discriminating against a person, based upon the use of a social credit score or other factors."[843]

Any financial institution that wishes to do business in Tennessee will not be allowed to cancel or deny banking services to, for example, firearms and ammunition manufacturers and sellers, gun owners, oil and gas exploration companies, pro-life or other Christian or politically conservative groups and individuals, or anyone else involved in legitimate commerce that the Left objects to. This is the kind of thing that could easily pass in Republican-led states. And as more and more people see GOP states encouraging and preserving freedom like this, the exodus from Democrat states already occurring will increase. The Left's agenda will die of starvation.

It is late, but it is never too late. There are actually some positive developments on the horizon like the above that are encouraging. But that should not be an excuse to do nothing. By the same token, discouragement never won a single battle, so that is a useless attitude. This conclusion will list many of those things we actually can do that may help save the day.

1. Pray. Ultimately, I believe the end result will be up to God. So for that and many other reasons, the most important thing we can do first is pray. While it may not be true for my readers, we as a nation have forgotten God. We have the gift of free will. We have the right to choose God as our guide or ignore God to pursue strictly worldly things. It is really a choice between living according to God's spirit and teachings or living according to our own personal pride—that is, we know better and don't need God's help. God gives us that choice and the consequences that go with it. And pride always comes before the fall. As described in Romans 1:28–32 (NKJV):

   > [28] And even as they did not like to retain God in *their* knowledge, God gave them over to a debased mind, to do those things which are not fitting; [29] being filled with all unrighteousness, sexual immorality, wickedness, covetousness, maliciousness; full of envy, murder, strife, deceit, evil-mindedness; *they are* whisperers, [30] backbiters, haters of God, violent, proud, boasters, inventors of evil things, disobedient to parents, [31] undiscerning, untrustworthy, unloving, unforgiving, unmerciful; [32] who, knowing the righteous judgment of God, that those who practice such things are deserving of death, not only do the same but also approve of those who practice them.

   That paragraph pretty much describes today's Left, doesn't it? But it really describes what happens to humans when they surrender to their own instincts without any moral code to restrain them. Our minds, souls, and behavior degenerate in every dimension. We become depraved, and Communism is simply the evolutionary endpoint to human depravity. You simply can't get closer to the bottom.

   Our nation was born a Christian nation. And yes, you can point to all the hypocrisy and failures of Christians, but that doesn't change the values embedded in the teachings of Christ. It simply acknowledges that all humans fail. "For all have sinned, and fall short of the glory of God." (Romans 3:23 NKJV)

To the extent that these values were practiced, we as a nation benefited. We became the greatest nation in the world, not because we are any better than anyone else, but because God's inspiration built the institutional structures of our society, and our culture largely followed them. As we turned away from that to choose our own "progressive" path forward, our nation was corrupted, and today it is circling the drain. That was a premeditated strategy of the Left, as you now should know. They knew that if they encouraged a cultural shift toward licentiousness, our natural tendencies would lead our culture toward corruption. Political, legal, and corporate corruption would follow soon after, and here we are.

So pray. Pray for God's mercy on us. Pray for his forgiveness, because "if God is for us, who can be against us?" (Romans 8:31 NKJV) Do you think he is for us now? I think not. But he could be again. And with his help, we can be confident. I think this is best described in Psalm 46 (KJV), one of the most beautiful passages in the Bible:

> ¹ God is our refuge and strength, a very present help in trouble.

> ² Therefore will not we fear, though the earth be removed, and though the mountains be carried into the midst of the sea;

> ³ Though the waters thereof roar and be troubled, though the mountains shake with the swelling thereof. Selah.

⁴ There is a river, the streams whereof shall make glad the city of God, the holy place of the tabernacles of the most High.

⁵ God is in the midst of her; she shall not be moved: God shall help her, and that right early.

⁶ The heathen raged, the kingdoms were moved: he uttered his voice, the earth melted.

⁷ The Lord of hosts is with us; the God of Jacob is our refuge. Selah.

⁸ Come, behold the works of the Lord, what desolations he hath made in the earth.

⁹ He maketh wars to cease unto the end of the earth; he breaketh the bow, and cutteth the spear in sunder; he burneth the chariot in the fire.

¹⁰ Be still, and know that I am God: I will be exalted among the heathen, I will be exalted in the earth.

The Lord of hosts is with us; the God of Jacob is our refuge. Selah.

2.   Be encouraged. People are fighting back. The Left has been very effective at stealing our resources so we cannot fill our armories with the kind of political war chest the Left has amassed. And they have no ethics. All the same, we are learning the game. Following are a few of our successes:

> The *Baltimore Sun* newspaper and numerous local papers throughout Maryland were purchased by David Smith, CEO of Sinclair Broadcasting. Sinclair owns many conservative TV and radio stations, and while Smith says the papers will be non-partisan, that will be a vast improvement over the existing situation. Most

newspapers in the state will hopefully no longer carry the rank bias they have for decades.[844]

Similarly, Elon Musk's purchase of Twitter (now X), has created a much less restrictive platform. In April, he was ordered to delete certain accounts embarrassing to Brazil's Communist government and/or share the profiles of everyone the government dislikes. Musk defied them, continues to publish, and refuses to hand over personal information.

The Left has controlled media since the 1930s. We tend to underestimate media power, saying that the media, for example, is "in the tank for Biden" or someone else. But the media is not a follower in this cultural war; it is a leader. Media leaders don't parrot the narrative; they set the narrative. More newspapers and especially TV networks, where most people continue to get their news, need to be purchased by conservatives.

Moms for Liberty is dramatically expanding its fight to change school boards and administrations nationwide to defeat toxic CRT and gender ideology taught in public schools. Its successes have brought in big donations to finance the fight. As described earlier, DEI programs are being shut down in some states. Encourage your legislators to do more.

Plaintiffs won a lawsuit against the FDA that will require the FDA to remove all advertisements, social media posts, and other public statements that warn of using ivermectin to treat COVID. The *Defender* magazine quoted Dr. Paul Marik, chief scientific officer of the Front Line COVID-19 Critical Care Alliance (FLCCC) and former chief of Pulmonary and Critical Care Medicine at Eastern Virginia Medical School, who said: "This is a landmark case and one of the most important wins in the whole COVID era."[845]

The military will no longer require troops to get the COVID shot.

3. Get to work.

There is no magic pill. Electing Donald Trump will be a critical first step. If a Democrat seizes the White House in 2024, we can kiss our country goodbye. So the most important issue right now is winning the presidential election, but also elections at all levels of government. This will not be an easy fight, but as President Trump said, we need to fight like hell.

In a recent post by conservative fundraising genius Richard Viguerie, he made the point that calling Democrats "liberal," "progressive," "woke," "Socialist," or even Communist (which most of them have become) will not help. Most people vote the party, not the individual, and that goes for independents as well. So instead we must start by branding the Democrats for what they do. Taken directly from his post, here is what he says:[846]

> The Democrats have moved so far toward socialism/Marxism that there are dozens and dozens of examples to use to BRAND the Democrat Party and candidates as dangerously out of step with the American people, including:
>
> - Democrats have opened wide our southern border.
> - Democrats' out-of-control government spending has led to high inflation.
> - Democrats want to defund the police.
> - Democrats are soft on criminals, including dangerous criminals.
> - Democrats believe in teaching Critical Race Theory (CRT) to school children (all whites are racists and minorities are victims).

- Democrats allow males in female sports, bathrooms, and showers.
- Democrats weaponize our government against conservatives/Republicans (FBI, IRS, DOJ, CIA, etc.).
- Democrats demand that abortion be legal up to the moment of birth and sometimes beyond.
- Democrats are acting like a communist dictatorship trying to put their opponents (Donald Trump and others) in jail and financially bankrupting them.
- Etc., etc., etc.

Viguerie makes a very good point. We see these activities every single day and they are upsetting to a vast majority of the American people, as numerous polls show. I refer to @ TheDemocrats in every post I make on X, reminding followers of every bad thing they try to do. But we need to do a lot more. Here are some suggestions:

- Get more people registered to vote who will vote our way. Democrats are confident most poor people will vote for them because they essentially buy votes with ever-expanding welfare. The job is harder for us because we have to find those who will vote on principle or at least to protect themselves from higher taxes. As taxpayers move closer to a minority, this is harder to do.
- Prevail on legislatures in key states to pass voter reform.
- Support or initiate multiple lawsuits to prevent mass mail-in, remote drop boxes, automatic voter registration (AVR), or any other voting agenda being pursued in your state by the Left.
- Engage in the process, for example, as election judges or poll watchers.

- Support or become involved in political campaigns for solid conservatives.

Voter ID is one important element, but there are many others. Some states have already implemented some. For example, Wisconsin passed a constitutional amendment to prevent a replay of 2020, when Facebook founder Mark Zuckerberg dumped $500 million into swing states to guarantee overwhelming voters for Biden—many of which were blatantly illegal. As of this writing, twenty-eight states have now banned or restricted private funding for elections a la Zuckerbucks. Those states are: Alabama, Arizona, Arkansas, Florida, Georgia, Idaho, Indiana, Iowa, Kansas, Kentucky, Louisiana, Mississippi, Missouri, Montana, Nebraska, North Carolina, North Dakota, Ohio, Oklahoma, Pennsylvania, South Carolina, South Dakota, Tennessee, Texas, Utah, Virginia, West Virginia, Wisconsin.[847] Other states have instituted more reforms, but regarding the presidency, the key swing states are Arizona, Georgia, Wisconsin, Michigan, Pennsylvania, and Nevada; New Hampshire, North Carolina, and Virginia are also important. Democrats believe that if they win the three "blue wall" states of Pennsylvania, Michigan, and Wisconsin, they can win the presidential election, so we need to concentrate forcefully on winning those states—not an easy task.[848]

In Pennsylvania, successive Democrat governors in 2018 and 2023 instituted changes to election law through executive order, illegally bypassing the legislature, which is where all election law is supposed to be made. A lawsuit by twenty-four legislators was thrown out of court by a district court judge who said they didn't have standing to bring the suit, a ridiculous ruling. If legislators responsible for election law do not have standing, who does? That ruling needs to be appealed. Left-wing activists are now urging the governor to assure that more government agencies get involved in performing AVR. Contact your PA legislator.

Similarly, in Wisconsin and Michigan, the Democrats, as everywhere, are utterly unethical, and they have Democrat governors and judges willing to twist law to support them. Wisconsin has majorities in both houses of the state legislature, but apparently, they are unwilling or unable to prevent Democrats from using extra-legal means, like the use of remote voting drop boxes and other devices to win. The constitutional amendment blocking Zuckerbucks may help, but they need to do much more. The Michigan legislature is controlled by Democrats in both houses. If we had to prioritize, I would put Michigan at the bottom of the list and focus on Pennsylvania and Wisconsin.

But President Trump needs a solid Republican majority in both houses of Congress if he is to pass meaningful reforms. In the Senate, Democrats face reelection in twenty-three seats, whereas Republicans only have eleven. At least seven Democrat seats are vulnerable. Thus there is a good chance of retaking the Senate. Four key races are in states also important for the presidential race including: Michigan (Debbie Stabenow's open seat), Nevada (Jacky Rosen), Pennsylvania (Bob Casey), and Wisconsin (Tammy Baldwin).

Senate Democrats are also up for election in three pro-Trump states: Montana (Jon Tester), Ohio (Sherrod Brown), and West Virginia (Joe Manchin, who is retiring). Manchin will likely be replaced by a Republican, but if you live in WV, make sure it's a good Republican!

All of the listed Democrat senators except Manchin are extreme leftists and have been supported by the Council for a Livable World.[849] The CLW was founded by Leo Szilard, a scientist on the Manhattan Project that developed the atom bomb. He was a Socialist and suspected Soviet agent—described by a defector as one of the Soviets' best sources for bomb information.[850] The CLW also helped Biden get elected to Congress. Despite his hyped image as a "moderate," Joe Biden has been a radical, anti-American leftist for his entire career.

The Senate makeup could possibly get a boost from Mitch McConnell's replacement as Senate GOP leader, given McConnell's welcome announcement he would step down from that role. My choice would be Tom Cotton, but it is more likely to be someone like John Cornyn, who would be just as bad, if not worse, than McConnell. In any event, a GOP majority in the Senate would be a major plus for a Trump presidency, even with all the squishies.

The House of Representatives is another matter. Due to redistricting in New York and court-ordered new districts, Democrats hold a good chance of retaking the House.[851] That would be a disaster. Republicans currently hold a six-seat margin. Space considerations prevent covering all of these races but, from a *USA Today* article, here is a list of those where Republicans are most vulnerable:[852]

- Rep. David Schweikert, R-AZ
- Rep. Juan Ciscomani, R-AZ
- Rep. John Duarte, R-CA
- Rep. David Valadao, R-CA
- Rep. Mike Garcia, R-CA
- Rep. Young Kim, R-CA
- Rep. Michelle Steel, R-CA
- Rep. Don Bacon, R-NE
- Rep. Tom Kean Jr., R-NJ
- Rep. Nick LaLota, R-NY
- Rep. Anthony D'Esposito, R-NY
- Rep. Mike Lawler, R-NY
- Rep. Marc Molinaro, R-NY
- Rep. Brandon Williams, R-NY
- Rep. Lori Chavez-DeRemer, R-OR
- Rep. Brian Fitzpatrick, R-PA
- Rep. Jen Kiggans, R-VA

There are five Democrat seats won in districts that went for Trump in the last election. These are vulnerable. Support their GOP challenger:

- Rep. Mary Peltola, D-AK
- Rep. Jared Golden, D-ME
- Rep. Marcy Kaptur, D-OH
- Rep. Matt Cartwright, D-PA
- Rep. Marie Gluesenkamp Perez, D-WA

The Cook Political Report is also a good source for campaign ratings: https://www.cookpolitical.com/ratings.

Given the Democrats' ability to play games in the elections, assume you need to get an extra 5 to 10 percent more votes to win in any race than you would have to in a clean election. So we have our work cut out for us.

Purging Voter Rolls

States can and have written their own laws to make purging voter rolls easier. But the Left goes out of the way to sabotage and undermine this as well. For example, in Wisconsin, state law calls for mailings to voters every four years when it is believed they are no longer active or present at their current address. The voter has thirty days to respond, to either confirm or update their records. If there is no response, the registration is removed from the rolls.

Prior to the 2020 election, the Wisconsin Elections Commission announced it would instead wait twelve to twenty-four months for a voter to respond. The Wisconsin Institute for Law & Liberty (WILL) sued, citing the thirty-day requirement. A circuit court judge ruled in WILL's favor, ordering the commission to immediately purge the rolls. Of course, the commission appealed, and the appeals court stayed the order. The state Supreme Court sided with the WEC, so over two hundred thousand obsolete voter records stayed on the rolls for 2020.

The following list borrows liberally from my 2021 book, *Who Was Karl Marx?* Very little has changed since then in terms of the road ahead of us, and the suggestions made then are just as relevant today. We are making headway though. So don't lose heart!

Elections

- <u>Restore election integrity in all red states</u>. Twenty-eight states are currently led by Republican legislatures. Alaska and Pennsylvania are split control. Voter ID and other ballot security, as well as *enforcing* heavy penalties for organized voter fraud, are essential. Be alert. Patriots must work to restore voting integrity first in the red states, then the red counties of the blue states—then after 2024, the whole nation. Get involved in this process. It's a top priority.
- <u>Restore majorities in both houses of Congress in 2024</u>. This is essential to limit the destruction the Democrats can accomplish. Key to that effort will be to prevent federalizing elections, which Democrats are attempting again.
- <u>Close Republican primaries</u>. This should be a no-brainer, but no one is talking about it. Only five US states have truly closed Republican primaries. This means that in most states, Democrats and Independents (even Communists) can vote in Republican primaries—and they do. In many states, the GOP's enemies vote in Republican primaries to pick the weakest candidate they can; and sometimes the candidate is actually a Democrat or other leftist who joins the GOP to dilute and undermine GOP political strength. Key Tactic: Don't give campaign donations to national parties. Give directly to the candidate or Super PACs dedicated to the candidate. *Pick good candidates!*
- <u>Maintain and increase majorities in state houses, governorships, and local government</u>. One of President Trump's major accomplishments was to appoint many good judges to federal courts. We saw how corrupt judges allowed Democrats in key states to violate state election law by changing the rules at the last minute. This was a big reason they were able to steal the presidential election in 2020.

- Elect competent jurists and sheriffs. Many of us overlook state and local judicial elections. The result is more bad decisions from leftist judges. Sheriffs also have immense power in some jurisdictions where they are the top law enforcement officer in the county. Support the Constitutional Sheriffs and Peace Officers Association (www.CSPOA.org), which seeks to restore the constitutional power sheriffs are supposed to have and still do have in some places. The purpose is to make all of these institutions of government answerable to We the People.
- Elect good leaders in local government. Local elections are critical. We tend to overlook them. This is why the Left wins. We need good candidates for school boards, mayors, executives, city/county councils, registrar of voters, judges, and sheriffs. No elective office should be ignored.
- Participate in elections as a volunteer, a candidate, or with money if you can.
- Create Super PACs. Make alliances with other candidate supporters and raise money.
- Support promising candidates. Identify and support strong candidates who commit to our issues.
- Demand that all candidates take a survey gauging their support for our issues. At the very least, they must commit to those and sign the survey saying so. Preferably, they have an existing track record that proves their allegiance.
- Advocate civil service reform to enable discipline of bureaucracies wildly out of control.
- Combat vote fraud:
  - All do good work in this area. Get involved!
    - True the Vote (www.truethevote.org)
    - Judicial Watch (www.judicialwatch.org)
    - Public Interest Legal Foundation (https://publicinterestlegal.org/)
    - Voter Integrity Project (https://voterintegrityproject.com/)
  - Develop/join an army of poll watchers/poll judges.

- ○ Develop/join an army of precinct captains (look up the Precinct Project).
- ○ Organize and support state Voter Integrity Projects (e.g., VA/MD, NC, CA, and other voting rights groups).
- ○ Volunteer for True the Vote (https://truethevote.org/).
- ○ Demand that voter rolls be purged as required by the NVRA (a step opposed by Democrats).
- ○ Demand prosecution of vote fraud.
- ○ Advocate for repeal of the NVRA to return full voting discretion to states.
- ○ Seek support from our media, Judicial Watch, Voter Integrity Project.
- ○ Demand checking green card registrations. Only a few states require citizenship proof.
- ○ Take legal action against illegal campaign coordination and other activities.

Education

- • Make public school taxes portable.

    State and local taxes used for public education should instead be used to pay tuition for whatever school parents choose for their kids. Refund education taxes to those who homeschool.

- • Replace school boards with solid people.
    - ○ Boards hire and fire bureaucrats, who exercise enormous power.
    - ○ Ban Critical Race Theory, Black Lives Matter, and radical sex education curricula.
    - ○ Restore critical learning skills and the three "Rs."
    - ○ Resurrect trade schools. Low-income community leaders have begged for this for years.
    - ○ Fight Islamization of public schools. After all, Christian groups cannot teach Christianity. Why is Islam being taught?

○ Restore prayer and the Pledge of Allegiance in public schools.

- Defund Universities.
    ○ Many universities receive state and federal tax dollars. Almost all universities impose speech codes, hire only leftist professors, and provide degrees in bogus curricula designed to indoctrinate our youth in the Left's destructive narratives. Conservative professors are silenced or fired.
    ○ Both federal and state governments should deny all subsidies, grants, or loans to universities that engage in any of these behaviors. This is working in Florida and forcing change.
    ○ Both federal and state governments should deny scholarships and loans to students who enroll in schools that refuse to drop leftist indoctrination.
    ○ Both federal and state governments should defund universities that allow transgender men to compete in women's sports.
    ○ Alumni must stop supporting those schools engaged in these behaviors. Tell them why.
    ○ Parents should not allow their children to attend these schools. Tell schools why.

Free Speech

- Stop the Left's full-throttle effort to silence opponents.
- Combat all efforts to suppress free speech.
- Fight efforts to enact stronger "hate crimes" laws that criminalize free speech.
- Flood town hall/city council meetings with supporters. Demand answers. Get there early.
- Launch defamation or tortious interference lawsuits against any individual or group that attempts to shut down events (see: "Lawfare" below).

Foundations

- The Left controls hundreds of billions in assets through a network of foundations dedicated to their various agendas, which are also funded with billions of dollars in federal, state, and local grants to leftist-run, tax-exempt 501(c)(3) and (c)(4) organizations. Almost no conservative organizations receive government funding. Defunding these organizations will destroy them.
- Provide a clearer definition of subversion in federal law and prosecute the insurrectionists. Urge lawmakers to strengthen laws against subversion. Dangers of Communism are acknowledged in federal law, but the law is rarely enforced. Enforce the law!
- Recruit candidates who will commit to ending government grants to leftists and support DOJ prosecution of left-wing foundations/organizations engaged in treasonous activities.
- Apply RICO law prosecution to George Soros, Open Society Institute, and other foundations that fund subversive organizations and activities.
- Sue Pew Charitable Trusts (violated federal law in its creation).
- Apply RICO law prosecution to foundations that act as subversive continuing criminal enterprises.
- Formerly conservative foundations have been infiltrated by the Left—remove leftists by retaking boards.

Immigration

- <u>Oppose amnesty in all forms</u>.
- Finish the wall along the US-Mexican border.
- Abolish the refugee program as currently constructed.
- End Diversity Visa lottery program.
- End chain migration.
- End anchor babies.
- End Temporary Protected Status.
- Enact mandatory E-Verify in all states.
- Add nations to State Department State Sponsors of Terror list.

- Make English the official language of the US.

Judeo-Christian Culture

- <u>Defend, restore, and celebrate our unmatched religious heritage</u>.
- Cultural Marxism's goal is to destroy Christianity, and the corruption of our society is the direct consequence. We as a nation have largely abandoned God.
- Leftist and Islamic allies seek destruction of Judeo-Christian values because it is our greatest source of strength and cultural stability.
- Discourage interfaith dialogue. It facilitates the Koranic Concept of War: detach the enemy from his faith. Christians and Jews are urged to accept Islam, but Islam is not urged to accept Christianity or Judaism.
- Support and defend religious liberty under attack. It's already lost in Europe and is on the way out in Canada.
- Join a faithful church if you are not a member already. Tithe regularly.
- Liberal churches and synagogues are apostates. If you are a member, leave.
- Pray daily for the salvation of our nation.

Language

- <u>Restore correct usage of language</u>.
- "Dreamers" are illegal aliens. Call them that.
- "Dreamers" are adults (all of the so-called dreamers are nineteen to over thirty years old). Stop calling them "children."
- "Undocumented immigrants" is a nonsense term. Use the correct legal term: illegal aliens.
- Men are men, and women are women. There is no such thing as sex reassignment surgery. It is simply extensive cosmetic surgery, augmented with hormone treatment.

- Change "compassion" to "dependency" and "special privilege" when speaking of interest group legislation. That kind of legislation is simply another form of vote buying.
- When Democrats talk about "democracy," they really mean Communism. We are not a democracy. We are a republic.

Lawfare

- <u>Countersue the Left</u>.
- Battle back against leftist groups' use of lawfare.
- Identify, support, and recruit legal organizations in this fight:
    - American Freedom Law Center (https://americanfreedomlawcenter.org)
    - American Center for Law and Justice (https://aclj.org/)
    - Judicial Watch (https://judicialwatch.org)
    - Thomas More Society (https://www.thomasmoresociety.org/)
- Donate to pro bono legal teams focusing on this fight.
- Oppose leftist claims that "civil rights" have precedence over civil liberties, e.g., Christian baker examples, Muslims demanding special privileges for Islam.

Media

- <u>Media is the Left's most critical source of power and control</u>. Our ability to message is limited by leftists who suppress news that challenges leftist orthodoxy and attack, vilify, defame, and destroy the reputations of those who disagree with them—especially the most effective and compelling voices.
- Strongly criticize groups like the Southern Poverty Law Center, which designates almost all conservative opponents as "haters" or "hate groups." They do not label violent left-wing organizations like Antifa, the Black Bloc, Black Lives Matter, or other groups as either violent or hateful.

- Purchase, take over, and create major media outlets, networks, or newspapers. (This is already happening to some extent, but much more is needed.)
- Try to avoid Hollywood productions that glorify the Left. Most Hollywood movies these days contain left-wing political messages. Boycott them. Keep children from them.

Islam

- Support investigation and prosecution of Muslim Brotherhood front organizations subverting our nation.
- Oppose Sharia (i.e., a parallel legal system antithetical to the US Constitution).
- Restore sane law enforcement that recognizes Islamic terrorism and trains to confront it.
- Restore and support law enforcement training on Islam.
- Ban the teaching of Islam in public schools.

Goals

Immediate Term:

- Support the reelection of Donald Trump in 2024.
- Take back both houses of Congress in 2024 and support elections of governors, state reps, state senators, judges, and local leaders. Pennsylvania's Supreme Court is five to two Democrats. The court won PA for Biden with its shoddy rulings.
- Get out the vote (GOTV) in all elections. We lose elections we could have easily won if more people just focused on that.
- State GOPs have failed to GOTV in many places. If they won't do their jobs, we have to do it for them. Many state party apparatuses need a serious makeover. Consider volunteering.

Medium/Long Term:

- Obtain, maintain, or increase majorities in Congress, state houses, judgeships, and local government.

Foundational:

- Enduring, ongoing effort to raise public awareness regarding the true nature of the threats we face (prioritize), defeat public corruption, restore our culture, faith, and commitment to constitutional republican government and the rule of law.

Prioritize Goals:

1. <u>Critical</u>: those we must win
2. <u>Salvageable</u>: those we can win with effort
3. <u>Low-hanging fruit</u>: wins easy to accomplish
4. <u>Long-term</u>: agendas we may win if successful with others

Strategies: Identify, expose, confront, subvert, organize, investigate, prosecute, defund, replace.

Tactics in Support of Strategies

Know Your Enemy:

- National Democratic Party
- Democratic Socialists of America (DSA)
- Establishment GOP (not all GOP)
- The "Swamp": a nickname for corrupt government infrastructure at all levels
- Left-wing organizations (e.g., SPLC, ACLU, NLG, CAP, IPS, IAF, Antifa, Revcom, Refuse Fascism, BLM)
- Islamist organizations: (e.g., CAIR, Muslim Brotherhood, Tablighi Jamaat, Jamaat ul Fuqra, Gulenists)
- Left-wing Foundations (e.g., Soros's Open Society, Ford, Rockefeller, and others)
- Obama Foundation/Organizing for Action, now All on the Line
- Mass media (they are not mainstream at all)
- Education establishment
- The Red-Green Axis (collusion between radical Left and Islamists, domestically and worldwide)

Expose: Campaign of education through speakers, forums, webinars, articles, letters, videos, social media to citizens, educators, and public officials to expose the Left agenda for what it is: violent, unprincipled, terrorist, and criminal—a threat to our very existence.

Confront: The Left engages in scorched-earth tactics to silence us. They threaten our venues with lawsuits, violence, and public humiliation. They engage in violent protests. They seek to enact "hate crime" laws that will criminalize our truth-telling. We need to expose and attack these groups and individuals with lawsuits, criminal charges, and public humiliation and seek legislative changes that will strengthen our cause.

- Democrats and the Left are the true insurrectionists. They are using their media mouthpieces to accuse us of everything that they are doing.
- Everything they say is exactly the opposite of the truth. Never let them get away with it. Ridicule them.
- Write letters to the editor regularly, even to liberal papers. If you are not confident on the subject, bone up on it.
- Write letters to your representatives. They do listen. Don't just fill out a preprinted postcard.
- Call your representatives. Go visit them.
- Participate in mass phone calls to legislators, *both Republican and Democrat*, when objectionable legislation comes up.
- Seek criminal convictions for violent protesters and others.
- Challenge their narratives in public debate.

Subvert: Burrow within to disrupt and expose their plans.

- Infiltrate enemy organizations.
- Expose their various plans.
- Create/support undercover videos (e.g., Project Veritas, https://www.projectveritas.com/; https://OKeefeMediaGroup.com).
- Attend their marches (Andy Ngo has bravely done this. Support his work: https://www.andy-ngo.com/).

- Develop network of public supporters who will alert us to town halls and other public meetings where we can show up early and pack the house.

Investigate and Prosecute: So much of what the Left does is criminal. As state and local political, law enforcement, and judicial institutions shift to principled, law-abiding control, these people need to face prosecution and conviction. Long sentences for a few of them would end this overnight. They are such cowards that most are unwilling to face any serious consequences for their actions. But as long as the justice system allows it, their insanity will continue and grow.

Replace: This is the most promising strategy. The Left's control of institutions like public education and media is overwhelming. The homeschooling movement is one very good answer to this. But we need much more. Governor DeSantis, South Dakota governor Kristi Noem, and a few others have demonstrated the kind of leadership needed. With such leadership, more will be encouraged to follow as our parallel society grows and flourishes.

"What then shall we say to these things? If God is for us, who can be against us?" (Romans 8:31 NKJV) Let's keep praying that he is on our side and join hand-in-hand in the effort to save our beloved country. We owe it to ourselves, our children, and all subsequent generations to do so. Hopefully I will meet you in spirit if not in person to see this done!

NOTES

1   "The only people responsible for the assassination attempt. Sebastian
    Gorka on AMERICA First." America First: Sebastian Gorka. July 16, 2024.
    Accessed July 23, 2024. https://www.sebgorka.com/video/the-only-people-
    responsible-for-the-assassination-attempt-sebastian-gorka-on-america-first.

2   McCue, Elise. "Trump May Have 'Staged' Own Shooting, Dem
    Adviser Tells Reporters." *Daily Signal.* July 14, 2024. Accessed
    July 15, 2024. https://www.dailysignal.com/2024/07/14/
    dem-political-adviser-pushes-trump-staged-shooting-media/.

3   Wallace, Danielle, and David Spunt. "Would-be Trump assassin had explosives in
    car parked near rally, bomb making materials at home: sources." Fox News. July 14,
    2024. Accessed July 15, 2024. https://www.foxnews.com/politics/would-be-trump-
    assassin-explosives-car-parked-near-rally-bomb-making-materials-home-reports.

4   "Did Thomas Matthew Crooks Act Alone?" SNCT.tv. July 23, 2024. https://
    salemnewschannel.com/watch/did-thomas-matthew-crooks-act-alone-66a00c4d1b4
    1860001f42ace.

5   Perez, Evan, Zachary Cohen, Natasha Bertrand, Kylie Atwood, and Kristen
    Holmes. "Exclusive: Secret Service ramped up security after intel of Iran
    plot to assassinate Trump; no known connection to shooting." CNN. July
    16, 2023. Accessed July 23, 2024. https://www.cnn.com/2024/07/16/
    politics/iran-plot-assassinate-trump-secret-service/index.html.

6   Loudon, Trevor. "Dyed in Red! the Sinister Background of 'Moderate' Kamala
    Harris, China's American Dream President." EpochTV. January 3, 2021. Accessed
    August 7, 2024. https://www.theepochtimes.com/epochtv/dyed-in-red-the-sinister-
    background-of-moderate-kamala-harris-chinas-american-dream-president-3746453.

7   Ibid.

8   "Herb and Marion Sandler." Discover the Networks. Accessed August 7, 2024.
    https://www.discoverthenetworks.org/individuals/herb-and-marion-sandler/.

9   Trujillo, Damian. "Why Are Some Murder Suspects Being Released
    With Little or No Bail?" NBC Bay Area. December 1, 2021. Accessed
    April 5, 2024. https://www.nbcbayarea.com/news/local/south-bay/

why-are-some-murder-suspects-being-released-with-little-
or-no-bail/2744550/.

10   Hanson, Victor Davis. "Is Biden Malicious, Incompetent, or Conniving."
American Greatness. February 5, 2024. Accessed February 7, 2024. https://
amgreatness.com/2024/02/05/is-biden-malicious-incompetent-or-conniving/.

11   Roberts, Katabella, "Nearly 40 Trucking Businesses Involved in
Canada's Freedom Convoy Protests Have Been Shut Down." *The Epoch
Times*. February 25, 2022. Accessed February 6, 2024. https://www.
theepochtimes.com/world/nearly-40-trucking-businesses-involved-in-
canadas-freedom-convoy-protests-have-been-shut-down-4301555.

12   Unruh, Bob. "Expert warns about move to impose life sentences for disfavored
speech." WND. March 14, 2024. Accessed March 18, 2024. https://www.wnd.
com/2024/03/expert-warns-move-impose-life-sentences-disfavored-speech/.

13   Fox, Michelle. "The U.S. national debt is rising by $1 trillion about every 100 days."
CNBC. March 1, 2024. Accessed May 9, 2024. https://www.cnbc.com/2024/03/01/
the-us-national-debt-is-rising-by-1-trillion-about-every-100-days.html.

14   Taylor, Jeff and Lynch, Michael. "Cox Report." *Reason*. August/September
1999. Accessed May 28, 2023. https://reason.com/1999/08/01/cox-reports/.

15   "David Horowitz>Quotes>Quotable Quote." *Goodreads*. Accessed July 10, 2023.
https://www.goodreads.com/quotes/1144588-an-sds-radical-once-wrote-the-issue-
is-never-the.

16   Bascom, James. "The Issue Is Never the Issue—The Real Issue Is the
Revolution." TFP.org. June 8, 2020. Accessed July 5, 2023. https://www.
tfp.org/the-issue-is-never-the-issue-the-real-issue-is-the-revolution/.

17   "The Tucker Carlson Encounter: Xi Van Fleet." *Tucker Carlson Show*. February 26,
2024. Accessed March 9, 2024. https://tuckercarlson.com/the-tucker-carlson-
encounter-xi-van-fleet-2/.

18   Nechayev, Sergey. "The Revolutionary Catechism." Marxists.
org. Accessed November 12, 2023. https://www.marxists.
org/subject/anarchism/nechayev/catechism.htm.

19   Simpson, James. *Who Was Karl Marx: The Men, the Motives and the Menace
Behind Today's Rampaging American Left*. Self-Published, Amazon, 2021.

20   Marx, Karl. "The Victory of the Counter-Revolution in Vienna." *Neue
Rheinische Zeitung*. No. 136, 1848. Translated by the Marx-Engels Institute.
Transcribed for the internet by director@marx.org, 1994. Accessed April 9,
2024. (http://www.marxists.org/archive/marx/works/1848/11/06.htm).

21   Karl Marx and Friedrich Engels. *The Communist Manifesto*.
New York: International Publishers, 1948. 44.

22   Wurmbrand, Richard. *Marx and Satan*. Bartlesville, Oklahoma:
Living Sacrifice Book Company, 1986. 27.

23   Lenin. As described by a foreign national and former high-level leftist insider who
remains anonymous for self-protection. James Simpson interview. July 7, 2014.

24   McMeekin, Sean. *The Red Millionaire: A Political Biography of
Willy Münzenberg, Moscow's Secret Propaganda Tsar in the West,
1917-1940*. New Haven: Yale University Press, 2004.

25   Koch, Stephen. *Double Lives: Spies and Writers in the Secret Soviet War
of Ideas Against the West*. New York: The Free Press, 1994. 5-6.

26   de Toledano, Ralph. *Cry Havoc: The Great American Bring-down and
How it Happened*. Washington, DC: Anthem Books, 2007. 13.

27   Ibid. 43.

28   Ibid. 13.

29   Amazon.com summary of *The Red Millionaire*. Accessed April 9, 2024. https://www.amazon.com/ Red-Millionaire-Political-M%C3%BCnzenberg-Propaganda/dp/0300098472/.

30   *Cry Havoc. Op. cit.* 43-45.

31   Ibid. 10.

32   Ibid. 11.

33   Lind, William, Ed. "'Political Correctness:' A Short History of an Ideology." Free Congress Foundation. November 2004. Accessed February 7, 2024. https://www. nationalists.org/pdf/political_correctness_a_short_history_of_an_ideology.pdf.

34   *Cry Havoc. Op. cit.* 86.

35   Crossman, Ashley. "Understanding Critical Theory." *ThoughtCo.* October 15, 2019. Accessed May 2, 2021. https://www.thoughtco.com/critical-theory-3026623.

36   Buchanan, Patrick. *The Death of the West: How Dying Populations and Immigrant Invasions Imperil Our Country and Civilization.* New York: St. Martin's Griffin, 2002. 80.

37   "Critical Legal Studies." Encyclopedia.com. Accessed February 7, 2024. https://www.encyclopedia.com/law/ encyclopedias-almanacs-transcripts-and-maps/critical-legal-studies.

38   "Critical Race Theory." Encyyclopedia.com. Accessed February 7, 2024. https:// www.encyclopedia.com/social-sciences-and-law/sociology-and-social-reform/ sociology-general-terms-and-concepts/critical-race-theory.

39   Toussaint, Etienne C. "The Purpose of Legal Education." *California Law Review.* February 2023. Accessed February 7, 2024. https://www. californialawreview.org/print/the-purpose-of-legal-education.

40   Mills, C. Wright. "Letter to the New Left." *New Left Review*, No. 5, September-October 1960. Accessed February 4, 2024. https://www. marxists.org/subject/humanism/mills-c-wright/letter-new-left.htm.

41   Rothman, Stanley. The End of the Experiment: The Rise of Cultural Elites and the Decline of America's Civic Culture. London and New York: Routledge, 2017. 177.

42   Gordon, Alex. "The red idol, or the destruction of the mind." New Eastern Europe. October 6, 2023. Accessed February 5, 2024. https://neweasterneurope. eu/2023/10/06/the-red-idol-or-the-destruction-of-the-mind/.

43   Cry Havoc. 63-64.

44   Isherwood, Christopher. *Down There on a Visit.* New York: Simon & Schuster, 1962. 35.

45   Pavy, Aimee. "Girls Will Be Boys." San Francisco Silent Film Festival. 2016. Accessed January 12, 2024. https://silentfilm.org/girls-will-be-boys/.

46   Ibid. 64.

47   Escoffier, Jeffrey. "Marcuse, Herbert (1898-1979)." glbtq. 2004. Accessed February 2, 2024. http://www.glbtqarchive.com/ssh/marcuse_h_S.pdf.

48   Costello, Anthony. "Race, Sex And Social Justice: The Impact Of Herbert Marcuse In America." *The Center That Holds.* October 16, 2022. Accessed February 4, 2024. https://www.patheos.com/blogs/theologicalapologetics/2022/10/race-sex-and-social-justice-the-impact-of-herbert-marcuse-in-america/.

49   Marcuse, Herbert. "Repressive Tolerance," in Wolff, Robert Paul, Barrington Moore, Jr., and Herbert Marcuse, *A Critique of Pure Tolerance.* Boston, MA: Beacon Press, 1965. Accessed February 5, 2024. https://www.marcuse.org/ herbert/publications/1960s/1965-repressive-tolerance-1969.pdf. 122.

50   Ibid. 119-120.

51   Brooks, Emily, and Joseph Simonson. "Pete Buttigieg's father was a Marxist professor who lauded the Communist Manifesto," *Washington Examiner.* April 2, 2019. Accessed May 4, 2021. https://

www.washingtonexaminer.com/news/pete-buttigiegs-father-was-a-marxist-professor-who-lauded-the-communist-manifesto.

52   Jennifer Crewe. "In Memory of Joseph Buttigieg, Translator of the Complete Prison Notebooks of Antonio Gramsci." Columbia University Press Blog, February 11, 2019. Accessed May 10, 2021. https://www.cupblog.org/2019/02/11/in-memory-of-joseph-buttigieg-translator-of-the-complete-prison-notebooks-of-antonio-gramsci/.

53   Cratty, Carol, and Michael Pearson. "DC shooter wanted to kill as many as possible, prosecutors say." CNN. February 7, 2013. Accessed March 17, 2024. https://www.cnn.com/2013/02/06/justice/dc-family-research-council-shooting/index.html.

54   Beard, Paul. "Support for Southern Poverty Law Center links Scalise, Family Research Council shooters." *Washington Examiner*. June 14, 2017. Accessed March 2, 2024. https://www.washingtonexaminer.com/news/washington-secrets/2142206/support-for-southern-poverty-law-center-links-scalise-family-research-council-shooters/.

55   "Grassley & Lankford Demand FBI Stop Using Biased Nonprofit As Source For Investigations." Press Release, Senator Chuck Grassley. October 12, 2023. Accessed January 5, 2024. https://www.grassley.senate.gov/news/news-releases/grassley-and-lankforddemand-fbi-stop-using-biased-nonprofit-as-source-for-investigations.

56   "Moms for Liberty listed as 'anti-government' group by extremism watchdog." *The Guardian*. June 6, 2023. Accessed April 9, 2024. https://www.theguardian.com/world/2023/jun/06/southern-poverty-law-center-moms-liberty-extremist.

57   Dillon, A.P. "US House Judiciary Republicans: DOJ labeled dozens of parents as terrorist threats." *North State Journal*. May 20, 2022. Accessed March 2, 2024. https://nsjonline.com/article/2022/05/us-house-judiciary-republicans-doj-labeled-dozens-of-parents-as-terrorist-threats/.

58   "Julian Bond." Discover the Networks. Accessed March 2, 2024. https://www.discoverthenetworks.org/individuals/julian-bond/.

59   "Angela Davis." Discover the Networks. Accessed March 2, 2024. https://www.discoverthenetworks.org/individuals/angela-davis/.

60   "About Us." *In These Times*." July 20, 2017. Accessed February 10, 2024. https://web.archive.org/web/20170720155249/http://inthesetimes.com/about/.

61   Reese, Charlie. "An Interview with Lenin Through the Magic of Historical Record." *Orlando Sentinel*. April 12, 1985. Accessed December 5, 2023. https://www.orlandosentinel.com/1985/04/12/an-interview-with-lenin-through-the-magic-of-historical-record/.

62   "Did Biden say the environmental crisis helps advance his agenda?" Blaze Media. April 22, 2022. Accessed February 10, 2024. https://www.theblaze.com/video/-2657200014.

63   Waller, J. Michael. *Big Intel: How the CIA and FBI Went from Cold War Heroes to Deep State Villains*. Washington, DC: Regnery Gateway, 2023. 192-194.

64   Ibid. 194.

65   "The Cloward-Piven Strategy." Wikipedia. Accessed March 3, 2024. https://en.wikipedia.org/wiki/Cloward%E2%80%93Piven_strategy.

66   Piven, Frances Fox, and Cloward, Richard. "The Weight of the Poor: A Strategy to End Poverty." *The Nation*. May 2, 1966. Accessed October 12, 2023. https://www.thenation.com/article/archive/weight-poor-strategy-end-poverty/.

67   Vadum, Matthew. *Subversion Inc. How Obama's ACORN Red Shirts are Still Terrorizing and Ripping Off American Taxpayers*. Washington DC: WND Books, 2011. 89.

68   "Weight of the Poor." 514.

69   "Weight of the Poor." *Op. cit.*

70   Ibid.

71   Rogin, Richard. "Now It's Welfare Lib; Welfare has come to be looked upon as a right and not a hidden shame or a gratuity." *New York Times*. September 27, 1970. 80.

72   Poe, Richard. "Cloward-Piven Strategy." Discover the Networks. Accessed January 5, 2024. http://www.discoverthenetworks.org/articles/theclowardpivenstrategypoe.html

73   Ibid.

74   Rogin. "Now It's Welfare Lib." *Op. cit.*

75   Poe. *Op. cit.*

76   Wiley, George. "The Nixon Family Assistance Plan - Reform or Repression." *National Black Law Journal*. 1971. Accessed March 15, 2024. https://escholarship.org/content/qt84t744wf/qt84t744wf.pdf.

77   "Median Family Income Up in 1970." U.S. Department of Commerce, Bureau of the Census. Series P-60, #78. May 20, 1970. Accessed April 9, 2024. http://www2.census.gov/prod2/popscan/p60-078.pdf.

78   Calculated with the CPI converted to a 2013 base year. Accessed April 9, 2024. https://www.in2013dollars.com/us/inflation/1970?amount=10000.

79   Guzman, George, and Melissa Kollar. "Income in the United States: 2022." United States Census Bureau. September 2023. Accessed January 10, 2024. https://www.census.gov/content/dam/Census/library/publications/2023/demo/p60-279.pdf.

80   Rogin. "Now It's Welfare Lib." *Op. cit.*

81   Carroll, Tamar W. "'To Help People Learn To Fight': New York City's Mobilization For Youth And The Origins Of The Community Action Programs Of The War On Poverty." Gotham Center for New York City History. October 8, 2015. Accessed March 25, 2024. https://www.gothamcenter.org/blog/to-help-people-learn-to-fight-new-york-citys-mobilization-for-youth-and-the-origins-of-the-community-action-programs-of-the-war-on-poverty.

82   Vadum. *Subversion Inc. Op. cit.* 76.

83   Ibid. 77.

84   Flanders, Stephanie. "Richard Cloward, Welfare Rights Leader, Dies at 74." *New York Times*. August 23, 2001. Accessed April 9, 2024. https://www.nytimes.com/2001/08/23/nyregion/richard-cloward-welfare-rights-leader-dies-at-74.html.

85   Piereson, James. "A Not-So-Great Society." *Washington Examiner*. September 30, 2016, accessed February 8, 2024. https://www.washingtonexaminer.com/magazine/1680878/a-not-so-great-society/.

86   Vadum. *Subversion Inc. Op. cit.* 79.

87   Williams, Juan. "Why not whites answering call for hot summer?" *Cleveland Plain Dealer*. June 17, 1982. 25-a.

88   "Thomas Sowell: Race-hustling results: Part III." Lima News. June 30, 2015. Accessed February 20, 2024. https://www.limaohio.com/archive/2015/06/30/thomas-sowell-race-hustling-results-part-iii-2/.

89   Stern, Sol. "Acorn's Nutty Regime for Cities." *City Journal*. Spring 2003. Accessed March 5, 2024. https://www.city-journal.org/article/acorns-nutty-regime-for-cities.

90   Beck, Glenn. "Cloward, Piven and the Fundamental Transformation of America." Fox News. January 5, 2010. Accessed April 9, 2024. http://www.foxnews.com/story/2010/01/05/cloward-piven-and-fundamental-transformation-america/.

91   "ACORN plans to shut down." CNN. March 22, 2010. Accessed April 9, 2024. https://www.cnn.com/2010/POLITICS/03/22/us.acorn.closing/index.html.

92   Vadum. *Subversion Inc. Op. cit.* 353.

93   "The sensational Giles and O'Keefe." *Washington Times*. September 16, 2009. Access April 9, 2024. http://www.washingtontimes.com/news/2009/sep/16/the-sensational-giles-and-okeefe/.

94   "ACORN." CNN. *Op. cit.*

95   Gordy, Cynthia. "Bertha Lewis on Life After ACORN." *The Root.* May 16, 2011. Accessed April 9, 2024. https://www.theroot.com/bertha-lewis-on-life-after-acorn-1790863961.

96   Vadum, Matthew. "A List if ACORN's 'New' Groups." MatthewVadum.com. July 1, 2012. Accessed April 9, 2024. http://matthewvadum.blogspot.com/p/acorn-new-groups.html.

97   Vadum. *Subversion Inc. Op. cit.* 19.

98   Rathke, Wade. "Power and Paradox of Cloward & Piven 'Breaking the Bank' Strategy." The Chief Organizer Blog. January 26, 2011. Accessed April 9, 2024. http://chieforganizer.org/2011/01/26/power-and-paradox-of-cloward-piven-%E2%80%9Cbreaking-the-bank%E2%80%9D-strategy/.

99   Ibid.

100 "Consolidated Minimum Wage Table." U.S. Department of Labor, Bureau of Labor Statistics. January 1, 2023. Accessed July 6, 2023. https://www.dol.gov/agencies/whd/mw-consolidated.

101 "Unemployment Benefits by State." World Population Review. 2023. Accessed July 6, 2023. https://worldpopulationreview.com/state-rankings/unemployment-benefits-by-state.

102 "Minimum wage in America: How many people are earning $7.25 an hour?" USAFacts. February 27, 2024. Accessed February 29, 2024. https://usafacts.org/articles/minimum-wage-america-how-many-people-are-earning-725-hour/.

103 Mills, Ryan. "California Fast-Food Franchisees Trying to Hang on after Minimum-Wage Law Takes Effect: 'The Pie's Only So Big.'" *National Review.* April 5, 2024. Accessed April 5, 2024. https://www.nationalreview.com/news/california-franchisees-warn-fast-food-industry-in-peril-after-minimum-wage-law-takes-effect-pies-only-so-big/.

104 Leonard, Thomas C. "Retrospectives Eugenics and Economics in the Progressive Era." *Journal of Economic Perspectives—Volume 19, Number 4.* Fall 2005. 207–224. Accessed April 9, 2024. https://www.princeton.edu/~tleonard/papers/retrospectives.pdf.

105 D'Souza, Dinesh. "Margaret Sanger's Racist Legacy." *The Epoch Times.* May 2, 2021. Accessed March 3, 2024. https://www.theepochtimes.com/opinion/margaret-sangers-racist-legacy-3788467.

106 Ibid.

107 "Watson Coleman Leads Introduction of Guaranteed Income Pilot Program." Press Release, Bonnie Watson Coleman. September 27 2023. Accessed April 9, 2024. https://watsoncoleman.house.gov/newsroom/press-releases/watson-coleman-leads-introduction-of-guaranteed-income-pilot-program.

108 Alfonseca, Kiara. "Guaranteed income embraced by leaders of some of largest U.S. counties." ABC News. February 15, 2023. Accessed January 12, 2024. https://abcnews.go.com/US/guaranteed-income-embraced-leaders-largest-us-counties/story?id=97190018.

109 Schmid, Valentin. "Universal Basic Income Explained." *The Epoch Times.* December 31, 2019. Accessed January 4, 2024. https://www.theepochtimes.com/opinion/universal-basic-income-explained-3185829.

110 Lipson, Charles. "The thirty-two-hour work week: another of Bernie's bad ideas." *American Spectator.* March 14, 2024. https://thespectator.com/topic/thirty-two-hour-work-week-bernie-sanders-bad-ideas/.

111 "U.S. Federal Government Spending Breakdown, 2023." US Government Spending. Accessed February 10, 2024. https://www.usgovernmentspending.com/breakdown_2023USrf_25rs5n.

112 "Weight of the Poor." *Op. cit.*

[113] Ibid.

[114] "Weight of the Poor." *Op. cit.*

[115] Lenin. *Op. cit.*

[116] "Weight of the Poor." *Op. cit.*

[117] Ibid.

[118] "Joe Biden says he's built most extensive "voter fraud" org in history." YouTube. November 5, 2020. Accessed March 5, 2024. https://www.youtube.com/watch?v=WGRnhBmHYN0.

[119] Carlson, Tucker. "Uncensored: Foreigners Will Be Able To Choose Our Next President" TCN. May 7, 2024. Accessed May 9, 2024. https://tuckercarlson.com/uncensored-catherine-engelbrecht/.

[120] 18 U.S. Code § 611 - Voting by aliens, subsection (c)3. Accessed May 9, 2024. https://www.law.cornell.edu/uscode/text/18/611.

[121] Binder, John. "Joe Biden Calls Illegal Aliens 'Model Citizens' While Promoting Amnesty." Breitbart. May 7, 2024. Accessed May 9, 2024. https://www.breitbart.com/politics/2024/05/07/joe-biden-calls-illegal-aliens-model-citizens-while-promoting-amnesty/.

[122] "Graham: Biden Abusing Immigration Parole To Implement An Open Borders Policy." Press Release, U.S. Senator Lindsay Graham. January 17, 2024. Accessed February 2, 2024. https://www.lgraham.senate.gov/public/index.cfm/press-releases?ID=787DA105-C7F0-43D0-BEBC-5A0AFD5656D9.

[123] Blankley, Bethany. "Report: DHS used over 50 airports worldwide to fly illegal foreign nationals into US." The Center Square. May 2, 2024. https://thedailybs.com/2024/05/02/report-dhs-used-over-50-airports-worldwide-to-fly-illegal-foreign-nationals-into-us/.

[124] Piven, Frances Fox, and Richard Cloward. *Why Americans Don't Vote.* New York: Pantheon Books, 1988. 209.

[125] Rodgers, Estelle. "The National Voter Registration Act: 15 Years On." American Constitution Society. 2009. Accessed April 9, 2024. https://www.acslaw.org/issue_brief/briefs-2007-2011/the-national-voter-registration-act-fifteen-years-on/.

[126] "Democrats 'plan to steal the vote.'" WND. January 13, 2010. Accessed March 2, 2024. https://www.wnd.com/2010/01/121878/.

[127] Vadum. *Subversion, Inc. Op. cit.* 41.

[128] Shawn, Eric. "ACORN Pleads Guilty to Voter Registration Fraud in Nevada." Fox News. December 23, 2015. Accessed February 12, 2024. https://www.foxnews.com/politics/acorn-pleads-guilty-to-voter-registration-fraud-in-nevada.

[129] "New Report Reveals the Truth About ACORN." Employment Policies Institute. June 2006. Accessed December 12, 2023. https://epionline.org/release/new-report-reveals-the-truth-about-acorn/.

[130] Vadum. *Subversion, Inc. Op. cit.* 87.

[131] MacIntosh, Jeane. "1 Voter 72 Registrations: ACORN paid me in cash and cigs." *New York Post.* October 10, 2008. Accessed April 9, 2024. https://nypost.com/2008/10/10/1-voter-72-registrations/. Another source claims there were 73 registrations.

[132] Vadum, Matthew. "Sentencing ACORN." FrontPageMag.com. August 17, 2011. Accessed April 9, 2024. https://www.frontpagemag.com/sentencing-acorn-matthew-vadum/.

[133] "ACORN is out of Ohio's elections." *Columbus Dispatch.* November 10, 2010. Accessed April 9, 2024. https://www.dispatch.com/story/news/2010/03/11/acorn-is-out-ohio-s/24156099007/.

[134] Phone conversation with Las Vegas Voter Registrar Harvard L. Lomax, March 7, 2012.

[135] Fund, John. "More ACORN vote fraud comes to light." *Wall Street Journal.* May 9, 2009. Accessed June 5, 2023. http://online.wsj.com/article/SB124182750646102435.html.

[136] Settlement Agreement, ACORN v Levy, Case No. 08-4084 (W.D. Mo). Plaintiff's lawyers included Project Vote, Demos, Lawyers Committee for Civil Rights Under Law and others. Accessed April 9, 2024. https://www.demos.org/sites/default/files/2019-04/Settlement%20Agreement%20in%20Missouri%20Voter%20Registration%20Lawsuit.pdf.

[137] "Partner: ACORN." Project Vote. Accessed March 23, 2024. https://www.projectvote.org/?partner=acorn.

[138] Rathke, Wade. "Why not Mandatory Voting and Registration?" The Chief Organizer Blog. March 1, 2012. Accessed November 12, 2023. http://chieforganizer.org/2012/03/01/why-not-mandatory-voting-and-registration/.

[139] *Why Americans Don't Vote. Op. cit.* 246-247.

[140] Feldman, Clarice. "ACORN, Fannie Mae and Motor Voter." *American Thinker.* September 16, 2008. Accessed January 4, 2024. http://www.americanthinker.com/blog/2008/09/acorn_fannie_mae_and_motor_vot.html.

[141] Jones, Terry. "3 out of 4 Americans worried about illegals voting in U.S. elections: I&I/TIPP Poll." The Daily BS. March 25, 2024. Accessed April 3, 2024. https://thedailybs.com/2024/03/25/3-out-of-4-americans-worried-about-illegals-voting-in-u-s-elections-ii-tipp-poll/.

[142] Hegeman, Roxana. "Court says Kansas can't require voters to show citizenship proof." *PBS News Hour.* April 29, 2020. Accessed March 2, 2024. https://www.pbs.org/newshour/politics/court-says-kansas-cant-require-voters-to-show-citizenship-proof.

[143] "Laws permitting noncitizens to vote in the United State." Ballotpedia. Accessed March 8, 2024. https://ballotpedia.org/Laws_permitting_noncitizens_to_vote_in_the_United_States.

[144] Cross, Alison. "Republicans Voice Outrage Over Non-Citizen Voting Bill." *Hartford Courant.* January 24, 2023. Accessed March 8, 2024. https://www.governing.com/now/republicans-voice-outrage-over-non-citizen-voting-bill.

[145] "Proof of Citizenship Requirements." Adrian Fontes, Arizona Secretary of State. Accessed March 4, 2024. https://azsos.gov/elections/voters/registering-vote/registration-requirements/proof-citizenship-requirements.

[146] Cupp, S.E., and Brett Joshpe. *Why You're Wrong About the Right: Behind the Myths.* New York: Threshold, 2008. 187.

[147] Fitzgerald, Jim. "Residents get 6 votes each in suburban NY election." Real Clear Politics. June 15, 2010. Accessed January 5, 2024. https://www.realclearpolitics.com/news/ap/politics/2010/Jun/15/residents_get_6_votes_each_in_suburban_ny_election.html.

[148] "Executive Order on Promoting Access to Voting." The White House. March 7, 2021. Accessed March 11, 2024. https://www.whitehouse.gov/briefing-room/presidential-actions/2021/03/07/executive-order-on-promoting-access-to-voting/.

[149] 18 U.S. Code § 611 - Voting by aliens, subsection (c)3. *Op. cit.*

[150] Fleetwood, Shawn. "DOJ Is Using Bidenbucks To Encourage Illegals And Felons To Vote, Says Mississippi Secretary Of State." *The Federalist.* March 13, 2024. Accessed March 18, 2024. https://thefederalist.com/2024/03/13/doj-is-using-bidenbucks-to-encourage-illegals-and-felons-to-vote-says-mississippi-secretary-of-state/.

[151] Fleetwood, Shawn. "Report: Biden Is Coordinating With ACLU, Other Left-Wing Groups To Interfere In Elections." *The Federalist.* June 8, 2023.

Accessed March 18, 2024. https://thefederalist.com/2023/06/08/report-biden-
is-coordinating-with-aclu-other-left-wing-groups-to-interfere-in-elections/.
152   Fleetwood. "DOJ Is Using Bidenbucks." *Op. cit.*
153   Ibid.
154   Olson, Kyle. "Illegals group claims credit for flipping state House – will get
drivers licenses as payoff?" *The Midwesterner.* June 5, 2023. Accessed March
18, 2024. https://www.themidwesterner.news/2023/06/illegals-group-
claims-credit-for-flipping-state-house-will-get-drivers-licenses-as-payoff/.
155   "We the People Michigan." IRS Form 990, Return of Organization
Exempt from Income Tax 2021. November 14, 2022. Accessed
January 10, 2024. https://pdf.guidestar.org/PDF_Ima
ges/2021/843/520/2021-843520391-202203189349313385-9.pdf.
      "We the People Action Fund." IRS Form 990, Return of Organization Exempt from Income
Tax 2021. November 14, 2022. Accessed January 10, 2024. https://pdf.guidestar.
org/PDF_Images/2021/843/528/2021-843528071-202203199349303655-9O.pdf.
156   Ibid.
157   Olson. "Illegals group claims credit." *Op. cit.*
158   "We the People Michigan." InfluenceWatch. Accessed March 18, 2024.
https://www.influencewatch.org/non-profit/we-the-people-michigan/.
159   Ibid.
160   "Table 6. Persons Obtaining Lawful Permanent Resident Status by Type
and Major Class of Admission: Fiscal Years 2013 to 2022." *2022 Yearbook
of Immigration Statistics.* U.S. Department of Homeland Security, Office
of Homeland Security Statistics. February 26, 2024. Accessed March 22,
2024. https://www.dhs.gov/ohss/topics/immigration/yearbook/2022.
161   McFadden, Cynthia, Sarah Fitzpatrick, Tracy Connor, and Anna Schecter.
"Birth tourism brings Russian baby boom to Miami." ABC News. January
9, 2018. Accessed July 11, 2024. https://www.nbcnews.com/news/
us-news/birth-tourism-brings-russian-baby-boom-miami-n836121.
162   Passel, Jeffrey S., and Paul Taylor. "Unauthorized Immigrants and Their
Unborn Children." Pew Research Center. August 11, 2010. Accessed July
10, 2024. https://www.pewresearch.org/race-and-ethnicity/2010/08/11/
unauthorized-immigrants-and-their-us-born-children/.
163   Montoya-Galvez, Camilo. "Trump vows to end birthright citizenship for
children of unauthorized immigrants if he wins in 2024." CBS News.
May 30, 2023. Accessed July 10, 2024. https://www.cbsnews.com/news/
trump-birthright-citizenship-children-unauthorized-immigrants/.
164   Gertz, Bill. "China's Intelligence Networks in United States Include
25,000 Spies: Dissident reveals up to 18,000 Americans recruited
as Chinese agents." *Washington Free Beacon.* July 11, 2017. Accessed
November 5, 2023. https://freebeacon.com/national-security/
chinas-spy-network-united-states-includes-25000-intelligence-officers/.
165   Tucker Carlson on vote fraud. X. March 7, 2024. Accessed March 8, 2024.
https://twitter.com/CitizenFreePres/status/1765954193418858658.
166   Jocelyn Benson on fighting attacks on democracy. X. March 6, 2024. Accessed
March 8, 2024. https://twitter.com/JackPosobiec/status/1765410842034508180.
167   Lyman, Brianna. "Secretaries Of State Won't Explain 'Coordinated' Effort To
Fight 'Common Adversary' In 2024." *The Federalist.* March 21, 2024. Accessed
March 25, 2024. https://thefederalist.com/2024/03/21/secretaries-of-state-
wont-explain-coordinated-effort-to-fight-common-adversary-in-2024/.

168   Wren, Adam, and Zach Montellaro. "Liberal group spends $4 million to boost secretary of state races." Politico. September 23, 2022. Accessed November 5, 2024. https://www.politico.com/news/2022/09/23/secretary-of-state-ivote-00058499.

169   Meier, Tiffany. "Michigan State Senator Raises Concerns About Secretary of State Jocelyn Benson, Election Integrity." *The Epoch Times.* October 26, 2022. Accessed March 1, 2024. https://www.theepochtimes.com/audio/us/michigan-state-senator-raises-concerns-about-secretary-of-state-jocelyn-benson-election-integrity-4821598.

170   "Nessel, FBI silent in face of obvious voter fraud discovered by clerks." Michigan House Republicans. February 14, 2024. Accessed March 10, 2024. https://gophouse.org/posts/nessel-fbi-silent-in-reply-to-obvious-voter-fraud-discovered-by-clerks.

171   "Vendor/Recipient: GBI Strategies." Open Secrets. February 1, 2021. Accessed March 19, 2024. https://www.opensecrets.org/campaign-expenditures/vendor?cycle=2020&vendor=GBI+Strategies.

172   Dunmire, Julie. "Documents detail MSP investigation into alleged Muskegon-area voter fraud." Fox 17. September 1, 2023. Accessed March 10, 2024. https://www.fox17online.com/news/local-news/lakeshore/muskegon/documents-detail-msp-investigation-into-alleged-muskegon-area-voter-fraud.

173   Ibid.

174   Davidson, Kyle. "8 Republicans introduce articles of impeachment against Democratic Attorney General Dana Nessel." Michigan Advance. November 10, 2023. Accessed March 4, 2024. https://michiganadvance.com/2023/11/10/8-republicans-introduce-articles-of-impeachment-against-democratic-attorney-general-dana-nessel/

175   Ibid.

176   "House Resolution No. 165." Michigan House of Representatives. November 9, 2023. Accessed March 10, 2024. https://www.legislature.mi.gov/documents/2023-2024/resolutionintroduced/House/pdf/2023-HIR-0165.pdf.

177   Letter to Jim Jordan. Sheriff Dar Leaf. Barry County Sheriff's Office. March 17, 2024. Accessed March 19, 2024. https://drive.google.com/file/d/1YTvKSLBETW6KXrMOuTm7UPo4_PtjCZ6k/view.

178   Silva, Ken. "Evidence of Foreign Nationals Accessing Dominion Voting Machines Leaked to Public." Headline USA. March 19, 2024. Accessed March 19, 2024. https://headlineusa.com/evidence-foreign-accessing-dominion-machines-leaked/.

179   Altimari, Dave, and Andrew Brown. "Bridgeport primary election overturned; new vote ordered." CT Mirror. November 1, 2023. Accessed March 10, 2024. https://ctmirror.org/2023/11/01/bridgeport-primary-election-ruling-ganim-gomes/.

180   Shawn, Eric. "Voter fraud a 'normal political tactic' in upstate New York." Fox News. January 17, 2012. Accessed January 5, 2024. http://www.foxnews.com/politics/2012/01/17/voter-fraud-normal-political-tactic-in-upstate-ny-city/.

181   "Alleged corruption uncovered inside Alaska Senator Lisa Murkowski's campaign ." Blaze Media. August 25, 2022. Accessed November 10, 2023. https://www.theblaze.com/video/alleged-corruption-murkowski-campaign.

182   Lott, John R. "Why Do Most Countries Ban Mail-In Ballots?: They Have Seen Massive Vote Fraud Problems." SSRN. August 3, 2020. Accessed March 10, 2024. https://papers.ssrn.com/sol3/papers.cfm?abstract_id=3666259.

183   "The Carter-Baker Commission, 16 Years Later: Voting by Mail." Baker Institute for Public Policy. Accessed March 12, 2024. https://www.bakerinstitute.org/event/carter-baker-commission-16-years-later-voting-mail.

184   Liptak, Adam. "Error and Fraud at Issue as Absentee Voting Rises." *New York Times.* October 6, 2012. Accessed March 10, 2024. https://www.nytimes.com/2012/10/07/us/politics/as-more-vote-by-mail-faulty-ballots-could-impact-elections.html.

185 Dzhanova, Yelena. "House Speaker Nancy Pelosi says the country must move toward vote by mail, setting up a fight with Trump." MSNBC. March 30, 2020. Accessed March 8, 2024. https://www.cnbc.com/2020/03/31/coronavirus-update-pelosi-says-country-must-move-to-vote-by-mail-taking-aim-at-trump.html.

186 "H.R.1604 - Universal Right to Vote by Mail Act of 2009." 111th Congress (2009–2010). Accessed April 9, 2024. https://www.congress.gov/bill/111th-congress/house-bill/1604.

187 Ozimek, Tom. "H.R. 1 Election Reform Bill 'Threat to American Democracy': Heritage Foundation Expert." *The Epoch Times*. March 15, 2021. Accessed March 8, 2024. https://www.theepochtimes.com/us/h-r-1-election-reform-bill-threat-to-american-democracy-heritage-foundation-expert-3734022.

188 "H.R.1439 - Vote at Home Act of 2023." 118th Congress (2023–2024). Accessed March 10. 2023. https://www.congress.gov/bill/118th-congress/house-bill/1439.

189 "Automatic Voter Registration." National Conference of State Legislatures. February 12, 2024. Accessed February 20, 2024. https://www.ncsl.org/elections-and-campaigns/automatic-voter-registration.

190 "Center for Tech and Civic Life (CTCL)." InfluenceWatch. Accessed March 5, 2024. https://www.influencewatch.org/non-profit/center-for-tech-and-civic-life/.

191 Anderson, Jillian. "Amistad Project Exposes Influence of Mark Zuckerberg's Dark Money Network in 2020 Election." December 16, 2020. Accessed April 9, 2024. https://www.einnews.com/pr_news/532866119/amistad-project-exposes-influence-of-mark-zuckerberg-s-dark-money-network-in-2020-election.

192 "Center for Technology and Civic Life." IRS Form 990, Return of Organization Exempt from Income Tax 2020. January 22, 2022. Accessed March 17, 2024. https://pdf.guidestar.org/PDF_Images/2021/472/158/2021-472158694-202240249349300769-9A.pdf.

193 "Center for Tech and Civic Life (CTCL)." InfluenceWatch. *Op cit.*

194 "Center for Election Innovation and Research." IRS Form 990, Return of Organization Exempt from Income Tax 2020. May 12, 2022. Accessed March 17, 2024. https://pdf.guidestar.org/PDF_Images/2021/813/815/2021-813815137-2022013 29349306200-9.pdf.

195 Center for Tech and Civic Life (CTCL)." InfluenceWatch. *Op cit.*

196 Ibid.

197 "Center for Technology and Civic Life." IRS Form 990, Return of Organization Exempt from Income Tax 2021. December 14, 2023. Accessed March 17, 2024. https://pdf.guidestar.org/PDF_Images/2023/472/158/2023-472158694-202313489349301851-9.pdf.

198 "Center for Election Innovation and Research." IRS Form 990. *Op cit.*

199 "CEIR 2020 Voter Education Grant Program." Center for Election Innovation & Research. March 2021. Accessed March 2, 2024. https://electioninnovation.org/research/ceir-2020-voter-education-grant-program/.

200 Marshall, Victoria. "Democratic Operatives Control Voter Rolls In 31 States, Report Shows." *The Federalist*. August 11, 2022. Accessed March 5, 2024. https://thefederalist.com/2022/08/11/democratic-operatives-control-voter-rolls-in-31-states-report-shows/

201 "Judicial Watch Study: 1.8 Million Extra Registered Voters." Judicial Watch. October 16, 2020. Accessed February 5, 2024. https://www.judicialwatch.org/judicial-watch-study/.

202 Michelle Obama. X. April 2, 2024. Accessed April 8, 2024. https://twitter.com/MichelleObama/status/1775250761766539438.

203 "Get Ready to Vote." When We All Vote. Accessed April 8, 2024. https://whenweallvote.org/takeaction/voter-resources-hub/.

204 "Register to Vote." When We All Vote. Accessed April 8, 2024. https://whenweallvote.org/register/.

205 Marshall. "Democratic Operatives Control Voter Rolls In 31 States." *Op. cit.*

206 Miele, Frank Daniel. "Zuckerberg-Funded Nonprofit Paid $11.8 Million to Democrat Political Consulting Firms for 'Nonpartisan Voter Education' in Michigan 2020 Election." Star News Network. August 5 2021. Accessed April 9, 2024. https://thestarnewsnetwork.com/2021/08/05/zuckerberg-funded-nonprofit-paid-11-8-million-to-democrat-political-consulting-firms-for-nonpartisan-voter-education-in-michigan-2020-election/.

207 Ibid.

208 Doyle, William. "The 2020 Election Wasn't Stolen, It Was Bought By Mark Zuckerberg." *The Federalist.* October 12, 2021. Accessed February 5, 2024. https://thefederalist.com/2021/10/12/the-2020-election-wasnt-stolen-it-was-bought-by-mark-zuckerberg/.

209 Piwowarczyk, Jim & Jessica McBride. "State Senators Call for Investigation Into Green Bay Election." Wisconsin Right Now. March 9, 2021. Accessed April 9, 2024. https://www.wisconsinrightnow.com/green-bay-election/.

210 Marshall. "Democratic Operatives Control Voter Rolls In 31 States." *Op. cit.*

211 Washburn, Logan. "Zuckbucks Group Teaches Election Offices How To Shut Down Speech And Influence Election Laws." *The Federalist.* March 15, 2024. Accessed March 18, 2024. https://thefederalist.com/2024/03/15/zuckbucks-group-teaches-election-offices-how-to-shut-down-speech-and-influence-election-laws/.

212 Ibid.

213 Ibid.

214 Ibid.

215 Ibid.

216 Center for Technology and Civic Life." IRS Form 990, Return of Organization Exempt from Income Tax 2021. December 14, 2023. Accessed March 17, 2024. https://pdf.guidestar.org/PDF_Images/2023/472/158/2023-472158694-202313489349301851-9.pdf.

217 "Center for Election Innovation and Research." IRS Form 990, Return of Organization Exempt from Income Tax 2021. May 4, 2023. Accessed March 17, 2024. https://pdf.guidestar.org/PDF_Images/2022/813/815/2022-813815137-202321249349302807-9.pdf.

218 "'Groups Hide in Greater Darkness': Foreign Nationals Using Charity Backdoor to Influence American Elections." Press Release, U.S. House of Representatives, Ways and Means Committee. December 15, 2023. Accessed March 12, 2024. https://waysandmeans.house.gov/2023/12/15/groups-hide-in-greater-darkness-foreign-nationals-using-charity-backdoor-to-influence-american-elections/.

219 Ibid.

220 Vogel, Kenneth P., and Shane Goldmacher. "Democrats Decried Dark Money. Then They Won With It in 2020." *New York Times.* January 29, 2022. Accessed January 31, 2024. https://www.nytimes.com/2022/01/29/us/politics/democrats-dark-money-donors.html.

221 Barnes, Ed. "Citizens' Group Helps Uncover Alleged Rampant Voter Fraud in Houston." Fox News. September 25, 2010. Accessed March 26, 2024. https://www.foxnews.com/politics/citizens-group-helps-uncover-alleged-rampant-voter-fraud-in-houston.

222 Ibid.

223 Morris, Andrea. "'True the Vote' Wins Big Case After Decade-Long Battle with IRS." CBN. June 7, 2019. Accessed March 26, 2024. https://www2.cbn.com/news/politics/true-vote-wins-big-case-after-decade-long-battle-irs.

224 Mahoney, Wendi Strauch. "Engelbrecht and Phillips Out of Jail: Incarcerated for Refusing to Reveal Sources." UncoverDC. November 7, 2022. Accessed March 25, 2024. https://www.uncoverdc.com/2022/11/07/engelbrecht-and-phillips-out-of-jail-incarcerated-for-refusing-to-reveal-sources/.

225 Asper, Jennifer. "Catherine Englebrecht of True the Vote with update on Konnech lawsuit h/t MidnightRider on Telegram." X. March 1, 2023. Accessed March 25, 2024. https://twitter.com/j3669/status/1630982648834277376.

226 "October 4, 2022: Head of Election Worker Management Company Arrested in Connection with Theft of Personal Data." Press Release, Los Angeles County District Attorney's Office. Accessed March 25, 2024. https://archive.fo/WaWc8.

227 Donohue, Shanna. "Charges dropped against election software CEO accused of data theft." *Washington Examiner*. November 10, 2022. Accessed March 25, 2024. https://www.washingtonexaminer.com/?p=2625092.

228 Huseman, Jessica. "Two leaders of True the Vote jailed by federal judge for contempt of court." The Texas Tribune. October 31, 2022. Accessed March 25, 2024. https://www.texastribune.org/2022/10/31/true-the-vote-leaders-jailed/.

229 Stieber, Zachary. "Election Software Firm Drops Case Against True the Vote." *The Epoch Times*. April 25, 2023. Accessed March 26, 2024. https://www.theepochtimes.com/us/election-software-firm-drops-case-against-true-the-vote-5219983.

230 Ibid.

231 Catherine Engelbrecht. Phone interview with James Simpson. March 24, 2024.

232 Faddis, Sam. "Is It Possible The Chinese Really Did Hack Our Elections?" *AND Magazine*. October 17, 2022. Accessed March 25, 2024. https://andmagazine.substack.com/p/is-it-possible-the-chinese-really.

233 Ibid.

234 McGuire, Mick. "Brnovich Ignoring Credible Concerns About Ballots Cast Through Arizona's Overseas Internet Portal." The Arizona Daily Independent. June 30, 2022. Accessed March 26, 2024. https://arizonadailyindependent.com/2022/06/30/brnovich-ignoring-credible-concerns-about-ballots-cast-through-arizonas-overseas-internet-portal/.

235 Ibid.

236 Richmond, Todd. "Jury finds former Milwaukee election official guilty of obtaining fake absentee ballots." AP News. March 20, 2024. Accessed March 26, 2024. https://apnews.com/article/wisconsin-ballot-fraud-trump-trial-c6b568d58e2ad7121566c3734ab5d851.

237 "Nechayev, Sergei Gennadievich." *The Free Dictionary, by Farlex*. Accessed January 5, 2021. http://encyclopedia2.thefreedictionary.com/Sergey+Nechayev.

238 Dinan, Stephen. "Biden got 255,000 'excess' votes in fraud-tainted swing states in 2020, study finds." *Washington Times*. March 28, 2022. Accessed March 26, 2024. https://www.washingtontimes.com/news/2022/mar/28/joe-biden-got-255000-excess-votes-fraud-tainted-sw/.

239 Ibid.

240 Matsumoto, Ryan. "Where did all the bellweather counties go?" FiveThirtyEight. February 1, 2021. Accessed March 27, 2024. https://fivethirtyeight.com/features/where-did-all-the-bellwether-counties-go/.

241 Villalovas, Eden. "Pennsylvania House Republican blasts automatic voter registration: 'Hasty.'" *Washington Examiner*. September 18, 2023. Accessed March 27, 2024. https://www.washingtonexaminer.com/news/2432546/

pennsylvania-house-republican-
blasts-automatic-voter-registration-hasty/.

242   Ibid.

243   The Center Square. "Pennsylvania Supports Licenses for Undocumented
      Immigrants." New Jersey 101.5. March 7, 2024. Accessed March 27, 2024.
      https://nj1015.com/penndot-supports-licenses-for-undocumented-immigrants/.

244   Cohen, Marshall, Katelyn Polantz, and Kelly Mena. "Pennsylvania Supreme
      Court election rulings are big wins for Biden." CNN. September 17, 2020.
      Accessed March 29, 2024. https://www.cnn.com/2020/09/17/politics/
      pennsylvania-supreme-court-green-party-presidential-ballot/index.html.

245   Bice, Daniel. "Members of the state Elections Commission deadlock
      on whether to let Green Party on presidential ballot." *Milwaukee
      Journal Sentinel.* August 20, 2020. Accessed March 29, 2024. https://
      www.jsonline.com/story/news/politics/elections/2020/08/20/
      election-commission-deadlocks-whether-let-green-party-ballot/3404370001/.

246   Saul, Stephanie, and Nick Corasaniti. "Wisconsin's Top Court Rules
      Against Reprinting of Ballots, Avoiding Election Chaos." *New York Times.*
      September 14, 2020. Accessed March 12, 2024. https://www.nytimes.
      com/2020/09/14/us/politics/wisconsin-ballots-reprinting-election.html.

247   Engelbrecht, Catherine. "The Aftermath: My Meeting With Raffensperger." True the
      Vote. August 21, 2023. Accessed March 25, 2024. https://open.ink/the-aftermath.

248   Ibid.

249   Ibid.

250   "Group will appeal court ruling that Georgia voter challenges don't violate
      federal law." AP News. February 2, 2024. Accessed March 27, 2024.
      https://apnews.com/article/georgia-voter-challenges-appeal-true-vote-40faf
      767628c4c291979c2c8416619ab.

251   Hemingway, Mollie. *RIGGED: How the Media, Big Tech, and the
      Democrats Seized Our Elections.* Washington, DC: Regnery, 2022.

252   "Voting by mail-in or absentee ballot is safe, secure, and easy." DOS
      Voting & Election Information. Accessed March 23, 2024. https://www.
      vote.pa.gov/Voting-in-PA/Pages/Mail-and-Absentee-Ballot.aspx.

253   "Court strikes down counting of 2,349 ballots in Allegheny County." Pittsburg
      Post-Gazette. November 19, 2020. Accessed March 12, 2024. https://
      www.post-gazette.com/news/politics-state/2020/11/19/Nicole-Ziccarelli-
      PA-state-Senate-vs-Brewster-election-ballots-Commonwealth-Court/
      stories/202011190151.

254   Ward, Paula Reed. "Pa. Supreme Court says undated mail-in ballots in Nicole
      Ziccarelli case can be counted." TribLIVE. November 23, 2020. Accessed March 5,
      2024. https://triblive.com/local/pa-supreme-court-says-undated-mail-in-ballots-
      in-ziccarelli-case-can-be-counted/.

255   Ibid.

256   "2020 Election, Official Returns." Pennsylvania Secretary of
      State. November 3, 2020. Accessed March 4, 2024. https://www.
      electionreturns.pa.gov/General/SummaryResults?ElectionID=83.

257   Knox, Brady. "Pennsylvania judge rules that undated mail-in ballots must be
      counted." *Washington Examiner.* November 21, 2023. Accessed March 5, 2024.
      https://www.washingtonexaminer.com/news/2440154/pennsylvania-judge-rules-
      that-undated-mail-in-ballots-must-be-counted/.

258   Hopkins, Daniel J., Marc Meredith, and Kira Wang. "How Many Naked
      Ballots Were Cast in Pennsylvania's 2020 General Election?" MIT Election Lab.

August 26, 2021. Accessed March 5, 2024. https://electionlab.mit.edu/articles/how-many-naked-ballots-were-cast-pennsylvanias-2020-general-election.

259 "America First Legal Files Landmark Lawsuit Against Maricopa County, Arizona Officials for Violating State Election Laws." America First Legal. February 7, 2024. Accessed April 6, 2024. https://aflegal.org/america-first-legal-files-landmark-lawsuit-against-maricopa-county-arizona-officials-for-violating-state-election-laws/.

260 Becket, Stefan, Melissa Quinn, Grace Segers, and Caroline Linton. "2020 election 'most secure in history,' security officials say." CBS News. November 13, 2020. Accessed March 12, 2024. https://www.cbsnews.com/live-updates/2020-election-most-secure-history-dhs/.

261 Ibid.

262 France, Emily. "US election 2020 results: which states are still counting votes?" Diario AS. November 12, 2020. Accessed March 3, 2024. https://en.as.com/en/2020/11/12/latest_news/1605218876_129970.html.

263 "All On The Line." KeyWiki. August 5, 2023. Accessed April 9, 2024. https://keywiki.org/All_On_The_Line.

264 "All On the Line." InfluenceWatch. Accessed April 9, 2024. https://www.influencewatch.org/non-profit/all-on-the-line/.

265 Assembly Speaker Robin Vos. Phone interview with James Simpson. 9–10 am Eastern Time, April 9, 2024.

266 Worstall, Tim. "Astonishing Numbers: America's Poor Still Live Better Than Most Of The Rest Of Humanity." *Forbes*. June 1, 2013. Accessed March 3, 2024. https://www.forbes.com/sites/timworstall/2013/06/01/astonishing-numbers-americas-poor-still-live-better-than-most-of-the-rest-of-humanity/.

267 Cordato, Roy. "Obama's Green Energy Failure List." Locke. October 30, 2012. Accessed January 22, 2023. https://www.johnlocke.org/obamas-green-energy-failure-list/; Bradley, Robert L., Jr. "Political Energy: We All Lose." *HuffPost*. October 22, 2012. Accessed January 5, 2023. https://www.huffpost.com/entry/political-energy-we-all-l_b_2001886/.

268 Whoriskey, Neil. "The New Civil Code: ISS and Glass Lewis as Lawmakers." CLS Blue Sky Blog. July 28, 2020. Accessed March 25, 2024. https://clsbluesky.law.columbia.edu/2020/07/28/cleary-gottlieb-discusses-the-new-civil-code-of-iss-and-glass-lewis/.

269 "ISS and Glass Lewis Proxy Voting Policy Updates for the 2024 Proxy Season." Sidley. February 2, 2024. Accessed February 12, 2024. https://www.sidley.com/-/media/update-pdfs/2024/02/iss-and-glass-lewis-policy-updates-for-2024.pdf?la=en&rev=00706484a18e4cd286633e4eb45d50c7.

270 Ibid.

271 Wheeler, Jack. "The Secret to the Suicidal Liberal Mind." *Newsmax*. January 21, 2002. Accessed April 2, 2024. https://www.newsmax.com/pre-2008/the-secret-the suicidal/
2002/01/20/id/664164/.

272 Ibid.

273 Ibid.

274 "A Republic, if you can keep it." *Respectfully Quoted: A Dictionary of Quotations*. 1989. Accessed April 9, 2024. http://www.bartleby.com/73/1593.html.

275 Kruta, Virginia. "Democrat Senator Admits His Party Needs Americans Divided If They Want To Win." The Daily Wire. March 13, 2024. Accessed March 14, 2024. https://www.dailywire.com/news/democrat-senator-admits-his-party-needs-americans-divided-if-they-want-to-win.

276   Inouye, Mie. "Frances Fox Piven on Why Protesters Must 'Defend Their Ability to Exercise Disruptive Power.'" *Jacobin*. June 17, 2020. Accessed April 9, 2024. https://www.jacobinmag.com/2020/06/frances-fox-piven-protests-movement-racial-justice.

277   "Public-private partnerships based on fascist economic model." *The Free Library*. 2014. Accessed January 16, 2024. https://www.thefreelibrary.com/Public-private+partnerships+based+on+fascist+economic+model.-a0198169101.

278   "National People's Action." Discover the Networks. Accessed April 9, 2024. https://www.discoverthenetworks.org/organizations/national-peoples-action-npa/.

279   Hunt, D. Bradford. "Redlining." *Chicago Encyclopedia*. Accessed April 9, 2024. http://www.encyclopedia.chicagohistory.org/pages/1050.html.

280   "1934—1968 FHA Mortgage Insurance Requirements Utilize Redlining." Fair Housing Center of Greater Boston. Accessed April 9, 2024. http://www.bostonfairhousing.org/timeline/1934-1968-FHA-Redlining.html.

281   Lacker, Jeffrey M. "Neighborhoods and Banking." *Federal Reserve Bank of Richmond Economic Quarterly*. Spring 1995. Accessed April 9, 2024. https://www.richmondfed.org/publications/research/economic_quarterly/1995/spring/lacker.

282   Schweizer, Peter. *Architects of Ruin: How Big Government Liberals Wrecked the Global Economy-and How They Will Do It Again If No One Stops Them*. New York: Harper, 2009. 29–30.

283   Vadum, Matthew, and Jeremy Lott. "In a Rotten Nutshell." Labor Watch. November 2008. Accessed April 9, 2024. https://capitalresearch.org/app/uploads/2013/07/LW1108.pdf.

284   Kurtz, Stanley. "Spreading the Virus." *New York Post*. October 13, 2008. Accessed April 9, 2024. http://nypost.com/2008/10/13/spreading-the-virus/.

285   Ibid.

286   Information Statement, Federal National Mortgage Association. December 31, 1994. Accessed April 9, 2024. https://www.fanniemae.com/media/27241/display. 6.

287   Zigas, Barry. "Fannie Mae and Minority Lending: Assessment and Action Plan." SWRO HCD Advisory Council Dallas. November 16, 2000. Accessed April 9, 2024. https://fcic-static.law.stanford.edu/cdn_media/fcic-docs/2000-11-16%20Fannie%20Mae%20and%20Minority%20Lending.pdf. 13.

288   Morrissey, Ed. "The quotes that explain the entire financial meltdown." Hot Air. October 12, 2008. Accessed April 9, 2024. https://hotair.com/ed-morrissey/2008/10/12/the-quotes-that-explain-the-entire-financial-meltdown-n157905.

289   Holmes, Steven A. "Fannie Mae Eases Credit to Aid Mortgage Lending." *New York Times*. September 30, 1999. Accessed April 9, 2024. http://www.nytimes.com/1999/09/30/business/fannie-mae-eases-credit-to-aid-mortgage-lending.html.

290   Vadum. *Subversion Inc. Op. cit.* 188.

291   Smith, Zach, and Paul Larkin. "Biden's DOJ Increases Power and Rewards Political Allies." The Heritage Foundation. July 21, 2022. Accessed April 9, 2024. https://www.heritage.org/crime-and-justice/commentary/bidens-doj-increases-power-and-rewards-political-allies.

292   "Rubio, Colleagues Call on Merrick Garland to Stop Sending Federal Funds to Partisan Organizations." Press Release, U.S. Senator Marco Rubio. July 12, 2022. Accessed March 14, 2024. https://www.rubio.senate.gov/rubio-colleagues-call-on-merrick-garland-to-stop-sending-federal-funds-to-partisan-organizations/.

293   "Justice Department's False Claims Act Settlements and Judgments Exceed $5.6 Billion in Fiscal Year 2021." Press Release, U.S. Department of Justice. February 1, 2022. Accessed February 5, 2024. https://www.justice.gov/opa/pr/justice-department-s-false-claims-act-settlements-and-judgments-exceed-56-billion-fiscal-year.

294 "U.S. Justice Department Moves to Reinstitute Supplemental
Environmental Projects as Part of Environmental Enforcement
Settlements." Sidley. May 8, 2022. Accessed February 5, 2024.
https://www.sidley.com/en/insights/newsupdates/2022/05/
us-justice-department-moves-to-reinstitute-supplemental-environmental-projects.

295 Ibid.

296 "Speech: Attorney General Merrick B. Garland Delivers Remarks on Significant
Milestone in Combating Redlining Initiative After Securing Over $107 Million in
Relief for Communities of Color Nationwide." U.S. Department of Justice. October
19, 2023. Accessed February 4, 2024. https://www.justice.gov/opa/speech/attorney-
general-merrick-b-garland-delivers-remarks-significant-milestone-combating.

297 Timiraos, Nick. "Rethinking Fannie, Freddie and the 30-Year Mortgage." *Wall
Street Journal.* September 22, 2013. Accessed April 9, 2024. http://online.wsj.
com/news/articles/SB10001424127887324807704579087072063293460.

298 Pinto, Edward. "Acorn and the Housing Bubble." *Wall Street Journal.*
November 12, 2009. Accessed April 9, 2024. https://www.wsj.com/
articles/SB10001424052748703298004574459763052141456.

299 Walliston, Peter J. "Dissenting Statement." Financial Crisis Inquiry
Commission. 2011. Accessed April 9, 2024. http://fcic-static.law.stanford.
edu/cdn_media/fcic-reports/fcic_final_report_wallison_dissent.pdf. 456.

300 "Countrywide: 1 in 3 Subprime Mortgages Delinquent." Reuters. January
29, 2008. Accessed April 9, 2024. http://www.cnbc.com/id/22877103.

301 Miga, Andrew. "Rep. Frank helped partner land Fannie Mae job." *San Diego Union
Tribune.* May 26, 2011. Accessed April 9, 2024. https://www.sandiegouniontribune.
com/sdut-rep-frank-helped-partner-land-fannie-mae-job-2011may26-story.html.

302 Sammon, Bill. "Lawmaker Accused of Fannie Mae Conflict of Interest."
Fox News. October 3, 2008. Accessed April 9, 2024. https://www.foxnews.
com/story/lawmaker-accused-of-fannie-mae-conflict-of-interest.

303 McCormack, John. "Barney Frank Blames Republicans for Freddie/Fannie Failure."
Washington Examiner. October 21, 2008. Accessed April 9, 2024. https://www.
washingtonexaminer.com/news/703040/barney-frank-blames-republicans-
for-freddie-fannie-failure/.

304 Mayer, Lindsay Renick. "Fannie Mae and Freddie Mac Invest in Democrats."
Open Secrets. July 16, 2008. Accessed April 9, 2024. http://www.
opensecrets.org/news/2008/07/top-senate-recipients-of-fanni.html.

305 Hagerty, James R. "US: Fannie Mae Ex-Officials Settle." CorpWatch. April 19,
2008. Accessed April 9, 2024. http://www.corpwatch.org/article/us-fannie-mae-ex-
officials-settle.

306 Smith, Ben. "Obama denies Raines ties, accuses McCain of throwing stones from
his 'seven glass houses.'" Politico. September 18, 2008. Accessed April 9, 2024.
http://www.politico.com/blogs/bensmith/0908/Obama_denies_Raines_ties_
accuses_McCain_of_throwing_stones_from_his_seven_glass_houses.html.

307 Walliston. *Op. cit.* 454.

308 "Goodlatte, Hensarling to Attorney General Holder: Why Does DOJ Require Banks
to Donate to Activist Groups?" Press Release, House of Representatives Judiciary
Committee. November 25, 2014. Accessed February 15, 2024. https://judiciary.
house.gov/media/press-releases/goodlatte-hensarling-to-attorney-general-holder-
why-does-doj-require-banks-to.

309 "UnidosUS (formerly National Council of La Raza)." InfluenceWatch.
Accessed February 16, 2024. https://www.influencewatch.org/
non-profit/unidosus-formerly-national-council-of-la-raza/.

310   Glazov, Jamie. "Unmasking the Real Culprits of the Housing Collapse." *FrontPage Magazine*. December 21, 2011. Accessed April 9, 2024. https://www. frontpagemag.com/unmasking-real-culprits-housing-collapse-jamie-glazov/.

311   "Judicial Watch Sues Justice Department for Records about Forcing Corporations to Fund Leftist Groups." Judicial Watch. June 12, 2017. Accessed February 16, 2024. https://www.judicialwatch.org/judicial-watch-sues-justice-department-records-forcing-corporations-fund-leftist-groups/.

312   Walliston. *Op. cit.* 445-446.

313   Thompson, Alex. "'Obama would be jealous': How Biden's rivalry with his ex-boss shapes his presidency." March 18, 2024. Accessed March 18, 2024. https://www.axios.com/2024/03/18/biden-obama-rivalry-presidency.

314   Pengelly, Martin. "Biden 'finishing the job' my administration started, Obama says." *The Guardian*. June 1, 2021. Accessed December 5, 2023. https://www. theguardian.com/us-news/2021/jun/01/biden-obama-finishing-the-job-president.

315   Markey, Lachlan. "Report: 80% of DOE Green Energy Loans Went to Obama Backers." The Heritage Foundation. November 14, 2011. April 9, 2024. http://blog.heritage.org/2011/11/14/ report-80-of-doe-green-energy-loans-went-to-obama-backers/.

316   Jackson, David. "Obama jokes about 'shovel ready' projects." *USA Today*. June 13, 2011. Accessed April 9, 2024. http://content.usatoday.com/communities/theoval/ post/2011/06/obama-jokes-about-shovel-ready-projects/1#.UoD7RydAcna.

317   Pethokoukis, James. "11 stunning revelations from Larry Summers's secret economics memo to Barack Obama." American Enterprise Institute. January 23, 2012. Accessed April 9, 2024. https://www.aei.org/economics/11-stunning-revelations-from-larry-summerss-secret-economics-memo-to-barack-obama/.

318   Ellerson, Lindsay. "Stimulus Legislation Could Be Introduced As Soon As Monday." ABC News. January 9, 2009. Accessed April 9, 2024. https://web.archive.org/web/20131107225723/http:// abcnews.go.com/blogs/politics/2009/01/stimulus-legisl/ .

319   Paley, Amit R. "Stimulus Provision May Inhibit Watchdog Investigations, Critics Warn." *Washington Post*. February 28, 2009. Accessed April 9, 2024. http://www. washingtonpost.com/wp-dyn/content/article/2009/02/27/AR2009022702846.html.

320   Plumer, Brad. "The U.S. labor force is still shrinking. Here's why." *Washington Post*. November 8, 2013. Accessed April 9, 2024. http://www.washingtonpost.com/blogs/ wonkblog/wp/2013/11/08/the-u-s-labor-force-is-still-shrinking-rapidly-heres-why/.

321   Simpson, James. "Cloward-Piven Government." *American Thinker*. November 23, 2009. Accessed March 12, 2024. https://www. americanthinker.com/articles/2009/11/clowardpiven_government.html.

322   Haq, Massoma. "Rules Committee Republicans Oppose Democrats' COVID-19 Relief Bill." *The Epoch Times*. February 27, 2021. Accessed February 2, 2024. https://www.theepochtimes.com/us/rules-committee-republicans-oppose-democrats-covid-19-relief-bill-3713149.

323   Andrzejewski, Adam. "Beverly Hills, Palm Beach, Key West— How Congress' $350 Billion Covid "Bailout" To States And Cities Gets Spread Around." *Forbes*. March 3, 2021. Accessed March 1, 2024. https://www. forbes.com/sites/adamandrzejewski/2021/03/03/350-billion-covid-bailout-to-states-cities-and-counties--here-are-the-details/?sh=f5d8ec9661c0.

324   Suderman, Peter. "Biden's $1.9 Trillion 'Rescue Plan' Isn't Saving the Economy. It's Holding It Back." *Reason*. May 13, 2021. Accessed February 5, 2024. https://reason. com/2021/05/13/bidens-1-9-trillion-rescue-plan-isnt-saving-the-economy-its-holding-it-back/.

325   Barr, Bob. "BARR: Biden's 'Infrastructure' Bill Contains Backdoor 'Kill Switch' For Cars." The Daily Caller. November 9, 2021. Accessed March 6, 2024. https://dailycaller.com/2021/11/29/barr-bidens-infrastructure-bill-contains-backdoor-kill-switch-for-cars/.

326   Moore, Steve. "Biden's Ban on Gas Cars." Unleash Prosperity Hotline. March 21, 2024. Accessed March 21, 2024. https://committeetounleashprosperity.com/hotlines/bidens-ban-on-gas-cars/.

327   Bakst, Daren *et. al.* "'Inflation Reduction Act' Is Euphemism for Big Government Socialism, Higher Prices." The Heritage Foundation. August 2, 2022. Accessed December 5, 2023. https://www.heritage.org/budget-and-spending/commentary/inflation-reduction-act-euphemism-big-government-socialism-higher.

328   Ibid.

329   Haglund, Larry. "How the Inflation Reduction Act would raise taxes while failing to reduce inflation." Americans for Prosperity. August 1, 2022. Accessed November 5, 2023. https://americansforprosperity.org/inflation-reduction-act-facts/.

330   Sobczyk, Nick, and Jeremy Dillon. "Manchin revives climate deal: What's in the $369B bill." *E&E News.* July 28, 2022. Accessed December 5, 2023. https://www.eenews.net/articles/manchin-revives-climate-deal-whats-in-the-369b-bill/.

331   Rogers, Cathy McMorris, Chair. "One Year Later, Even President Biden Admits the 'Inflation Reduction Act' Failed to Lower Costs for Americans." Energy and Commerce Blog. August 16, 2023. Accessed November 10, 2023. https://energycommerce.house.gov/posts/one-year-later-even-president-biden-admits-the-inflation-reduction-act-failed-to-lower-costs-for-americans.

332   "Top Picks: Consumer Price Index for All Urban Consumers (CPI-U)." U.S. Bureau of Labor Statistics. March 13, 2024. https://data.bls.gov/cgi-bin/surveymost?cu.

333   "Databases, Tables & Calculators by Subject: Gasoline, all types." U.S. Bureau of Labor Statistics. March 13, 2024. https://data.bls.gov/timeseries/APU00007471A?amp%253bdata_tool=XGtable&output_view=data&include_graphs=true.

334   Bannister, Craig. "Bidenomics after 36 Months: Six Charts the Media Don't Want You to See." MRCTV. February 16, 2024. Accessed March 1, 2024. https://mrctv.org/blog/craig-bannister/bidenomics-after-36-months-six-charts-media-dont-want-you-see.

335   Ibid.

336   Moore, Steve. "Under Biden's Budget the Federal Government Would Spend a World Record $57,000 Per Household." Committee to Unleash Prosperity. March 21, 2024. Accessed March 21, 2024. https://committeetounleashprosperity.com/hotlines/under-bidens-budget-the-federal-government-would-spend-a-world-record-57000-per-household/.

337   "BIDEN'S TRILLIONS: House GOP Blasts Joe's Budget, 'Roadmap to Accelerate America's Decline.'" Hannity. March 11, 2024. Accessed March 12, 2024. https://hannity.com/media-room/bidens-trillions-house-gop-blasts-joes-budget-roadmap-to-accelerate-americas-decline/.

338   Moore, Art. "Obama classmate audited 2 years ago now 'vindicated.'" WorldNet Daily. May 14, 2013. Accessed December 4, 2023. http://www.wnd.com/2013/05/obama-classmate-see-i-told-ya-so-about-irs/.

339   Wheeler, Dr. Jack. "This Is No Accident, Comrades." To The Point News. July 8, 2010. http://www.tothepointnews.com/content/view/4143/2/.

340   Morrow, Robert. "What My Father Told Me About LBJ and 'Niggers.'" *Economic Policy Journal.* August 13, 2013. Accessed April 9, 2024. https://web.archive.org/web/20170629151406/http://www.economicpolicyjournal.com/2013/08/what-my-father-told-me-about-lbj-and.html.

341 "Black Party Affiliation." BlackDemographics.com. Accessed April 9, 2024. http://blackdemographics.com/culture/black-politics/.

342 Hisle, Janice. "The Rise of Black Support for Trump." *The Epoch Times*. December 22, 2023. Accessed January 5, 2024. https://www.theepochtimes.com/article/the-rise-of-black-support-for-trump-5515133.

343 "Black Party Affiliation." *Op.cit.*

344 Between 1933, when FDR took office, and 1939, federal spending increased 99 percent, from $4.6 billion to $9.1 billion. Interestingly, after harshly criticizing President Hoover for his policies, FDR's New Deal only expanded on them. Hoover had already increased federal spending 47 percent between 1929 and 1933. Source: White House Office of Management and Budget, Historical Tables, Table 1.1. Summary of Receipts, Outlays and Surpluses or Deficits, 1789–2019.

345 "Civil Rights Act of 1964." U.S. Senate. Accessed March 16, 2024. https://www.senate.gov/artandhistory/history/civil_rights/cloture_finalpassage.htm.

346 Stern. "Acorn's Nutty Regime for Cities." *Op. cit.*

347 Phrankleen. "What do Africans think about African-Americans and Vice Versa?" YouTube. Accessed May 1, 2022. https://www.youtube.com/watch?v=jIvJcRGx1HU.

348 Abua, Joseph. "The Fiasco between Africans and African-Americans." UAB Institute for Human Rights. June 10, 2020. Accessed March 12, 2023. https://sites.uab.edu/humanrights/2020/06/10/the-fiasco-between-africans-and-african-americans/.

349 Washington, Booker T. *Up from Slavery, an Autobiography.* Louisiana: Pelican Publishing, 2010. vii.

350 *Up from Slavery.* ix–x.

351 Young, Mary, and Gerald Horne (eds.). *W. E. B. Du Bois: An Encyclopedia.* Westport: Greenwood, 2001. 7.

352 Reese, Charlie. "An Interview with Lenin Through the Magic of Historical Record." *Orlando Sentinel.* April 12, 1985. Accessed April 9, 2024. https://www.orlandosentinel.com/1985/04/12/an-interview-with-lenin-through-the-magic-of-historical-record/.

353 Gannon, Francis X. "N.A.A.C.P." in *Biographical Dictionary of the Left, Vol I.* Massachusetts: Western Islands, 1969. 141.

354 Hill, Herbert. *Citizen's guide to desegregation: a study of social and legal change in American life.* Westport: Greenwood Press, 1979. 57. https://search.worldcat.org/title/634013084.

355 "Roger Baldwin." Discover the Networks. Accessed February 2, 2024. https://www.discoverthenetworks.org/individuals/roger-baldwin/.

356 Gannon. *Op. cit.* 2.

357 "American Civil Liberties Union (ACLU)." Discover the Networks. Accessed February 26, 2024. https://www.discoverthenetworks.org/organizations/american-civil-liberties-union-aclu/.

358 "The American Negro in the Communist Party." Committee on Un-American Activities, U.S. House of Representatives. December 22, 1954. 13.

359 Jackson, James E., ed., "W.E.B. DuBois to Gus Hall: "Communism Will Triumph. I Want to Help Bring That Day." *The Worker.* November 26, 1961. Accessed July 10, 2023. https://www.peoplesworld.org/article/from-the-peoples-world-archives-w-e-b-dubois-joins-the-communist-party/.

360 Gannon. *Op. cit.* 142.

361 Ibid.

362 "W.E.B. Du Bois." Discover the Networks. Accessed February 10, 2024. https://www.discoverthenetworks.org/individuals/william-edward-burghardt-w-e-b-du-bois.

363 Gannon. *Op. cit.* 143.

364 "NAACP." Discover the Networks. Accessed February 10, 2024. https://www.discoverthenetworks.org/organizations/national-association-for-the-advancement-of-colored-people-naacp/.

365 Johnson, Manning. *Color, Communism and Common Sense.* New York: Alliance Inc., 1958. https://www.heritage-history.com/site/hclass/secret_societies/ebooks/pdf/johnson_
color.pdf.

366 Gannon. *Op. cit.* 145.

367 Ibid. 142–143.

368 Ibid. 143.

369 Lynn, Denise. "When W. E. B. Du Bois Went to the Masses." *Jacobin.* December 27, 2019. Accessed April 9, 2024. https://jacobin.com/2019/12/web-du-bois-jefferson-school-
pan-africanism-communist-party.

370 Du Bois, W.E.B. "Memo on My Teaching at the Jefferson School." CREDO. May 12, 1954. Accessed July 10, 2023. https://credo.library.umass.edu/view/pageturn/mums312-b142-i444/#page/1/mode/1up.

371 DuBois, "Memo."

372 Gannon. *Op. cit.* 148.

373 Ibid. 150-151.

374 "NAACP." Discover the Networks. *Op. cit.*

375 Ibid.

376 "Know the Issues." NAACP. Accessed March 29, 2024. https://naacp.org/know-issues.

377 Slisco, Alia. "Black Lives Matter Leader Endorses Trump: 'Everybody Else Sucks.'" *Newsweek.* November 8, 2023. Accessed April 3, 2024. https://www.newsweek.com/black-lives-matter-leader-endorses-trump-everybody-else-sucks-1842100.

378 Schweizer, Peter. *Blood Money: Why the Powerful Turn a Blind Eye While China Kills Americans.* New York: HarperCollins, 2024. 70.

379 Ibid.

380 Kozar, Ronald J. "Six years of BLM Killed More Blacks than 86 Years of Lynchings." *American Thinker.* April 25, 2022. Accessed April 10, 2024. https://www.americanthinker.com/articles/2022/04/six_years_of_blm_killed_more_blacks_than_86_years_of_lynchings.html.

381 "Black Conservatives Ask the NAACP to Condemn Progressive Racism at the Orlando Annual Convention." Press Release, FreedomWorks. July 12, 2013. Accessed March 29, 2024. https://www.freedomworks.org/press/black-conservatives-ask-the-
naacp-to-condemn-progr/.

382 Chantrill, Christopher. "Welfare Spending." US Government Spending. Accessed July12, 2023. https://www.usgovernmentspending.com/welfare_spending.

383 Ibid.

384 Harrington, John, and Grant Suneson. "What were the 13 most expensive wars in U.S. history?" *USA Today.* June 13, 2019. Accessed March 31, 2024. https://www.usatoday.com/story/money/2019/06/13/cost-of-war-13-most-expensive-wars-in-us-history/
39556983/.

385 Tanner, Michael D. "Poverty and Welfare: 2022 • CATO HANDBOOK FOR POLICYMAKERS." Cato Institute. Accessed March 5, 2024. https://www.cato.org/cato-handbook-policymakers/cato-handbook-policymakers-9th-edition-2022/poverty-welfare.

386   Begody, Candace. "50 important welfare statistics for 2023." Lexington Law. April 10, 2023. Accessed December 4, 2023. https://www.lexingtonlaw.com/blog/finance/welfare-statistics.html.

387   "Welfare and Medicaid Spending." US Government Spending. Accessed March 30, 2024. https://www.usgovernmentspending.com/.

388   Cato Handbook. *Op. cit.*

389   Cato Handbook. *Op. cit.*

390   "Federal Poverty Level." Healthcare.gov. Accessed April 9, 2024, https://www.healthcare.gov/glossary/federal-poverty-level-fpl/.

391   Cato Handbook. *Op. cit.*

392   Ibid.

393   Ibid.

394   Calculated with the CPI converted to a 2013 base year. https://www.in2013dollars.com/us/inflation/1970?amount=10000.

395   Berg, Austin. "Illinois' Warped Welfare System Traps Families in Poverty." Illinois Policy Institute. June 15, 2015. Accessed July 6, 2023. https://www.illinoispolicy.org/illinois-warped-welfare-system-traps-families-in-poverty/.

396   "How Many People Participate in the Social Safety Net?" ASPE. January 20, 2023. Accessed March 4, 2024. https://aspe.hhs.gov/sites/default/files/documents/18eff5e45b2be85fb4c350176bca5c28/how-many-people-social-safety-net.pdf.

397   "Welfare Recipient Statistics 2023: Insights and Trends." Gitnux. July 12, 2023. Accessed July 12, 2023. https://blog.gitnux.com/welfare-recipient-statistics/.

398   Dautovic, G. "Straight Talk On Welfare Statistics." Fortunly. October 11, 2023. Accessed March 4, 2024. https://fortunly.com/statistics/welfare-statistics/.

399   "Small Towns and Rural Areas Hit Hard by Opioid Crisis." CBHA. August 2020. Accessed March 12, 2024. https://www.cbha.org/about-us/cbha-blog/2020/august/small-towns-and-rural-areas-hit-hard-by-opioid-c/.

400   "Fifty-Four Defendants Charged in $18 Million WIC and Food Stamp Fraud Conspiracy. Thirty-Four Additional Defendants Charged with Allegedly Selling Their Federal Food Benefits for Cash." Press Release, Federal Bureau of Investigation. June 10, 2014. Accessed April 9, 2024. http://www.fbi.gov/atlanta/press-releases/2014/fifty-four-defendants-charged-in-18-million-wic-and-food-stamp-fraud-conspiracy.

401   "$250 Million Minnesota Fraud Suit Rattles Somali Community." *Som Tribune.* September 21, 2022. Accessed March 30, 2024. https://www.somtribune.com/2022/09/21/250-million-minnesota-fraud-suit-rattles-somali-community/.

402   "Payment Integrity Scorecard: Medicaid." Center for Medicare and Medicaid Services. Q3 2023. Accessed April 9, 2024. https://www.cfo.gov/wp-content/uploads/scorecards/FY23-Q3/Centers%20for%20Medicare%20_%20Medicaid%20Services%20(CMS)%20Medicaid.pdf.

403   "SNAP Data Tables. National Level Annual Summary 1969-2023." U.S. Department of Agriculture, Food and Nutrition Service. Accessed March 28, 2024. https://www.fns.usda.gov/pd/supplemental-nutrition-assistance-program-snap.

404   "Survey of Income and Program Participation (SIPP) Detailed Program Receipt Tables: 2020." U.S. Census Bureau. Accessed March 4, 2024. https://www.census.gov/data/tables/2020/demo/public-assistance/sipp-receipts.html.

405   Zagorsky, Jay L. and Patricia K. Smith. "Does the U.S. Food Stamp Program contribute to adult weight gain?" *Economics and Human Biology.* Vol 7. May 16, 2009. 246–258.

406   Ver Ploeg, Michelle and Katherine Ralston. "Food Stamps and Obesity: What Do We Know?" U.S. Department of Agriculture, Economic

Research Service. March 2008. Accessed April 9, 2024. https://www.ers.
usda.gov/webdocs/publications/44221/12196_eib34_1_.pdf?v=0.

407   "The Temporary Assistance for Needy Families (TANF) Block Grant:
Responses to Frequently Asked Questions." Congressional Research
Service. March 20, 2024. https://sgp.fas.org/crs/misc/RL32760.pdf.

408   "Characteristics and Financial Circumstances of TANF Recipients Fiscal Year
(FY) 2022." U.S. Department of Health and Human Services, Administration
for Children and Families. Accessed March 12, 2024. https://www.acf.
hhs.gov/sites/default/files/documents/ofa/fy2022_characteristics.pdf.

409   "Supplemental Security Income: Disability Program Vulnerable to Applicant
Fraud When Middlemen Are Used." GAO. August 31, 1995. Accessed
April 9, 2024. https://www.govinfo.gov/content/pkg/GAOREPORTS-
HEHS-95-116/html/GAOREPORTS-HEHS-95-116.htm.

410   "Policy Basics: Supplemental Security Income." Center on Budget
and Policy Priorities. Accessed March 20, 2024. https://www.cbpp.
org/research/social-security/supplemental-security-income.

411   "National Health Expenditures by type of service and source of funds, CY 1960-
2021." Centers for Medicaid and Medicare Services. Accessed July12, 2023. https://
www.cms.gov/Research-Statistics-Data-and-Systems/Statistics-Trends-and-Reports/
NationalHealthExpendData/NationalHealthAccountsHistorical.

412   "Distribution of Medicaid/CHIP enrollees in the United States in 2021,
by ethnicity." Statista. 2023. Accessed July 12, 2023. https://www.statista.
com/statistics/1289100/medicaid-chip-enrollees-share-by-ethnicity.

413   "Immigrants and the Affordable Care Act." National Immigration
Law Center. January 2014. Accessed April 10, 2024. https://
www.nilc.org/issues/health-care/immigrantshcr/.

414   "State-Funded Health Coverage for Immigrants as of July
2023." KFF. July 26, 2023. Accessed March 10, 2024. https://
www.kff.org/racial-equity-and-health-policy/fact-sheet/
state-funded-health-coverage-for-immigrants-as-of-july-2023/.

415   Williams, Walter E. "Black Unemployment." *Townhall.* April
10, 2013. Accessed January 5, 2024. https://web.archive.
org/web/20130413104052/http://townhall.com/columnists/
walterewilliams/2013/04/10/black-unemployment-n1561096/page/full.

416   Wiessner, Daniel. "Biden's $15 minimum wage for federal contractors blocked by
US judge." Reuters. September 27, 2023. Accessed March 3, 2024. https://www.
reuters.com/legal/bidens-15-minimum-wage-federal-contractors-blocked-
by-us-judge-2023-09-27/.

417   Ibid.

418   U.S. Bureau of Labor Statistics. "Labor Force Participation Rate - 20
Yrs. & over, Black or African American Men (LNS11300031)."
Retrieved from FRED, Federal Reserve Bank of St. Louis. Accessed
April 2, 2024. https://fred.stlouisfed.org/series/LNS11300031.

419   "Labor force participation rate by sex, race and Hispanic
ethnicity." Women's Bureau. Accessed March 12, 2024. https://
www.dol.gov/agencies/wb/data/lfp/lfp-sex-race-hispanic.

420   U.S. Bureau of Labor Statistics. "Unemployment Rate - 20 Yrs. &
over, Black or African American Women (LNS14000032.)" Retrieved
from FRED, Federal Reserve Bank of St. Louis. Accessed April
2, 2024. https://fred.stlouisfed.org/series/LNS14000032.

421   U.S. Bureau of Labor Statistics. "Unemployment Rate - 20 Yrs. & over, White
Men (LNS14000028)," retrieved from FRED, Federal Reserve Bank of St.

Louis, March 29, 2024, https://fred.stlouisfed.org/series/LNS14000028; and "Labor Force Participation Rate - 20 Yrs. & over, Black or African American Men (LNS11300031)," retrieved from FRED, Federal Reserve Bank of St. Louis, April 2, 2024, https://fred.stlouisfed.org/series/LNS11300031.

422 Moynihan, Daniel Patrick. "The Negro Family: The Case for National Action." Office of Policy Planning and Research, U.S. Department of Labor. March 1965.

423 McElroy, Wendy. "The Welfare State Did What Slavery Couldn't Do." Mises Institute. September 9, 2020. Accessed April 3, 2024. https://mises.org/mises-wire/welfare-state-did-what-slavery-couldnt-do.

424 Ibid.

425 Krumholz, Willis. "Family Breakdown and America's Welfare System." IFS. October 7, 2019. Accessed March 5, 2024. https://ifstudies.org/blog/family-breakdown-and-americas-welfare-system.

426 Rahmann, Kenya. "The truth about black parents, Welfare and the man-in-the-house rule." The Child Support Hustle. Accessed March 25, 2024. https://www.thechildsupporthustle.com/the-truth-about-black-parents-welfare-and-the-man-in-the-home-requirement/.

427 "Was Welfare Used To Destroy Black Families?" Medium. January 20, 2024. Accessed February 10, 2024. https://medium.com/illumination/was-welfare-used-to-destroy-black-families-2fe59379f4bb.

428 "Births: Final Data for 2021: Table 9. Births to unmarried women, by age and race and Hispanic origin of mother: United States." *National Vital Statistics Report, Vol 72, No. 1.* January 31, 2023. Accessed February 5, 2024. https://www.cdc.gov/nchs/data/nvsr/nvsr72/nvsr72-01.pdf.

429 Rector, Robert. "Marriage: America's Greatest Weapon Against Child Poverty; Special Report #117 on Poverty and Inequality." The Heritage Foundation. September 5, 2012. Accessed April 10, 2024. http://www.heritage.org/research/reports/2012/09/marriage-americas-greatest-weapon-against-child-poverty.

430 Carleson, Marcia J. "Trajectories of Couple Relationship Quality after Childbirth: Does Marriage Matter?" Center for Child Wellbeing, Working Paper #2007-11-FF, April 2007. Accessed April 10, 2024. https://citeseerx.ist.psu.edu/document?repid=rep1&type=pdf&doi=5f68b9f1e16c0ecea81110129dddc0565c9989f1. Cited in Rector, Special Report #117, footnote 38.

431 Op. cit.

432 Langan, Patrick A, Ph.D. "Race of Prisoners Admitted to Federal and State Institutions, 1926-1986." U.S. Bureau of Justice Statistics. NCJ-125618, May 1991. 7.

433 "Prisoners in 2022 – Statistical Tables." U.S. Department of Justice, Office of Justice Programs. November 2023. Accessed March 4, 2024. https://bjs.ojp.gov/library/publications/prisoners-2022-statistical-tables.

434 Thomas, Ginni. "Former Louisiana Democrat: Democratic Party Moving Too Far Left [VIDEO]." The Daily Caller. July 30, 2013. Accessed April 10, 2024. http://dailycaller.com/2013/07/30/former-louisiana-democrat-democratic-party-moving-too-far-left-video/.

435 Thomas, Ginni. "Rush Limbaugh's Call Screener: 'What Liberalism Has Done To Black Communities Is Horrific.'" The Daily Caller. September 21, 2014. Accessed April 10, 2024. http://dailycaller.com/2014/09/21/rush-limbaughs-call-screener-what-liberalism-has-done-to-black-communities-is-horrific/.

436 Ibid.

437 "*Notes from the Field:* Firearm Homicide Rates, by Race and Ethnicity — United States, 2019–2022." Centers for Disease Control and

Prevention. October 20, 2023. Accessed January 5, 2024. https://www.cdc.gov/mmwr/volumes/72/wr/mm7242a4.htm.

438 Garger, Kenneth. "Man wrongly accused of killing 7-year-old Jazmine Barnes found dead in jail cell." *New York Post.* July 29, 2019. Accessed April 5, 2024. https://nypost.com/2019/07/29/man-wrongly-accused-of-killing-7-year-old-jazmine-barnes-found-dead-in-jail-cell/.

439 Lapin, Tamar. "Man charged in fatal shooting of 7-year-old girl." *New York Post.* January 6, 2019. Accessed April 5, 2024.https://nypost.com/2019/01/06/man-charged-in-fatal-shooting-of-7-year-old-girl/.

440 Garger. *Op. cit.*

441 FBI Uniform Crime Reports, Expanded Data Table 6. 2010–2019. Accessed April 10, 2024. https://www.fbi.gov/how-we-can-help-you/more-fbi-services-and-information/ucr/publications.

442 Ibid.

443 Bunn, Curtis. "Report: Black people are still killed by police at a higher rate than other groups." MSNBC. March 3, 2022. Accessed April 3, 2024. https://www.nbcnews.com/news/nbcblk/report-black-people-are-still-killed-police-higher-rate-groups-rcna17169.

444 "Number of people shot to death by the police in the United States from 2017 to 2024*, by race." Statista Research Department. March 11, 2024. Accessed March 15, 2024. https://www.statista.com/statistics/585152/people-shot-to-death-by-us-police-by-race/.

445 Liu, Helena. "Dismantling the imperialist white supremacist capitalist patriarchy." TransformingSociety. Accessed March 5, 2024. https://www.transformingsociety.co.uk/2020/01/31/dismantling-the-imperialist-white-supremacist-capitalist-patriarchy/.

446 "How many nonprofits are there in the U.S.?" USAFacts. November 16, 2023. Accessed March 16, 2024. https://usafacts.org/articles/how-many-nonprofits-are-there-in-the-us/.

447 "Southern Poverty Law Center." IRS 990 Return of Organization Exempt From Income Tax. January 15, 2023. Accessed April 10, 2024. https://pdf.guidestar.org/PDF_Images/2022/630/598/2022-630598743-202320469349300512-9.pdf.

448 "Ways & Means Seeks Public Input on Tax-Exempt Organizations: Potential Violations of Rules on Political Activities, Inappropriate Use of Charitable Funds, & Rise in Foreign Sources of Funding." Ways and Means Committee, U.S. House of Representatives. August 14, 2023. Accessed March 16, 2024. https://gop-waysandmeans.house.gov/ways-means-seeks-public-input-on-tax-exempt-organizations-potential-violations-of-rules-on-political-activities-inappropriate-use-of-charitable-funds-rise-in-foreign-sources-of-funding/.

449 "George Soros: The main obstacle to a stable and just world order is the United States." AZ Quotes. 2007. Accessed February 10, 2024. https://www.azquotes.com/quote/656312.

450 Blumer, Tom. "Politico Lets Bill Clinton Whine for More Credit for Welfare Reform, Balanced Budget." NewsBusters. October 1, 2011. Accessed April 10, 2024. https://www.newsbusters.org/blogs/nb/tom-blumer/2011/10/01/politico-lets-bill-clinton-whine-more-credit-welfare-reform-balanced.

451 Haskins, Ron. "Welfare Reform, Success or Failure? It Worked." Brookings. March 15, 2006. Accessed April 10, 2024. https://www.brookings.edu/articles/welfare-reform-success-or-failure-it-worked/.

452 Rector, Robert. "Welfare Reform: Impact on Marriage, Abortion, Poverty, and Dependence." The Heritage Foundation. August 11, 2023. Accessed January 5, 2024. https://www.heritage.org/welfare/report/

welfare-reform-impact-marriage-abortion-poverty-and-dependence.

453   Rector, Robert. "Stimulus bill secretly overturns welfare reform." TwinCities.com. September 23, 2009. Accessed April 10, 2024. http://www.twincities.com/opinion/ci_11766079.

454   Rector, Robert. "How Obama has gutted welfare reform." *Washington Post*. September 6, 2012. Accessed April 10, 2024. https://www.washingtonpost.com/opinions/how-obama-has-gutted-welfore-reform/2012/09/06/885b0092-f835-11e1-8b93-c4f4ab1c8d13_story.html.

455   Madison, James. "Opinions, Selected From Debates in Congress, From 1789 to 1836, Involving Constitutional Principles: On the Memorial of the Relief Committee of Baltimore, for the Relief of St. Domingo Refugees." U.S. House of Representatives, January 10, 1794. Constitution.org. Accessed April 10, 2024. https://constitution.org/1-Constitution/je/je4_cong_deb_14.htm.

456   Calder, Rich. "Thousands of migrants in NY quietly collecting 'welfare' through Hochul rule change." *New York Post*. February 10, 2024. Accessed April 4, 2024. https://nypost.com/2024/02/10/metro/thousands-of-migrants-get-cash-aid-through-hochul-policy-change/.

457   "Need help with basic expenses? You may be eligible for Cash Assistance from NYC's Department of Social Services." NYC DSS Human Resources Division. Accessed April 4, 2024. https://www.nyc.gov/assets/immigrants/downloads/pdf/FLY-1136-MLF-Need-Help-with-Basic-Expenses.pdf.

458   Lind, Michael. "Our Open Border Policy Is Not an Accident." *Tablet*. January 28, 2024. Accessed April 4, 2024. https://www.tabletmag.com/sections/news/articles/open-border-policy-not-accident.

459   Salzmann, Karl. "FLASHBACK: Biden Tells Migrants To 'Surge to the Border.'" *Washington Free Beacon*. May 10, 2023. Accessed March 10, 2024. https://youtu.be/rYwLYMPLYbo?si=kjNcXsMGCpy7oAmh.

460   Simpson, James. *The Red/Green Axis 2.0: An Existential Threat to America and the World*. Washington, DC: Center for Security Policy Press, 2019.

461   "How Close Was Merkel to the Communist System?" Spiegel. May 14, 2013. Accessed April 17, 2024. https://www.spiegel.de/international/germany/new-book-suggests-angela-merkel-was-closer-to-communism-than-thought-a-899768.html.

462   Huggler, Justin. "10 moments that define German chancellor Angela Merkel." *The Telegraph*. October 9, 2015. Accessed April 17, 2024. https://www.telegraph.co.uk/news/worldnews/europe/germany/angela-merkel/11920552/10-moments-that-define-German-chancellor-Angela-Merkel.html.

463   Roosevelt, Col. Archibald. "Conquest via Immigration." Georgia: The Alliance, 1956. 5, 7.

464   "Select Committee Unveils Findings into CCP's Role in American Fentanyl Epidemic - REPORT & HEARING." Press Release, U.S. House of Representatives, Select Committee on the CCP. April 16, 2024. Accessed April 17, 2024. https://selectcommitteeontheccp.house.gov/media/press-releases/select-committee-unveils-findings-ccps-role-american-fentanyl-epidemic-report.

465   "'Terrifying Situation': Fmr national security adviser says this is keeping him up at night." Fox News. March 29, 2024. April 2, 2024. https://www.foxnews.com/video/6349973285112.

466   Chang, Gordon G. "China's Infiltrators: 'They Are Coming Here to Kill Us.'" Gatestone Institute. February 13, 2024. Accessed April 3, 2024. https://www.gatestoneinstitute.org/20388/china-infiltrators-us.

467   Ibid.

468   "Rubio: FBI Director 'Confirmed To Me' A Trafficking Network Exists That Smuggles ISIS-Linked People Into U.S." The Daily Wire. March 24, 2024. Accessed April 3, 2024. https://www.dailywire.com/news/rubio-fbi-director-confirmed-to-me-a-trafficking-network-exists-that-smuggles-isis-linked-people-into-u-s.

469   "FACTSHEET: RECORD-BREAKING BORDER ENCOUNTERS UNDERSCORE SECRETARY MAYORKAS' REFUSAL TO COMPLY WITH THE LAW, BREACH OF PUBLIC TRUST." House of Representatives. Committee on Homeland Security. February 8, 2024. Accessed April 3, 2024. https://homeland.house.gov/2024/02/08/factsheet-record-breaking-border-encounters-underscore-secretary-mayorkas-refusal-to-comply-with-the-law-breach-of-public-trust/.

470   Senate Cloakroom. "Not agreed to, 45-51: Motion to concur in the House amendment to the Senate amendment to H.R.4366, with Hagerty amendment #1634." X. March 8, 2024. https://twitter.com/SenateCloakroom/status/1766253399111094658.

471   Elon Musk. X. March 8, 2024. Accessed April 3, 2024. https://twitter.com/elonmusk/status/1766309014827061326..

472   "'This is insane!' Every Senate Dem votes to continue using taxpayer funds to fly illegal migrants to US town." The Daily BS. March 25, 2024. Accessed April 3, 2024. https://thedailybs.com/2024/03/25/this-is-insane-every-senate-dem-votes-to-continue-using-taxpayer-funds-to-fly-illegal-migrants-to-us-towns/.

473   "Statement by President Joe Biden on Refugee Admissions." The White House. May 3, 2021. Accessed April 3, 2024. https://www.whitehouse.gov/briefing-room/statements-releases/2021/05/03/statement-by-president-joe-biden-on-refugee-admissions/.

474   "DHS Rescinds Prior Administration's Termination of Temporary Protected Status Designations for El Salvador, Honduras, Nepal, and Nicaragua." Press Release, U.S. Department of Homeland Security. June 13, 2023. Accessed April 3, 2024. https://www.dhs.gov/news/2023/06/13/dhs-rescinds-prior-administrations-termination-temporary-protected-status.

475   Moslimani, Mohamad. "How Temporary Protected Status has expanded under the Biden administration." Pew Research Center. March 29, 2024. Accessed March 30, 2024. https://www.pewresearch.org/short-reads/2024/03/29/how-temporary-protected-status-has-expanded-under-the-biden-administration/.

476   Spredermann, August. "Illegal Immigrants Leave US Hospitals With Billions in Unpaid Bills." The Epoch Times. March 14, 2024. Accessed May 2, 2024. https://www.theepochtimes.com/article/illegal-immigrants-leave-us-hospitals-with-billions-in-unpaid-bills-5604492.

477   Ibid.

478   Ibid.

479   Rappaport, Nolan. "Are Biden's immigration policies allowing dangerous diseases into our country?" The Hill. August 28, 2023. Accessed May 2, 2024. https://thehill.com/opinion/immigration/4171403-are-bidens-immigration-policies-allowing-dangerous-diseases-into-our-country/.

480   Wilson, Jacque, and Greg Botelho. "Enterovirus D68 found in 4 patients who have died, including 10-year-old girl." CNN. October 1, 2014. Accessed May 2, 2024. https://www.cnn.com/2014/10/01/health/enterovirus-68-death/index.html.

481   For reference, see my 2021 book Who Was Karl Marx? I devote an entire subchapter to Noel Ignatiev, a CPUSA member who coined the term "white skin privilege" and spent his life promoting the concept while teaching at Harvard and other prominent universities.

482   Holloway, Matthew. "REVEALED: Eight non-government organizations are funneling illegal immigrants into America, using taxpayer dollars." Law Enforcement Today. February 24, 2024. Accessed April 4, 2024. https://lawenforcementtoday.com/authors/matthew-holloway.

483   Bensman, Todd. "UN Budgets Millions for U.S.-Bound Migrants in 2024." Center for Immigration Studies. January 24, 2024. Accessed April 4, 2024. https://cis.org/Bensman/UN-Budgets-Millions-USBound-Migrants-2024.

484   Ibid.

485   Rogers, Zachary. "Cartels making $13 billion a year smuggling migrants across border, report says." ABC15 News. July 26, 2022. Accessed April 4, 2024. https://wpde.com/news/nation-world/cartels-making-13-billion-a-year-off-smuggling-migrants-through-border-nyt-report-says-mexio-immigrants-coyote-texas.

486   "Funding the United Nations: How Much Does the U.S. Pay?" Council on Foreign Relations. February 29, 2024. Accessed April 5, 2024. https://www.cfr.org/article/funding-united-nations-what-impact-do-us-contributions-have-un-agencies-and-programs#chapter-title-0-3.

487   "Secrets, Lies and Atomic Spies: Alger Hiss." NOVA Online. January 2002. Accessed March 5, 2024. http://www.pbs.org/wgbh/nova/venona/dece_hiss.html.

488   Fang, Frank. "Venezuela Empties Prisons, Sends Criminals to US Border: House Republicans." *The Epoch Times.* September 23, 2022. Accessed April 5, 2024. https://www.theepochtimes.com/us/venezuela-empties-prisons-and-sends-criminals-to-us-border-house-republicans-4750105.

489   "Texas Criminal Illegal Alien Data." Texas Department of Public Safety. Accessed April 4, 2024. https://www.dps.texas.gov/section/crime-records/texas-criminal-illegal-alien-data.

490   Dorgan, Michael. "Illegal migrant deported 8 times with 11 arrests now charged with murder in Ohio: 'Our border is broken.'" Fox News. April 5, 2024. Accessed April 6, 2024. https://www.foxnews.com/us/illegal-migrant-deported-8-times-11-arrests-now-charged-murder-ohio-border-broken.

491   Bialik, Kristen, Alissa Scheller, and Kristi Walke., "6 facts about English language learners in U.S. public schools." Pew Research Center. October 25, 2018. Accessed November 5, 2023. http://www.pewresearch.org/fact-tank/2018/10/25/6-facts-about-english-language-learners-in-u-s-public-schools/.

492   "Portland Public Schools EL Local Plan 2015-17." Oregon Department of Education. June 5, 2015. Accessed April 10, 2024. https://www.pps.net/cms/lib/OR01913224/Centricity/Domain/181/PPS_EL_Plan_-_June_5_2015.pdf.

493   Analysis of city education budgets conducted by author in 2015 and published Lewiston School budgets.

494   Morris, Lisa, and Amy F. Johnson. "Analysis of Essential Programs and Services Components: English Language Learners." Maine Education Policy Research Institute, University of Southern Maine. December 2019. Accessed April 4, 2024. https://www11.maine.gov/doe/sites/maine.gov.doe/files/inline-files/ELL%20component%20review%201.8.20Update.pdf.

495   Volokh, Eugene. "Cultural Defense Accepted as to Nonconsensual Sex in New Jersey Trial Court, Rejected on Appeal." The Volokh Conspiracy. July 23, 2010. Accessed July 24, 2024. https://volokh.com/2010/07/23/cultural-defense-accepted-as-to-nonconsensual-sex-in-new-jersey-trial-court-rejected-on-appeal/.

496   Ibid.

497   Hill, Bailee. "'Shocking' California bill to protect violent illegal immigrants from deportation draws fierce backlash." Fox News. March 12, 2024. Accessed April 4, 2024. https://www.foxnews.com/media/shocking-california-bill-protect-violent-illegal-immigrants-deportation-draws-fierce-backlash.

498 Simpson, James. "Joe Biden's Hand in Corruption, Subversion and Crime in Guatemala." *American Thinker*. October 31, 2020. Accessed April 5, 2024. https://www.americanthinker.com/articles/2020/10/joe_bidens_hand_in_corruption_subversion_and_crime_in_guatemala.html.

499 Landau, David. "Obama's Ambassador Plays Caligula South Of The Border." The Daily Caller. May 6, 2016. Accessed April 5, 2024. https://dailycaller.com/2016/05/06/obamas-ambassador-plays-caligula-south-of-the-border/#ixzz4UpcYLIJI.

500 Simpson. *Op. cit.*

501 "Southwest Border Unaccompanied Alien Children Statistics FY 2015." U.S. Customs and Border Protection. Accessed April 5, 2024. https://www.cbp.gov/newsroom/stats/southwest-border-unaccompanied-children/fy-2015.

502 Scher, Brent and Joe Schoffstall. "Secretive Liberal Donor Network Plots 2020 Strategy in DC." *Washington Free Beacon*. November 16, 2018. Accessed November 22, 2023. https://freebeacon.com/politics/secretive-liberal-donor-network-plots-2020-strategy-d-c/.

503 "Memo: Strategic Outlook for the 2008 Elections." Scribd. September 27, 2007. Accessed April 10, 2024. https://www.scribd.com/document/329671653/NYC-Meeting-2007-Final-Draft-4#from_embed.

504 "SEIU's Eliseo Medina wants immigration reform for 8 million new progressive voters." YouTube. January 31, 2013. Accessed July 25, 2023. https://youtu.be/pSCG8TVgfh8.

505 Baker, Bryan. "Estimates of the Unauthorized Immigrant Population Residing in the United States: January 2014." U.S. Department of Homeland Security, Office of Immigration Statistics. July 2017. Accessed April 3, 2024. https://www.dhs.gov/sites/default/files/publications/Unauthorized%20Immigrant%20Population%20Estimates%20in%20the%20US%20January%202014_1.pdf.

506 "How Many Illegal Aliens Are in the United States? 2023 Update." FAIR. June 22, 2023. Accessed December 5, 2023. https://www.fairus.org/issue/illegal-immigration/how-many-illegal-aliens-are-united-states-2023-update.

507 Passel, Jeffrey S. and Jens Manuel Krogstad. "What we know about unauthorized immigrants living in the U.S." Pew Research Center. November 16, 2023. Accessed December 20, 2023. https://www.pewresearch.org/short-reads/2023/11/16/what-we-know-about-unauthorized-immigrants-living-in-the-us/.

508 Justich, Robert, and Betty Ng, CFA. "The Underground Labor Force is Rising to the Surface." Bear Stearns. January 3, 2005. Accessed April 3, 2024. https://cdn.factcheck.org/UploadedFiles/Bear_Sterns_20_million_illegal.pdf.

509 Fazel-Zarandi, Mohammad M., Jonathan S. Feinstein and Edward H. Kaplan. "The number of undocumented immigrants in the United States: Estimates based on demographic modeling with data from 1990 to 2016." *PLOS One*. September 21, 2018. Accessed November 12, 2023. https://doi.org/10.1371/journal.pone.0201193.

510 "U.S. Border Patrol and Office of Field Operations Encounters by Area of Responsibility and Component." U.S. Customs and Border Protection. June 20, 2024. Accessed July 14, 2024. https://www.cbp.gov/newsroom/stats/nationwide-encounters.

511 Martosko, David. "Up to 34 MILLION blank 'green cards' and work permits to be ordered ahead of Obama illegal immigrant 'amnesty.'" *Daily Mail*. October 28, 2014. Accessed April 3, 2024. http://www.dailymail.co.uk/news/article-2800356/us-immigration-authorities-prep-order-34-million-blank-green-cards-work-authorization-papers-obama-readies-executive-order-illegal-aliens.html.

512 "Table 10. Persons Obtaining Lawful Permanent Resident Status by Broad
Class of Admissions and Region and Country of Birth: Fiscal Year 2022."
2022 Yearbook of Immigration Statistics. U.S. Department of Homeland
Security, Office of Homeland Security Statistics. November 2023. Accessed
December 20, 2023. https://www.dhs.gov/sites/default/files/2024-
02/2023_0818_plcy_yearbook_immigration_statistics_fy2022.pdf.

513 "Table 6. Persons Obtaining Lawful Permanent Resident Status By Type
and Major Class of Admission: Fiscal Years 2013 to 2022." Ibid.

514 "Table 2. Persons Obtaining Lawful Permanent Resident Status by Region and
Selected Country of Last Residence: Fiscal Years 1820 to 2022." *2022 Yearbook of
Immigration Statistics.* U.S. Department of Homeland Security, Office of Homeland
Security Statistics. Accessed April 10, 2024. https://www.dhs.gov/sites/default/
files/2024-02/2023_0818_plcy_yearbook_immigration_statistics_fy2022.pdf.

515 Dorfman, Zach. "How Silicon Valley Became a Den of Spies: The West Coast
is a growing target of foreign espionage. And it's not ready to fight back."
Politico. July 27, 2018. Accessed November 12, 2023. https://www.politico.
com/magazine/story/2018/07/27/silicon-valley-spies-china-russia-219071.

516 Gertz, Bill. "China's Intelligence Networks in United States Include
25,000 Spies: Dissident reveals up to 18,000 Americans recruited
as Chinese agents." *Washington Free Beacon.* July 11, 2017. Accessed
November 5, 2023. https://freebeacon.com/national-security/
chinas-spy-network-united-states-includes-25000-intelligence-officers/.

517 Dorfman. *Op. cit.*

518 "Illegal Aliens Quietly Being Relocated Throughout US on
Commercial Flights." Judicial Watch. January 19, 2018. Accessed
January 21, 2024. https://www.judicialwatch.org/blog/2018/01/
illegal-aliens-quietly-relocated-throughout-u-s-commercial-flights/.

519 Ibid.

520 Western Lensman. "WATCH: The Democrat Open Borders Plan
to Entrench Single-Party Rule | Explained in Under Two Minutes."
X. March 19, 2024. Accessed March 19, 2024. https://twitter.
com/WesternLensman/status/1769883941878571505.

521 Morley, James III. "Federal Judge: Illegal Immigrants Can Carry Guns." *Newsmax.*
March 18, 2024. Accessed March 19, 2024. https://www.newsmax.com/newsfront/
second-amendment-illegal-immigration-chicago/2024/03/18/id/1157731/.

522 Sonneland, Holly K. " Chart: How U.S. Latinos Voted in the 2020 Presidential
Election." AS/COA. November 5, 2020. Accessed January 5, 2024. https://www.
as-coa.org/articles/chart-how-us-latinos-voted-2020-presidential-election.

523 Whitely, Jason. "Non-citizens registered to vote in Texas, some cast ballots." KVUE.
August 23, 2018. Accessed March 5, 2024. https://www.kvue.com/article/news/
non-citizens-registered-to-vote-in-texas-some-cast-ballots/269-586817236.

524 "California's immigrants and the homeless population in the state: Letters." *Los
Angeles Daily News.* January 3, 2024. Accessed March 4, 2024. https://www.
dailynews.com/2024/01/03/californias-immigrants-and-the-homeless-
population-in-the-state-letters/.

525 Ohanian, Lee. "Newsom Wants to Add $6.4 Billion to California's
$1.6 Trillion Debt with Proposition 1." Hoover Institution. February
13, 2024. Accessed March 12, 2024. https://www.hoover.org/research/
newsom-wants-add-64-billion-californias-16-trillion-debt-proposition-1.

526 Pollak, Joel B. "Jerry Brown Blames 'Low-Life Politicians' for
'Sanctuary State' Backlash." Breitbart. April 17, 2018. Accessed
August 20, 2023. https://www.breitbart.com/politics/2018/04/17/

jerry-brown-blames-low-life-politicians-sanctuary-
state-backlash/.

527 Skelton, George. "Governors' tough talk can't block refugees." *Los Angeles Times.*
November 23, 2015. Accessed August 15, 2023. https://www.latimes.com/
local/politics/la-me-pol-sac-cap-brown-refugees-20151123-column.html.

528 Elliot, Debbie. "A Lesson in History: Resettling Refugees of Vietnam."
NPR. January 14, 2007. Accessed April 4, 2024. https://www.npr.
org/2007/01/14/6855407/a-lesson-in-history-resettling-refugees-of-vietnam.

529 Gabbay, Tiffany. "Founder of Judge Curiel's La Raza Group: Whites Go Back to
Europe, California to Be 'Hispanic State.'" Breitbart. June 9, 2016. Accessed April 4,
2024. https://www.breitbart.com/border/2016/06/09/whites-go-back-europe-
california-hispanic-state-said-founder-judge-curiels-group/.

530 Pollock, Richard. "FLASHBACK: Democrats Tried To Block Thousands
Of Vietnam War Refugees, Including Orphans." The Daily Caller. January
29, 2017. Accessed April 4, 2024. https://dailycaller.com/2017/01/29/
flashback-when-liberal-democrats-opposed-refugees-and-even-orphans/.

531 Panzar, Javier. "It's official: Latinos now outnumber whites in California."
Los Angeles Times. July 8, 2015. Accessed April 4, 2024. https://www.
latimes.com/local/california/la-me-census-latinos-20150708-story.html.

532 Lind. "Our Open Borders Policy Is Not an Accident." *Op. cit.*

533 Oxford, Dwayne. "Why are Black voters backing Donald Trump
in record numbers?" Al Jazeera. March 18, 2024. Accessed
April 4, 2024. https://www.aljazeera.com/news/2024/3/18/
why-are-black-voters-backing-donald-trump-in-record-numbers.

534 Billot, James. "NYT: Trump support among black voters grows nearly 500%."
UnHerd. March 3, 2024. Accessed April 4, 2024. https://unherd.com/
newsroom/ny-times-trump-support-among-black-voters-grows-nearly-500/.

535 Gordy, Cynthia. "Vice President Biden Fires Up the NAACP: Blogging
the Beltway: He described the election as a fight for the heart and soul of
America." *The Root.* July 12, 2012. Accessed April 10, 2024. https://www.
theroot.com/vice-president-biden-fires-up-the-naacp-1790884286.

536 Nelson, Steven. "Biden could owe as much as $500K in back
taxes, government report indicates." *New York Post.* September 23,
2021. Accessed March 12, 2024. https://nypost.com/2021/09/23/
biden-could-owe-as-much-as-500k-in-irs-taxes-report/.

537 York, Erica. "Summary of the Latest Federal Income Tax Data, 2024 Update."
Tax Foundation. March 13, 2024. Accessed March 27, 2024. https://
taxfoundation.org/data/all/federal/latest-federal-income-tax-data-2024/.

538 Ibid.

539 Boortz, Neal. "How About the Democrats' Secret Plan?" *Newsmax.*
March 20, 2002. Accessed March 27, 2024. https://www.newsmax.com/
Pre-2008/How-About-the-Democrats-/2002/03/20/id/666012/.

540 "Table A-8. Employed persons by class of worker and part-time status." U.S.
Department of Labor, Bureau of Labor Statistics. March 8, 2024. Accessed
March 27, 2024. https://www.bls.gov/news.release/empsit.t08.htm.

541 "State and Local Government Spending Details for 2023." US
Government Spending. Accessed March 27, 2024. https://www.
usgovernmentspending.com/piechart_2023_US_total.

542 "What is the Total National Debt?" US Government Spending. Accessed
March 27, 2024. https://www.usgovernmentspending.com/national_debt.

543 Weiss, Rusty. "Dem Councilwoman: Ferguson Shows Government Is Going To
'Round Up and Execute' Blacks." *The Mental Recession.* September 2, 2014. Accessed

April 10, 2024. https://web.archive.org/web/20140905030722/http://menrec.com/dem-councilwoman-ferguson-shows-government-going-round-execute-blacks/.

544 McMahon, Mike. "Should 'aggressive' Street Crimes Unit, racial profiling return to Troy?" *The Oneida Daily Dispatch*. August 29, 2014. Accessed April 10, 2024. http://www.oneidadispatch.com/general-news/20140829/should-aggressive-street-crimes-unit-racial-profiling-return-to-troy.

545 Huerta de Soto, Jesus. "Economic Thought in Ancient Greece." Ludwig von Mises Institute. September 15, 2010. Accessed April 10, 2024. https://mises.org/mises-daily/economic-thought-ancient-greece.

546 Urban, George. "Djilas on Gorbachev (II): Milovan Djilas and George Urban in Conversation." *Encounter*. November 1988. 24.

547 Ibid. 25.

548 Gardner, Llew. Interview with Prime Minister Margaret Thatcher. *This Week*. Thames TV, February 6, 1976. Accessed April 10, 2024. http://www.margaretthatcher.org/document/102953.

549 Roche, John P. *The History and Impact of Marxist-Leninist Organizational Theory*. Institute for Foreign Policy Analysis, Foreign Policy Report. April 1984. ix.

550 "Poneros." *Blue Letter Bible*. Accessed March 21, 2024. https://www.blueletterbible.org/lexicon/g4190/kjv/tr/0-1/.

551 Lobaczewski, Dr. Andrew M. *Political Ponerology: The Science of Evil, Psychopathy, and the Origins of Totalitarianism*. Otto, NC: Red Pill Press, 2022.

552 Ibid. xxiv–xxv.

553 Ibid. xi.

554 White, Kaylee McGhee. "Don't let Andrew Cuomo squirm out of his responsibility for New York's nursing home deaths." *Washington Examiner*. June 23, 2020. Accessed February 13, 2024. https://www.washingtonexaminer.com/opinion/1634420/dont-let-andrew-cuomo-squirm-out-of-his-responsibility-for-new-yorks-nursing-home-deaths/.

555 Shrikant, Aditi. "Youth suicide rates rose 62% from 2007 to 2021: 'People feel hopeless,' one recent grad says." CNBC. December 7, 2023. Accessed January 20, 2024. https://www.cnbc.com/2023/12/05/youth-suicide-rates-rose-62percent-from-2007-to-2021.html .

556 Saunders, Heather and Panchal, Nirmita. "A Look at the Latest Suicide Data and Change Over the Last Decade." KFF. August 4, 2023. Accessed February 12, 2024. https://www.kff.org/mental-health/issue-brief/a-look-at-the-latest-suicide-data-and-change-over-the-last-decade/.

557 DeSimone, Danielle. "Concerns Rise Over Military Suicide Rates; Here's How the USO is Trying to Help." USO. September 6, 2023. Accessed February 13, 2024. https://www.uso.org/stories/2664-military-suicide-rates-are-at-an-all-time-high-heres-how-were-trying-to-help.

558 Associated Press. "Suicides in the U.S. reached all-time high in 2022, CDC data shows." NBC News. August 10, 2023. https://www.nbcnews.com/health/mental-health/cdc-data-finds-suicides-reached-time-high-2022-rcna99327.

559 Braye, KaMaria. "U.S. military sees record breaking low recruitment numbers." WAVY.com. December 27, 2023. Accessed March 2, 2024. https://www.wavy.com/news/military/u-s-military-sees-record-breaking-low-recruitment-numbers/.

560 Stéphane Courtois, ed. *The Black Book of Communism*. Boston: Harvard University Press, 1999. 747.

561 Dziak, John J. *Chekisty: A History of the KGB*. New York: Ivy Books; 1988. 29.

562 Kropotkin, Peter. "The Third Chapter." Chapter 3 in *The Terror in Russia*. London: Methuen & Co., 1909. 4th Ed. Accessed April 10, 2024. http://dwardmac.pitzer.edu/ANARCHIST_ARCHIVES/kropotkin/terror/chapter3.html.

563   "Assassination of Alexander II of Russia." Wikipedia. Accessed March 7, 2024. https://en.wikipedia.org/wiki/Assassination_of_Alexander_II_of_Russia.

564   Courtois. *The Black Book of Communism*. 14.

565   "The Red Terror." Alpha History. Accessed April 10, 2024. https://alphahistory.com/russianrevolution/red-terror/.

566   Merridale, Catherine. *Red Fortress: History and Illusion in the Kremlin*. Kindle Edition, Macmillan, 2013.

567   Lincoln, Bruce. *Red Victory: A History of the Russian Civil War*. New York: Da Capo Press, 1999. 374.

568   *Red Victory. Op. cit.* 383-386.

569   Dziak. Op. cit.

570   Ibid. 15.

571   *Oxford English Dictionary*. "communism." Accessed April 10, 2024. https://www.oed.com/search/dictionary/?scope=Entries&q=communism.

572   The Free Dictionary by Farlex. "communism." Accessed April 10, 2024. http://www.thefreedictionary.com/communism.

573   *Merriam-Webster*. "communism." Accessed April 10, 2024. http://www.merriam-webster.com/dictionary/communism.

574   Dictionary.com. "communism." Accessed April 10, 2024. http://dictionary.reference.com/browse/communism.

575   *Merriam-Webster. Op. cit.*

576   Shafarevich, Igor. *The Socialist Phenomenon*. Foreword by Aleksandr I. Solzhenitsyn. Translated from the Russian by William Tjalsma. Originally published in 1975, by YMCA Press. An English translation was subsequently published in 1980 by Harper & Row. Transcribed for the internet by Robert L. Stephens. viii.

577   Voslensky, Michael. *Nomenklatura: The Soviet Ruling Class*. New York: Doubleday, 1984. 289.

578   Ibid.

579   V. Ilyin (a pseudonym). "Certain Features of the Historical Development of Marxism." *Zvezda* (The Star). No. 2. December 28, 1910. Accessed April 10, 2024. Cited in https://www.marxists.org/archive/lenin/works/1910/dec/23.htm#bkV17E024.

580   Michelle Obama. X. April 2, 2024. Accessed April 8, 2024. https://x.com/MichelleObama/status/1775250757798736122.

581   Donaldson, Chris. "FAA seeks to hire people with 'severe intellectual' and 'psychiatric' problems in DEI push – what could go wrong?" BizPac Review. January 15, 2024. Accessed April 5, 2024. https://www.bizpacreview.com/2024/01/15/faa-seeks-to-hire-people-with-severe-intellectual-and-psychiatric-problems-in-dei-push-what-could-go-wrong-1427713/.

582   Ibid.

583   Cogan, Marin. "How to think about Boeing's recent safety issues." Vox. March 25, 2024. Accessed April 6, 2024. https://www.vox.com/2024/3/15/24100817/boeing-crash-safety-aviation-flying.

584   Nelson, Steven. "Secret Service Director Kim Cheatle landed job after push by Jill Biden's office, sources say." *New York Post*. July 15, 2024. Accessed July 21, 2024. https://nypost.com/2024/07/15/us-news/secret-service-director-kim-cheatle-landed-job-after-push-by-jill-bidens-office-sources/.

585   Hazlett, Thomas W. "Apartheid." Econlib. Accessed April 4, 2024. https://www.econlib.org/library/Enc/Apartheid.html/.

586   Barnes, Katie. "Transgender athlete laws by state: Legislation, science, more." ESPN. August 24, 2023. Accessed April 10, 2024. https://www.espn.com/espn/story/_/id/38209262/transgender-athlete-laws-state-legislation-science.

587 "About: Partners." Campus Pride. Accessed April 10, 2024. https://www.campuspride.org/about/partners/.

588 Hipkins, Julian III. "Teaching About Ferguson." Teaching for Change. August 21, 2014. Accessed April 10, 2024. http://www.teachingforchange.org/teaching-about-ferguson.

589 Libs of TikTok. March 10, 2024. Accessed March 20, 2024. https://twitter.com/libsoftiktok/status/1766982044859478191.

590 Richardson, John. "Europe: Let's End Free Speech! Are European Countries Now Police States?" Gatestone Institute. November 17, 2016. Accessed March 3, 2024. https://www.gatestoneinstitute.org/9311/europe-free-speech.

591 Leesman, Madeline. 'I'm So Sick of This S***' : J.K. Rowling Fires Back After Outlet Describes Trans Killer As a 'Woman.'" *Townhall*. February 27, 2024. Accessed March 7, 2024. https://townhall.com/tipsheet/madelineleesman/2024/02/27/jk-rowling-trans-comment-n2635793.

592 Ibid.

593 Ibid.

594 Settles, Gabrielle. "There is no growing 'trend' of transgender, nonbinary shooters, experts say | Fact check." *USA Today*. February 23, 2024. Accessed March 7, 2024. https://www.msn.com/en-us/news/us/there-is-no-growing-trend-of-transgender-nonbinary-shooters-experts-say-fact-check/ar-BB1iMFcb.

595 Brock, Megan and Kate Anderson. "EXCLUSIVE: Prominent Psychologist Talks Nonstop About Gender-Transitioning 3-Year-Olds During Medical Training Course." The Daily Caller. January 8, 2024. Accessed March 7, 2024. https://dailycaller.com/2024/01/08/exclusive-prominent-psychologist-talks-nonstop-about-gender-transitioning-3-year-olds-during-medical-training-course/.

596 Bawer, Bruce. "A Certain Madness Amok." *City Journal*. April 1, 2021. Accessed March 7, 2024. https://www.city-journal.org/article/a-certain-madness-amok.

597 Duro, Israel. "Canadian father jailed for objecting to daughter's gender change wins in Court of Appeal." Voz Media. August 30, 2023. Accessed March 7, 2024. https://voz.us/canadian-father-jailed-for-objecting-to-daughters-gender-change-wins-in-court-of-appeal/?lang=en.

598 Aoraha, Claudia. "Republican Montana Gov Greg Gianforte defends state's decision to remove 14-year-old teen from her parents who disagreed with her wish to transition." *Daily Mail*. January 31, 2024. Accessed February 10, 2024. https://www.dailymail.co.uk/news/article-13028345/Montana-Greg-Gianforte-defends-states-decision-remove-teen-parents.html.

599 Ibid.

600 Andrzejewski, Adam. "University of Virginia Spends $20 Million On 235 DEI Employees, With Some Making $587,340 Per Year." Open the Books. March 5, 2024. Accessed March 10, 2024. https://openthebooks.substack.com/p/university-of-virginia-spends-20.

601 Newman, Alex. "Calif. Schools Give Taxpayer Cash to Children for Far-Left Activism." *The Liberty Sentinel*. March 19, 2024. Accessed March 19, 2024. https://libertysentinel.substack.com/p/media-propaganda-is-literally-killing.

602 "DEI Conquers Stanford." Christopher F. Rufo. Accessed April 30, 2024. https://christopherrufo.com/p/dei-conquers-stanford.

603 "Equity and Inclusion Strategic Plan." Stanford Physics Department, School of Humanities and Sciences. Accessed April 30, 2024. https://physics.stanford.edu/inclusion/equity-and-inclusion-strategic-plan.

604 Thomas, Zoey. "UF eliminates diversity: What's known and what remains unclear." *The Independent Florida Alligator*. March 4, 2024.

Accessed March 16, 2024. https://www.alligator.org/article/2024/03/
uf-eliminates-diversity-whats-known-and-what-remains-unclear.

605   Haggerty, Kevin. "DEI dominoes continue to fall; another red state passes laws,
woke students wail over closures." American Wire. April 3, 2024. Accessed
April 6, 2024. https://americanwirenews.com/dei-dominoes-continue-to-
fall-another-red-state-passes-laws-woke-students-wail-over-closures/.

606   Ibid.

607   The New American. "Conversations That Matter | Media Propaganda is
Literally Killing Americans - Emerald Robinson." Rumble. March 14, 2024.
Accessed March 19, 2024. https://rumble.com/v4j2fml-conversations-
that-matter-media-propaganda-is-literally-killing-americans-e.html.

608   Newman. "Calif. Schools Give Taxpayer Cash." Op. cit.

609   "Conversations that Matter." Op. cit.

610   Schwab, Klaus. "Davos 2024: Rebuilding trust in the future." World
Economic Forum. January 16, 2024. Accessed March 21, 2024. https://www.
weforum.org/agenda/2024/01/rebuilding-trust-collaberation-future/.

611   Aldrick, Philip. "Cost-of-Living Crisis Is Top Immediate Risk for
Davos Elite." Bloomberg. January 11, 2023. Accessed January 13,
2024. https://www.bloomberg.com/news/articles/2023-01-11/
cost-of-living-crisis-is-top-immediate-risk-for-davos-elite.

612   Dmitry, Baxter. "Klaus Schwab's WEF Issues Edict to Global
Leaders: 'Gas Prices Aren't High Enough.'" NewsPunch. July
14, 2022. Accessed April 10, 2024. https://newspunch.com/
klaus-schwabs-wef-issues-edict-to-global-leaders-gas-prices-arent-high-enough/.

613   Schwab. "Davos 2024." Op. cit.

614   Stocklin, Kevin. "The WEF Says It Wants to 'Rebuild Trust'; Consumer Advocates
Suggest How." The Epoch Times. January 18, 2024. Accessed March 21, 2024.
https://www.theepochtimes.com/us/the-wef-says-it-wants-to-rebuild-trust-
consumer-advocates-suggest-how-5567493.

615   "Javier Milei Address at the 54th Annual Meeting of the World Economic Forum."
American Rhetoric. January 17, 2024. Accessed February 5, 2024. https://www.
americanrhetoric.com/speeches/javiermileiworldeconomicforum54.htm.

616   "AMERICA FIRST: President Trump Says AMERICA Will Never Be A
SOCIALIST Country." YouTube. January 21, 2020. Accessed February
5, 2024. https://www.youtube.com/watch?v=GeJqmV7KzPI.

617   Brundtland, Gro Harlem. "Report of the World Commission on Environment
and Development: Our Common Future." Oxford: Oxford University
Press, 1987. Accessed December 2, 2023. https://sustainabledevelopment.
un.org/content/documents/5987our-common-future.pdf. 5.

618   "XX Congress of the Socialist International, New York, The World Economy:
A Common Responsibility." Socialist International. September 9–11,
1996. Accessed November 23, 2023. https://www.socialistinternational.
org/congresses/xx-congress-of-the-socialist-international-new-york/.

619   "Education for Sustainable Development." UNESCO.
Accessed November 23, 2023. https://en.unesco.org/themes/
education-sustainable-development/what-is-esd/sd.

620   Brundtland. "Our Common Future." 5.

621   Brundtland. "Our Common Future." 22.

622   "Report of the United Nations Conference on the Human Environment,
Stockholm, 5-6 June, 1972." United Nations Digital Library. 1973. Accessed
December 31, 2023. https://digitallibrary.un.org/record/523249?ln=en.

623   "Short Biography." MauriceStrong.net. Accessed January 5, 2024. https://www. mauricestrong.net/index.php?option=com_content&view=article&id=15& Itemid=24.

624   Runnalls, David. "Remembering Maurice Strong, pioneering environmental champion." IIED. December 4, 2015. Accessed January 21, 2024. https://www. iied.org/remembering-maurice-strong-pioneering-environmental-champion.

625   "IIED's founder: Barbara Ward." IIED. August 20, 2014. Accessed January 21, 2024. https://www.iied.org/iied-founder-barbara-ward.

626   "Summary of the sixth biennial high-level meeting of the Development Cooperation Forum." United Nations Economic and Social Council. July 9–18, 2018. Accessed January 5, 2024. http://old.cdc-crdb.gov.kh/cdc/ Donor_Development_Cooperation_Programs/undaf/docs/dcf.pdf.

627   Allison, Emily. "Border Deception: How the US and UN are Quietly Running the Border Crisis." *The Epoch Times*. October 13, 2022. Accessed December 5, 2023. https://www.theepochtimes.com/border-deception-how-the-us-and-un-are-quietly-running-the-border-crisis-2_4782317.html.

628   "The Vancouver Action Plan: Recommendation A.4 More Equitable Distribution." United Nations Conference on Human Settlements, June 11, 1976. Accessed April 10, 2024. https://habitat76.ca/the-vancouver-action-plan/.

629   Ibid.

630   "United Nations Conference on Environment & Development Rio de Janeiro, Brazil, 3 to 14 June 1992: AGENDA 21." United Nations Sustainable Development. Accessed October 25, 2023. https:// sustainabledevelopment.un.org/content/documents/Agenda21.pdf.

631   "Agenda 21." UN Department of Economic and Social Affairs, Division for Sustainable Development. Accessed December 5, 2023. https://www.un.org/esa/dsd/agenda21/.

632   H.Con.Res.353 — 102nd Congress (1991-1992). Congress.Gov. Accessed November 10, 2023. https://www.congress.gov/bill/102nd-congress/house-concurrent-resolution/353.

633   "Support the APA Foundation." APA Foundation. Accessed December 15, 2023. https://www.planning.org/foundation/.

634   "Transforming our world: the 2030 Agenda for Sustainable Development." United Nations Department of Economic and Social Affairs: Sustainable Development. Accessed November 10, 2023. https://sdgs.un.org/2030agenda.

635   Melville, James. "The WEF published this video in 2018: 8 predictions for the world in 2030." X. August 5, 2022. Accessed April 10, 2024. https:// twitter.com/JamesMelville/status/1555470357846532096?lang=en/.

636   Anderson, Jack, and Dale Van Atta. "TREE SPIKING AN 'ECO-TERRORIST' TACTIC." *Washington Post*. March 5, 1990. Accessed January 10, 2024. https://www.washingtonpost.com/archive/local/1990/03/05/ tree-spiking-an-eco-terrorist-tactic/a400944c-a3a0-4c03-ab99-afada6f44e7a/.

637   "Dave Foreman Quotes." AZ Quotes. Accessed January 22, 2024. https://www.azquotes.com/author/26203-David_Foreman.

638   AZ Quotes.

639   "What are the Principles for Responsible Investment?" PRI: Principles for Responsible Investment. Accessed January 23, 2024. https://www.unpri. org/about-us/what-are-the-principles-for-responsible-investment.

640   "Sustainable Finance – the new frontier for investment banking growth." Acuity Knowledge Partners. Accessed December 5, 2023. https://www.acuitykp.com/ sustainable-finance-the-new-frontier-for-investment-banking-growth/.

[641] Atkins, Betsy. "Demystifying ESG: Its History & Current Status." *Forbes*. June 8, 2020. Accessed November 23, 2023. https://www.forbes.com/sites/betsyatkins/2020/06/08/demystifying-esgits-history--current-status/?sh=16a12eba2cdd.

[642] "About the PRI." PRI. Accessed March 21, 2024. https://www.unpri.org/about-us/about-the-pri.

[643] "Climate Action 100." InfluenceWatch. Accessed January 5, 2024. https://www.influencewatch.org/non-profit/climate-action-100/.

[644] "G20 BALI LEADERS' DECLARATION Bali, Indonesia." G20 Indonesia 2022. November 15–16, 2022. Accessed January 24, 2024. http://www.g20.utoronto.ca/2022/G20%20Bali%20Leaders-%20Declaration,%2015-16%20November%202022,%20incl%20Annex.pdf.

[645] "G20 New Delhi Leaders' Declaration." G20 Research Group. September 9, 2023. Accessed March 5, 2024. http://www.g20.utoronto.ca/2023/230909-declaration.html#G.

[646] Schwab, Klaus. "Davos Manifesto 1973: A Code of Ethics for Business Leaders." World Economic Forum. December 2, 2019. Accessed January 20, 2024. https://www.weforum.org/agenda/2019/12/davos-manifesto-1973-a-code-of-ethics-for-business-leaders/.

[647] "KPMG ESG." KPMG. Accessed November 14, 2023. https://www.kpmg.us/services/kpmg-esg.html.

[648] Chumley, Cheryl K. "Stakeholder Capitalism is Communism in Disguise." *Washington Times*. September 28, 2021. Accessed December 5, 2023. https://www.washingtontimes.com/news/2021/scp/28/stakeholder-capitalism-communism-disguise/.

[649] "Measuring Stakeholder Capitalism: Towards Common Metrics and Consistent Reporting of Sustainable Value Creation." World Economic Forum. September 22, 2020. Accessed January 20, 2024. https://www.weforum.org/reports/measuring-stakeholder-capitalism-towards-common-metrics-and-consistent-reporting-of-sustainable-value-creation.

[650] Stakeholder Capitalism Metrics Initiative.

[651] Pollard, Amelia. "BlackRock Is Caught in the ESG Crossfire and Struggling to Get Out." *Bloomberg*. December 15, 2022. Accessed January 10, 2024. https://www.bloomberg.com/news/features/2022-12-15/blackrock-is-caught-in-the-esg-crossfire-and-struggling-to-get-out#xj4y7vzkg.

[652] Revell, Eric. "ESG fallout: BlackRock CEO Larry Fink should resign, says state treasurer." Fox News. December 9, 2022. Accessed January 12, 2024. https://www.foxbusiness.com/markets/esg-fallout-blackrock-ceo-larry-fink-should-resign-says-state-treasurer.

[653] Stocklin, Kevin. "IN-DEPTH: BlackRock CEO Says He'll No Longer Use 'ESG' Term." *The Epoch Times*. July 4, 2023. Accessed March 4, 2024. https://www.theepochtimes.com/business/blackrock-ceo-says-hell-no-longer-use-esg-term-5359830.

[654] Catenacci, Thomas. "Texas pulls $8.5B from BlackRock in stunning blow to ESG movement." Fox Business. March 19, 2024. Accessed March 21, 2024. https://www.foxbusiness.com/politics/texas-pulls-8-5-billion-blackrock-stunning-blow-esg-movement.

[655] Stocklin. "IN-DEPTH." *Op. cit.*

[656] Ibid.

[657] "Bachelors in Sustainability Program Guide." BestColleges.com. January 21, 2022. Accessed January 26, 2024. https://www.bestcolleges.com/features/sustainability-degree-programs/.

658   White, Olivia, et al. "Digital Identification: A key to inclusive growth." McKinsey Digital. Accessed January 5, 2024. https://www.mckinsey.com/capabilities/mckinsey-digital/our-insights/digital-identification-a-key-to-inclusive-growth.

659   "G20 BALI LEADERS' DECLARATION." *Op. cit.*

660   "G20 New Delhi Leaders' Declaration." G20. September 9–10, 2023. Accessed March 5, 2024. https://www.mea.gov.in/Images/CPV/G20-New-Delhi-Leaders-Declaration.pdf. 9.

661   "Judge's Ruling Alters Path to Verdict in Trump NY Case; WHO Pandemic Treaty Fails." *The Epoch Times.* May 28, 2024. Accessed July 22, 2024. https://www.theepochtimes.com/epochtv/who-pandemic-treaty-fails-world-waits-on-trump-trial-results-5657941.

662   Meyer, Warren. "The Man Who Saved the Whales." *Forbes.* Nov 5, 2010. Accessed November 12, 2023. https://www.forbes.com/sites/warrenmeyer/2010/11/05/the-man-who-saved-the-whales/?sh=4b1bb1fb596f.

663   Ehrlich, Dr. Paul R., and Ann Howland Ehrlich. *Population Bomb.* New York: Ballantine Books, 1968.

664   "New Report on Replacement Migration Issued by UN Population Division." Press Release, United Nations. March 17, 2000. Accessed December 21, 2023. https://press.un.org/en/2000/20000317.dev2234.doc.html.

665   Wheelock, David. "How Bad Was the Great Depression? Gauging the Economic Impact." St. Louis Federal Reserve Bank. July 11, 2013. Accessed December 5, 2023. https://www.stlouisfed.org/the-great-depression/curriculum/economic-episodes-in-american-history-part-3.

666   Rich, Robert. "The Great Recession." Federal Reserve History. November 22, 2013. Accessed December 12, 2023. https://www.federalreservehistory.org/essays/great-recession-of-200709.

667   Carroll, Conn. "Kerry-Boxer: 10% unemployment is just the beginning." The Daily Signal. October 1, 2009. Accessed December 4, 2023. http://blog.heritage.org/2009/10/01/kerry-boxer-10-unemployment-is-just-the-beginning/

668   "Kerry on how to keep climate goals alive: 'Money, money, money, money, money, money.'" Associated Press. January 17, 2023. Accessed January 20, 2024. https://www.marketwatch.com/story/kerry-on-how-to-keep-climate-goals-alive-money-money-money-money-money-money-money-01673958211.

669   Hoffman, Andrew J., and Douglas M. Ely. "Time to Put the Fossil-Fuel Industry Into Hospice." *Stanford Social Innovation Review.* Fall 2022. Accessed January 12, 2024. https://ssir.org/articles/entry/time_to_put_the_fossil_fuel_industry_into_hospice.

670   Neufeld, Dorothy. "Visualizing the $94 Trillion World Economy in One Chart." Visual Capitalist. December 22, 2021. Accessed December 20, 2023. https://www.visualcapitalist.com/visualizing-the-94-trillion-world-economy-in-one-chart/.

671   Henderson, David R. and Hooper, Charles L. "Flawed Climate Models." Hoover Institution. April 24, 2017. Accessed January 26, 2024. https://www.hoover.org/research/flawed-climate-models.

672   "The Business Case." Climate Action 100. Accessed January 26, 2024. https://www.climateaction100.org/business-case/.

673   "Time to Put the Fossil-Fuel Industry Into Hospice." *Op. cit.*

674   Schwab, Klaus. "Maurice Strong: An Appreciation." World Economic Forum. November 29, 2015. Accessed January 20, 2024. https://www.weforum.org/agenda/2015/11/maurice-strong-an-appreciation/.

675   Gordon, Anita. "A tribute to the founding giant of the global environment movement." World Bank Blogs. December 8, 2015.

Accessed April 5, 2024. https://blogs.worldbank.org/climatechange/
tribute-founding-giant-global-environment-movement.

676   "Maurice Strong." AZ Quotes. Accessed January 5, 2024. https://
www.azquotes.com/author/14256-Maurice_Strong.

677   Bell, Larry. "Let's Be Very Clear Mr. Kerry: No Scientific Evidence Of 'Dangerous'
Human Climate Influence Exists." *Forbes*. February 24, 2014. Accessed January
20, 2024. https://www.forbes.com/sites/larrybell/2014/02/24/lets-be-very-clear-
mr-kerry-no-
scientific-evidence-of-dangerous-human-climate-influence-exists/?sh=2a44b5b226f5.

678   "Maurice Strong." AZ Quotes. Accessed January 22, 2024.
https://www.azquotes.com/quote/595340.

679   Wood, Daniel. "The Wizard of Baca Grande." *West*. May 1990. Accessed January 12,
2024. https://vdocuments.site/maurice-strong-wizard-baca-grande-1990.html. 10.

680   "The Wizard of Baca Grande." *Op cit.* 10.

681   Ibid.

682   Samuels, Brett. "George Soros at Davos: Trump 'a danger to the world.'" *The
Hill*. January 25, 2018. Accessed March 10, 2024. https://thehill.com/policy/
technology/370757-soros-calls-for-stricter-regulations-on-facebook-google/.

683   Duigon, Lee. "The High Priest of Humanism: Meet the UN's Maurice Strong."
Chalcedon. March 22, 2004. Accessed January 23, 2024. https://chalcedon.edu/
resources/articles/the-high-priest-of-humanism-meet-the-uns-maurice-strong.

684   Schwab, Klaus. "Now is the time for a 'great reset.'" World Economic
Forum. June 3, 2020. Accessed January 22, 2024. https://www.
weforum.org/agenda/2020/06/now-is-the-time-for-a-great-reset/.

685   "The Great Reset." World Economic Forum. September 21, 2020. Accessed January
5, 2023. https://www.weforum.org/videos/series/the-great-reset-863c8ea2d4/.

686   Rectenwald, Michael. "What Is the Great Reset?" *The Epoch
Times*. May 15, 2022. Accessed April 10, 2024. https://www.
theepochtimes.com/opinion/what-is-the-great-reset-4467659.

687   Mallis, Athena. "A catastrophic global cyber-attack could happen in the next two
years: World Economic Forum." Digital Nation. January 19, 2023. Accessed January
21, 2023. https://www.digitalnationaus.com.au/news/a-catastrophic-global-cyber-
attack-could-happen-in-the-next-two-years-world-economic-forum-589902.

688   Feingold, Spencer. "Experts at Davos 2023 call for a global response
to the gathering 'cyber storm.'" World Economic Forum. January
18, 2023. Accessed January 19, 2024. https://www.weforum.org/
agenda/2023/01/cybersecurity-storm-2023-experts-davos23/.

689   Betz, Bradford. "World Economic Forum chair Klaus Schwab declares on Chinese
state TV: 'China is a model for many nations.'" Fox News. November 23, 2022.
Accessed January 5, 2024. https://www.foxnews.com/world/world-economic-
forum-chair-klaus-schwab-declares-chinese-state-tv-china-model-many-nations.

690   Hubert, Antoine. "Why we need to give insects the role they deserve in our food
systems." World Economic Forum. July 12, 2021. Accessed January 20, 2024.
https://www.weforum.org/agenda/2021/07/why-we-need-to-give-insects-the-role-
they-deserve-in-our-food-systems/.

691   Chisholm, Paul. "Your Ancestors Probably Ate Insects. So What's Bugging
You?" NPR. July 16, 2018. Accessed January 26, 2024. https://www.npr.org/
sections/thesalt/
2018/07/16/628989973/many-of-our-ancestors-ate-insects-so-what-s-bugging-you.

692   Melville, James. The WEF published this video in 2018. *Op. cit.*

693 Heller, Tony. "Climate Scientists Knew!" Real Climate Science. September 11, 2018. Accessed March 29, 2024. https://realclimatescience.com/2018/09/climate-scientists-knew/.

694 "1972 CBS News: Walter Cronkite Warns of Coming Ice Age." KEEL. Accessed March 29, 2024. https://710keel.com/1972-cbs-news-walter-cronkite-warns-of-coming-ice-age-video/.

695 Saul, Josh. "Goldman Sees Biden's Clean-Energy Law Costing US $1.2 Trillion." Bloomberg. March 23, 2023. Accessed March 29, 2024. https://archive.ph/LhiL1.

696 Moore, Patrick. Invisible Catastrophes and Threats of Doom. Comox, BC, Canada: Ecosense Environmental, 2021. 26.

697 Moore, Patrick. "The Truth About CO2." Prager University. July 26, 2015. Accessed April 1, 2024. https://www.prageru.com/video/the-truth-about-co2.

698 Conversations That Matter. "A Dearth of Carbon (w/ Dr. Patrick Moore, environmentalist)." YouTube. September 16, 2016. Accessed April 1, 2024. https://youtu.be/TjlmFr4FMvI.

699 Conversations That Matter. "World In Midst of Carbon Drought (w/ Prof. William Happer, Princeton University)." YouTube. June 22, 2015. Accessed April 1, 2024. https://www.youtube.com/watch?v=U-9UlF8hkhs.

700 "A Dearth of Carbon." Op. cit.

701 Ibid.

702 Ibid.

703 Bowden, John. "Ocasio-Cortez: 'World will end in 12 years' if climate change not addressed." The Hill. January 22, 2019. Accessed February 10, 2024. https://thehill.com/policy/energy-environment/426353-ocasio-cortez-the-world-will-end-in-12-years-if-we-dont-address/.

704 Hays, Gabriel. "Al Gore goes on 'unhinged' rant about 'rain bombs,' boiled oceans, other climate threats at Davos." Fox News. January 18, 2023. Accessed March 29, 2024. hhttps://www.foxnews.com/media/al-gore-goes-unhinged-rant-about-rain-bombs-boiled-oceans-other-climate-threats-davos.

705 Fischer, Hubertus, Martin Whalen, Jesse Smith, Derek Mastroianni, and Bruce Deck. "Ice Core Records of Atmospheric CO_2 Around the Last Three Glacial Terminations." Science. March 12, 1999. Accessed March 22, 2024. https://www.science.org/doi/10.1126/science.283.5408.1712.

706 "Al Gore Net Worth." Celebrity Net Worth. January 12, 2024. Accessed February 24, 2024. https://www.celebritynetworth.com/richest-politicians/democrats/al-gore-net-worth/.

707 Plumer, Brad. "Climate Change Is Speeding Toward Catastrophe. The Next Decade Is Crucial, U.N. Panel Says." New York Times. March 20, 2023. Accessed March 22, 2024. https://www.nytimes.com/2023/03/20/climate/global-warming-ipcc-earth.html.

708 Catenacci, Thomas. "UN calls for mass fossil fuel shutdowns to prevent 'climate time bomb." Fox News. March 20, 2023. Accessed April 1, 2024. https://www.foxnews.com/politics/un-calls-mass-fossil-fuel-shutdowns-prevent-climate-time-bomb.

709 "Disclaimer." IPCC. Accessed March 26, 2024. https://www.ipcc.ch/disclaimer/.

710 Harvey, Fiona. "Equivalent of Covid emissions drop needed every two years – study." The Guardian. March 3, 2021. Accessed March 20, 2024. https://www.theguardian.com/environment/2021/mar/03/global-lockdown-every-two-years-needed-to-meet-paris-co2-goals-study.

711 Morano, Marc. "Great Reset By Marc Morano – Chapter 12 Excerpt: 'COVID Lockdowns Morph to Climate Lockdowns'" Climate Depot. September 8, 2022.

Accessed April 2, 2024. https://www.climatedepot.com/2022/09/08/great-reset-by-marc-morano-chapter-12-excerpt-covid-lockdowns-morph-to-climate-lockdowns/

712 "Energy Sec. Granholm claims U.S. can 'learn' from China on climate change." Fox News. March 10, 2023. Accessed March 26, 2024. https://www.foxnews.com/video/6322321567112.

713 Ly, Mimi Nguyen. "China Building New Coal Plants Equal to Entire US Capacity." *The Epoch Times*. October 7, 2018. Accessed March 29, 2024. https://www.theepochtimes.com/china-building-new-coal-plants-equal-to-entire-us-capacity_2679901.html.

714 "New Report Examines Costs to U.S. Industrial Sector of Obama's Paris Pledge." Press Release, U.S. Chamber of Commerce, Global Energy Institute. March 16, 2017. Accessed March 3, 2024. https://www.globalenergyinstitute.org/new-report-examines-costs-us-industrial-sector-obamas-paris-pledge.

715 Friedrich, Johannes, Mengpin Ge, Andrew Pickens, and Leandro Vigna. "This Interactive Chart Shows Changes in the World's Top 10 Emitters." World Resources Institute. March 2, 2023. Accessed July 23, 2024. https://www.wri.org/insights/interactive-chart-shows-changes-worlds-top-10-emitters.

716 Koprowski, Gene. "Czech President Klaus: Global Warming Not Science, but a 'New Religion.'" Fox News. December 18, 2009. Accessed April 5, 2024. https://www.foxnews.com/science/czech-president-klaus-global-warming-not-science-but-a-new-religion.

717 Schweizer, Peter. *Throw Them All Out: How Politicians and Their Friends Get Rich Off Insider Stock Tips, Land Deals, and Cronyism That Would Send the Rest of Us to Prison*. New York: Houghton Mifflin Harcourt, 2011. 87–88.

718 *Throw Them All Out*. 80–81.

719 Ibid.

720 Howley, Patrick. "Bundler of Sunshine." *Washington Free Beacon*. May 22, 2012. Accessed April 2, 2024. https://freebeacon.com/national-security/bundler-of-sunshine/.

721 Phillips, Jack. "Federal Judge Blocks Key Biden Climate Change Executive Order. *The Epoch Times*. February 14, 2022. Accessed April 5, 2024. https://www.theepochtimes.com/us/federal-judge-blocks-key-biden-climate-change-executive-order-4276911.

722 Kasperowicz, Peter. "Navy Secretary Cited Climate Change as Top Priority as Biden Proposes Shrinking the Fleet." Fox News. March 18, 2023. Accessed March 29, 2024. https://www.foxnews.com/politics/navy-secretary-cites-climate-change-top-priority-biden-proposes-shrinking-fleet.

723 Blase, Brian. "Learning From CBO's History Of Incorrect ObamaCare Projections." *Forbes*. January 2, 2017. Accessed March 29, 2024. https://www.forbes.com/sites/theapothecary/2017/01/02/learning-from-cbos-history-of-incorrect-obamacare-projections/?sh=4bc6e60346a7.

724 Saul, Josh. "Goldman."

725 "Production Tax Credit and Investment Tax Credit for Wind Energy." WINDExchange. Accessed March 28, 2024. https://windexchange.energy.gov/projects/tax-credits.

726 Stacy, Thomas F., and George S. Taylor PhD. "The Levelized Cost of Electricity from Existing Generation Resources." Institute for Energy Research. June 2019. Accessed March 28, 2024. 2. https://www.instituteforenergyresearch.org/wp-content/uploads/2019/06/IER_LCOE2019Final-.pdf.

727 Lesser, Jonathan A. "Out to Sea: The Dismal Economics of Offshore Wind." Manhattan Institute. August 25, 2020. Accessed March 29, 2024. https://www.manhattan-institute.org/dismal-economics-offshore-wind-energy.

728   Calma, Justine. "The US offshore wind boom will depend on these ships."
       The Verge. February 23, 2021. Accessed February 30, 2024. https://www.
       theverge.com/22296979/us-offshore-ships-wind-boom-installation-vessels.

729   "Offshore Wind Outlook 2019." IEA. November 2019. Accessed March
       30, 2024. https://iea.blob.core.windows.net/assets/495ab264-4ddf-
       4b68-b9c0-514295ff40a7/Offshore_Wind_Outlook_2019.pdf.

730   "Challenges in the Installation and Repair of Offshore Wind Turbines."
       PMI Industries. Accessed March 29, 2024. https://pmiind.com/challenges-
       installation-repair-
       offshore-wind-turbines/.

731   Merriman, Joel. "How Many Birds Are Killed by Wind Turbines?"
       American Bird Conservancy. January 26, 2021. Accessed March 28,
       2024. https://abcbirds.org/blog21/wind-turbine-mortality/.

732   De la Garza, Alejandro. "U.S. Fishermen Are Making Their Last Stand
       Against Offshore Wind." *Time*. September 30, 2021. Accessed February
       30, 2024. https://time.com/6102900/offshore-wind-fishing/.

733   Wanna, Carly, Jennifer Dloughy, Josh Saul, and Bloomberg. "A 40-ton problem
       is weighing on the $100 billion offshore wind industry." *Fortune*. February
       18, 2023. Accessed March 29, 2024. https://fortune.com/2023/02/18/
       offshore-wind-turbines-whales-dying-oceans-environment/.

734   "Conflicts of Interest: Environmental Organizations Take Offshore Wind Industry
       Money." Save Right Whales Coalition. April 26, 2022. Accessed March 28, 2024.
       https://drive.google.com/file/d/1cKoO-4s369hKf4Z3RaVcopEmrHpGob7d/view.

735   Woods Hole Oceanographic Institution. Return of Organization
       Exempt from Income Tax (Form 990), 2019, Part I, line 22. November
       2, 2022. Accessed April 10, 2024. https://pdf.guidestar.org/PDF_Ima
       ges/2019/042/105/2019-042105850-17843243-9.pdf.

736   New England Aquarium Corporation. Return of Organization Exempt from Income
       Tax (Form 990), 2019, Part I, line 22. October 27, 2020. Accessed April 10, 2024.
       https://pdf.guidestar.org/PDF_Images/2019/042/297/2019-042297514-
       202013119349301106-9.pdf.

737   Environmental League of Massachusetts. Return of Organization Exempt from
       Income Tax (Form 990), 2019, Part I, line 22. April 18, 2020. Accessed April 10,
       2024. https://pdf.guidestar.org/PDF_Images/2019/042/760/2019-042760271-
       202041019349300909-9.pdf.

738   National Fish and Wildlife Foundation. Return of Organization Exempt from
       Income Tax (Form 990), 2019, Part I, line 22. February 13, 2021. Accessed April
       10, 2024. https://pdf.guidestar.org/PDF_Images/2020/521/384/2020-521384139-
       202132089349300708-9.pdf.

739   National Audubon Society. Return of Organization Exempt from Income Tax (Form
       990), 2019, Part I, line 22. March 3, 2022. Accessed April 10, 2024. https://pdf.
       guidestar.org/PDF_Images/2021/131/624/2021-131624102-19761276-9.pdf.

740   "Wind Power and Birds: Properly sited wind power can help protect
       birds from climate change." Audubon. July 21, 2020. Accessed March
       28, 2024. https://www.audubon.org/news/wind-power-and-birds.

741   Larson, Christina, Jennifer McDermott, Patrick Whittle, and Wayne Parry.
       "Contrary to politicians' claims, offshore wind farms don't kill whales. Here's
       what to know." WHYY PBS. December 27, 2023. Accessed April 5, 2024.
       https://whyy.org/articles/offshore-wind-farms-whale-deaths-what-to-know/.

742   "US Wind Announces Key Partnerships With Local Conservation Groups."
       Press Release, US Wind. December 2, 2021. Accessed March 23, 2024. https://
       drive.google.com/file/d/19Zxq2cLNCrcIU5-2HW4MCIa3W5plZJ-i/view.

743   Bauder, David. "Climate grant illustrates growth in philanthropy-funded news." Associated Press. February 16, 2022. Accessed March 28, 2024. https://apnews.com/article/science-business-arts-and-entertainment-journalism-united-states-087d1d5dd7189c529fe5d7a21a1ffb5f.

744   "From Russia With Love? Examining Links Between US Environmental Funder and the Kremlin." Environmental Policy Alliance. 2015. Accessed March 29, 2024. https://www.biggreenradicals.com/wp-content/uploads/2015/12/Klein_Report_12-2015.pdf.

745   Catenacci, Thomas. "Green group influencing Biden admin has deep ties to Chinese government." Fox News. September 26. 2022. Accessed March 29, 2024. https://www.foxnews.com/politics/green-group-influencing-biden-admin-deep-ties-chinese-government.

746   Cambria, Antonino. "Biden Admin Hands $750,000 To China-Linked Group Behind Push To Ban Gas Stoves." The Daily Caller. February 15, 2023. Accessed March 29, 2024. https://dailycaller.com/2023/02/15/biden-admin-hands-750000-to-china-linked-group-behind-push-to-ban-gas-stoves/.

747   Parry, Wayne. "US offshore wind energy industry faces blowback from locals." AP News. November 15, 2022. Accessed March 30, 2024. https://apnews.com/article/business-new-jersey-wind-power-energy-industry-climate-and-environment-8cd2f697f8d53e4a979bf7359ab6b29a.

748   Moore, Stephen. "How the First 'Green New Deal' Flopped." The Heritage Foundation. March 28, 2019. Accessed March 30, 2024. https://www.heritage.org/environment/commentary/how-the-first-green-new-deal-flopped.

749   Simpson, James. "A Better Way to Restore the Chesapeake Bay." Maryland Public Policy Institute. October 27, 2014. Accessed April 2, 2024. https://www.mdpolicy.org/research/detail/a-better-way-to-restore-the-chesapeake-bay.

750   Kurtz, Josh. "Gansler Says His Experience Makes Him Best-Equipped to Tackle Climate Change in Md." Maryland Matters. November 11, 2021. Accessed April 3, 2024. https://www.marylandmatters.org/2021/11/11/gansler-says-his-experience-makes-him-best-equipped-to-tackle-climate-change-in-md/.

751   Fears, Darryl. "Will dredging alleviate the Conowingo Dam sediment issue?" *Washington Post*. April 7, 2015. Accessed April 2, 2024. https://www.washingtonpost.com/national/health-science/will-dredging-alleviate-the-conowingo-dam-sediment-issue/2015/04/05/fec9cb0e-c025-11e4-9271-610273846239_story.html.

752   "MICHAEL R. ENRIGHT: Chief of Staff, 2007-09, Senior Advisor to Governor, 2009-10." Maryland Manual Online. Accessed April 2, 2024. https://msa.maryland.gov/msa/mdmanual/08conoff/staff/former/html/msa14641.html.

753   Associated Press. "Easton-based firm proposes solar farm near state prison." *The Daily Record*. May 20, 2011. Accessed April 2, 2024. http://thedailyrecord.com/2011/05/20/easton-based-firm-proposes-solar-farm-near-state-prison/.

754   Associated Press. "Board approves solar project on prison land in Western Md." *The Daily Record*. July 27, 2011. Accessed April 2, 2024. http://thedailyrecord.com/2011/07/27/board-approves-solar-project-on-prison-land-in-western-md/.

755   2012 Maryland total housing stock = 2,341,000. See: "Construction and Housing: Housing Units and Characteristics." 2012 Statistical Abstract, National Data Book, U.S. Census Bureau. Accessed April 2, 2024. https://www.census.gov/library/publications/2011/compendia/statab/131ed/construction-housing.html.

756   "Governor O'Malley Celebrates Groundbreaking on State's Largest Solar Power Project." Press Release, First Solar. July 7, 2012. Accessed April 2, 2024. https://s202.q4cdn.com/499595574/files/doc_news/2012/07/1/7b92485d-e080-4baf-946d-8722e509103f.pdf.

757   "Governor O'Malley Celebrates Groundbreaking." *Op. cit.*

758   Associated Press. "Board approves solar project." *Op. cit.*

759   Pichaske, Pete. "Maryland counties grapple with controlling growth of solar farms." *The Daily Record*. July 23, 2021. Accessed April 2, 2024. https://thedailyrecord.com/2021/07/23/maryland-counties-grapple-with-controlling-growth-of-solar-farms/.

760   Dantzler, Nicole. "Prince George residents voice opposition to proposed solar farm." ABC8 News. December 4, 2023. Accessed April 5, 2024. https://www.wric.com/news/prince-george/prince-george-residents-voice-opposition-to-proposed-solar-farm/.

761   Greenfield, Sherry. "Frustration surrounds Carroll commissioners' vote to disallow community solar projects on farmland." *The Baltimore Sun*. May 22, 2023. Accessed April 5, 2024. https://www.baltimoresun.com/2023/05/22/frustration-surrounds-carroll-commissioners-vote-to-disallow-community-solar-projects-on-farmland/.

762   Maryland Solar; Data Current Through: Q4 2023." SEIA. Accessed April 2, 2024. https://www.seia.org/state-solar-policy/maryland-solar.

763   Nehls, Grace. "U.S. DOE announces $30 million wind turbine materials, manufacturing funding opportunity." Composites World. February 14, 2023. Accessed March 25, 2024. https://www.compositesworld.com/news/us-doe-announces-30-million-wind-turbine-materials-manufacturing-funding-opportunity.

764   Ozimek, Tom. "Alexandria Ocasio-Cortez's Green New Deal Could Cost $93 Trillion: Think Tank." *The Epoch Times*. February 26, 2019. Accessed April 2, 2024. https://www.theepochtimes.com/alexandria-ocasio-cortezs-green-new-deal-could-cost-93-trillion-think-tank_2815980.html.

765   Thomas-Blate, Jessie. "69 Dams Removed in 2020." American Rivers. February 18, 2021. Accessed April 2, 2024. https://www.americanrivers.org/2021/02/69-dams-removed-in-2020/.

766   Dears, Donn. "Net-zero carbon goal is unattainable." *Washington Examiner*. June 20, 2022. Accessed March 25, 2024. https://www.washingtonexaminer.com/restoring-america/courage-strength-optimism/net-zero-carbon-goal-is-unattainable.

767   Michael, Joshua P. "'Clean Energy Transition' Part 2." Full Broadside. March 30, 2023. Accessed April 2, 2024. https://fullbroadside.substack.com/p/clean-energy-transition-part-2.

768   Owens, Josh. **"Is it possible to make steel without fossil fuels?"** Greenbiz. September 24, 2020. Accessed April 2, 2024. https://www.greenbiz.com/article/it-possible-make-steel-without-fossil-fuels**.**

769   Dears. "Net-zero carbon goal is unattainable." *Op. cit.*

770   Ibid.

771   Schultz, Kenneth. "Logistics and Costs for Australia to Achieve Net Zero Carbon Dioxide Emissions by 2050." What's Up With That? July 10, 2021. Accessed April 2, 2023. https://wattsupwiththat.com/2021/07/10/logistics-and-costs-for-australia-to-achieve-net-zero-carbon-dioxide-emissions-by-2050/.

772   Michaux, Simon P. "Assessment of the Extra Capacity Required of Alternative Energy Electrical Power Systems to Completely Replace Fossil Fuels." Geological Survey of Finland. August 20, 2021. Accessed April 2, 2024. https://www.researchgate.net/publication/354067356_Assessment_of_the_Extra_Capacity_Required_of_Alternative_Energy_Electrical_Power_Systems_to_Completely_Replace_Fossil_Fuels.

773   Ibid. 328.

774   "MINERAL COMMODITY SUMMARIES 2023." U.S. Department of the Interior, U.S. Geological Survey. January 31, 2023. Accessed April 2, 2024. 109. https://pubs.usgs.gov/periodicals/mcs2023/mcs2023.pdf.

775   Michaux. *Op. cit.* 351-354.

776   Ibid. 638.

777   Ibid. iii.

778   Parry, Wayne. "Wind farm off New Jersey likely to 'adversely affect' but not kill whales, feds say." AP News. December 19, 2023. Accessed April 5, 2024. https://apnews.com/article/offshore-wind-atlantic-shores-new-jersey-noaa-554891da8670f75e21042bbdad907797.

779   Kunzelman, Michael, Lindsay Whitehurst, and Allana Durkin Richer. "Proud Boys' Enrique Tarrio gets record 22 years in prison for Jan. 6 seditious conspiracy." AP News. September 6, 2023. Accessed April 8, 2024. https://apnews.com/article/enrique-tarrio-capitol-riot-seditious-conspiracy-sentencing-da60222b3e1e54902db2bbbb219dc3fb.

780   Ibid.

781   Naylor, Brian. "Read Trump's Jan. 6 Speech, A Key Part Of Impeachment Trial." NPR. February 10, 2021. Accessed April 7, 2024. https://www.npr.org/2021/02/10/966396848/read-trumps-jan-6-speech-a-key-part-of-impeachment-trial.

782   Ibid.

783   "Fact check: Men who stormed Capitol identified by Reuters are not undercover Antifa as posts claim." Reuters. January 10, 2021. Accessed April 7, 2024. https://www.reuters.com/article/idUSKBN29E0QH/.

784   Waller, J. Michael. "Covert Cadre: What I saw leading up to the US Capitol attack. Center for Security Policy." January 13, 2021. Accessed April 7, 2024. https://centerforsecuritypolicy.org/covert-cadre-what-i-saw-leading-up-to-the-us-capitol-attack/.

785   Ibid.

786   Ibid.

787   Ibid.

788   Powe, Alicia. "Use Of Force Expert Says Capitol Police 'Set One Man On Fire' With Concussion Grenades On January 6." *The Gateway Pundit.* February 24, 2024. Accessed April 7, 2024. https://www.thegatewaypundit.com/2024/02/use-force-expert-capitol-warns-police-set-one/.

789   Ibid.

790   "FBI affirms Center for Security Policy analyst's account of Capitol pre-attack." Center for Security Policy. March 5, 2021. Accessed April 7, 2024. https://centerforsecuritypolicy.org/fbi-affirms-center-for-security-policy-analysts-account-of-capitol-pre-attack/.

791   Written Testimony of USCP Former Chief of Police Steven A. Sund before the Senate Committee on Rules and Administration and the Senate Homeland Security and Government Affairs Committee Tuesday, February 23, 2021. Accessed April 7, 2024. https://www.rules.senate.gov/imo/media/doc/Testimony_Sund.pdf.

792   "Proof That January 6 Was Not An Insurrection." The Great American Email. January 7, 2023. Accessed April 7, 2024. https://greatamericanmail.substack.com/p/proof-that-january-6-was-not-an-insurrection.

793   Ibid.

794   "A Democrat Coup, Part 2: January 6 as Democrats' mechanism to disqualify Republican rivals from Federal and State office." The Great American Email. January 6, 2022. Accessed April 7, 2024. https://greatamericanmail.substack.com/p/a-democrat-coup-part-2-january-6?s=w.

795   "Capitol Police Commander Present During Jan. 6 Says It 'Was Not An Insurrection.'" Republican Daily. Accessed

April 7, 2024. https://republicandaily.com/2023/12/
capitol-police-commander-present-during-jan-6-says-it-was-not-an-insurrection/.

796   Ibid.

797   Carlson, Tucker. "Ep. 61 This the smartest, best informed account of what
       actually happened on January 6th." X. January 6, 2024. Accessed April 8,
       2024. https://twitter.com/TuckerCarlson/status/1743724117113602512.

798   Ibid.

799   "Videos taken by journalist Tayler Hansen prove Ashli Babbitt was
       not violent inside US Capitol." YouTube. January 25, 2022. Accessed
       April 8, 2024. https://www.youtube.com/watch?v=hSt2LJWokI0.

800   Carlson. "Ep 61." *Op. cit.*

801   Beheshti, Vahid. "Breaking: The Leaked Top-Secret Letter of the
       Intelligence Organisation of the Islamic Revolutionary Guard
       Corps." X. April 15, 2024. Accessed May 2, 2024. https://twitter.
       com/Vahid_Beheshti/status/1779786659229298775.

802   Chernik, Ilanit. "Activists get violent during Reservists on
       Duty event at York University." *Jerusalem Post.* November 28,
       2019. Accessed May 2, 2024. https://www.jpost.com/diaspora/
       activists-get-violent-during-reservists-on-duty-at-york-university-608617.

803   Hubbard, Madeline. "Cuba spent years training anti-Israel activists behind campus
       protests." Just the News. May 7, 2024. https://justthenews.com/accountability/
       watchdogs/cuba-spent-years-training-anti-israel-activists-behind-campus-protests.

804   The Editors of Encyclopaedia Britannica. "First International."
       Encyclopedia Britannica. June 18, 2017. Accessed April 6, 2024.
       https://www.britannica.com/topic/First-International.

805   The Editors of Encyclopaedia Britannica. "Second International."
       Encyclopedia Britannica. August 21, 2019. Accessed April 6, 2024.
       https://www.britannica.com/topic/Second-International.

806   The Editors of Encyclopaedia Britannica. "Third International."
       Encyclopedia Britannica. February 2, 2024. Accessed April 6, 2024.
       https://www.britannica.com/topic/Third-International.

807   *Blood Money. Op. cit.* 42-43.

808   Figueroa, Ariana. "Watch out for China buying U.S. farmland, Noem tells U.S.
       House panel." *Nebraska Examiner.* March 20, 2024. Accessed April 6, 2024. https://
       nebraskaexaminer.com/2024/03/20/watch-out-for-china-buying-u-s-farmland-
       noem-tells-u-s-house-panel/.

809   Goldstein, Adam. "Limits on foreign ownership of U.S. farmland gain support
       in Congress, despite skepticism." *Wisconsin Examiner.* March 20, 2023. Accessed
       April 7, 2024. https://wisconsinexaminer.com/2023/03/20/limits-on-foreign-
       ownership-of-u-s-farmland-gain-support-in-congress-despite-skepticism/.

810   "Chinese billionaire is second-biggest foreign owner of US land."
       Times of India. January 10, 2024. Accessed April 6, 2024. http://
       timesofindia.indiatimes.com/articleshow/106694381.cms

811   Alfonsi, Sharyn. "Chinese migrants are the fastest growing group crossing from
       Mexico into U.S. at southern border." CBS News. February 4, 2024. Accessed April
       7, 2024. https://www.cbsnews.com/news/chinese-migrants-fastest-growing-
       group-us-mexico-border-60-minutes-transcript/.

812   Leonard, Tom. "Are the thousands of Chinese 'migrants' flooding into the
       U.S. really a sleeper army of spies and soldiers preparing for war?" *Daily
       Mail.* March 8, 2024. Accessed April 7, 2024. https://www.dailymail.
       co.uk/news/article-13175093/thousands-Chinese-migrants-flooding-
       sleeper-army-spies-soldiers-preparing-war-tom-leonard.html.

813   "About Us." The State Legislative Leadership Foundation.
       Accessed April 6, 2024. https://www.sllf.org/about-us/.

814   Ross, Chuck. "'Whatever You Need': How Hunter Biden Helped the
       CCP's Premier Influence Group Gain a US Foothold." *Washington Free
       Beacon.* August 18, 2022. Accessed April 6, 2024. https://freebeacon.
       com/biden-administration/whatever-you-need-how-hunter-biden-
       helped-the-ccps-premier-influence-group-gain-a-us-foothold/.

815   "Full Text: Outcome list of President Xi Jinping's state visit to the United
       States." #39. Ministry of Foreign Affairs of the People's Republic of China.
       September 26, 2015. Accessed April 6, 2024. https://www.fmprc.gov.cn/
       mfa_eng/wjdt_665385/2649_665393/201509/t20150926_679414.html.

816   "Conference of State Majority Leaders." June 20–22. State Legislative
       Leadership Foundation. Accessed April 6, 2024. https://www.sllf.org/
       leadership-programs/2024-conference-of-state-majority-leaders/.

817   State Legislative Leadership Foundation. IRS form 990 Return
       of Organization Exempt from Taxes, 2022, A7. November 14,
       2023. Accessed April 6, 2024. https://pdf.guidestar.org/PDF_Ima
       ges/2022/237/148/2022-237148478-202303189349313415-9.pdf.

818   "Martin M. Looney." KeyWiki. Accessed April 6, 2024.
       https://keywiki.org/Martin_M._Looney.

819   Assembly Speaker Robin Vos. Phone interview with James Simpson. *Op cit.*

820   "SLLF and the Chinese People's Association for Friendship with Foreign
       Countries sign historic pact." SLLF. December 11, 2015. Accessed July 23,
       2024. https://web.archive.org/web/20160304114425/http://www.sllf.org/.

821   Husebo, Wendell. "Exclusive: Republican Wisconsin Assembly Speaker Robin Vos
       on Board of CCP Front Group." Breitbart. March 8, 2024. Accessed April 9, 2024.
       https://www.breitbart.com/politics/2024/03/09/republican-wisconsin-assembly-
       speaker-robin-vos-board-ccp-front-group/.

822   "International Programs: China." SLLF. December 11, 2015. Accessed July
       23, 2024. https://web.archive.org/web/20160307041022/http://www.sllf.org/
       leadership-
       programs/international-programs/.

823   "Minister Counselor Zhang Min Attends First China-US Sub-national
       Legislatures Cooperation Forum." Embassy of the People's Republic of China
       in the United States of America. June 30, 2016. Accessed April 9, 2024. http://
       us.china-embassy.gov.cn/eng/ggwjhd/201606/t20160630_4409962.htm.

824   Little, Thom, PhD. "SLLF at Fifty: Looking Forward to Fifty More!" SLLF.
       December 9, 2022. Accessed April 9, 2024. https://www.sllf.org/sllf-at-fifty-looking-
       forward-to-fifty-more/.

825   "SLLF at COP 28. SLLF. December 13, 2023. Accessed
       April 9, 2024. https://www.sllf.org/sllf-at-cop-28/.

826   Ross. "Whatever You Need." *Op. cit.*

827   "2023 ASSEMBLY BILL 269." Wisconsin State Legislature. May 17, 2023.
       Accessed April 9, 2024. https://docs.legis.wisconsin.gov/2023/proposals/ab269.

828   "2021 Wisconsin Statutes & Annotations Chapter 710 - Miscellaneous property
       provisions. 710.02 - Limitation on nonresident aliens and corporations." Justia.
       https://law.justia.com/codes/wisconsin/2021/chapter-710/section-710-02/.

829   "Barrasso to Sec. Granholm: End Department's Support for Communist China."
       Senate Committee on Energy and Natural Resources, Republican News. March
       5, 2024. Accessed April 9, 2024. https://www.energy.senate.gov/2024/3/
       barrasso-to-sec-granholm-end-department-s-support-for-communist-china,

830   Shideler, Kyle. "FBI alleges black identity extremist groups were acting as 'instruments of the Russian government.'" Center for Security Policy. August 4, 2022. Accessed April 6, 2024. https://centerforsecuritypolicy.org/fbi-alleges-black-identity-extremist-groups-were-acting-as-instruments-of-the-russian-government/.

831   Nal, Renee. "Infiltration Alert: Russia's Aleksandr Dugin's Sinister Plot to Destroy Trump's MAGA Movement (Exclusive Interview)." RAIR Foundation USA. July 23, 2024. Accessed July 24, 2024. https://rairfoundation.com/infiltration-alert-russias-aleksandr-dugins-sinister-plot-destroy/.

832   "Richard Spencer." KeyWiki. March 22, 2024. Accessed April 7, 2024. https://keywiki.org/Richard_Spencer.

833   Loudon, Trevor. "Brenton Tarrant: Is the Christchurch Mosque Shooter a 'National Bolshevik'?" *The Epoch Times*. April 8, 2019. Accessed April 7, 2024. https://www.theepochtimes.com/opinion/brenton-tarrant-is-the-christchurch-mosque-shooter-a-national-bolshevik-2850960.

834   Nal, Renee. "Try to Wrap Your Head Around 'MAGA Communism.'" Spider and the Fly. March 2024. Accessed April 7, 2024. http://www.spider-and-the-fly.com/maga-communism.html.

835   Hinkle, Jackson. "I am a Christian Communist American Patriot, and I stand with Putin!" X. February 9, 2024. Accessed April 7, 2024. https://twitter.com/jacksonhinklle/status/1755962253776388320.

836   Dugin, Alexander. "Against Post-Modern World." The Fourth Political Theory. Accessed April 7, 2024. https://web.archive.org/web/20240308221020/https:/www.4pt.su/en/content/against-post-modern-world.

837   Nal. "Infiltration Alert." *Op. cit.*

838   Nal. "Try to Wrap Your Head Around 'MAGA Communism.'" *Op. cit.*

839   Nal. "Infiltration Alert." *Op. cit.*

840   "Great Again: The Trump Boom vs the Biden Bust." Unleash Prosperity Now. Accessed July 17, 2024. https://unleashprosperitynow.com/#pdf-great-again-book/.

841   Smith, Justin O. "America Is Hurtling Toward a Full Blown Hot Civil War." The Burning Platform. April 6, 2024. Accessed April 8, 2024. https://www.theburningplatform.com/2024/04/06/america-is-hurling-toward-a-full-blown-hot-civil-war/.

842   Martin, Naomi. "Security guard injured in Garland terror attack tormented by belief that FBI knew of ISIS plot." *Dallas Morning News*. May 26, 2017. Accessed April 8, 2024. https://www.dallasnews.com/news/crime/2017/05/26/security-guard-injured-in-garland-terror-attack-tormented-by-belief-that-fbi-knew-of-isis-plot/.

843   D'Abrosca, Peter. "Tennessee General Assembly Passes Landmark Bill Against De-Banking." *Tennessee Star*. March 29, 2024. Accessed May 12, 2024. https://tennesseestar.com/news/tennessee-general-assembly-passes-landmark-bill-against-de-banking/pdabrosca/2024/03/29/.

844   "The Baltimore Sun purchased by Sinclair's David D. Smith." *The Baltimore Sun*. January 15, 2024. Accessed April 8, 2024. https://www.baltimoresun.com/2024/01/15/baltimore-sun-media-sold-david-d-smith/.

845   Baletti, Brenda, Ph.D. "'Blood on Its Hands': FDA Will Remove Anti-ivermectin Social Media, Website Posts Under Lawsuit Settlement Agreement." *The Defender*, Children's Health Defense. March 25, 2024. Accessed April 8, 2024. https://childrenshealthdefense.org/defender/fda-ivermectin-covid-treatment-lawsuit-social-media/.

846   Viguerie, Richard. "IT'S NOT ABOUT DEMOCRAT CANDIDATES — IT'S ABOUT THE DEMOCRAT PARTY." Go Right Go Big. Accessed April 9, 2024. https://links.gorightgobig.com/a/2111/preview/21492/1494087/c6146e4934066ba

a6857b32572a6bfabf60de254?message_id=IjFkNjk0ZDQwLWQ4OWYtMDEzYy00MWU2LTQyMDEwYTgwMDEwYkBnb3JpZ2h0Z29iaWcuY29tIg==.

847   Lee, Sarah, Jon Rodeback, and Hayden Ludwig. "States Banning or Restricting 'Zuck Bucks'—UPDATED 4/10/2024." Capital Research Center. Accessed May 2, 2024. https://capitalresearch.org/article/states-banning-zuck-bucks/.

848   Jewell, Zach. "Dems Counting On 3 Battleground States To Deliver 2024 Win For Biden." The Daily Wire. April 8, 2024. Accessed April 9, 2024. https://www.dailywire.com/news/dems-counting-on-3-battleground-states-to-deliver-2024-win-for-biden.

849   "Jon tester: Supported by Council for a Livable World." KeyWiki. Accessed March 7, 2024. https://keywiki.org/Jon_Tester#Supported_by_Council_for_a_Livable_World.

850   *Special Tasks: The Memoirs of an Unwanted Witness-A Soviet Spymaster*, New York: Little, Brown and Company, 1994, 172, as quoted in "Leo Szilard," KeyWiki. Accessed April 10, 2024. https://keywiki.org/Leo_Szilard#cite_note-9.

851   Parsnow, Luke, and Jack Arpey. "Hochul signs New York Legislature's own set of new congressional maps into law." *Spectrum News*. February 28, 2024. Accessed March 7, 2024. https://spectrumlocalnews.com/nys/central-ny/politics/2024/02/28/new-york-legislature-passes-new-congressional-maps.

852   Tran, Ken. "Who will control the House after 2024? From Michigan to California, these are the tight races to watch." *USA Today*. February 21, 2024. Accessed April 8, 2024. https://www.usatoday.com/story/news/politics/elections/2024/02/21/who-will-control-house-2024-races-to-watch/72686388007/.

ABOUT THE AUTHOR

James Simpson is an economist, successful businessman, investigative journalist, and bestselling author. He was a former candidate for the US Congress in 2020, and in his earlier career worked as an economist and budget analyst for the White House Office of Management and Budget. He received his master's degree in economics from the University of Delaware and taught at the university as an adjunct instructor.

Made in the USA
Middletown, DE
23 September 2024

60979624R00216